A SPARK OF REVOLUTION
(1734–1775)

A SPARK
OF REVOLUTION
(1734–1775)

Thomas Jefferson, James Watt, and William Small

MARTIN CLAGETT

Clyde Hill Publishing
Bellevue • 2021

Meis uxori et filio et filiae

Elizabeth et Richard et Alexandra

Meis bonis amicis

John Casten atque Keith Thomson et Harry Dickinson

In Memoriam

Sir Nicholas Proctor Goodison (1934-2021)
Gillian Christina Hull (1936-2021)

Old paint on a canvas, as it ages, sometimes becomes transparent. When that happens it is possible, in some pictures, to see the original lines: a tree will show through a woman's dress, a child makes way for a dog, a large boat is no longer on an open sea. That is called pentimento because the painter "repented," changed his mind. Perhaps it would be as well to say that the old conception, replaced by a later choice, is a way of seeing and then seeing again. That is all I mean about the people in this book. The paint has aged and I wanted to see what was there for me once, what is there for me now.

Lillian Hellman. *Pentimento*.

Contents

A Two-Continents Job: Garry Wills.   ix

Preface.   xv

Introduction   xix

Editorial Method   xxv

Acknowledgments.   xxvii

Chapter 1: Early Life and Family Background   1

Chapter 2: Small's Early Education   19

Chapter 3: The College of William and Mary   49

Chapter 4: The Replacements.   84

Chapter 5: The Williamsburg of Small and Jefferson   105

Chapter 6: Friends and Societies.   123

Chapter 7: Small and Instruction at William and Mary   148

Chapter 8: William Small and Thomas Jefferson   172

Chapter 9: Leaving Virginia   191

Chapter 10: Small and London and Franklin   206

Chapter 11: Boulton, Birmingham, and the Lunar Society .   221

Chapter 12: William Small and James Watt.   248

Chapter 13: Conclusion: The Importance of Being Small . .   274

Chapter 14: Post Scripta—Doctor Small   289

William Small Timeline 303

Dramatis Personae (1734–1758)...................... 307

Dramatis Personae (1758–1764)...................... 317

Dramatis Personae (1764–1775)...................... 321

Bibliography 327

Index... 345

A Two-Continents Job

Garry Wills

It is not surprising that William Small is little known today. He died young (age 41) and wrote nothing important. He lived in four disjunct periods and places, with no family or associates to accompany him in the transitions from the second to the third, or from the third to the fourth (in the times of life when he was most formed and influential).

From birth to age twenty-one he lived in his native Scotland, graduating from Marischal College in Aberdeen. From twenty one to twenty-six, he was a medical student, doctor, and intellectual explorer in London—and here his Scottish connections did play a role in the increase of his qualifications and recognition. From twenty-six to thirty he was a professor in America (at the College of William and Mary). From thirty to his death he was a medical doctor and aspiring inventor in England.

He managed, in this short and peripatetic life, to become a footnote to the story of two revolutions, one political, one economic. He was important for the American Revolution as the teacher of Thomas Jefferson. He was important to the Industrial Revolution as part of the manufacturing intelligentsia in Birmingham, where he was a close ally of Matthew Boulton, James Watt and Erasmus Darwin. He was a subordinate figure in both places, not a principal. So why does Martin Clagett consider his life worthy of close study and delayed attention?

Jefferson left moving testimony to Small's impact on him. He says Small "probably fixed the destinies of my life." Clagett supplies good reason to consider that this was an entirely accurate estimate of Small's importance to Jefferson. It is frightening to consider what might have become of Jefferson if he had not met Small in 1760 when Jefferson arrived at William and Mary. The college had, until that very moment, been a profound disappointment, with its clergymen-professors snarling at each other, drinking, neglecting their duties, and defying all correction. The acting governor of Virginia, Francis Fauquier, intellectually distinguished himself, was dismayed by the anarchy in the college faculty. He encouraged the recruitment of a qualified layman as the new professor of mathematics.

Jefferson tells us what happened next. "Fortunately the philosophical chair became vacant soon after my arrival at college, and he [Small] was appointed to fill it per interim; and he was the first who ever gave regular lectures in ethics, rhetoric & belles letters." In effect, Small taught all the courses in the two years Jefferson was enrolled in the college, and during the two years the two of them remained in Williamsburg, in close and mutually stimulating contact with each other. Instead of the stultifying and vicious Anglican priests who might have taught him, Jefferson enjoyed the closest friendship with, as he put it, "a man profound in the most useful branches of science, with a happy talent of communication, correct and gentlemanly manners, and an enlarged and liberal mind." Small brought with him up-to-date news of the Enlightenment that was then exciting Scotland. Small thus had both the new ideas of Scotland and the social polish of London, a combination Jefferson had not encountered to that date.

Nor was it Small alone who opened a new world for Jefferson. Small had little time or use for his disappearing colleagues at the college, but he was a great admirer of George Wythe, who became Jefferson's legal teacher for the last two years of Small's time in America. Francis Fauquier, starved for intellectual company in the little village of Williamsburg, invited Small, Wythe and Jefferson to frequent dinners at the Governor's Mansion, where Jefferson was proud to be a member of this "partie quarree." As the youngest man admitted into this company on an equal basis, Jefferson could not have found a more sophisticated and cosmopolitan circle for the formation of his questing mind. He wrote: "At those dinners I have heard more good sense, more rational and philosophic conversations, than all my life besides. They were truly Attic societies."

In this circle, it was clearly Small who mattered most to Jefferson—enough for him to say, later on, that "Dr. Small was . . . to me as a father." But this was a father close enough to his own age (they were twenty-six and seventeen when they met) to be a friend and equal. "He most happily for me, became soon attached to me & made me his daily companion when not engaged in school; and from his conversations I got my first views of the expansion of science & and of the system of things in which we are placed." Small was still exploring the meaning of Enlightenment, and Jefferson was in the enviable spot of contributing to his mentor's growth along with his own. This can be the most rewarding of intellectual exchanges, as I know—I was taught in my teens by a group of Jesuit "scholastics" who were in their mid-twenties, still learning themselves as they taught me and my fellows.

Jefferson so cherished Small's memory that when relations between America and England were threatened, in 1775, he tried to firm up their relationship by sending Small a gift of six dozen bottles of his best Madeira, with "my constant wishes for your happiness." He signed off: "I shall still hope that amidst public dissension private friendship may be preserved inviolate, and among the warmest you can ever possess is that of your obliged humble servant, Th. Jefferson." But even while Jefferson was packing up his precious cargo, Small lay buried in Birmingham. It is clear that William and Mary, which could have been a disappointment for the young Jefferson, became a shining memory he cherished all his life. Small was a secular guide who looked to the future, and his memory nurtured Jefferson's later plans for his own University of Virginia.

Nor was Jefferson the only beneficiary of Small's inspiration. Jefferson's friend John Page called Small his "ever to be beloved professor." Another student, Walter Jones, said he had learned from Small "all the arts that will be serviceable in life." Robert Carter, who said that he had been corrupted by previous study in England, was happy that under Small he "discovered the cruel tyrannical designs of the British government," and became "a true and steady patriot." This suggests that Jefferson did not have to fear division from Small as the Revolution was looming. Small was training patriots at William and Mary. Indeed, Small cannot claim to be the schoolmaster to the Revolution—a title that rightfully belongs to John Witherspoon of Princeton. But Small is a worthy second to that great man.

Small wanted to return to England, but Fauquier was naturally reluctant to let him go. Small at last was freed on an errand for the college—to acquire scientific instruments and return with them. He made sure the instruments were acquired and delivered, but he did not go back himself. He began a successful medical practice in Birmingham, but his heart was in the work of his new friends in Matthew Boulton's experimental factories. He was the one who introduced James Watt to Boulton, and he was the social glue in that informal set of relationships that was formalized after his death as the famous "Lunar Society" celebrated by Jenny Uglow and others.

Small clearly had a genius for friendship, shown in the Fauquier gatherings as well as in the Boulton ones. Samuel Johnson coined a new word for his young friend James Boswell, "clubbable." He did not put it in his dictionary, but he should have, since the eighteenth century prized sociability in striking and innovative ways. Johnson did define club as "an assembly of good fellows, meeting under certain [i.e., regularized] conditions." Though Small was successful in his medical practice, he obviously felt most at home with his scientific fellows, whom he helped lobby for an extension on their patent for the steam engine. He said that he desired to be a "projector"—in Johnson's definition, "one who forms schemes or designs." There could be no better description of the Boulton circle than as a team of projectors. Clagett plausibly surmises that fame and fortune would have come to Small had he lived to see the success of the steam engine he promoted so enthusiastically.

Any book on Small must be a two-continents job. Consequently, Clagett has spent years, and shown dogged persistence, going through official records both in Scotland and America. As a result of his patient detective work, we know about his Virginia life more than his friends in Birmingham ever did, and more about his Birmingham life than Jefferson or Page could have learned. He at last gives Small his due, which was long overdue.

Historical accidents have long kept Small hidden from most of us. But not from Clagett.

Portrait of William Small by Tilly Kettle. 1766. Unrestored.

Preface

Over the fireplace in the office of the president of the College of William and Mary hangs a portrait of a gentleman in powdered wig. His Roman nose separates inquisitive eyebrows, the wide span of forehead bespeaks an expansive intellect, and the piercing blue eyes, surrealistically lifelike, seem to be searching for answers. He wears the academic gown and Geneva bands that were de rigueur for graduates of Scottish universities in the eighteenth century. The portrait, by

Tilly Kettle, came to the college in a way as mysterious and convoluted as the professor himself. The provenance of the portrait is as nebulous and amorphous as the history of the sitter. The sale of the portrait was first promoted by a relatively obscure auction house in Maine and, when asked about the origin of the picture, the provenance officer was hesitatingly vague. The auction house maintained that the portrait had come to it by way of an old Boston bishop with a Philadelphia pedigree and had been in the possession of his family for almost two centuries. The only information provided by the bishop was that the sitter had been a professor at the College of William and Mary, and died at the age of forty-one. From this scant information, the provenance officer immediately pinpointed the subject as William Small, and identified the painter as Tilly Kettle. Gradually, by gleaning odd bits of information and by consulting experts, it was determined that indeed the painting had not been collecting dust these many years in Philadelphia but had resided in England and even recently been offered for sale there. The seller in England had represented the painting to a Birmingham society as William Small painted by the celebrated Tilly Kettle. The skeptical society, however, rejected the painting and the sitter as a fake—since in England, only clerics dressed in black gowns and wore the distinctive ties known as Geneva bands, or preaching bands. Since Small was not a cleric, the sitter could not be Small and the portrait, by necessity, must be a fraud.[1]

Having been rejected in England, the online salesman sent the portrait to the aforesaid auction house in Maine, where it was offered to the University of Virginia, Monticello, and the College of William and Mary. Background research by this author showed that the biographical details of both the artist and the sitter found them to be in the same city for only three years (1765–1768) and that Kettle had painted a number of Small's friends and associates. An analysis of the portrait by Philip Mould, art consultant to Parliament, determined that the artist was indeed Tilly Kettle. An auction was held in January 2005 and an alumnus of the college, having been sent to bid on the picture (and being the only bidder), purchased the portrait for the minimum bid of $5,000.

The portrait was packed up and sent to Williamsburg, where art experts at the college determined the age and nature of the paints and canvas used in its composition. From there, Small's portrait was forwarded to Richmond and the Fine Art Conservation of Virginia.

The portrait having been blurred by centuries of smoke and ash and touched up and modified several times presented a feeble version of its former self. In a surprising development, however, in the process of cleaning and restoration, a mottled mustard smear at the bottom right of the painting came into focus and clarified the questions associated with its origin. The words "Kettle pinxit" emerged, along with a date—"66." William Small and Tilly Kettle were only in the same place at the same time for three years—in the town of Birmingham, England, from 1765 to 1768.

This study, like the portrait, at first obscured by the effluvia of time and conjecture, became, bit by bit, a clearer and more compelling story. For the first time, the *complete* life of William Small has been investigated; his family and education in Scotland, his influence and impact on a young Thomas Jefferson in Virginia, his friendship and association with Benjamin Franklin, the partnership and affiliation with Matthew Boulton, his collaboration and support of James Watt, the pivotal role that he played as an apostle of the tenets of the Scottish Enlightenment, as the co-founder of the Birmingham Lunar Society, and as a promoter of talent and enterprise.

NOTE

1. See Martin Clagett, "The Portrait of William Small," privately printed for presentation at the Meeting of Eighteenth-Century Scottish Studies Conference. Funded by the Earhart Foundation. The monograph follows the history of the portrait from 1766 until its purchase by the College of William and Mary in 2005.

Introduction

The life of William Small is as extraordinary, as mysterious, as elusive as the provenance of his portrait. Here is a man who served as a mentor not only to Thomas Jefferson but also to a whole host of leaders of the American Revolution and the New Republic. A colleague of the inventor who led the Western world out of the agricultural milieu of the Middle Ages into the progressive world of the Industrial Revolution. The confidant and friend to many of the most influential individuals of the late eighteenth century. And yet, there has been virtually no investigation into his personal life, the people and ideas that influenced him, nor a systematic study of his impact on those around him.

Even to those who were tangentially touched through the muddle of time—students at the College of William and Mary, scholars at the International Center of Jefferson Studies, members of the New Birmingham Lunar Society—Small remained "a riddle, wrapped in a mystery, inside an enigma."

The strange lack of information regarding this elusive figure may stem from several sources—most important, from Small's own personal reluctance to publish and promote himself. Small's greatest contribution to both the American Revolution and the Industrial Revolution was his ability to bring together the right people at the right time to engage in critical instruction, illuminating demonstration, and the successful completion of several projects.

In America, through his infectious enthusiasm, Small transformed the intellectually flaccid and politically internecine College of William and Mary into an institution on the cutting edge of educational innovation and its students into the adolescent vanguard of the Revolution. Back in England, Small secured employment with one of Britain's earliest, wealthiest, and most avant-garde industrialists, Matthew Boulton.[1] Small's scientific insights energized Boulton to recruit kindred scientists and engineers and to join with them in a scientific society. Small, together with Boulton transformed the sleepy town of Birmingham into a dynamic hive of industrial experimentation, innovation, and economic enterprise.

Small, with Boulton's financial and political backing, carefully selected academics, mechanics, inventors, chemists, and men of science, brought them into close proximity, and let the sparks fly. Genius often seeks out and revels in the insight of others, and, by kindred and kinetic energy, feeds on and is increased by simultaneous epiphanies. It was not until Small died that the members of this fledgling scientific think tank found it necessary to formalize their organization with an official title and set of regulations.

A second cause of the inexplicable lack of information concerning Small's life stems from the agenda of historical research—which often tends to be nationalistic. British scholars concentrated on Small's life as a leading figure in the Birmingham Lunar Society and his relationships with the leading figures of the Industrial Revolution—James Watt, Erasmus Darwin, Joseph Priestley, and Matthew Boulton. American scholars, conversely, have focused on Small's time in Williamsburg and his influence on Thomas Jefferson.

Until recently, therefore, we knew very little about Small's personal background, his education, or his early life. Small seems to have burst forth, as Athena from the skull of Zeus, at a meeting of the President and Masters of the College of William and Mary in the autumn of 1758; or conversely, as a stranger arriving in Birmingham seeking a job with the famous Matthew Boulton and armed only with his charm and an introduction from Benjamin Franklin.

In both the American version and the British version, the story of Small himself is incidental to other great men. His story is not usually told as his own, but only as an extraneous appendage of Thomas Jefferson, Matthew Boulton or James Watt. It is difficult to understand why this is the case. After having "fixed the destinies" of Jefferson's life and playing a pivotal role in the development of the steam engine, virtually no research has been conducted into Small's personal life, his family's background, and the influence that formed his vision of the "system of things in which we are placed" had on his multiple friends and disciples.

Therefore, it is crucial to know the basis of Small's intellectual foundations in order to understand the philosophy that he expounded, his method of instruction, and the ultimate impact of his scientific and intellectual lessons. Inextricably tied into Small's life are the underpinnings of his comprehension of the universe and his commitment to reason, the desire for order, the scientific method, and the improvement of life on earth.

Small's brief life may be conveniently compartmentalized into three distinct periods. The first, his family background and education, the second, his recruitment and tenure at the College of William and Mary, and the third, his return to Britain and his collaboration with Matthew Boulton and James Watt and the improved steam engine.

The examination of Small's life in Scotland includes a history of his family background, which was derived from primary source documentation buried in Scottish archives and never investigated in depth before. William Small came from a distinguished line of ministers and academics with connections to Aberdeen, Dundee, and St. Andrews. Perhaps more important to the story of Small's intellectual background are the institutions that fostered his system of beliefs and the men who directed him as a young man. In Scotland, he underwent a rigorous curriculum at Dundee Grammar School for seven years. Later, Small matriculated at Marischal College in Aberdeen, where he followed a systematic study of the scientific method, bolstered by the pragmatic tenets of William Duncan's *Elements of Logick* and Thomas Reid's *School of Common Sense Philosophy*.

Small followed his mentor John Gregory to London, where Gregory worked as a physician at St. George's Hospital. Having 'walked the wards' for several years, Small was recruited by the Right Reverend Samuel Nichols, the Bishop of London's assistant, to take up a post in far-off Virginia as the Professor of Mathematicks. Small entered into an academic situation in which the entire faculty, except for the Master of the Indian School and the President, had been summarily sacked by the Board of Visitors. The reduced staff was comprised of William Small as Professor of Natural Philosophy, Jacob Rowe as Professor of Moral Philosophy, and Goronwy Owen as the Grammar School Master. Small taught subjects related to science and mathematics; Rowe, as Professor of Moral Philosophy, lectured on ethics, rhetoric, and belles lettres; and Owen prepared the younger students, or scholars, in classical languages, elementary mathematics, and writing.

Soon after arriving, Small's colleagues took up the same contentious politics and raucous personal behavior responsible for the dismissal of their predecessors. In 1760, Jacob Rowe was expelled and Goronwy Owen resigned, leaving William Small as the only collegiate professor at the very moment that Thomas Jefferson was riding into Williamsburg from the mountains of Virginia. Small was Jefferson's only professor at the college, although he was later instructed in law privately by George Wythe. In the autumn of 1764, likely at the instigation of Benjamin Franklin, Small departed for England.

In London, he became Franklin's protégé and was introduced to the leading figures of science and medicine. In May 1765, Small made a journey to Birmingham to interview for a position as family physician and scientific advisor to the great industrialist Matthew Boulton. Boulton, impressed, immediately engaged Small, and thus began the last phase of Small's short life.

Small and Boulton formed the nucleus of the famous Birmingham Lunar Society; Small encouraged Boulton to include an increasing coterie of comrades to investigate scientific and industrial questions, persistently pestered Boulton to engage his new friend James Watt as an engineer, and assisted Watt in developing the improved steam engine. Small lobbied tirelessly for the passage of a bill granting a monopoly for Watts's invention, which, in the end, not only made Boulton and Watt infinitely wealthy but also ushered in the Industrial Revolution.

Small was an essential part of The Age of Enlightenment, which heralded the American Experiment, the Industrial Revolution, and the International Republic of Letters. It is in this time of skepticism, cynicism, and confusion that a story of reason, amiability, and common sense should be told and should be heard.

NOTES

1. Matthew Boulton, born in 1728, took over his father's toy business in Birmingham, England, at an early age and became one of the earliest and most innovative entrepreneurs of the Industrial Age. In 1765, with the encouragement of his friend Benjamin Franklin, Boulton hired William Small as his family physician and scientific advisor. By the following year, the two had established a society comprised of the foremost scientists and inventors in the English Midlands, which in time would be known as the Birmingham Lunar Society.

Editorial Method

In terms of textual editing, the guiding principle of this work has been to follow Julian Boyd's advice as reflected in the title of his article on this subject, "God's Altar Needs Not Our Polishings" (*New York History* 39 [January 1958]). All citations have been left as originally reflected in primary source documents or as recorded where the originals have not been available unless editorial intervention was unavoidable. With these things having been said, please note the following peculiarities of eighteenth-century manuscripts.

Spelling and misspelling have been retained as written. Archaic and obsolete forms have not been altered, frequently past tenses reflect a –'d instead of an –ed, and spelling is erratic. Often nouns of consequence are capitalized no matter their position in the sentence.

Punctuation is idiosyncratic—commas pop up in unusual places and periods are sometimes forgotten. A period is frequently inserted after number; virgules and periods often elide. Oftentimes, an extended blank space is inserted at the end of a sentence in the middle of a paragraph—usually indicating a change in the direction of thought or subject content. A "favor" is a letter, "ultro" usually refers to last month—"instant" is this month. If the form of the spelling is likely to confuse the reader, the correct spelling will be inserted in square brackets [ ].

Words inserted into the original document by the original writer are noted by carets < >; words omitted by the writer but essential for understanding the text are expressed also with brackets [ ]; torn or missing text and illegible or unintelligible words are noted.

Acknowledgments

No man is an island and no work of consequence is done in isolation but is the result of the efforts of many individuals and institutions; so it has been with the life of William Small. The three main areas of support and collaboration that have made this work possible have been financial, academic, and personal. I would like to acknowledge each group in its turn. It is not unusual, however, for the boundaries of defined fields to overlap, evolve, elide. In particular, many contributors, who have assisted either with financial encouragement or those who have been instrumental in research inquires, have evolved into cherished friends and advisers. For sake of clarity and convenience, however, I will acknowledge and thank those without whom this narrative would not have been possible within the parameters mentioned above.

Much of the investigation on this subject was made possible through the financial largesse of various institutions by way of a series of grants, scholarships, and posts. The first was a scholastic grant from Virginia Commonwealth University through the intercession of my dissertation chair, Dr. Samuel Craver. When the investigation into the life of William Small became known to Dr. Ingrid Gregg of the Earhart Foundation, a travel grant made it possible to archive dive through Scotland and England; Andrew O'Shaughnessy, Saunders Director of the Robert H. Smith International Center for Jefferson Studies, further encouraged the development of the theme of Small's influence on Jefferson by endorsing my application for a

Gilder-Lehrman fellowship at the ICJS; and John Casteen, president of the University of Virginia, procured for me the position of visiting lecturer at that institution with the purpose of researching the impact of William Small on Thomas Jefferson's scientific enthusiasms and endeavors. Hank Wolf, Rector of the College of William and Mary, through his endorsements made possible a visiting scholar's post at that critical institution.

Formerly, information concerning the early life and education of William Small was minimal and primary source documentation was essential. Two works by James Muirhead, *The Origin and Progress of the Mechanical Inventions of James Watt* and *The Life of James Watt*, provided hints of Small's family background and early life in Scotland. The scant information in these works furnished clues to the repositories that potentially held the documentation to fill in the details for that unexamined portion of Small's life. The sites and institutions were to be found at the University of St. Andrews, the University of Dundee, the University of Aberdeen, the University of Edinburgh, the University of Glasgow, the National Archives of Scotland, and the New Register House in Edinburgh.

Much of the background for Small's immediate family background was centered in Fife, around the quaint town of St. Andrews. The staff at the university and many scholars associated with that institution were most helpful in the investigation including the archivists of the institution, Rachel Hart and Norman Reid, and Professors David Allen, Peter Maxwell-Stuart, J. J. Haldrane, Robert Smart, and Vice Principal Stephen Magee. In addition, the Emeritus Archivist of St. Andrews, Robert Smart became a cherished friend and a valuable resource for matters dealing with the university's archival history. In Dundee, both Ian Fleet and Charles McKean pointed the ways to rich sources of information concerning Dundee Grammar School, where both William and his brother studied before matriculating into college.

William Small's formative years were spent at Marischal College, which now is a part of the University of Aberdeen. It is here that Small first learned about the "expansion of science & the system of things in which we are placed." It is at Marischal that Small encountered the professors who introduced him to the scientific method and the tenets of Common Sense Philosophy—concepts integral to his influence at the College of William and Mary and his contributions to the development of the steam engine—the archivists Jane Pirie and Michelle Gait were of great assistance in finding and accessing pertinent information about Small and his mentors during his residence at Marischal.

Edinburgh is the home of the National Archives and a central clearinghouse of primary source documentation for Scottish history. An interesting and important cache of documentation for the early history of the Small family is located at the Lord Lyon's Office, a division of the New Register House of the National Archives of Scotland. I am grateful to the archivist there, Mrs. Elizabeth Rhodes, who brought out the account of the Small family coat of arms; at the Royal College of Physicians, Ian Milne pointed out the newly accessible notebooks of Sir John Pringle. I am exceedingly indebted to Professor Harry Dickinson of the University of Edinburgh, who was instrumental in piecing together various pieces of the puzzle and provided excellent advice and encouragement throughout the whole process. I would also like to thank, for his clarity on issues involving Scots Law, Professor John Cairns, Chair in Civil Law, at the University of Edinburgh.

At the University of Glasgow, the archivists Sarah Hepworth and Leslie Richmond provided assistance and access to important records. Derek Alexander, Director at the National Trust of Scotland, took me to various sites important to Small's history. Near Perth, Gillian Hull, who was the first researcher into Small's medical background, provided new information and for many years acted as an informed sounding board with respect to Small's early career in Scotland. At the University of St. Andrews, Maynard Garrison introduced me to scholars and administrators—including Vice Principal Stephen Magee—who connected me to resources and faculty knowledgeable about the story of St. Andrews and the father of William, James Small. Maynard and his lovely wife Mary also hosted me during my first stay in that town and facilitated an appointment as a visiting scholar to the university.

The most-helpful resources for shedding light on Small's career at the College of William and Mary came from Special Collections at Swem Library at that institution. I am very grateful for the assistance of Miss Margaret Cook, whose encyclopedic knowledge of the archival collections at Swem and razor-sharp ability for making connections between disparate items, led to discoveries connected to Small's career at the college. In addition, Thad Tate, an emeritus professor of history and former director of the Omohundro Institute, provided a deep well of knowledge from which to draw information and inferences. I owe a deep debt of gratitude the Henry Wolf (former Rector of the College of William and Mary) and his kind wife Dixie for both their encouragement and support while I was at William and Mary and afterwards.

In Charlottesville, John Casteen, then president of the University of Virginia, was a crucial source of support and encouragement, as were his staff: Linda Birkhead, Sean Jenkins, and Nancy Rivers. The specialists at both the Harrison Institute and the Alderman Library, especially Regina Rush, were accommodating and efficient in locating the records of the *Virginia Gazette Daybooks* and a revealing letter from Dudley Digges to the Bishop of London. Professor A. E. Dick Howard, the White Burkett Miller Professor of Law at the University, was, and is, a constant source of advice and knowledge.

At Monticello, Elizabeth Chew and Susan Stein advised on curatorial items that reflected the relationship between Thomas Jefferson and William Small. Andrew O'Shaughnessy, the Saunders Director of the International Center for Jefferson Studies, made possible my stay as Gilder-Lehrman Fellow and [I] was [fortunate] to [have experienced] at Kenwood Plantation an environment that was gracious and inviting and provided a venue for the exchange of ideas, interactive collaboration, the adding and vetting of new information, and seeing old history in a different light. Kenwood is also a congenial headquarters for individuals with like interests in related subjects; it provides an important and revolving opportunity for meeting just the right person with the specific knowledge that is sought. ICJS also maintains a celebrated staff of scholars, researchers, and associates: Jefferson Looney, Editor of the *Retirement Series of the Papers of Thomas Jefferson*; Endrina Tay, Cinder Stanton, Sue Perdue, Jack Robertson, Gaye Wilson, Mary-Scott Fleming, and Peter Onuf, Professor Emeritus of the University of Virginia and Senior Research Fellow at the ICJS.

In New Jersey, at Princeton, Barbara Oberg, editor of *The Papers of Thomas Jefferson*, and her staff at the Firestone Library Archives, were able to point me in the right direction on many issues reflecting the influence of Small. In Philadelphia, I am grateful for the help of Richard Shrank in special collections and indebted to Keith Thomson, Executive Director for the American Philosophical Society for his attention to and enthusiasm for this project. I am also thankful for the counsel and kind reception of Professor Michael Zuckerman of the University of Pennsylvania regarding connections between William Small and Benjamin Franklin.

In Richmond, I am owe a debt of gratitude to Dr. Samuel Craver, who urged me to delve deeper into the provocative but incomplete narrative of William Small; to Francis Pollard formerly at the Virginia Historical Society (now the Virginia Museum of History and Culture); to Professor John Kneebone for promoting my project, to Daniel Grenier, who, through his knowledge of digital graphics discovered the signature so critical to the identification of the portrait of William Small by Tilly Kettle, and, most especially, to Brent Tarter, of the Library of Virginia, who read and reread the numerous iterations of the narrative and provided advice and inspiration. Finally, I want to thank Emily Jones Salmon, former senior copy editor for the former Publications Division of the Library of Virginia, and her husband, John Salmon, whose combined expertise in reviewing and correcting forms and formats has led to a cleaner and more coherent copy.

Back in England, where Small spent his final years, the repositories of London and Birmingham allowed insight into Small's involvement with the political, financial, and medical communities in London and his impact on the formation and character of the famous Birmingham Lunar Society, his persuasive influence on the industrialist Matthew Boulton, and his critical collaboration with James Watt and the part that he played in the refinement and promotion of James Watt's improved steam engine that ushered in the Industrial Age.

In London, I am thankful for the expert analysis of Tilly Kettle's portrait of William Small by Philip Mould, art consultant for the Houses of Parliament; to the staff of the Fulham Palace Archives for its assistance in locating colonial records dealing with appointments to the College of William and Mary; and to Celine Fox for her advice in regard to Tilly Kettle's portrait. Jenny Uglow, author of the award-winning tome *The Lunar Men*, was instrumental in providing the big picture of the interaction of the members of the Birmingham Lunar Society. Sir Nicholas Goodison, former Chairman of the London Stock Exchange and Courtland Institute of Art and renowned expert on Matthew Boulton, was critical in networking with people in Britain and locating the authorities who were most knowledgeable about the intricacies of the Birmingham Lunar Society, Matthew Boulton, James Watt, and the development of Watt's steam engine. Sir Nicholas, himself, is a lodestone of knowledge concerning this era in British history, the art and industry of Matthew Boulton, and the individuals with whom both Boulton and Small associated.

In Birmingham, the main source of the details of the life and activities of Small, the Birmingham Lunar Society, Matthew Boulton, James Watt, and the evolution of the steam engine are found in the archives of the Birmingham Central Library. I am obliged to Fiona Tate for her infinite patience and expertise in locating specific documents in the massive Matthew Boulton, James Watt, and Boulton-Watt collections held by the library, and to Sally Baggott at the Birmingham Assay Office. In a surprising development, it came to light that the archives of Cobbett's Law Firm (formerly Lee Law Firm) held the personal records and documents of many members of the Lunar Society, including James Watt, William Withering, and Joseph Priestley (all friends and colleagues of William Small). The Director of Cobbett's at the time, Stephen Gilmore, was the gatekeeper who make it possible for me to access these unique and important documents—thank you, Stephen. John Rimmer, Stephen's partner in the firm, made available to me a mass of unpublished and undocumented letters of James Watt Jr. that were important in following the loose threads of the Boulton-Watt partnership.

There are many individuals to whom I am grateful not only for their professional involvement, but I am also beholden to them on a personal level. Maynard and Mary Garrison, Hank and Dixie Wolf, Keith and Linda Thomson, all of whom opened doors for me that likely would have remained shut without their intercession. Brent Tarter, Harry Dickinson, and Keith Thomson read and advised on the various manifestations of the Small narrative with patience, provided articulate and helpful criticism, and critical insights over an extended period of time. John Casteen has not only overseen the progress of the project over the years but has also line-edited text. I am extremely grateful to Garry Wills for both his guidance in moving forward with my research and his kind permission to append his preface to this work.

I also wish to express my thanks to my many assistants including my son, Richard Graham Clagett II, and my daughter, Alexandra Helena Bowen Clagett; my many assistants: Clint Oaster, Gray Walker, Eric Marquis, Laura Harvey, Andrew Stites, Kyle Grubb, Whitley Lee, Adam Rodabaugh, and David Lowzinski for their dedication, investigatory and technical skills and insights. I want especially to mention my late father-in-law, Arnold Egon Pristenik, my recently departed mother, Dorothy Potter Clagett, and my long-enduring wife, Elizabeth Ann Clagett.

Last but not least, I am thankful for the intercession of Greg Shaw, my literary agent, for wedging me and my research into his very busy schedule and being the "projector" that William Small always strived to be and to his son, Ryan Shaw for his fresh set of eyes which made for a more comprehensive and comprehensible reading of Small's life, and to my daughter, A.H.B. Clagett for her practical advice and logical recommendations.

I also am compelled to mention my long since gone dog "Sparky" whose name, in part, was the inspiration for the title of this work.

CHAPTER I

Early Life and Family Background

In 1734, just as British colonists in Virginia were beginning to advocate for greater autonomy, a child was born to a country cleric in a rural hamlet of Scotland. This child would become a mentor to Thomas Jefferson, an advisor to James Watt, a co-founder of the celebrated Birmingham Lunar Society, and a protégé of the most famous promoter of the goals of the Republic of Letters—Benjamin Franklin. This child was named William Small.

The most important factors in determining the direction of William Small's life were formed during his early years in Scotland. These included the traditions of his Scottish ancestors, the advanced instruction he received at Dundee Grammar School, the expertise and philosophical orientations of his professors and mentors at Marischal College in Aberdeen, and the medical expertise he obtained through his training with the Gregory brothers in Aberdeen and medical apprenticeships in London.

To date, little has been reported about Small's formative years in Scotland. James Patrick Muirhead (author and authority on James Watt) noted that Small's father had been a minister in a small hamlet of Carmylie located near the east coast of Scotland between Arbroath and Dundee, and that he had a brother, Robert, who became a minister in the latter town. There is also a long trail of clergymen and scholars among his ancestors; their names and accomplishments, however, were so deeply embedded in dusty local archives and collections of church papers that until recently they escaped the notice of interested parties. Indeed, the identity of William's paternal grandfather and his branch of the family were matters of speculation and hotly contested between descendants and those claiming to be directly related to William Small down to the present day.

Knowledge of Small's family tree is only presently known back to the time of his great-great-grandfather George Small, of whom little is known. His great-grandfather Thomas Small brought the family into prominence by skill and an advantageous marriage. His grandfather, it turns out, was not the wealthy and patrician minister of Forfar who was "driven from his church without so much as a shadow of a charge," but rather, the younger son of Thomas—a

ANCESTORS OF WILLIAM SMALL

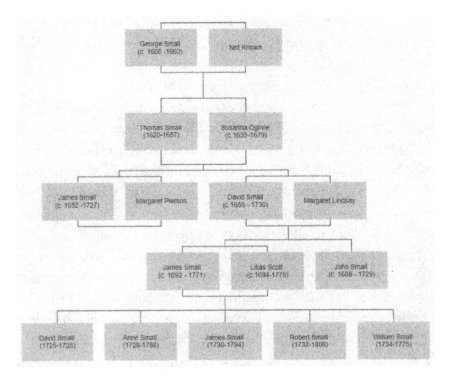

A. H. B. Clagett

kind, indulgent and successful merchant of Dundee—David Small. William's father, James Small, was something of a prodigy who during his academic session at University of St. Andrews became its librarian, living his life as a clergyman somewhere between expectation and despair.

GEORGE SMALL (CA. 1600–1660). GREAT-GREAT-GRANDFATHER OF WILLIAM SMALL.

The earliest-recorded ancestor of William Small was his great-great-grandfather George Small. A weaver from Aberdeen who lived in the nearby hamlet of Foveran, the elder Small was described in a contemporary survey as "a citizen with a "wyff, two bairnes (children) and [a] servant." His occupation was listed as a wobster (weaver)."[1] Not much more is known of his history at present.

THOMAS SMALL (CA. 1620–1687). GREAT-GRANDFATHER OF WILLIAM SMALL.

One of the two "bairnes" was William's great-grandfather Thomas Small (1620–1687). His birthplace, Foveran, is a small village located just north of Aberdeen and several places nearby bear the name Fardine. According to Sir Samuel Forbes, the Fardine parish derived its name from the sweet spring, which issues from the ruins of Foveran Castle. Forbes claimed that Foveran is Celtic for the stream of springs.[2] Among the roster of place-names in the 1870 Valuation Roll for the County of Aberdeen and Parish of Foveran, there are several entries that reflect variants of the name Fardine; croft of South Fardine, Hill of Fardine, and Farm and Inn of South Fardine.[3] Presently both South Farden Croft and South Fardine Farm can be found in the area.[4] Thus, it is very likely that Thomas Small was the son of a weaver in Old Aberdeen whose ancestral home had for some time been located a few miles north of that city.

Academic and Professional Life

Thomas Small likely took his early education at the kirk school and progressed to the Aberdeen Grammar School. He entered the University of St. Andrews, probably the College of St. Mary's, in 1636, at the age of sixteen, and graduated with a Master of Arts in 1640.[5] Soon afterward, he began a successful career in the Church.[6]

Thomas Small's first-recorded position was as schoolmaster and reader at the Parish of Meigle, where he received a gift of two chalders of victuals from the teinds [tithes] of that parish.[7] The church of Meigle was dedicated to St. Peter and Thomas was a prebend (church official) of Dunkeld.[8] On October 23, 1649, he was transferred to the Church at Lintrathen,[9] which was dedicated to St. Medan and held the ancient and venerated Bell of St. Medan.[10]

Near Lintrathen was the Parish of Forfar, a wealthy district that brought with it substantial responsibilities, respect, and income. In 1658, Alexander Robertson, the intense and aggressive minister of Forfar, initiated a campaign to eradicate witchcraft in his district. From 1658 to 1662, Robertson persecuted the scourge of witchcraft vigorously and without mercy. He divided Forfar into eight districts, each with "gaird for the witches," which consisted of six men to be vigilant against the companions of the devil. Between 1660 and 1663, at least forty-three persons were accused of witchcraft and nine were executed. Both the townspeople and the government soon tired of this zealotry. Robertson was deprived of his office by an Act of Parliament in June 1662,[11] and removed by a Decree of the Privy Council on October the first of the same year.[12]

In July 1662, Thomas Small became one of the three candidates named to replace the erstwhile witch-killer and on July 12 a delegation "had gone to St Andreus with Mr Thomas Small for getting a colatione[13] for the admission of Mr Tho: Small."[14] The Archbishop of St. Andrews affirmed the decision to choose Thomas Small and within eight days the decision was finalized and Thomas Small's "presentatione [was] being p[rin]tit & red" by the Council.[15]

The office of Minister of Forfar produced a substantial income. On May 21, 1667, Thomas Small and his wife received a letter of alienation[16] from John Robertsone, writer (lawyer) of Forfar for "all and hail the lands of Corrilhill, lying in the barony and forest of Platon and the parish of Tannadice."[17] Less than a year later he increased his holdings in the area by purchasing the wadset[18] "in the lands of Wolflaw and westward of Quarrelhill in the barony and forest of Platon, as well as the teinde sheaves."[19]

On April 22, 1668, Thomas Small bought the "lands of Wolflaw and westward of Quarrelhill in the barony and forest of Platon, as well as the teind sheaves" from John Mortimer for the sum of £1,000.[20] On May 14, 1668, Small also received a "Tak"[21] from the "Colledge of St Andreus," which was issued by the Principal of St. Mary's, Walter Conrie, and Professor of Divinity, James Tyrie.[22]

Thomas Small served in his capacity as Minister of Forfar, although not without arguments with his congregation until the beginning of 1687, when he had become so infirm that his eldest son James came over to Forfar from his parish in Cortachy to help his father. The magistrate formally asked "Mr James Small minister of Cortachy son of Mr Thomas Small at Forfar to be ane [an] assister and helper to the sd [said] Mr Thomas inregard of his infirmitie and old age and not a capacitie to discharge that deutie as former."[23]

Before April of that year, Thomas Small died and, notwithstanding the differences between certain members of the committee and their former minister, the Forfar Town Council sent a delegation to "speake to Mr. James Small minister att Cortache And to gitt up from him the presentarne granted be the magistrats and counsell as patrons of the church at fforfar in favour of the sd Mr James ... to be sole and only minister of the sd church."[24] Thus, James Small continued in his father's footsteps until 1716 when he was "driven from his church without so much as a shadow of a charge against him."[25]

Thomas Small's Personal Life

In 1650, Thomas Small married Susanna Ogilvie, the daughter of the powerful and influential Earl of Airlie, James Ogilvie. Through his family connection, Small was able to increase his properties and advance his career in the church. By 1656, Thomas Small and Susanna Ogilvie were wealthy enough to lend 1,000 merks Scot, a substantial sum, to David Ogilvie.[26] Susanna Small's father, James, the Earl of Airlie, paid 2,000 merks Scot for the wadset for lands in "barony of Lintrathen and the Mill of Ingzean" for the couple on June 9, 1658, and must have added additional property in March 1660 as he made an additional payment in their favor for another 300 merks Scot.[27]

As a display of his wealth and increasing status within the community, in 1680, Thomas Small greatly enhanced the status of his family by obtaining a coat of arms and becoming a member of the landed gentry. The document reads, "Mr Thomas Small of Corrihall minister of Forfar descended from the familie of Faderines[.] Bears parted perfess waved gules and argent over all, a Lyon passant sable pearced with a dagger proper hefted & pomelled, of the second heft appearing betwixt the shoulders & the point under the bellie tending towards the hind legs. On ane helmet befitting his degree with a mantle gules doubled argent & torse of his collours is set for his crest a branch of palme proper[.] The motto in ane ecroll Ratione non Ira.[28]

Ratione non Ira – By Reason not by Anger.

SMALL FAMILY COAT OF ARMS (1680), LORD LYONS OFFICE: MOTTO–BY REASON NOT BY ANGER

About 1652, Susanna Small gave birth to their first son, James; another son, David, followed about three years later. The older son, James, followed his father's career and offices in the church. Thomas Small assigned his younger son, David, to be apprenticed in the Dundee merchant trade.

David Small (1655–1730?). Grandfather of William Small.

The presumption that James Small, the elder son of Thomas Small was the grandfather of William was dispelled when Professor Harry Dickinson ran across a revealing, albeit brief, mention in the records of William's father's parish of Carmylie, which told a different story.

The only-known connection between James Small of Carmylie, William Small's father, and any other family member is the following: "The Minister having told the session that he could not be present with them upon the 18th of this month being called to Fife to witness the funeral of his Brother, enquired of the elders what they had done at that meeting."[29] This statement was followed by a search of the funeral records of the Forgan Parish, which was nearest church to the residence of David Small in Westhouse, Leuchers, Fife. In the Forgan Parish records it was noted, "John Small, buried 18 June 1729, abode Leuchars, Westhouse."[30]

William Small's father, James Small of Carmyllie, was the son of David Small and his wife, Margaret Lindsay. There is listed in parish records that David Small of Westhouse was married to Margaret Lindsay and the couple had six children who were baptized in Leuchars, near the town of St Andrews. James was their third son born on July 12, 1689. Until recently the identity of James's father (and William's grandfather) had been in doubt with competing claims of potential descendants bantered back and forth between continents.

The enigma has finally been settled by the fine detective work of Professor Harry Dickinson of the University of Edinburgh.[31]

It is most probable that James Small attended the parish school at Forgan Kirk and proceeded to the celebrated Dundee Grammar School. It is not unlikely that his sons (and David Small's grandsons) Robert and William, were legacies at that school.

David Small's home was located in a part of Leuchars known as Westhouse, just opposite the present-day St. Andrews golf course at the Eden estuary, and close by Forgan Kirk and Newport-on-Tay, which was a ferry station for passengers crossing the Tay River to Dundee. Other circumstantial evidence indicating David Small's parentage and James Small's connections to Leuchars and therefore David Small include 1) after completing his courses at St. Andrews, James took his Presbytery trials, an examination to become a minister in the Presbyterian church. After which, it was recorded. "The Presbytery appoints for supplies to the Brethren who were chosen to represent them in the ensuing General Assembly as follows viz.... For Leuchars Mr James Russel Sabbath first and Mr James Small Sabbath second, as also they appoint Mr James Small to preach at Forgan for Mr James Russel the third Sabbath of May next."[32]

Leuchars was the family parish and Forgan Kirk was the family church where James Small's brother John was buried. First ministers had seniority, second ministers were junior in experience and rank. The fact that James Small, William's father, was to be second minister at Leuchars and to preach for the first minister at Forgan, suggests to a robust degree that Leuchars was James Small's home district and Forgan his home church.

Thus, both by the relationship of James and John Small, with Leuchars listed as David Small's place of residence, and the strong correlation between the Forgan as both the site of James Small of Carmylie's early clerical affiliations and John Small's place of internment, a logical conclusion is that David Small of Leuchars was the father of James Small of Carmylie and the grandfather of William Small.

In any case, the elder son of Thomas Small received the plum position of following in his father's fortunes and footsteps, while the younger son, David, was destined for the trades. Nevertheless, Thomas Small seemed to have made a prudent and practical choice for his younger son, for on September 6, 1669, a contract of indenture was made "betwixt Henry Crawford, merchant burgess of Dundee on the one part and David Small, lawful son of Mr Thomas Small, minister at Forfar, for himself and with the special advice and consent of his said father." The contract provided that David Small would become "bound prentice and servant ... to the said Henry Crawford, his master in the merchant trade" for the "hail [whole] space, years and term of five years ... the said David ... binds and obliges himself ... to be a leal [loyal] true and faithful servant ... both by night and by day." He further promised to reveal anything he heard that might be injurious to this master, and to do everything in his power to prevent it from doing reputational harm. Further, if he was absent more than two days without his master's permission, his master could demand "the sum of 12 shillings for each day's leave." The agreement also stated that he shall refrain from "carding, dyceing, night walking ... or fall into any sort of fornication" and that if caught doing any of these things his term of service would return to the full five years. Thomas Small further promised to pay a substantial "prentice fee" and "to furnish and provide his said son with sufficient clothes and [bedding?] suitable to his condition." Henry Crawford, for his part, was to "educate and instruct" his prentice "in the merchant trade and whole points, so far as he himself knows ... and to conceal no points thereof from him." Crawford was also obliged "to sustain and entertain his said prentice at bed and board suitable to his rank, quality and condition and that he shall send his said prentice with a considerable stock for Holland."[33]

Thomas Small certainly must have paid a substantial sum to Mr. Crawford for his tutelage and, by all available evidence, David Small became a member of the Dundee merchant guild, thereby obtaining both a comfortable living and a well-respected position in society.

JAMES SMALL (1689-1771).
FATHER OF WILLIAM SMALL.

Early Life and Education

William Small's father, James Small of Carmyllie, was born in 1689. Although no documentation has been located, it is not unlikely that he attended the parish school at Forgan Kirk and progressed to the celebrated Dundee Grammar School. David Small's status as a prosperous merchant would have enabled him to provide his sons with the best education available. David Small's home was conveniently located at Westhouse, close by Newport-on-Tay, where ferryboats made the short trip to Dundee and back on regular schedules. Although James Small's records for Dundee Grammar School have not as yet come to light, it is known for certain that James Small was a student and employee in two of the four colleges that made up the University of St. Andrews.[34]

A Student at St. Andrews

James Small is listed as a "minus potens" in the records of St. Andrews University[35] that indicates that he was either the younger son of a landowner or of common stock. Although the records of St. Andrews show James Small as entering the university in 1707,[36] he appears on the Bursar's Diet in 1706.[37] James may have either been ill or lost the bursary in 1707, for the records imply that he missed some time at school and returned to college on March 3, 1708,[38] as is recorded in the Bursar's diet on the "Die Dom(ini) 7 Martii 1708 along with James Fleeming—redierunt [they have returned]."[39] In 1709 James Small received a BA from the University,[40] and applied for a bursary in the spring of 1710.

James Small was selected for one of these bursaries and graduated with an MA by the end of the year.[41] In 1710, he applied and won a place as a divinity student at St. Mary's College in the United Colleges of St. Andrews.[42] In 1712 Small applied again for a bursar's diet and other funds,[43] and was granted both. His teachers at St. Mary's included the principal, James Hadow, as second master or Professor of the New Testament, from 1710 to 1712; Thomas Halyburton, followed by Alexander Scrymgeour, as Professor of Old Testament; Patrick Haldane, Professor of Hebrew, and John Syme.[44] Small is listed in the records of St. Andrews as a student at St. Mary's again from 1716 to 1719.[45]

In addition to his duties as a student, James Small had the rare honor of being nominated for the post of Library Keeper in 1718 after the resignation of Mr. John Crie. The faculty considered different candidates for the post, and then proceeded "to the election of one to serve in that office," and "by a plurality of votes Mr James Small was chosen."[46] In May, the decision was confirmed as the University appointed "Mr James Smal to be admitted as Library Keeper,"[47] and he was ratified by a vote of the entire Senatus the following week as Keeper of the Publick Library "being satisfied with the qualifications and fitness of Mr James Small Library Keeper for discharging that office."[48]

Ecclesiastical Career

After a successful turn as bursar, divinity student, and librarian, James Small began to turn his ambitions to the ministry in 1719. Evidently, he garnered the approval and encouragement of the university, for at least three members of the faculty Senatus of St. Andrews—Joseph Drew, James Hadow, and William Vilant—were also members of the St. Andrews Presbytery that presided over trials, ordinations, and assignments of ministers.[49] Principal Drew arranged it so that James Small would be included in the upcoming trials for the Presbytery.

Principal Drew reported that "Mr James Small, student in Divinity, had been mentioned at the last synod at Coupar the order to pass tryalls which was allowed as also the ministers in St. Andrews reported that they had conversed with him and were satisfied that

the Presbytery should proceed to enter him on Tryalls, where-
upon the Presbytery presented for him a homily: 2 Cor(inthians)
4 Chap(ter): Verse 5."[50]

In the autumn of 1719, Small delivered "his homily formerly proscribed viz: second of the Corinthians fourt and fifth verse ... which
were approven and got presented to him a common head."[51] His second lecture was presented in the spring of 1720: "This Day Mr James
Small Delivered the Lecture on Judges the nineteenth Mr Melvil
got presented to him a lecture on Judges the twentieth chapter and
Mr James Small the popular sermon on Acts the second and thirtie
ninth verse ... which they are to deliver the next Presbytery."[52]

About a month after his homily, the Presbytery of St. Andrews
received a request from the parish of Meigle for both James Small
and Robert Moldrum to supply the vacancies in their kirk.[53] This is
both geopolitically interesting, for the parish of Meigle lies close to
Forfar and Airlie Castle, and within the sphere of influence of the
powerful Ogilvie clan. Coincidentally, Meigle had also been the first
ecclesiastical post for Thomas Small in the 1640s.

In June 1720, the Presbytery of St. Andrews appointed James
Small to represent the parish of Leuchers, about four miles from
St. Andrews, in the "ensuing General Assembly by preaching the
Sabbath second" and also "to preach for Mr Russel of Leuchers the
following May."[54] The Presbytery of St. Andrews ordered an offi-
cial license to be issued to James Small in July.[55] Small was called to
Carmylie on July 20, 1720, and ordained on September 23, 1720.[56]
Carmylie would be his home parish until he died in 1771.

Family Life in Carmylie

As James Small was making an aggressive start to his administration
of Carmylie parish, his personal life also took a turn in a positive
direction, for he soon met and married Lillias Scott on August 22,
1723.[57]

The couple produced five children in uniform and pragmatic fashion, one every two years, from 1726 through 1734. The first was David, who was baptized on March 25, 1725, but he died shortly thereafter.[58] A girl, Anne, followed in 1728,[59] and James was baptized on December 13, 1730.[60] Robert, who would become a notable figure in the history of Dundee and a Moderator of the General Assembly, is recorded as having been born on December 12, 1732, and baptized on the 17th.[61] The last child, William, was born on October 13, 1734, and baptized on October 20, 1734.[62]

According to Scottish-naming tradition, the eldest son is named for the paternal grandfather (David), the eldest daughter was named after Lillias's mother (Anna), and the second eldest son was named after the mother's father (James). This tradition of naming adds collateral confirmation to the theory that James Small of Carmylie was the son of David Small, the Dundee merchant.

NOTES

1. *Scottish Notes and Queries* 7, no.1 (June 1893): 1.

2. Alexander Smith, *A New History of Aberdeenshire* (Aberdeen: Lewis Smith, 1875), 572.

3. Personal communication, Janet Jones to Martin Clagett, March 28, 2008.

4. Personal communication, the Reverand Gerald Stranraer-Mull to Martin Clagett, April 14, 2008. The Reverend Stranraer-Mull is the minister at St. James, Cruden Bay, Scotland, nearby Foveran and a local historian.

5. Index of Matriculations and Graduations in the University of St. Andrews (1579–1747), Archives. St. Andrews University, St. Andrews, Scotland (hereafter cited as St. Andrews University).

6. Thomas Small's first-recorded position was as schoolmaster and reader at Meigle. See Hew Scott, ed., *Fasti Ecclesiae Scoticanae* (Edinburgh: Oliver and Tweed, 1925), 5:285. On October 23, 1649, he was transferred to the Church at Lintrathen. See 02023-GD16-46-32-1, National Archives of Scotland, New Register House, Edinburgh, Scotland (hereafter cited as National Archives of Scotland).

7. Scott, *Fasti Ecclesiae Scoticanae*, 5:285.

8. Ibid., 5:269.

9. MSS 02023-GD16-46-32-1, National Archives of Scotland.

10. Scott, *Fasti Ecclesiae Scoticanae*, 5:267.

11. Ibid., 5:285.

12. Ibid.

13. Colation: the formal admission to a benefice by the proper ecclesiastical authority.

14. "Transcripts of the Forfar Town Council Minute Book," July 12, 1662, Transcript Reference number 33352.1(p38), Original F/1/1. Courtesy of Mrs Fiona Scharlau, Angus Archives, Restenneth, Scotland.

15. Ibid.

16. Letter of alienation: document that transferred ownership of land from one party to another.

17. RS35/3 f.255, National Archives of Scotland.

18. Wadset: the conveyance of land in pledge for or in satisfaction of a debt or obligation.

19. RS35/3 f.436, National Archives of Scotland. Sheave: a portion or part; Teind: 10 percent of the produce set aside for support of the church.

20. RS35/3 f.436, National Archives of Scotland.

21. Tak or Tack: a leasehold tenure of a piece of land.

22. SM110-5R31-36, Archives, University of St. Andrews; Walter Conrie, 1648–1662, Minister at St. Leonard's; 1662–1666, Professor of Divinity St. Mary's College, University of St. Andrews; admitted Principal of St. Mary's, October 23, 1666; Principal, 1666–1686; Robert Blair and William Row, *Life of... Robert Blair... Containing His Autobiography, From 1593 to 1636, With Supplement to His Life, And Continuation of the History of the Times to 168*, Publications, 11, ed. Thomas McCrie. (Edinburgh: Wodrow Society, 1848), 395; James Tyrie, admitted Professor of Divinity, St. Mary's College, 1667, McCrie, *Life of... Robert Blair*, 410.

23. "Transcripts of the Forfar Town Council Minute Book," January 22, 1687, Transcript Reference number 33:352.1 (p.35), Original F/1/2, Angus Archives, Restenneth, Scotland.

24. "Transcripts of the Forfar Town Council Minute Book," January 22, 1687, Transcript Reference number 33:352.1 (p.39), Original F/1/2, Angus Archives, Restenneth, Scotland; CC20/4/15 f.265, St. Andrews Commissary Court, Testament Dative, Recorded October 22, 1687.

25. Scott, *Fasti Ecclesiae Scoticanae*, 5:286.

26. RS35/7 f.445, National Archives of Scotland.

27. RS35/7 f.19, National Archives of Scotland.

28. Small Family Coat of Arms in Register of All Arms and Bearings in Scotland, 1680, Lord Lyon's Office, New Register House, Edinburgh, Scotland.

29. CH2/558/2, "Minutes and Accounts of the Carmylie Parish," June 23rd, 1729, National Archives of Scotland.

30. Old Parish Records, OPR445-2, Leuchars, Vol. 2. Courtesy of Mrs. Rachel Hart, Archivist, University of St. Andrews.

31. Leuchar Parish Records show that David Small married Margaret Lindsay. The couple had six children who were baptized in Leuchars, near the town of St. Andrews. James was their third son, born on July 12, 1689. The direct connection between David Small and William's father James was discovered by Professor Harry Dickinson of the University of Edinburgh, "The Minister having told the session that he could not be present with them upon the 18th of this month being called to Fife to witness the funeral of his Brother, enquired of the elders what they had done at that meeting" (CH2/558/2/128-32, Minutes and Accounts of the Carmylie Parish, June 23rd 1729, National Archives of Scotland) and confirmed by the death record of his brother John in Leuchars. "John Small, buried 18 June 1729, abode Leuchars, Westhouse," Old Parish Records, OPR445-2, Leuchars, Vol. 2. Courtesy of Mrs. Rachel Hart, Archivist, University of St Andrews, St Andrews, Scotland (hereafter cited as University of St. Andrews).

32. CH2/1132/2, St. Andrews Presbytery Minutes, 1714–1723, June 20, 1720, Archives, University of St. Andrews (230).

33. NAS 02023 RD3/4/1/000389, National Archives of Scotland. I am indebted to John G. Harrison for rendering the document from the Scottish secretarial hand of the mid-seventeenth century. Personal communication, John G. Harrison to Martin Clagett, February 23, 2008.

34. As an undergraduate, James Small attended professors' lectures in St. Salvator's College; as a theology student and a librarian in St. Mary's, he undoubtedly was familiar with St. Leonard's as well. The University of St. Andrews was comprised of three colleges—St. Salvator's, St. Leonard's, and St. Mary's— each college having its own history and functionality. The collective institution, then as now, dominated the town, both structurally and economically.

35. Records of the University of St. Andrews: Index of Matriculations and Graduations (1579–1747), 176, Archives, University of St. Andrews.

36. Records of the University of St. Andrews. Archives, University of St. Andrews.

37. "From the twentieth of Novr to the first of ffebry," SS 516/1706.1, Accompts for Bursars Diets (1706–1707), Archives, University of St. Andrews. SS indicates San Salvators College and 1706 the year.

38. SS 530/1/46v, Archives, University of St. Andrews.

39. Recorded by Mag: Car: Gregory, Math: proff"—Magister Charles Gregory, Professor of Mathematics, SS 516/1706.1, Accompts for Bursars Diets, Archives, University of St. Andrews.

40. Records of the University of St. Andrews: Index of Matriculations and Graduations (1579–1747), 176, Archives, University of St. Andrews.

41. Ibid.

42. He was listed as a 1st year "RB" (1710–1711); in 1711–1712 as a 2nd year "RB"; 1712–1713 as a 3rd year "RB"; and in 1713–1714 as a 4th year "RB." SM 310/1, Archives, University of St. Andrews. RB stands for Royal Bursar.

43. St. Andrews Senatus Minutes, Vol. 2 (1698–1718), September 8, 1712 (224), Archives, University of St. Andrews.

44. Courtesy Robert Smart, Archivist Emeritus, St. Andrews University, personal communication, May 18, 2007.

45. SM 310/1, Archives, University of St. Andrews. It was not unusual for a student to remain at the college even after his normal course of study. "There could be any number of reasons for this—having a tutor's post, having yet to satisfy the presbytery regulations for licence, expecting or hoping for some particular post etc., etc. … It was by no means uncommon for some divinity students to stick around after completing their normal courses." Personal communication from Robert Smart, Archivist Emeritus to the University of St. Andrews, May 18, 2007.

46. St. Andrews Senatus Minutes, UY 452/2/299, Vol 2 (1698–1718), April 16, 1718, Archives, University of St. Andrews

47. St. Andrews Senatus Minutes, UY 452/2/300, Vol 2 (1698–1718), May 12, 1718, Archives, University of St. Andrews.

48. St. Andrews Senatus Minutes, UY 452/2/304, Vol 2 (1698–1718), Archives, University of St. Andrews. The salary for this post was substantial as revealed by a 1720 receipt by James Small for salary "received from James Torny factor for the New College the sum of an Hundred pounds Scots as an years Sallary." SM110/ S887.276, Archives, University of St. Andrews.

49. James Hadow was Principal of St. Marys (1707–1749), Joseph Drew was Principal of St. Leonard's (1708–1738), and William Vilant was curator of Library materials and brother of Colin Vilant, former Principal of St. Leonard's. All three names are listed as "sederunt" on July 27, 1718, in the St. Andrews Senatus Minutes, Vol. 2 (1698–1718), 304. All three are also listed as "sederunt" at a Presbytery meeting on April 20, 1720, which concerned the Presbytery "tryall" of James Small. St. Andrews Presbytery Records, CH2/ 1132/ 2)226, Archives, University of St. Andrews.

50. St. Andrews Presbytery Minutes (1714–1723), July 15, 1719, CH2/1132/2, 202, Archives, University of St. Andrews. "For we preach not ourselves, but Christ Jesus the Lord; and ourselves your servants for Jesus' sake." 2 Corinthians, Chapter 4, Verse 5, King James Version.

51. CH2/1132/2 (213). St. Andrews Presbytery Minutes (1714–1723), October 20, 1719, Archives, University of St. Andrews.

52. CH2/1132/2 (223), St. Andrews Presbytery Minutes (1714-1723), March 17, 1720, Archives, University of St. Andrews. "For the promise is unto you, and to your children, and to all that are far off, *even* as many as the Lord our God shall call." Acts, Chapter 2, Verse 39, King James Version.

53. Personal communication, Robert Smart to Martin Clagett, May 9. 2007. "We cannot say what kind of jobs the presbytery of Meigle was seeking Meldrum and Small for—they could either have been seeking schoolmasters or probationer ministers, which latter was the stage they were at in their careers. Robert Meldrum was slightly older than James Small being baptized 4 August 1688 son of Robert Meldrum, tenant in Balmullo (Leuchars parish). He was licensed by St. Andrews Presbytery 24 April 1717 and became minister at Kemback 1730—5 September 1733 (died). It is not known what he was doing during the 23 years between license and ordination, but I would guess he was most likely a parish schoolmaster."

54. "The Presbytery appoints for supplie to the Brethren who were chosen to represent them in the ensuing General Assembly as following, viz: for St. Andrews Mr William Cunningham to preach there Sabbath first and Mr William Vilant Sabbath second For St. Leonards Mr James Knox Sabbath first and Mr Andrew Melvil Sabbath second For Kilrenny Mr William Dalyiesh Sabbath first and Mr Joseph Pitcairn Sabbath second For Leuchers Mr James Russel Sabbath first and Mr James Small Sabbath second; as also they appoint Mr James Small to preach at Forgan for Mr James Russel the third Sabbath of May next." June 1720, CH2/1132/2 (230), St. Andrews Presbytery Minutes (1714–1723).

55. July 27, 1720, "The Presbytery appoints the Clerk to give Mr James Small his licence and testifecit when called for, and appoints Mr William Harvie and him to subscribe the same in their name. CH2/1132/2 (240), St. Andrews Presbytery Minutes (1714–1723).

56. Scott, *Fasti Ecclesiae Scoticanae*, 5:432.

57. James Small married Lillias Scott (1694–1775) September 24, 1723. Scott, *Fasti Ecclesiae Scoticanae*, 5:432.

58. Old Parish Records, Carmylie Baptism Records, Baptism, March 7, 1727. "To Mr James Small Minister in Carmylie, his son David bapt by Mr Charles Charters Min[r] in Arbirtet before this Witness David Kyd in Carmylie." A naming

tradition in Scottish families was regularly applied. It consisted of naming the eldest son after the paternal grandfather, the eldest daughter after the maternal grandmother, the next son after the maternal grandfather, and the next daughter after the paternal grandmother. Therefore, it is collateral evidence that James Small's father was David Small rather than James Small.

59. Old Parish Records, Carmylie Baptism Records, Baptism, "March 31, 1728. "Baptised to Mr James Small Minister in this paroch by Mr Robt Trail Minr in Panbride, his Daughter Anne Small. Witnesses Da Kyd in Carmylie and George Kerd in Moncheir."

60. James's date of birth, December 6, 1730, in Scott, *Fasti Ecclesiae Scoticanae*, 5:432; date of baptism given as December 13, 1730. Old Parish Records, Carmylie Baptism Records. "Baptized James Small son to Mr James Small Minister here, bapd by Mr Robt Trail Minister at Panbride David Kid and George Kerd Elders Witnesses."

61. Robert's date of birth was given as December 12, 1732, in Scott, *Fasti Ecclesiae Scoticanae*, 5:316; Carmylie Baptism Records Dec 17th "Decr 17th Bapt'd by Mr Robert Trail Minister at Panbride to Mr James Small Minister here his Son ROBERT."

62. William's date of birth is given as October 13, 1734, in Scott, *Fasti Ecclesiae Scoticanae*, 5:432; Old Parish Records, Carmylie Baptism Records, "October 20th Bapd to Mr James Small Min.r in this paroch by My Robert Trail Min.r in Panbride his son WILLIAM SMALL. David Kid and George Kerd Elders witnesses."

CHAPTER 2

Small's Early Education

HALF A WORLD AWAY

At the very time when the colonists in America began to consider their own political situations and their relationships with the mother country, when vestries were politely defying the Anglican establishment, and when native assemblies were asserting their constitutional prerogatives, a son who would help change the face of the Western world was born to a country cleric. This child would become a mentor to Thomas Jefferson, a collaborator and friend of Benjamin Franklin, a partner of the industrialist Matthew Boulton, and a promoter and collaborator of James Watt.

Small was born in the rural hamlet of Carmylie, located halfway between the ancient town of Arbroath and the busy port of Dundee. The ruins of the abbey at Arbroath rise impressively from the middle of the ancient town, leaving behind hints of what must have been. In the spring of 1320, within the lofty walls of the abbey, the Declaration of Arbroath, which expressed the contractual relationship between the ruler and the ruled, was drafted. Many believe that the Declaration of Arbroath was an inspiration for the American Declaration of Independence; not proved would be the verdict under Scottish law, but it is indeed a neat circumstance of fate that almost within shouting distance of the abbey is the tiny parish of Carmylie.

Carmylie Parish[1]

The Milton of Carmylie and its church are ensconced by the soft glove of a verdant field, sheltered on three sides from the crisp winds that blow down from the mountains, and the fourth side stretching out toward the variations of the North Sea. The lights from St. Andrews can be seen signaling, in turns, at night from a ridge near the kirk.

It has been recorded that both Robert and William Small became students at the well-known and highly respected Dundee Grammar School[2] some fifteen miles distant from Carmylie. As the journey from Carmylie to Dundee would have been arduous in an age of poor transportation, with impassible roads and unpredictable weather, Robert and William likely lived with their grandfather, David Small, in Leuchars during the school year and made the short ferry ride across the Tay River to Dundee each day.

DUNDEE GRAMMAR SCHOOL

By the eighteenth century, Dundee Grammar School was already well known as a rigorous training ground for academics and intellectuals, alongside future leaders of church and state. Robert and William Small found themselves in an institution that emphasized mathematics and the practical sciences as well as the traditional subjects of Latin, religion, basic math, and writing. Its preeminent position among institutions of its kind and the thoroughness of its instruction were attested to by the aggressive competition for positions among its faculty and the length of its course of studies—seven years instead of the customary five.[3]

Dundee Grammar School's early history is literally lost in the mists of antiquity.[4] About 1225, Gilbert, the Bishop of Brechin, granted a charter to the Abbot of Lindores to appoint a master or masters of the school in Dundee. A number of disputes arose between the masters of the school and ecclesiastical authorities until 1555 when control of Dundee Grammar School passed from the church to the Town Council of Dundee. The Town Council jealously guarded its rights to the school after its move from private to public ownership.[5]

In 1589, the Town Council provided Dundee Grammar School with its first permanent home, between Adam's Town House and St. Clement's Church, where it would remain for the next two hundred years. It was here that William and Robert Small attended school. The building included a hall raised on a vaulted basement, reached by an outside stair where the masters, janitors, and rector could shout at their classes simultaneously.

The extended period of seven years rather than five years speaks to the rigor of the curriculum and thoroughness of instruction at that institution. When Robert and William attended Dundee Grammar School, the customary age to enter was eight and to graduate was fifteen. Since William was born in 1734, he probably entered grammar school in 1743, and exited in his sixteenth year, 1750.

In most respects the administration of Dundee Grammar School was similar to other schools in Scotland. The school was controlled by the town council. Hiring of masters, curriculum, and all texts had to be approved by the council. The tenure of the masters was generally "*ad vitam aut ad culpam*" (for life or until fault is found), and salaries were derived from local funding.

INSTRUCTORS AT DUNDEE GRAMMAR SCHOOL

The teaching staff at Dundee Grammar School consisted of a rector (or headmaster), a janitor, and several masters, whose number was determined by the fortunes and the needs of the institution. The rector was in charge of setting school policies, establishing the curriculum, selecting the texts, administering scholarships, scheduling times for classes and vacations, fixing regulations and punishments, and teaching the senior class. The janitor was in charge of maintenance and instructing the entrant class, and the masters were assigned to the intervening years. The masters most likely to have instructed William and Robert were Gilbert Lundie, George Blair, John Mearns, and the notorious William Lauder.

Town Council records show that Gilbert Lundie, or Lundy, as janitor in 1743 and he would likely have been William's first formal teacher. Lundie, frustrated by the lack of a promised raise from the Town Council, resigned in 1747 and took up residence in Spott, Haddingtonshire. The funds for his raise were supposed to come from "Bruce's Mortification," a fund that disappeared when Lord Gray, to whom it was entrusted, went bankrupt.[6]

George Blair, minister of the Gospel at Abernyte, was appointed rector for life in 1738 and served in that capacity until the spring of 1749, when he not only heard the call of the ministry but was resettled in it.[7] As rector, he instituted many changes during his administration: the school acquired a more substantial reputation, men of distinguished backgrounds applied for teaching positions, irregular payments to the masters were changed into a "scholar's fee," or fifth-quarter payment, and a library and the Office of Librarian were established.[8]

When George Blair returned to the ministry in 1749, the Dundee Town Council appointed John Coutts as rector. Coutts previously was the rector of the famous school in Herriot's Hospital in Edinburgh.[9] One of his first changes as rector was in the method of teaching English.

During much of Blair's administration, the number of masters was generally three, for Blair believed that it was too much for any one of the masters to have charge of three classes. William Small's most likely instructors at Dundee were John Mearns and William Lauder—less likely were John Knox, John Pitcairn, and John Davidson. John Mearns was a master for the entire time of William's stay at Dundee Grammar School and one of the more-qualified teachers. John Mearns, who had a reputation as an excellent classical scholar, served as one of the masters of the Latin School. Stymied in his ambitions for greater salary and a more respectable position, however, Mearns became unhappy. Soon thereafter, he accepted a position as master at the Latin School at Dunkold.

William Lauder was probably the most highly regarded of the classical scholars, although he possessed a sanguine temper and a persecution complex. He may have been one of William's earlier teachers. Although he began his career with great promise, William Lauder had some serious deficiencies. In 1743, he accepted a position as a master at Dundee Grammar School, but before he could take his post "a [golf] ball unluckily struck him on the knee, which festering from careless inattention, it became necessary to amputate the leg."[10] After he had undergone the operation, there was also a change of personality. A contemporary described him as having a "rolling eye, stentorian voice, shallow complexion and ungovernable temper [that] created difficulties of their own." In an attempt to enhance his literary reputation, Lauder falsely attacked the reputation of the dead poet Milton, but his deception was soon detected and documented. He was forced to sign a confession dictated by Dr. Samuel Johnson admitting his duplicity. After this humiliation, he left Britain[11] and moved to Barbados, where he established a school; and, it is said that he subjected his own daughter to the most infamous treatment from which strangers rescued her.[12] He died in Barbados about 1771, a despised and discredited figure.[13]

SUBJECTS, SCHEDULES, AND EXPECTATIONS

Despite the transgressions of some of its masters, the reputation of Dundee Grammar School made great strides, as demonstrated by some of the candidates who applied for positions there. In addition to a gifted and dedicated staff, the students also benefited from rigorous discipline and a challenging course of studies.

Classes were held almost continuously throughout the year. The exceptions were sporadic breaks, which extended from the day before the fair in August until the day after the fair in September, a day at New Year, a day at spring and autumn fasts, days at both Christmas and Easter (which were considered Popish or pagan festivals), one or two sports half-holidays, and orations and occasional plays transmuted into weekly half-holidays.[14]

The curriculum was rigorous and considered progressive for grammar school students of the time. It focused primarily on the study of the major branches of Latin, including grammar, prose, poetry, disputations, and rhetoric. The school also taught religion (including church music), physical recreation, writing, and basic math. Favorite texts at the school were James Kirkwood's *Grammatica Despauteriana* and Thomas Ruddiman's *Rudiments of Latin Grammar*.[15]

The students were trained not only to be scholars, but also gentlemen. The more recalcitrant students were found to be swearers, breakers of the Sabbath, rebels to their masters, truants from school and fugitives from discipline. For the first offense they were to be "publickly whiped," for the second "flogged," and for the third transgression they were expelled until assurances could be made for better behavior in the future. Also not tolerated were those students "who disturbed the walk below the Town House by playing hand or football, those that rode horses, especially in time of mercat [market], those that frequented the shoer [shore] boats or ships, and those senior scholars who had been found speaking English instead of Latin and been betrayed by the clandestine captors." On five out of the six school days there was no corporal punishment, but on Monday morning all delinquents presented themselves to the rector for their condign reward.[16]

Thus, William Small began his life with the lessons of academic rigor and monastic discipline imposed by the masters at Dundee Grammar School. Small finished his studies about 1750 and matriculated at Marischal College, Aberdeen, in 1751.

MARISCHAL COLLEGE

Given both the long-standing relationship between the Small family and the University of St. Andrews and the proximity of the Small family home at Westhouse, Small's matriculation at Marischal College in the relatively remote city of Aberdeen is somewhat surprising. Although Small's family originated in the tiny hamlet of Foveran, near Aberdeen, and both the Smalls and the Ogilvies (the Earl of Airlie) had connections in Aberdeen, the choice of Marischal probably depended more on finances than on family traditions.[17]

The independent nature of Scotland in the eighteenth century was due, in part, to its isolated and remote location. There was a lack of central infrastructure, and towns were separated from one another with few reliable roads, canals, or means of transportation between them, which created an archipelago of isolated communities connected primarily by the sea. Because of its coastal location on the North Sea, its disconnect with the interior of the country, and the influences of its primary trading partners Holland and France, Aberdeen contained the most progressive and scientifically oriented institutions of learning in Scotland at that time. The clientele of

Marischal College, in particular, was drawn from the middle class of noveaux riche merchants interested in the pragmatic aspects of education, and the advantages that a scientific and utilitarian curriculum would provide to their sons. In an age when there were only two universities in England, Scotland boasted five: the University of Glasgow, the University of Edinburgh, University of St. Andrews, King's College, and Marischal College.

Aberdeen, a city of granite and gulls, is located in the northeastern section of Scotland and was described in the mid-eighteenth century as being "pleasantly situated near the sea being a tolerable harbour into which the Ships come up under the Castle, almost close to the town."[18] The city was divided into two sections—the Old Town and the New Town—with a college located in each. King's College was situated in Old Town and Marischal College in New Town. The denominations for the sections of the city also accurately reflected the natures of the institutions. Proximity, among other factors, provided for a love-hate relationship between the two colleges and their characters and histories were images of opposites. Marischal was originally a Presbyterian foundation, while King's was Episcopalian; Marischal emphasized a curriculum dominated by science and practical subjects, while King's stressed a more-traditional curriculum of law, medicine, and theology; Marischal drew the majority of its clientele from the merchant families of New Aberdeen and Aberdeenshire, while King's students came primarily from the old and traditional families of the Highlands. Marischal also seems to have produced more competitive and ambitious students, while those from King's seemed more contentious, litigious, and conservative in outlook.[19]

As a result of the increase in trade and the economic advantages that were brought about by the Union of 1707, the middle class in the northern kingdom expanded exponentially. With that prosperity came an increased desire by the bourgeoisie to provide their children with an advanced education. The unquenchable thirst for pragmatic knowledge was also encouraged by abundant trade opportunities, and nurtured by the tenets of the Scottish Enlightenment. It was at this happy juncture of time and place that Aberdeen was transformed from a quiet and traditional town into a city teeming with enthusiasm, new blood, and new ideas. It was during this happy juncture of time and place that William Small matriculated into Marischal College. Small had been born into a region that both topographically and psychologically nurtured strict morality, stubborn pride, and a resistance to authority. He came of age during a time that polished those traits with intelligence, sophistication, and intellectual curiosity.

Marischal College was one of the most scientifically and philosophically advanced institutions in Britain. Scottish universities were more democratic than their English counterparts and demonstrated a more utilitarian mission. English universities were characterized as elitist institutions that catered to a small percentage of the population, and their mission was to turn out classically trained gentlemen. Life at Oxford and Cambridge has been described as port-mellowed and it has been noted that "eighteenth-century English university life centered in residential colleges where wit and indolence were more characteristic than purpose and industry."[20] Scottish universities, by contrast, were available to almost any student of talent regardless of finances or social status. John Knox had formulated a plan and instituted a tradition of extending educational opportunities to the entire population. A myriad of bursaries and mortifications were established to help students from less affluent backgrounds attain training and erudition. The mission of the universities of Scotland was also directed toward a more progressive and pragmatic clientele.

Marischal's status rose consistently during the eighteenth century. In addition to the increasing population from which to draw students, Marischal also seems to have benefited from its close connection to national politics, its location in an urban setting, and with a lack of faculty strife that plagued King's.

Marischal College[21]

After the demise of Charles I, both colleges in Aberdeen flourished under the patronage of the Puritans and Oliver Cromwell, and the size of the institutions increased dramatically. The end of the eighteenth century saw even-greater catalysts for the growth of Scottish universities.

First, the end of the Stuarts and the ascension of William and Mary in 1688 brought with it a renewed interest in the expansion and support of Protestant institutions. Second, the Act of Union of 1707 not only accomplished its goal of lessening the threat of a return of the Stuarts, but also had the unintended consequence of opening up trade with the American colonies. Scottish merchants were especially interested in the tobacco trade and bartered directly with colonial farmers to their own advantage and to the detriment of the London merchants. Naturally this added to the revenues of the northern kingdom.

In addition to the newly found wealth of the middle class, the Union of 1707 also had the effect of siphoning off Scottish nobility. So that they might not lose position and influence, many Scottish nobles went to London, thus creating a social and political vacuum soon taken up by nouveaux riche merchants. The initial trappings of wealth and respectability were material objects—clothes, fine houses, and ostentatious carriages, but the more-lasting attributes of gravitas stemmed from comprehensive education. Thus, the enlarged and energetic middle class in Scotland hungered after knowledge and polish. The new class of students was also more receptive to the ideals of the Enlightenment. At this juncture in history, with Aberdeen transformed from a quiet and traditional village into a city teeming with enthusiasm, new blood, and new ideas, William Small matriculated to Marischal College.

Many of the customs and habits of tradition, the innovations of change, and the philosophical orientations that Small would bring to America were inculcated during his years in Aberdeen and are important factors in understanding Small's instructional approaches, his scientific and metaphysical orientations, and the mindset and methodology that he would disseminate to students, colleagues, and friends throughout his lifetime. Teachers most often instruct in the same way that they were taught and gravitate to those the areas of study in which they have studied. Men of science often make use of their instruction to enhance and expand the boundaries of understanding. Innovators synthesize what they know and what is possible in the hope of creating what might be. For William Small, this process began in Aberdeen.

ACADEMICS AT MARISCHAL COLLEGE

During the eighteenth century, Marischal College began sessions at "the end of October or beginning of November" and competitions for bursaries took place on the last Monday of October, classes ended in April with a fortnight of vacation at Christmas.[22] In their first year, a student was known as a bejan, from the French *bec-jaune*, a baby bird; in the second year they were called semi-bejani, or more commonly semis; in the third year, they were known as baccalaurei, or tertians; students in their fourth and final year were termed magistrands.

Marischal College typified Scottish institutions in its modus operandi and, until 1753, retained the outdated regenting system. In their first year, all students studied under a fixed Professor of Greek, and, as Greek was seen as the foundation of all learning, the most experienced tutor was assigned this duty. After the first year, a single professor, or regent, instructed a single class of students throughout its college career, teaching all subjects and conducting all exams. Professors lived at the college and were responsible not only for their students' educational progress but also for their moral development and behavior. It was not uncommon in this era for a young man to leave home and enter college as early as the age of ten, and as the boy was so young, the regent served both as guardian and teacher, with specified duties including closing the gates in the evening, "perlustrating" through the dorms at night, and conducting evening prayers.[23]

Common in Scottish universities at this time was the catechetical or lecture system, in which the professor lectured for part of the class and then spent additional time questioning the students about the material covered. By way of reinforcement, the professors would often begin the next class with a Socratic examination of the previous day's lesson. Often in this system, primary materials were notes taken in class and frequently the notes remained unchanged from year to year. Naturally, these class notes were frequently passed down from father to son, as it was common for the eldest son to inherit his father's post. In order to avoid controversy, the lecturer often read these notes verbatim and any deviation from the expected order might lead to foot-scraping—the universal sign of disapproval.

The lecture system, while standard in practice, was varied in practical application. In Scottish universities there were many incentives for a professor to be popular with his students—not only could a lecturer avoid being the target of a pelting from peashooters but could also increase the size of their classes. Professors in Scotland received a modest salary that was augmented by entrance fees and lecture tickets sold to the students. Thus, a popular teacher could easily double or even triple his salary with fees from students. In addition to the unwavering nature of the text of many lectures, the professors frequently printed and sold copies of their lecture notes to the students for proficiency and profit.

Another way in which the professors added to their salaries was to lecture to extramural or ungowned classes and to give demonstrations not only to students from other schools but also to locals and other interested parties. Particularly popular were lectures in natural philosophy (or science) and some distinguished scholars made a living out of entertaining crowds with exhibitions of curiosities, new inventions, and especially demonstrations of electricity and magnetism.

Small was blessed with many accomplished instructors. One of the most influential was Alexander Gerard, who fundamentally changed the way in which students progressed through their classes In 1753, Gerard presented a plan that proposed the abandonment of the old *regenting* system and adopt the more progressive professorial system. The recommendation was approved by the Senatus of Marischal College, who voted that his recommendations be put in place immediately.

The expressed advantages of the regenting system (in which an incoming class of students remained with their initial fixed instructor through the remaining years of their college career) were that the professor bonded with his students, knew their individual strengths and weaknesses, and could modify his lessons for maximum results. The disadvantages became more apparent as the base of knowledge expanded and became more topically specific—in other words, one regent could not be the most qualified instructor in every subject. The exposure to both systems of instruction—regenting and professorial—helped William Small develop an approach to pedagogy that allowed him to be both a generalist and a specialist, a personal guardian and a detached lecturer, a friend, and a master, all of which was essential background for his career at the College of William and Mary as the young Professor of Mathematicks.

SMALL'S PROFESSORS AND CLASSES

For the first two years of William Small's college career, 1751–1753, Marischal College remained under the regent system. Thomas Blackwell (who taught all first-year students) was his bejan professor of Greek; Francis Skene was his semi-bejan professor of history and chronology.[24] The new professorial system commenced in the 1753–1754 session and it was decreed that "Mr. Francis Skene shall constantly teach the Semi Class, Mr. William Duncan the Tertian, and Mr. Alexander Gerard the Magistrand."[25]

This change put Small into the classroom of William Duncan (1753–1754) the teacher who arguably most profoundly established his philosophical orientations. Following Duncan, Small attended Alexander Gerard's class in his final year (1754–1755). William Duncan set forth some of the seminal precepts of Common Sense Philosophy in his celebrated work, *Elements of Logick*; Alexander Gerard was in the forefront of the study of belles lettres, which reinforced the goal of improvement central to Common Sense tenets through the examination and creation of fine literature. If this change in the instructional format at Marischal had not taken place, Small would have missed the opportunity to study and learn under both professors, each with their own specific styles of teaching and areas of expertise.

The change in the system of instruction was also accompanied by a new curriculum. While maintaining the importance of the classics, it also included a greater emphasis on the sciences and practical studies. The first year continued to be devoted to the study of Greek, the second year introduced "History, Geography, Chronology, and Natural History, commonly called special physics, and ... students of this class shall attend the lessons of the Professor of Mathematics."[26]

The third year was devoted to scientific studies such as natural philosophy, general physics, mechanics, hydrostatics, pneumatics, optics, and astronomy. The final year was spent in the abstract sciences, moral philosophy, logic, ethics, and "the philosophy of the human mind and the sciences that depend on it—which included politics and law, and what we would now call psychology."[27]

In addition to his duties as the Professor of Greek, Thomas Blackwell was elected principal in 1748. In 1750, Blackwell introduced a new course for the instruction of the students in ancient history, geography, and chronology, which informed students about the principles of natural bodies and about "the rise and fall of states, and of the great revolutions that have happen'd in the world"[28]

Francis Skene, Small's semi-bejan professor, had tutored Lord Monboddo (known as the Father of Evolutionary Linguistics) and was the first to teach civics (how governments are formed and under which conditions they work most efficiently) and natural history (which concerned itself with the developmental stages of society and the contractual relationships between those governed and the government). The content and context of these studies and their innovative approaches were likely transferred to Small's charges in Williamsburg.

William Duncan, Small's tertian professor, taught natural and experimental philosophy, criticism and belles lettres, and mathematics. Natural and experimental philosophy included mechanics, hydrostatics, pneumatics, optics, astronomy, magnetism, and electricity. The mathematical component was probably devoted to trigonometry, geometry, and algebra.

Duncan was Aberdeen-born, attended the grammar school in that town, and graduated from Marischal College in 1737. After graduation he migrated to London where he was an author of several well-received translations of Caesar and Cicero. His most famous work and the one that is most likely to have made an impression on the young William Small, however, was his *Elements of Logick ... Designed ... for Young Gentlemen at the University and to prepare the Way of the Study of Philosophy and the Mathematick,* which was first published in Dodsley's *Preceptor* in 1748. Samuel Johnson, in the preface to *The Preceptor,* advised the student to advance to Isaac Watt's *Logick: or, the Right Use of Reason in the Enquiry After Truth* once he mastered Duncan's volume. Johnson considered William Duncan and Isaac Watts to be two of the most-important rhetorical theorists of the age, and John Collard, in his work *The Essentials of Logic* published in 1796, called Watts and Duncan "the two logical writers in the highest esteem at our universities."[29] Several authors maintain that Thomas Jefferson was heavily influenced by the work of William Duncan, in that the Declaration of Independence contains similar sentiments, logical arrangements, and many of the same words.[30]

From 1750 to 1752, Small was assigned the classes of Dr. Fordyce, Professor of Natural Philosophy at Marischal. When Dr. Fordyce drowned, Alexander Gerard was appointed Professor Of Logic and Moral Philosophy.[31] Although a junior member of the faculty, he was chiefly responsible for the changes that took place at Marischal College in 1753.[32] In 1756, Gerard, an early promoter of the study of belles lettres, was recognized for his contributions to the new field of study.

Thus, records at Marischal College suggest that William Small's professors were Thomas Blackwell, Francis Skene, William Duncan, and Alexander Gerard. John Gregory, who taught at King's College and co-founded the Aberdeen Philosophical Society, has long been considered Small's mentor in Aberdeen. Although Gregory was teaching at King's while Small was a student at Marischal, there were institutional and collegial bonds that conjoined the two institutions, so this is entirely plausible.

THE INFLUENCE OF MARISCHAL COLLEGE AND THE SCHOOL OF COMMON SENSE

The importance of Small's experience at Marischal was not only in the mechanics of its instruction but also in his orientation and grounding in the philosophical tenets of a distinctive branch of metaphysical thought—those of the Scottish Enlightenment.

Although variations on the Enlightenment manifested themselves in different manners across the world, all versions shared the common belief in the supremacy of reason and the betterment of the human condition. The teachings of Francis Bacon and the illustrations of Isaac Newton made clear the importance of reason and scientific method in man's attempts to understand the cosmos. The Scottish version of this new perspective stressed the concrete rather than the abstract, the utilitarian rather than the metaphysical, and solid scientific methodology rather than nebulous intellectual argumentation. The central tenet of this philosophy can be summed up in the word *improvement*. The process of enlightened improvement was all-encompassing, involving physical, moral, and aesthetic dimensions. The study of divergent aspects of improvement was divided into natural and moral philosophy. Natural philosophy, often a synonym for science, dealt with the definition, description, and material causes of natural phenomena. Moral philosophy dealt with the metaphysics of values, meanings, and purposes—of what nature ultimately is and how we know it.[33]

The true beginnings of this movement took their origins in the *Philosophiae Naturalis Principia Mathematica* of Sir Isaac Newton. Newton's view of the logical and sequential structure of nature gave form and clarity not only to the physical aspects of the universe, but also to life itself. If there were a logical nature to being, if it were sequential, then it could be controlled. If the terror of the randomness of life was lessened, man could better direct the flow of his own destiny. The patterns of life had a natural, almost mathematical flow to them, and scientific method was the tool by which these patterns could be most effectively discerned. Once the pattern was discovered, a destructive flow could be altered into a beneficial stream, by reason and design. This process produced results that were purposeful and beneficial. And, even though the primary goal pertained to man's physical well-being, the tenets of the Enlightenment extended this ambition to a more extended approach that embraced the economic advancement, political stability, and moral development of man.

While Enlightenment movements in Europe shared many common characteristics, in Scotland they seem to have taken on more democratic, more utilitarian, more scientific attributes. The most pressing concern of early Scottish Enlightenment pioneers was the physical well-being of the people. The most evident way to make life better and the future more secure was to increase the food supply. They believed that the key to a nation's self-sufficiency was the ability to feed its citizens, and thus, the first goal of improvement should be agriculture. The best method to achieve this was by employing scientific methodology. According to the scientific method, the first step towards improvement is observation or data collection, which was the means by which to discern the pattern that would lead to maximum production and distribution.[34]

During the late seventeenth century, the enlightened elite, or virtuosi, commissioned clergymen to take statistical surveys of their parishes. The surveys recorded who was producing what crops or goods and how they were processed and distributed. The statistical surveys were a means by which economic patterns could be discovered, natural resources could be used in more effective ways, productivity could be increased, and labor could be lessened. The result would be a benefit to individuals, to the community, and to society at large.

The ministers, being the social and religious fulcrum of the community, more easily enlisted the help and trust of the local citizenry and thereby were able to produce the most reliable and functional reports. In being a part of the process, the ministers also became advocates and proponents of the enlightenment cause.

Scottish clergymen were among the most convincing voices of Newtonian precepts, and by participating in this movement, deflected charges of irreverence and heresy. Instead of seeing science as a tool to diminish the relevance of God and the intercession of the church, participation by men of the cloth encouraged the belief that a cosmos ordered on scientific principles was an affirmation of the existence and power of God. The scientific method requires a null hypothesis to begin investigations. In this case the null hypothesis would state, "there is no God." The hypothesis would then be: "How can a universe so perfectly balanced and so logically constructed exist without the intervention and inspiration of an all-powerful God?" That God allows man the opportunity to better his life and the lives of his fellow creatures through science is not a refutation of his being, but rather an affirmation.

Scotland was fertile soil to plant the seeds of an enlightened society, for it had a long history of support for a universal system of education that would benefit not only the individual but also the nation. The educational system of eighteenth-century Scotland had its origins in the Scottish Reformation. In 1560, John Knox's democratic plan for the reformation of education in Scotland, the *First Book of Discipline*, was introduced to the General Assembly of the Church of Scotland. The ambitious program called for every parish to have a school and every town of considerable size a grammar school. Its intention was to establish a national system of universal education, including elementary schools, grammar schools, and universities that would be supported by the wealth wrested from the deposed Roman Catholic establishment and with taxes on wealthy landlords.

These combined efforts made Scotland, although a relatively poor country, one of the best-educated nations in Europe during the seventeenth and eighteenth centuries. John Knox's plans made education in Scotland more accessible, and often made classmates of the gentleman's son and the poor scholar. As a consequence, the Scottish system promoted both a democratic tradition and encouraged a rigorous curriculum.

The result of the importance of education in Scottish psyche, and its near-universal application was the ironic situation in which one of the best-educated citizenries in Europe dwelt in one of the most economically impoverished nations in the West. An unintended consequence of that plan was a proliferation of young, educated Scots who came to America seeking opportunity, and who stayed to tutor and teach their colonial cousins. These ubiquitous Scots, among whom John Witherspoon, James Wilson, and William Small are conspicuous, helped to spread the concept of equal opportunity, and made the Common Sense Philosophy of Thomas Reid a core tradition of the American Enlightenment.[35] This phenomenon was what historian Perry Miller called "the official metaphysic of America."[36]

The source of Small's scientific and philosophical mindsets—his *modus philosophandi*, *modus operandi*, and *modus vivendi*—all stem from his time and associations in Aberdeen. His greatest sources of inspiration were his professors—William Duncan, Alexander Gerard, and John Gregory. Small likely also had his classical skills sharpened by his association with Duncan, whose translations of Cicero and Caesar had received favorable notice in London. Small, in turn, may be partially responsible for Jefferson's elegant style of writing, which resonated with the rhythmic clausulae of Cicero's *Orations*.

Alexander Gerard was not only an original member of the Aberdeen Philosophical Society, where the tenets of Common Sense Philosophy were developed and refined, but was also on the cutting edge of the study of refined literature and polite language as a primary sense in determining truth and promoting social advancement. In 1755, The Edinburgh Society for the Encouragement of Arts, Sciences, Manufactures and Agriculture conferred a prize on Gerard for his "An Essay on Taste," the very year that Small was a student in his Moral Philosophy class.[37]

JOHN GREGORY:
SMALL'S MOST INFLUENTIAL MENTOR

Although John Gregory never taught at Marischal College, but rather at the neighboring and rival school, King's College, he is frequently mentioned as Small's mentor in college.[38] There are several plausible scenarios that may explain this situation.

Despite their rivalry, Marischal College and King's College cooperated with and complemented each other in many ways. The first accommodation pertained to lectures and notes. John Gregory, who was a recipient of a M.D. from Marischal, a regent in King's College, and the Mediciner at the University of Edinburgh, used his grandfather's notes, verbatim, to teach a course in *materia medica*. Often the texts of the courses came directly from the notes and were used by multiple professors, even in successive generations. From the evidence available through class notes, it seems that parallel courses existed at both institutions. Christine Shepherd maintains that there "is the probability of a standard course being taught at King's and Marischal"[39] and that identical sets of lecture notes were "being used at Marischal and King's."[40]

A second example of institutional cooperation involved students from one institution auditing classes at the other. This was a way to extend the choices of the students and the quality of their education. Professors were able to enroll ungowned or private students, who paid for classes that were not a part of their requirements but on topics that they wished to study. This was another way for a popular teacher to augment his salary.[41]

The third collaboration was between the professors themselves, who, despite having come from rival institutions, formed an influential intellectual association called the Aberdeen Philosophical Society, or as it was known locally, the Wise Club.

The symbiotic relationship between the two institutions allowed Small access to Dr. John Gregory. Indeed, although Gregory is frequently cited as Small's mentor, no documentary evidence exists to support the contention that Small attended any of Gregory's classes. In fact, Gregory was in London training as a practicing physician during Small's final year at Marischal College.

In 1746 Gregory was elected a regent, taught natural philosophy at King's College, and lectured there for three years on mathematics, moral philosophy, and natural philosophy.[42] In 1747 he began a medical practice in Aberdeen with his brother James.[43] In 1749, he resigned from his position at King's to devote himself solely to medicine. In 1752, he married Elisabeth, the daughter of Lord Forbes, and moved to London to look for more-challenging work two years later. As late as 1756, Gregory's wife wrote to Elizabeth Montagu, her aunt and influential founder of the Bluestockings Club, for assistance in securing a position for her husband at St. George's Hospital in London.[44] When John Gregory's brother James died on October 16, 1755, Gregory's friend Professor Thomas Gordon urged him to apply for the vacant chair. On November 13, 1755, John Gregory was elected "Mediciner" in his brother's place.[45]

Although there is little likelihood that John Gregory ever taught a class at Marischal College, there are several reasons to believe that a mentor-student relationship did exist between Gregory and Small. The first reason is the recommendation by which William Small obtained his medical degree from Marischal College. The two recommending doctors were John Gregory and Sir John Elliot.[46] Gregory, who himself had been granted an M.D. in absentia in 1746, recommended other candidates for degrees. It is assumed that both physicians had personal knowledge of Small's abilities and training.[47] Andrew Doig, a Gregory expert, indicated that if Small's recommendation were found, it would likely give a full account of the candidate's medical training and knowledge.[48]

The second reason to believe such a relationship existed is contained in two letters from William Small to James Watt in 1773 after the death of John Gregory. The first referred to Gregory as "my amiable friend of 22 years,"[49] which dates the relationship to 1751, the year Small came to Aberdeen. The second letter stated, "Had Dr G lived and another died, and I could have been a colleague to G., I should have liked that very much."[50] The second letter implied that Small was close to Gregory and, if one reads between the lines, that they had worked together.

There is other circumstantial evidence that assumes a connection between the two men; both the Gregory family and the Small family had a long and intimate involvement with the University of St. Andrews, and it is unlikely that the two families did not know each other. William's brother Robert, his father, James, his grandfather, James, and his great-grandfather, Thomas, all attended St. Andrews. Small's father was treasurer there from 1710 to 1720. The Gregory family was strongly represented at St. Andrews and King's College. John was also the grandson of James Gregorie, the inventor of the reflecting telescope and first Chair of Mathematics at St. Andrews. He was also a cousin to David Gregory, who taught astronomy at Oxford. His father, James, was mediciner at King's, and he was succeeded by his own son, James the Younger, and finally, by John himself.

It is not unlikely that John Gregory took a special interest in the son of a family friend. It was recorded that John and James Gregory of Aberdeen employed apprentices in the 1750s[51] and it has been suggested that Gregory took Small into his home and acted as a tutor to him.[52]

There has been little primary source documentation uncovered that concerned Small's activities between the time that he graduated from Marischal in 1755[53] until the time that he was recruited for a position at the College of William and Mary in 1758. It has been proposed by several reputable historians that Small apprenticed with John Gregory and his brother James while still in Aberdeen.[54] Moreover, information from collateral sources leaves little doubt that he was apprenticing at the medical trade during this period.

Gregory moved to London in 1754 in order to establish himself as a physician at St. George's Hospital.[55] It seems clear that Small followed his old mentor to the metropolis to learn the medical trade as well. In the papers of John Pringle (only recently made available to the public), there are references to Small which place him at dissections attended by Pringle and performed by John Hunter, two of the most-distinguished British physicians of the era. The first demonstration took place in 1757, when Small was training at St. George's Hospital in London.[56] Small may have also worked with another prominent London physician Sir John Eliot at the Greenwich Hospital, who signed an attestation for Small's M.D. from Marischal College in 1765.[57]

At the very time that Gregory and Small were working in London at St. George's Hospital, the College of William and Mary was desperately seeking a replacement for its Professor of Mathematics.

One of the many duties of the Bishop of London was to select qualified individuals to fill academic vacancies at the College of William and Mary in Virginia. The college's Board of Visitors had sacked the entire faculty in 1757, and, although Nichols had procured a professor for moral philosophy and a Master of the Grammar School, he had been unsuccessful in obtaining "a professor of mathematicks" for the institution. There was a great reluctance among capable candidates to accept such a post in a faraway colony, bereft of friends and family and the comforts of home, and to serve at the pleasure of a board of governors who "in a pique" had recently sacked their entire faculty.

During the same time as the bishop was searching for a replacement, John Gregory was sharpening his medical skills at St. George's Hospital. He and his wife resided at the home of her aunt, Elizabeth Montagu. The connection had intriguing implications, as Montagu was the doyenne of the celebrated Bluestocking Club (a society that attracted all the influential social, political, and literary figures of the capital). Her husband, Edward, was the Virginia Assembly's representative to Parliament. All the most important people attended Mrs. Montagu's literary salons, including prominent members of the clergy.

It is not unlikely that William Small came to the attention of the bishop's assistant, the Right Reverend Doctor Samuel Nichols, through his association with the Montagus and the Gregorys, and that when he became aware of Small's training and qualifications, he immediately summoned Small to Fulham Palace for an interview. This favorable interview led to the recruitment for Small for a new adventure and the beginning of many changes.

NOTES

1. Photograph by Martin Clagett, 2007.

2. William's brother, the Reverend Robert Small, wrote in his *History of Dundee* that he had seen more than fifty years before a copy of a certain charter and its translation, rendered by Mr. George Bruce, then Rector of the Grammar School. While this statement does not specifically say that Robert went to the Grammar School—given the date 1742 and the fact that that Bruce was then the recently retired rector of the school—it certainly implies the connection. See Robert Small, *History of Dundee from its Origin Down to the Present Time with a Statistical Account of the Parish and Town in the Year 1792* (Dundee: J. Chalmers, 1842), 57.

3. Classes were held almost continuously throughout the year, the exceptions being the "vacances," which extended from the fair day in August until after the fair in September, a day at New Year, a day at spring and autumn fasts, days at both Christmas and Easter, one or two sports half-holidays, and orations and occasional plays transformed regular school days into weekly half-holidays. (J. W. W. Stephenson, *Education in the Burgh of Dundee in the Eighteenth Century* [Dundee: Dundee City Council, 1969], 25, 43; *Dundee High School Magazine*, no. 60 [June 1934]: 8.) Not only were the semesters extended but also the regular class days were arduous as well. School opened at six o'clock in the summer and seven o'clock in the winter; prayers and religious instruction in English preceded breakfast. After breakfast, at about ten in the morning, scheduled lessons commenced and continued until lunch, around noon. At one o'clock classes would resume and continue until about four. (Courtesy of the author Iain Flett. Iain Flett, "Dundee Grammar School in the Eighteenth Century," in *Seven Hundred & Fifty Glorious Years: Some Facts and Facets of the High School of Dundee* [Dundee: Dundee City Council, 1994], 15). And the work continued every day of the week; Saturday was a regular school day on which disputations

were scheduled and once a month the senior boys debated a subject prearranged by the master. Even on Sundays, sessions were held, *laborare est orare*; students and masters attended service, after which they convened in the school and the students were questioned on various aspects of the sermon. Stephenson, *Education in the Burgh of Dundee*, 8.

4. *Dundee High School Magazine*, no. 60 (June 1934): 6.

5. Two centuries later, in 1434, it was recorded that the master of the school, Gilbert Knight or Knycht, at odds with the Bishop of Brechin, appealed to the Abbot of Lindores to settle the argument. After discovery that the bishop was the real authority in the matter, Knight hurried back, apologized profusely, and confident that the bishop would be touched by his penitence, resigned. The bishop, however, took the headstrong priest at his word and assigned another master. A century later, in 1555, another dispute arose between the master and his ecclesiastical superiors. This time the Abbot of Lindores accused Thomas MacGibbon of preaching Protestant doctrines to his charges. Dundee was the first town in Scotland to profess openly the Protestant faith and the Town Council backed MacGibbon against the Abbot. The Abbot retaliated by excommunicating the Town Council but, in the end, "the dog it was that died." *Dundee High School Magazine*, no. 60 (June 1934): 7.

6. *Dundee High School Magazine*, no. 60 (June 1934): 41.

7. Ibid., 42.

8. Ibid.

9. Ibid., 45.

10. George Chambers, *The Life of Thomas Ruddiman* (London: J. Stockdale, 1794), 146.

11. Stephenson, *Education in the Burgh of Dundee*, 36.

12. Ibid.; Chambers, *Life of Thomas Ruddiman*, 146.

13. Details concerning Lauder can be found in Chambers, *Life of Thomas Ruddiman, Anecdotes of Buchannan* (London: 1794), *Gentleman's Magazine* 20 (London: January 1749): 535, and a more extensive account in Paul Baines, *The House of Forgery in Eighteenth-Century Britain* (Aldershot: Ashgate Publishing Ltd., 1999), 81–103.

14. Baines, *The House of Forgery in Eighteenth-Century Britain*, 25; Stephenson, *Education in the Burgh of Dundee*, 36.

15. *Dundee High School Magazine*, no. 60 (June 1934): 11–12.

16. Ibid., 8.

17. Records from the University of Aberdeen Archives indicate that in February 1750 a number of bursaries were unclaimed, and a substantial mortification had been recently made by Sir Alexander Irving. Perhaps of more significance

to Small were the vacant bursaries that were available from the neighborhood of Carmylie. The following indicates that there were unclaimed bursaries, some of which originated from sources geographically near the home of William Small; indeed, Small's mother, Lillias Scott Small, was from Montrose and married James Small in Montrose. "The Faculty appoint Dr Gordon to commune wt Mr Strahan at Montrose and Sir Alex Ramsey when he meets wt them Anent [concerning] ye Money due the College upon account of Sir Ramseys vacant Bursarys. And Referr the Consideration of Drums Vacant Bursarys due Likewise." Minutes signed by Thomas Blackwell, Principal Marischal College, February 20, 1750, MS M 41 /33, University of Aberdeen Archives, Aberdeen, Scotland.

18. Richard Pocoke, *Tours in Scotland: 1747, 1750, 1760*, ed. Daniel Kemp (Edinburgh: T. and A. Constable, 1887), 201.

19. Roger Emerson, "Aberdeen Professors, 1690–1880: Two Structures, Two Professoriates, Two Careers," in Jennifer Carter and Colin McLaren, *Crown and Gown: An Illustrated History of the University of Aberdeen* (Aberdeen: Aberdeen University Press, 1995), 68; Jennifer Carter and Joan Pittock, *Aberdeen and the Enlightenment: Proceedings of a Conference Held at the University of Aberdeen* (Aberdeen: Aberdeen University Press, 1987), 161, 164.

20. Robert Polk Thompson, "The Reforms at the College of William and Mary, 1763–1780," *Proceedings of the American Philosophical Society* 115, no. 3 (June 1971): 189.

21. Marischal College, Aberdeen, Courtesy of Michelle Gait, Archivist, University of Aberdeen.

22. *Evidence, Oral and Documentary . . ., Volume IV, University of Aberdeen* (London: Clowes and Sons, 1837), 284.

23. J. M. Bulloch, *A History of the University of Aberdeen, 1495–1895* (London: Hodder and Stoughton, 1895), 148–150.

24. P. J. Anderson, ed., *Fasti Academicae Mariscallanae Aberdonensis* (Aberdeen: New Spalding Club, 1898), 2:592.

25. P. J. Anderson, ed., *Studies in the History and Development of the University of Aberdeen* (Aberdeen: Aberdeen University Press, 1906), 8.

26. The specific courses are listed in H. Lewis Ulman's work *The Minutes of the Aberdeen Philosophical Society, 1758–1773* (Aberdeen: Aberdeen University Press, 1990), 22. First year—Classics; second year—Classis, Natural and Civic History, Geography, Chronology, Arithmetic, Algebra, and Plain Geometry; third year—Criticism and Belles Lettres, Natural and Experimental Philosophy, Spherical Trigonometry, Spherical Geometry, and higher Algebra; fourth

year- Logic, Metaphysics, Pneumatology, Natural Theology, Moral Philosophy, higher Algebra, Quadratre of Curves, Fluxions, and Newton's Principles
of Philosophy.

27. Carter and McLaren, *Crown and Gown*, 59.

28. Paul Woods, "Science and the Aberdeen Enlightenment," in *Philosophy
and Science in the Scottish Enlightenment*, ed. Peter Jones (Edinburgh: John Donald
Publishers, 1988), 46.

29. Steven Lynn, "Johnson's Rambler and Eighteenth-Century Rhetoric,"
Eighteenth-Century Studies 19, no.4 (Summer 1986): 466.

30. See Wilber S. Howell, "The Declaration of Independence and Eighteenth-Century Logic," *William and Mary Quarterly*, 3rd series, vol. 18, no. 4
(October 1961):463–484; Garry Wills, *Inventing America: Jefferson's Declaration
of Independence* (Garden City, N.Y.: Doubleday, 1978).

31. Ulman, *Minutes of the Aberdeen Philosophical Society*, 35.

32. In 1755, Gerard's *Plan of Education in the Marischal College and University
of Aberdeen, with the reasons of it* advocated a change from the regenting system
to the professorial system; it was printed by order of the faculty. Anderson, *Fasti
Academicae Mariscallanae Aberdonensis*, 2:45.

33. Keith Thomson. *Before Darwin: Reconciling God and Nature* (New Haven:
Yale University Press, 2005), 40.

34. Martin Clagett, *Scientific Jefferson: Revealed* (Charlottesville: University of
Virginia Press, 2009), iii.

35. Donald H. Meyer, *The Democratic Enlightenment* (New York: G. P. Putnam's
Sons, 1976), 189.

36. Ibid.

37. Ulman, *Minutes of the Aberdeen Philosophical Society*, 35.

38. James McCash, "Dr. William Small: Note 4 on A Man of Little Showing,"
College Courant 20 (January 1969): 29–31; Gillian Hull, "William Small, 1734–
1775: No Publications, Much Influence," *Journal of the Royal Society of Medicine*
90 (February 1997): 102–105.

39. Carter and Pittock, *Aberdeen and the Enlightenment*, 151.

40. Ibid.

41. Ibid., 58.

42. Leslie Stephens and Sidney Lee, eds., *Dictionary of National Biography*
(London: Smith, Elder & Co., 1908), 8:545.

43. Paul Lawrence, "Occasional papers," no.1 (Edinburgh: Royal Society of
Edinburgh), 4; Francis McDonnell, ed., *List of Apprentices for Aberdeen, 1750–1780*
(St. Andrews: University of St. Andrews, 1994).

44. Lawrence B. McCullough, *John Gregory's Writings on Medical Ethics and Philosophy of Medicine* (London: Kluwer Academic Publisher, 1998), 57:47.

45. Paul Lawrence, "The Gregory Family" (PhD diss., University of Aberdeen, 1971), 154.

46. Medical degrees in Scottish universities were generally issued on the attestations of two physicians before the nineteenth century.

47. Personal communication, Dr. Dorothy Johnston, University of Nottingham, to Martin Clagett, December 7, 2001. "The MD of 1765 was at the attestation of Dr. Gregory and Dr. Elliot. I expect that [this] is the basis for [the idea] that he [Small] did this apprenticeship with Gregory."

48. Personal communication, Dr. Andrew Doig to Martin Clagett, August 24, 2000.

49. William Small to James Watt, March 15, 1773, MS 3782/12/76/143, Archives, Birmingham Central Library, Birmingham, England.

50. William Small to James Watt, May 1, 1773, in James Patrick Muirhead, *The Origins and Progress of Mechanical Inventions of James Watt*, Letter 112 (London: John Murray, 1854), 2:46.

51. Frances G. McDonnell, ed., *Roll of Apprentices of Aberdeen, 1751–1796* (St. Andrews: University of St. Andrews, 1994).

52. Lawrence, "The Gregory Family," 154.

53. Album Studiosorum, 1755, MS M 3 (25), Special Collections, University of Aberdeen, Aberdeen, Scotland.

54. Hull, "William Small, 1734–1775," 102–105.

55. Elizabeth Gregory to Elizabeth Montagu, June 28, 1756, MO 1063, Courtesy of Mary Robertson, Archives, Huntington Library, San Marino, California.

56. Personal correspondence, August 26, 2008, Courtesy of Simon Chaplin, Director of Museums and Special Collections. Citation from the Pringle Papers at the Royal College of Physicians in Edinburgh. Pringle: 1/4/f.157 (c.1757). Courtesy of Mrs. Estela Dukan and Iain Milne of the RCPE Special Collections.

57. John Eliot was born in Edinburgh in 1736 and went to London to become an apothecary's assistant. Enticed by the lure or adventure and booty, he signed on to a privateer's ship and returned home with a substantial premium. Eliot then determined to become a physician, graduated from Christ College, Oxford, and established himself in Cecil Street, London. In 1771, Eliot married the seventeen-year-old daughter of Hugh Dalrymple, a wealthy Edinburgh barrister, and took her back to London. Elliot's wife, Grace Dalrymple Eliot, having discovered the pleasures of the flesh, ran off with Lord Valentia in 1773. Her father paid Eliot £12,000 in compensation. Grace was later to bear a child to the Prince of Wales,

for whom Eliot became physician in 1778. Elliot was as successful profession-
ally as he was socially and was listed as Senior Physician at Greenwich Hospital
in 1779. He died in 1786. *Dictionary of National Biography*; and courtesy of P. J.
and R. V. Wallis, *Eighteenth Century Medics* (Newcastle upon Tyne: Project for
Historic Bibliography, 1988). See also James W. Singer, "Painting of the Week:
Thomas Gainsborough, Grace Dalrymple Elliott," July 19, 2020, https://www
.dailyartmagazine.com/grace-dalrymple-elliott/ (accessed July 27, 2021).

CHAPTER 3

The College of William and Mary

As William Small was gaining a firm foundation in science, mathematics, and Common Sense Philosophy, events were unfolding in Virginia that would set the stage for such a seemingly unconventional choice of William Small as the new "Professor of Mathematicks" at the College of William and Mary.

Following the form and function of the times, William and Mary, the second-oldest institution of higher learning in British North America, was established for the expressed purpose of producing native-born clergymen for the colony of Virginia. From the beginning, with few exceptions, the faculty was comprised exclusively of Anglican churchmen who had graduated from Oxford or Cambridge, and the guardian of the institution was none other than the Bishop of London himself.

In these ecclesiastic and political traditions, the appointment of a lay son of a Presbyterian minister and an all-too-recent graduate of a college located in close proximity to the remote and primitive highlands of Scotland must have raised many eyebrows. Yet in many ways, the recruitment of William Small was the most logical and uncomplicated answer to the vexing problems that had beset the Board of Visitors of the College of William and Mary.

Several distinct but interconnected sets of circumstances intersected to carry Small across the ocean and land him in Williamsburg in the autumn of 1758. The conditions both separately and conjointly were political, religious, economic, and social in nature. The first concerned a series of confrontations between members of the English establishment in Virginia and local authorities; the second a series of events that involved the control over the leadership of the Anglican church in the colony and the rise of "New Light" Protestantism; the third, and most explosive issue, centered on elements of self-governance and taxation; and finally, there came to pass a period of nationalistic self-identification during which Virginians incrementally and, perhaps, hesitatingly began to define themselves as Americans and not as Englishmen by proxy.

The final issue, not only for Small but also for many educators in this time and in this place, was a pragmatic one—employment. English clerics viewed a teaching position in the colonies as one that was distant and disadvantageous, daunting and dangerous, destructive and demeaning. It meant a post far away from friends, family, and familiar sights, working in a land "of masters and slaves" where there were few opportunities for advancement and many for dismissal, and under the control of a junta of sensitive and self-important "farmers." Tutoring and teaching positions in the colonies were increasingly being subsumed by Scots, who having been raised in one of the best-educated but most-impoverished nations in Western Europe, were anxious to seek out a new life in the New World. The unintended consequence of these collateral conditions was a nation, waking up in a half-conscious state, to the philosophical lullabies of academic nannies nurtured on nationalism, utilitarianism, Presbyterianism, and educated in a system based on egalitarian principles.

The first and underlying of these conditions was the nature and history of the college itself that created the platform from which the other conflicts between the establishment forces of the Church in Virginia and the local population would emanate.

In addition to the structure and nature of the college itself the contributing factors that most clearly demonstrate the internal struggle between the nativist forces (the local elite or plantocracy) and the establishment forces (Anglican clergymen and British officials) can best be demonstrated in the cases of the Reverend Mr. William Kay, Lieutenant Governor Robert Dinwiddie's imposition of the Pistole Fee, the contentious passage of the Two-Penny Act, and the dismissal of the ushers Matthew Hubard and Cole Digges by the faculty.

The confluence of these events would make a person with William Small's unique qualifications all-the-more attractive to the governing body of the college, the Board of Visitors.

THE COLLEGE OF WILLIAM AND MARY

In 1685, James Blair, who had been educated in Aberdeen at Marischal College and at the University of Edinburgh (both Scottish institutions), went to Virginia as the rector of Henrico Parish. He had advanced so much in reputation and popularity that by 1689, the Bishop of London appointed him as Commissary in the colony. Shortly after Blair's arrival an unexpected endowment of twenty-five hundred pounds was made by a consortium of wealthy Virginians and London merchants for the purpose of establishing a school to train clergymen for the colonies. Blair and Lieutenant Governor Francis Nicholson quickly seized on the opportunity for establishing a college in Williamsburg.

While Governor Nicholson was pitching the proposal for the establishment of the college to the House of Burgesses, James Blair set sail for England to secure a royal charter. Although Blair was opposed by several factions in Britain, nevertheless he was able to obtain the charter and return to Virginia in 1691. He was also able to fashion the charter in such a way as to make himself a determining force in the destiny of the institution; Blair became both the President and the Rector of the College. In addition, the Bishop of London bestowed on him the office of Commissary, which carried the authority of the Church in the colony. His prominence in the founding of the college and the longevity of his administration assured that the institution would be, in large part, a reflection of both his experience and his ambitions.

The College of William and Mary was created as a hybrid institution with elements of both the Scottish prototype and the traditional English university. It was Scottish in its structure, administration, scientific emphasis, role of the professorate, and constitution. It followed the English model with regard to academic traditions, progression of classes, freedom in the selection of classes, and the question of yearly exams.

Although it has often been said that the College of William and Mary was a direct reflection of English universities of the time, nevertheless, many of elements of the administrative structure of the College of William and Mary seem to have been based on Scottish models in general, and in some particulars, on Blair's alma mater, Marischal College.

The first of these distinctions was the organization of the institution. In England the term university connoted an institution that consisted of "the Chancellor, Masters, and scholars, that is one corporation, and each of the colleges were distinct and independent societies with their separate codes of law."[1] The governance of the English university is analogous to that of the government of United States: each of the colleges legislated for itself and sent representatives to the council that legislated for the university as a whole.

By contrast, in Scotland the "system of colleges as autonomous places for residence for undergraduates, with their separate endowments and governing Heads and Fellows, in separate and imposing buildings never took root"[2] and because, in general, Scottish institutions possessed only one college, whereas Oxford and Cambridge were comprised of a number of colleges, governance in Scottish institutions was usually more uniform and directed. The terminologies college and university, however, became synonymous, indeed, Marischal College's elder and more distinguished sister at Aberdeen was known as "King's University and College."[3]

The second characteristic of the College of William and Mary, which was patterned after Marischal College and was responsible for much of the troubles and contentious relationships within the college during the mid-eighteenth century, was the creation of a dual set of controlling boards within the institution. The conflict between these two competing groups, the Society (or Faculty and President) and the Board of Visitors, was to a significant degree responsible for the conditions that led to the recruitment of William Small. Bailey Cutts, a historian of educational issues wrote:

> The source of the continuing conflict was implicit in the charter of the College. William and Mary was entrusted with the functions of a mission school, a grammar school, and a university, yet its organizational arrangements were approximate copies of the traditional collegiate forms at Oxford. By language and regulations, the new college created the illusion that it would function like an English university. Yet its purpose and circumstances assured that could never be the case. The disjunction between function and form made disagreements and misunderstandings inevitable. William and Mary had no exact counterpart in England or America.[4]

Cutts asserted that although the differences between the College of William and Mary and English universities were often credited to colonial ingenuity, nevertheless, "Scotland and Ireland possessed post-Reformation universities that were prototypes, in all essentials, of the colonial institutions of higher learning."[5]

> The President and the Masters constituted a corporation, called the Society. The charter gave this corporation the power to hold and manage property and revenues granted to the College, the power to elect a burgess to the Virginia legislature, and the power to act as the provincial office of the surveyor general with the authority to license surveyors. A lay governing board, the Visitors and Governors, had the power to select the faculty and make statutes that delineated the structure of the institution and embodied the rules by which it was

to be operated. Eighteen in number, this self-perpetuating board annually elected its own head, the Rector. It also had the power to choose a chancellor, whose term was set at seven years.[6]

The potentially explosive nature of the dual controls of the College of William and Mary was at the center of the internecine feuds at the institution; as chancellor, the Bishop of London was often relegated to the role of a referee.

Besides the structural ambiguities and the unavoidable conflicts implicit in the Charter, other, and more recent developments contributed to the sacking of the entire faculty, the necessity of immediate replacements and the desire of the Board of Visitors to have faculty members unencumbered by the social and political agenda of Anglican clerics who often turned to the sympathetic ear of the Chancellor of the College—the Bishop of London.

A CONFLICT OF INTEREST: THE LOCAL ELITE AND THE BRITISH ESTABLISHMENT IN VIRGINIA

Besides the vagaries of power and control inherent in the structure and Charter of the College of William and Mary, there was also the contrasting attitudes, ambitions and acrimony that existed between the native-born elite and the imported establishment authorities who vied for status, position, and authority within the colony. The differences had religious, political, and social dimensions.

The first concerned a series of confrontations between members of the English establishment in Virginia and local authorities; the second centered around the control of Anglican Church leadership in the colony and the rise of "New Light" Protestantism; the third and most explosive issue involved the local and self-important plantocracy of Virginians and the condescending and paternalistic authorities in England.

From the beginning, the faculty had been composed of English clerics who viewed a teaching position in the colonies as one that was daunting and dangerous. It meant a post far away from friends, family, and familiar sights, where there were few opportunities for advancement and many for dismissal. Further, control of the institution was in the hands of local officials with penchants for constrictive control. Teaching and tutoring positions in America were increasingly subsumed by Scots, who having been raised in one of the best educated but most impoverished nations in Western Europe were anxious to seek out a new life in the New World. During this critical period in the nation's history, the unintended consequences of these collateral conditions was a generation of students instructed by men who had been raised on the sentiments of nationalism, utilitarianism, and educated in a system based on egalitarian principles.

While establishment forces of the clergy, the faculty, and officials appointed by the Crown were determined to maintain the status quo, locals were adamant about controlling their own destiny. The middle of the eighteenth century brought a growing struggle for political power, social status, and economic influence in the colony of Virginia. The three major players in this tug of war were the clergy, the local elite, and the lieutenant governor. Two of the three sides were diametrically opposed on philosophical and constitutional grounds. The clergy represented the English colonial establishment and fought fiercely for the rights and prerogatives arrogated to themselves and the Crown. The native plantocracy, on the other hand, expressed the viewpoint that being in situ, they could best determine the course of domestic matters.

The gentry and members of the House of Burgesses made legal and philosophical arguments that advocated for a system in which local authorities would manage local affairs. Their position was centered around the claim that officials could not make sound decisions regarding Virginian affairs from England, given the great geographic distance and time it took to relay those decisions across the Atlantic. Richard Bland, a major player in the early controversies, used the phrase *"salus populi est suprema lex"*[7] (the welfare of the people is the highest law), to underscore his position. He maintained that needs could be ascertained and administered best by local officials familiar with regional matters, rather than being handled by distant and disinterested entities.

The odd man out was the lieutenant governor, who usually supported whichever group was most closely aligned with his own agenda or political philosophy. If the lieutenant governor wanted to initiate a new tax, he might enlist the help of Anglican clergy; if he wanted to establish a legal precedent that deprived the clergy of some of their rights, and thereby increase his own authority, he might align himself with local leaders. Any decision he might make could, however, be overturned by various authorities in England.

The clergy walked in lockstep with the government at home for several reasons—primarily because they came directly from England and thought of themselves as Englishmen, not as Virginians. Clergymen viewed their presence in the colony as a performance of patriotic duty, and understood that their authority and influence, as well as their commissions, came directly from the Bishop of London.

The ties that bound the faculty of the college to England were philosophical, emotional, and pragmatic. The clergy and, in particular, the faculty of William and Mary, believed themselves to be more enlightened, more sophisticated. and more erudite than their country cousins and more capable of making the correct decisions for the colony. Recruited directly from Oxford or Cambridge, they fraternized together and usually spoke with one voice on the major issues affecting the governance of the college and their own positions.

By the middle of the eighteenth century, the first families of Virginia had already put down deep and intertwined roots, and began to develop and influence the passage of laws that reflected both their own personal needs and those of the community. The more influential they became, the more jealous they were of any infringement on their newly found power. It was not unusual for a gentleman to simultaneously maintain both a seat in the House of Burgesses and a position on the Board of Visitors at the college—the two civil institutions that most directly controlled the governance of the College of William and Mary.

At the time, Virginia was a hazardous place for Englishmen. Virginians (who considered themselves to be Englishmen but were considered by the English establishment as something less) suffered from a perception of inferiority. As a consequence, any injury, either real or imagined, could be conflated from an ember into a wildfire, and an unwitting visitor could unintentionally stir up a storm of ill will by a chance comment or action. To make matters worse, the local luminaries were often related to each other by complex ties of multiple marriages, and to offend one gentleman was to offend the whole of his extended family.[8]

As administrators, the clergy and the faculty of William and Mary were advocates of the status quo. In contrast, members of the Virginian aristocracy, who sat on the governing Board of Visitors, were agents for change. As a result, constant and bitter conflicts erupted between the two groups. Although these flashpoints emerged from disparate sources, the combined effect was to produce an atmosphere in which a man with William Small's unusual résumé contained the precise qualifications desired by an oft-frustrated Board of Visitors—he was a Scot, not an Englishman; he was a layman, not a cleric; and he was the son of a Presbyterian minister, not an Anglican priest. In short, Small was cut from a very different cloth than his present and previous colleagues.

In addition to the general and natural tug of war that was continually in play between native and imported authorities, there were specific, separate but interconnected incidents that led to the dismissal of the entire faculty; thereby, requiring a new set of replacements with a divergent and dissimilar set of qualifications.

The conditions both separately and conjointly were political, religious, economic, and social. Among the most important and defining of these incidents was the Case of the Reverend Mr. Kay, Lieutenant Governor Robert Dinwiddie's imposition of the Pistole

Fee, the contentious Two-Penny Act, and the dismissal by the faculty of two school ushers—Matthew Hubard and Cole Digges.

THE CASE OF THE REVEREND
MR. WILLIAM KAY

Out of these events was born not only the determination of Virginians to be counted as equals and be in command of local affairs, but also to obtain the instruments, both philosophic and pragmatic, of doing so. Chronologically, the case of the Reverend Mr. William Kay set up an initial confrontation between the native authorities, as represented by the vestries, and especially Colonel Landon Carter, and the English establishment, as represented by officials of the Anglican Church. In 1744, Colonel Landon Carter, feeling that the Reverend Kay, newly arrived from England and installed by church authorities, had publicly humiliated him with a sermon directed against sin of pride and was determined to unseat this newcomer foisted on his parish by distant sources. Landon Carter, by ties of consanguinity and influence of wealth, tossed the Reverend Kay out of his church, locked him out of his glebe house, stopped his salary, and stole away his wife. Kay appealed to the Privy Council and sued the powerful Colonel Carter and was awarded a verdict of £80, "the highest costs that were ever given by that Board on hearing an appeal."[9] The verdict and supplemental awards to the Reverend Kay made not only the Colonel but also many in the community determined to contain the oppressive control from abroad.

THE PISTOLE FEE

The second event in the series that both took William Small to Virginia and established an atmosphere of rebellion was the Pistole Fee, an attempt by the clever tax-collector-turned-lieutenant-governor,

Robert Dinwiddie, to increase the revenues for the Crown and at the same time supplement his own salary.

Dinwiddie and Parliament viewed the fee (which was a tax on the acquisition of property) as a legitimate and customary imposition, while the colonists viewed the exceptional assessment by the incoming lieutenant governor as a dangerous legal and constitutional precedent. The result of this confrontation both hardened the positions of the administration in England and sharpened the opposition of the colonial subjects against intrusions into local affairs. Because of the unexpected reluctance of the Virginians to the introduction of the fee and the stubborn insistence of Dinwiddie for its collection, the first tangible signs of the coming revolution appeared in the guise of a separate and independent agent to represent the views of the General Assembly and the toast publicly proposed by William Stith, the President of the College of William and Mary, for "Liberty and property and no pistole."

The toast put the president and the members of the Board of Visitors in direct opposition to the governor and the English colonial authorities; the controversy, in the words of Governor Dinwiddie, put the people "very much in a republican way of thinking."[10] Although Dinwiddie dismissed the controversy over the "silly Fee of a Pistole" and John Blair called the fee "moderate and reasonable,"[11] the Burgesses contended that "the Rights of the subject are so secured by law, that they cannot be deprived of the least part of their property, but by their own consent."[12] It was feared that once such a tax was instituted that a "small spark ... will gain ground ... and blaze into an irresistible flame."[13]

Until this time the colony of Virginia had but one agent in London to represent the interest and concerns of Virginia in Parliament, this agent was appointed by the governor and the Council (the upper chamber of the General Assembly appointed by the governor); the House of Burgesses was determined to have its own and separate agent as often their agenda and that of the governor conflicted. As early as 1756, the House of Burgesses began to call for its own permanent representation in London, for as John Blair wrote to Council's agent, James Abercrombie, "I find they cannot digest your opposition to them in the affair of the Pistole Fee."[14]

Lieutenant Governor Francis Fauquier would later assert that the initial demand of the Burgesses to have their own agent "resulted from the desire on the part of the members of the House of Burgesses to have someone to represent them in England in case there should arise in the future a dispute similar to that of Governor Dinwiddie's days in reference to the pistole fee. Then a special agent, Peyton Randolph, was sent over at great expense to lay before the authorities in England the views of the people of Virginia."[15] Dinwiddie prorogued the assembly for its high-handed response and their demand for an independent agent.

As the exigencies of the French and Indian War were becoming more alarming, however, the governor found it imperative to recall the chastened assembly in order to obtain additional funding for defense. After several versions of an appropriation bill made their ways through the legislature, each attaching a rider that provided for funds to retain their separate agent in London, the bill passed and was begrudgingly signed by the governor. Through Peyton Randolph's efforts in London, a compromise concerning the controversial fee of a pistole was finally reached—the Privy Council decided that the Pistole Fee was legitimate but made several important exclusions to its execution.

In 1759, the Burgesses appointed Edward Montagu of Middle Temple, as the agent in London to represent their viewpoints and take up any other matter "that may either affect or be of interest in this colony."[16] He was to be under the direction of a committee of correspondence, composed of members of both the Council and the House of Burgesses,[17] and transact such business as had been passed on to the committee by the assembly. The committee in return was to lay before the assembly both the correspondence of the agent and the results of his actions taken on their behalf.[18]

Although the term *committee of correspondence* has usually been associated with Samuel Adams and Massachusetts, the original Committee of Correspondence had been established in Virginia in 1759.[19] The committee acted as a liaison between the legislature and their own agent in London but quickly took on collateral matters of more serious consequence. In the summer of 1763, information was communicated to the committee through its agent, Edward Montagu, concerning bills proposed by Parliament for taxing the internal commerce of the colonies. The Virginia General Assembly was not scheduled to meet until the end of October; nevertheless, the committee directed its agent to "oppose with all his weight and influence as far as he might venture to insist on the injustice of laying any duties on the colony and the particular injustice of taxing the internal trade of the colony without its consent."[20] The committee not only gave the agent directions without officially consulting the assembly but also began to disperse information about the intentions of Parliament. These communications to Montagu in essence constituted the de facto beginnings of an American foreign office.[21]

On November 4, 1764, the Virginia General Assembly directed the Committee of Correspondence to communicate with the General Assembly of Massachusetts in respect to the proposed stamp act.[22] And as early as 1768, Richard Henry Lee suggested to John Dickinson of Pennsylvania that committees of correspondence be established in all the colonies "to secure union of counsel and action" against the oppressive activities of the British government.[23] The consequences of the Pistole Fee were unintended but substantial—a scenario was established in which the British government, formerly seen as paternalistic and protective, now became regarded as unlawful and oppressive; a counsel for the native legislature was created separate from that of the home government in the colony, setting up an independent agency and further emphasizing the divisions between the colonists and the Parliament; and, a committee of correspondence rapidly evolved from a group charged with secretarial duties into one with ad hoc deliberative functions, including instructing the agent in

London, disseminating information, and coordinating resistive activities among all the colonies. These Committees of Correspondence became the telegraphs of the American Revolution.

THE TWO-PENNY ACT

At the same time that the Pistole Fee pitted the Burgesses against the governor, another controversy arose and this time the establishment clergy created a critical mass of ill will against itself. The salary for public servants was traditionally paid in pounds of tobacco; weather conditions and the war with the French had made the price of tobacco skyrocket and just at the moment the clergy thought there would be an unexpected windfall, the House of Burgesses snatched it away and substituted in its place a much-lower payment, and that in the form of paper money. The clergy complained to the Privy Council that "an Act lately pass'd in that Colony, whereby their Salaries hitherto paid in Tobacco, are now to be discharged at about half the Value in a paper Currency of no intrinsic worth of itself and of no value at all out of the said Colony of Virginia."[24] The unseemly agitation appeared to the colonists, who were paying taxes in tobacco, as an unholy attempt by the clergy to take advantage of the situation.

A visiting cleric, the Reverend Andrew Burnaby wrote that "an unhappy disagreement has lately arisen between the clergy and the laity, which, it is to be feared, may be of serious consequence. The cause of it was this. Tobacco being extremely scarce from a general failure of the crop, the assembly passed an act to oblige the clergy and all public officers to receive their stipends in money instead of tobacco. This the clergy remonstrated against.... They sent over an agent to England, and the law was repealed."[25] The clerical agent was John Camm, whom Governor Fauquier described as "a man of some abilities but of a turbulent spirit ... whose delight it is ... to raise the Flame and live in it."[26]

The ministers believed that they were only seeking just compensation but the perception of ordinary citizens, who had previously been well disposed towards the clergy, changed to the viewpoint that all the establishment ministers were cut from the same self-serving cloth, since other civil servants whose wages were also being paid in tobacco, endured the same hardships as the Anglican priests, and without complaint. The clergy was now "jumbled together in one general and undistinguished mass, under the common denomination of parsons," who acted, "as if they were the only members of the community, who [were] divested of all ... rights and privileges."[27]

Indeed, most Virginians felt that the actions of the home government in its support of the established clergy against the rights of the native vestries in the case of Mr. Kay and the imposition of a tax in the case of the Pistole Fee were rapidly eroding their traditional rights as free Englishmen, and increasingly important, as free Americans. "In their opinion, this little band of able and self-willed clergymen, most of them natives of England, had deliberately and selfishly brought up an issue that still threatened to destroy the right of the people to govern themselves by laws of their own making."[28]

The ill-conceived edict of the Privy Council was stated in such an ambiguous fashion that it was unclear whether it was ordering the nullification of a legislative act that was already defunct, or it was asserting that the act was to be rescinded ab initio. In other words, if the fiat was declaring the Two-Penny Act illegal on its passage, the result would be that the complaining clergymen were owed their back wages. The uncertainty caused several of the plaintiffs to take their case to trial, with negative or minimal outcomes, and concluding with the famous Parson's Cause, which made Patrick Henry an unexpected hero of the people.

Burnaby suggested that these unremitting remonstrations "greatly exasperated the people; such is the mutual animosity at this time, that, I fear, it will not easily subside or be forgotten."[29] The loyalty of Americans toward their mother country was diminished by the seeming indifference of British authorities to the concerns of the colonists and the perception on the part of many Virginians that they were being exploited as a resource for British imperial expansion, and were not being treated as beloved members of a family but as easily expendable dependents. These injuries and insults manifested themselves in political, religious, and economic spheres and often overlapped and collided with the Virginians on one side and the Parliament, royal officials, British merchants, and the Anglican clergy on the other. Many of these disputes revolved around the clergy and more specifically those clergy who constituted the faculty of the college; therefore, it was not helpful to the reputation of the Anglican Church when reports circulated concerning the immoral behavior of men of the cloth. The most notorious case involved a minister from Hamilton Parish, John Brunskill, Jr.

THE REVEREND MR. BRUNSKILL

It was noted in a meeting of the Council held on April 21, 1757, that "this Day a Complaint [has been] made by the Vestry of Hamilton Parish in Prince William County against the Rev^d Mr. John Brunskill for divers Immoralities, such as profane Swearing, Drunkenness, and immodest Actions."[30] Fauquier described Brunskill (whose father was also a Virginia clergyman) as "not only a Reproach to the Clergy but a Scandal to Human Nature."[31] And, inasmuch as John Brunskill Sr. had a similar habit of inactivity, a reputation for indecent behavior, and a history of antagonizing members of his congregation, the son came by his behavior honestly.[32]

Both colonists and colonial authorities were prone to leniency, providing the offender showed remorse and mended his ways—Brunskill had more than several opportunities to reform himself and despite "having received Reproof, Advice, and Exhortation, continued to persist in a most abominable Course of Life, to the great Scandal of his Profession, and evil Example of all good Christians."[33] In a letter to the Bishop of London, Dinwiddie said that Brunskill was "a Person almost guilty of every Sin except Murder, and this last he had very near perpetrated on his own Wife by tying her up by the Leggs to the Bed Post and cuting her in a cruel Manner with Knives, and guilty of so many Indecencies, that Modesty forbids my troubling You with a Detail of."[34]

According to Governor Dinwiddie, the hearing at first was proposed to be closed to the public, as the proceedings might very well throw "many reflections on the church." But "Mr. Brunskill said No, he would vindicate himself publickly."[35] Brunskill maintained, "If I be prov'd a Liar, let me Suffer the Disgrace & Shame due to Liars. If not, let the Slanderer be rebuk'd & receive his Reward."[36] The trial, again according to Dinwiddie, "was conducted with great Impartiality, and every Thing was prov'd in a much more heinous Manner than was in the Original Complaint, which greatly surpriz'd the Council and myself."[37] Both the Council and the governor thought that it would be wise to research the legalities of the problem as the Bishop of London had not supplied an official response to the situation.

Dinwiddie deemed it his duty both as the governor and as a Christian and by the authority of the Bishop of London's 81st Instruction—"If any parson already prefered to any Benefice shall appear to have given Scandal, either by Doctrine or Manners, You are to use the best means for the Removal of him."[38] The governor's orders to the Vestry of Hamilton Parish were: "You are hereby required and commanded not to admit Mr. John Brunskill to officiate in your Church as Minister, I having thought fit by and with the advice of His Majesty's Council to remove and absolutely deprive him of acting as a Clergyman in any Church within this Dominion."[39]

The decision caused an immediate uproar among the clergy as an intrusion of secular authorities into ecclesiastic matters. Commissary Dawson, who was both the Bishop of London's representative in the colony and the President of the College, considering the awkward position in which he might find himself, hesitated to take action. In the meantime, Brunskill had posted on the door of his church and all around town numerous statements declaring Governor Dinwiddie's order "a <u>Forgery</u> otherwise a <u>Nullity</u>," and that despite the fiat and the actions of the Hamilton Parish vestry, "I am still lawful Minister of Hamilton Parish and shall continue to officiate as formerly."[40] John Camm and William Robinson, the incandescent leaders of the protest even arranged for deposed Brunskill to preach from their own pulpits in order to express their unwillingness to accept Dinwiddie's usurpation of ecclesiastic authority. Camm may have gone too far this time for he invited the deposed Brunskill to preach "before two members of the Council who had assisted in his Deprivation."[41]

"The Brunskill case revealed the central issue as it appeared to the leading clericalists. Personal gain was not involved, nor is it to be supposed that Camm and Robinson readily endorsed immorality. It is evident, therefore, that they considered clerical independence, without which genteel rank could not be secured, of overriding importance for the well-being of the church."[42] Although Virginia law, in regard to jurisdiction in this case, ran contrary to canon law, nevertheless, "the Bishop of London ... did not interfere."[43] The bishop perhaps wished to extricate himself from both the potential liabilities and problems of interceding in the affairs of the colonial church, for he "evidently sustained the governor in his proceeding; at any rate, any future discipline of the clergy was undertaken, if at all, by the lay, not by the ecclesiastical authorities."[44]

John Brunskill was translated (given a new church position) to remote Amelia County in 1759, where he continued until his death in 1803 and is reported to have lived out his years "a dead weight upon the church."[45]

The contentious behavior of the establishment clergy, in general, and the condescension of the faculty of William and Mary, in particular, compelled Governor Dinwiddie and the Visitors, pro tempore, to put aside their dispute about the Pistole Fee and speak with one voice.

The primary ecclesiastical agitators were to be found among the faculty at the college with John Camm being the ringleader.

The faculty, urged on by William Preston and John Camm, had vociferously supported the rights of the clergy against the intrusions of the native vestries; they had opposed the provisions of the Two-Penny Act, invited a minister disgraced by his actions and dismissed by the governor and Council to speak from their pulpits, and been defiantly noncompliant to the requests of the Board of Visitors. It was the opinion of many in the colony that the professors spent more time in agitating than in educating. The reasons for the acrimony, with the governor, the Council, the Burgesses, and the Visitors on the one side and the faculty on the other, were both personal and political. Next, however, a seemingly routine and unremarkable event set ablaze the tinderbox of bad feelings that resulted in the dismissal of the entire faculty at the college.

HUBARD AND DIGGES

The Master of the Grammar School was provided with an usher to help in the governance and education of the boys in the grammar school—ushers were from local families, often the products of the same grammar school in which they were serving, were paid a generous salary, and were frequently related by varying degrees of consanguinity to members of the Board of Visitors. The role of the usher was much like the duties assigned to janitors in the Scottish grammar schools—teach the lower levels of students, assist the master in preparation of classes and discipline of the students, and provide for the physical upkeep of the school itself. Although it was rare for an usher to become a master, nevertheless, this happened in the case of Emmanuel Jones.[46]

Even though there are always two sides to a story, accessible documents relate the faculty's perspective; nevertheless, they have the ring of truth and there is little doubt that the outcome had more to do with the underlying wish of the Visitors and the community to be rid of the pesky parsons than it did with any specific or technical infractions. The Masters may have felt immunized against repercussions by the regulations of the charter, by the recent and consistent support from the Bishop of London, and by the decisions of the Privy Council. Thus, on May 3, 1756, they dismissed two ushers—Cole Digges and Matthew Hubard, both of whom were related to powerful members of the Board of Visitors.[47] The resolution to expel the two ushers was unanimous, the reason given was "not only for yir [their] remarkable Idleness & bad Behaviour in general, but particularly for whipping ye little Boys in ye Gramar School, … for Obstinacy & Disrespect to ye Grammar master, & refusing to answer before the President & Masters of Complaints made of them."[48]

The Masters further resolved that "any young Gentleman, who shall keep Company with the said Cole Digges & Matthew Hubard, or shew any Countenance, shall be looked upon to be Abettors & punished accordingly." And, it stated finally, that the parents of the chastised ushers "be acquainted with ye above Resol[ve] & to keep ym [them] fm coming within ye College Bounds."[49]

During the disciplinary trial, which took place on the second floor of the Wren Building, Matthew Hubard's brother James anxiously listened to the deliberations through the door, and when the above resolutions were read, he burst into the room and dragged his brother away. Although the ushers may have been guilty of the offenses, the punishments not only bespoke a mean and vindictive spirit of the Masters, but could also easily be interpreted as a personal insult by members of the faculty to several of the Visitors and a direct challenge to the group as a whole. The intention may well have been to take the Visitors down a notch and to reestablish the real center of control in the faculty.

The Masters must have thought that the statutes would protect them from any retribution on the part of the Visitors, but those gentlemen likely initiated strategies to remove the professors from the very day of the trial. In a subsequent letter to the Bishop of London, Professor William Robinson noted, "There are two things very observable in the Orders of the Visitors, They generally consist of something that bears hard upon the Masters and the information upon which they are built is conceal'd. Two points which make it but too plain that instead of taking their notions of the conduct of the Masters from the Inspection and public declaration of the President, they take it from the private information of the Boys in the Grammar School. And what the Professors can do in the College, where they are more properly under the care of their Pupils than vice versa I leave to your Lordships consideration."[50] During the next seventeen months the Visitors furtively conspired and refined a sophisticated plan that took the Masters completely by surprise in the autumn of 1757.

THE SACKING OF THE FACULTY

In dispatches to the Bishop of London and others, Dinwiddie also criticized the faculty members of the college for their performance in the classroom as well as their extracurricular activities. The governor added his editorial along with parental concerns; he observed that the "professors of the Colledge took it in their heads to make Resentment against the President of the Colledge your Comissary, using him with much ill Manners, & when the poor gentleman was sick & weak, he having been much afflicted with the Fever & Ague this Summer, they have refus'd him any Assistance in his ministerial Duty" and that for the past six months "not One of them have come to Church (the Place where the Society always attend on Sundays & holydays), w.ᶜ was ever esteem'd part of their Duty in Order to See that the Scholars behav'd well."[51]

He further maintained that the dissatisfaction with the faculty was not his alone but was both widespread and long-standing. Specifically, he said that "the Visitors of the Colledge, and indeed the Country in general, have for many Years have been greatly dissatisfied with the Behavior of Professor of Philosophy and the master of the Grammar School, not only on Acct of Intemperance & Irregularity laid to their Charge, but also because they had married, and contrary to all Rules of Seats of Learning, kept their Wives, Children & Servants in College, w^c must Occasion much Confusion & Disturbance. And the Visitors having often express'd their Disapprobation of their Families remaining in College, about a year ago they remov'd them into Town, & Since that time, as if they had a Mind to shew their Contempt of the Visitors, they have liv'd much at home, And negligently attended their Duty in Colledge."[52] More damning, he injected that their "Neglect of Duty & immoral Conduct, being often drunk & very bad Examples to the Students."[53] He concluded that the continuation of this particular group of professors had instead of improving the status of the college "have quite ruin'd this Seminary of Learning, the People declaring they will not Send their Child^n to the Colledge till there is a new Sett of professor's & many of them sent their Children to Philadelphia for Education w^c is 300 miles from this, & attended with double the Charges for Education as that of the Colledge of William & Mary."[54] Therefore, the Visitors instructed the President to write to the Bishop of London "to be So kind as to recommend & send over two proper Persons in their Room."[55]

The impetus for the request for a new "sett" of professors derived from a combination of personal animosity and political convenience. The personal animosity was primarily on the side of the Board of Visitors and the local gentry who were inflamed at the constant complaints of faculty members to London and the insults, cunningly inserted into the editorials of the *Virginia Gazette* in transparent anonymity by several members of the faculty against the local elite. Therefore, it was beneficial the governor and Council to rid themselves of the most obnoxious of their critics. Jack Morpurgo, in his work *Their Majesties' Royall Colledge*, describes the attendant circumstances of the times in the following accurate and amusing way:

So the Williamsburg factions flailed away at each other—the Governor, the Council, the Burgesses, the Commissary, the President, the Visitors, the Faculty—the alliances shifting, the Montagues not all or consistently antagonistic to the Capulets; the ring not decently ordered with the consequence that on occasion the political boxing-matches spilled out from the central arena and developed into three, or even four-sided brawls in which every contestant hit out at whoever was in sight, eager for effect but unconsidering of cause. The mêlée was so continuous and so chaotic that it was not easy to mark the moment when a contestant turned from pummeling one opponent and took to battering another, but the bell for the opening of the toughest round between the Visitors and the Faculty was struck, clearly and definitely on 13 May 1756 when the faculty decided to expel two students, Matthew Hubard and Cole Digges.[56]

Their opportunity for retribution came in the spring when the very Grammar School Master who had effected the dismissal of Matthew Hubard and Cole Digges took sick. The stratagem was not only intended to take personal revenge on the offending master and act as a deterrent to the other professors but also to drive a wedge into the solidarity of the establishment block. The Visitors and Governors of the College of William and Mary maintained that Thomas Robinson, "Master of the Grammar School, by Reason of Bodily Infirmities, is become incapable of discharging the Duty of that Office" be demitted and requested that another professor "be speedily provided." The Visitors further requested that as the Visitors had often observed that "appointing a Clergyman ... has often proved "a Means of the School being neglected" because of "the frequent Avocations as a Minister" that his Lordship be pleased that "the Person to be sent over be a LayMan, if such a one may be provided" and if such a person could not be found then "a Clergyman."[57]

Seeing the proverbial writing on the wall, the Professor of Moral Philosophy, William Preston, informed the Visitors that he intended to return to England. This decision set off a chain reaction among the faculty that would precipitate a string of events concluding with the whole faculty, except the pliant President and the native Master of the Indian School, being sacked and replaced with even more colorful candidates.

Robinson and his colleagues decried the decision that had been obviously precipitated by personal motives and political advantage. Robinson admitted that he "had a Fit of Sickness this last Spring, which rendered me incapable of attending my Business for several Weeks," nevertheless, he maintained that his illness did not affect instruction in his school since "that Deficiency was made up by the Kindness of the other Masters, who took the Care of my School by Turns, as was most convenient to each of them."[58] He also asserted that his pastoral duties were restricted to an occasional Sunday ride into the country where he preached to a friend and returned the same evening. He wrote to the Bishop of London that the real reason behind the actions of the Visitors was that they were "so very desirous of having a Lay-man ... [in order that] ... they may have him more under their Thumbs, and make him so supple as a Slave. For should such a one give the least Offense to any of them, or indeed any of their Children or Relations ... out he must go."

He added that a laymen would be more vulnerable to the manipulations of the Visitors, for at least, if a clergyman is deposed from his position at the college, he "may stand a Chance to find Refuge in a Parish" but, a layman is not on the same footing since "the poor Man will have Nothing else left him to do, but to ship himself Home again and surprise all England with the strange Adventures of his Travels."[59] William Robinson also maintained that the secret and arbitrary nature of the dismissal of Thomas Robinson on a "private pique" "shewed" the Visitors' "rashness and cruelty" and if this deprivation was to stand as a precedent, he doubted whether "any Person, sent hither from England to a Professorship" would accept the offer.[60]

The Visitors, however, were not satisfied with the dismissal of Robinson but also wanted to make clear in no uncertain terms their control over the institution that they felt had been put into question by the removal of the ushers. Therefore, in the November following the dismissal of the Grammar School Master a meeting of the

Visitors was called, in response to complaints by the expelled usher, to determine if he had been ousted without cause. The aggrieved usher was allowed to be present, and the Visitors asked the convened Masters, one by one, to give their reasons for the expulsion of Hubard and Digges; each one "refus'd to give their particular reasons, because they look'd upon that as giving up their right to the ordinary government of the College."[61]

John Camm added that although he was bound not to answer by the oath that he had taken to obey the statutes; for the satisfaction of the usher and his family and friends" he would be happy to give them to the Publick Gazette. Upon which the Usher step'd forward and beg'd that he would not."[62] Although the chairman told the masters that the statutes did give the masters the "right to put in and turn out an Usher by Statute, that he could read English, but the Statutes were not the Laws of the Medes and the Persians, To wch the Masters made no reply and the Committee broke up."[63] The Committee determined that there should be a future meeting at which a deprivation should be ordered, and set the meeting for the very same day.[64]

When the Committee next met, the Charter was examined to determine if the Masters had violated its terms and nothing could be found, nevertheless, it was put to a vote "whether the Masters had transgressed the Charter & Statutes and carried in the Affirmative by a majority."[65] The masters were sent for and "not suffer'd to say any thing, but only to answer this question, whether they adhered to their former opinion … (that they were not required to answer to the Board of Visitors for their actions) upon their answering in the affirmative, they were order'd to withdraw."[66] The Visitors thereupon resolved that "M^r. Camm, M^r. Graham and M^r. Jones be removed on Wednesday the 14th of next Month; and that other Masters be provided in their Room, who will submit the Reasons of their Conduct, to the Consideration of this Visitation, agreeably to the said Charter and Statutes."[67] To make a point the Visitors also resolved to increase the usher's salary to £75 Sterling per annum, as much as the salary of several of the deprived professors.

Emmanuel Jones, the only native-born and -educated member of the faculty, thought better of his intransigence and made a separate peace with the Visitors. On December 14, 1758, Jones was "distinguished from the rest of the offenders and call'd in. He was ask'd whether he acknowledg'd the Power of the Visitors to enquire into the ordinary Government of the College. He answer'd Yes; and was immediately restored to his Place."[68] When the rest of the Masters were told this, they replied that they would have answered in the same way had the questioned been posed to them in such a fashion. Jones' family connections almost certainly interceded in his behalf. The Visitors, however, ordered President Thomas Dawson to write to the Bishop of London and request that he "procure and send over Masters to supply the Places of M^r. Camm and M^r. Graham late Masters of Divinity and Mathematical Schools."[69]

THE DISMISSAL OF THE RELUCTANT FACULTY MEMBERS

The deprived masters refused to recognize the authority of the Visitors to dismiss them and ignored their summons to vacate throughout December and January. On February 7, 1758, the Visitors met again and ordered President Dawson and Emmanuel Jones to call on John Camm, Richard Graham, and Thomas Robinson to comply with the commands of the Visitors. The following week Dawson and Jones sent for their recent colleagues and demanded "that they remove from the College, & deliver up their Keys of their Schools, & Appartments, which they absolutely refus'd to do. The President likewise demanded of Mr. Graham the Seal & Papers belonging to the College, which he also refus'd to deliver."[70] President Dawson called in the housekeeper and the steward as witnesses and to inform that the housekeeper was "not to supply them with any Provisions;

the Servants not to obey their Orders; & other Measures in their said Order appointed."[71] At this same meeting it was further resolved that Mr. Graham lay his accounts before the President and 'Masteres' in order to have them examined.

Although the deposed Master of the Grammar School still refused to acknowledge his interim replacement, William Davis, the Bishop of London's assistant, the Reverend Samuel Nichols, had already found a replacement for Robinson in a pastor and poet named Goronwy Owen. Owen arrived on March 23, 1758, shortly after this exchange. The Minutes of President and Masters of the College of William and Mary reflect that "the President sent to Mr. Robinson, and desired the Keys of the Grammar Master's Apartments, in order to put Mr. Owen in Possession of them: Mr. Robinson refused, and said, that nobody had a better Right to these Chambers than himself. Upon which Refusal, the President ordered Hasps with Staples & Padlocks to be put upon the Doors of the several Apartments, & Schools, and two new Locks upon the Wicket Doors."[72]

The reluctant retirees, worn down by no meals, no servants, no students, and no pay, at long last conceded their keys and returned to England. Dawson, dispirited from the dispute (probably partly in sympathy with his former colleagues and partly because he had betrayed them), was despised by even the men whom he served and increasingly took refuge in the bottle. Although Camm and Graham would receive a deferred vindication, Robinson died shortly after his return to England, and for the present the Visitors were triumphant.

Meanwhile, Lieutenant Governor Dinwiddie was writing to Thomas Dawson, the President of William and Mary, about his meeting with Thomas Sherlock (the Bishop of London and Chancellor of William and Mary), and his assistant, Dr. Samuel Nichols,[73] concerning the replacements who would soon reach Virginia.

Lieutenant Governor Dinwiddie, who was in England at the time, informed President Dawson that he had met with his successor, "Francis Foukier Esq. ... [who] is a Gentlemn of good Sense & Interest here &

hope he will be Agreeable to the people & make a good Govr wch will give me much pleasure." He also reported that the Bishop of London was "So infirm that he cannot properly deliver himself without an Interpreter, however, I have had two interviews with Doct^r Nichols."[74]

Nichols, the Prebend of St. Paul's and Sherlock's assistant, dispatched Goronwy Owen overseas to serve as Master of the Grammar School. Owen had been recommended for William Preston's post as Professor of Moral Philosophy, but Nichols must have had reservations. Owen was instead offered the lesser post of Grammar School Master because Dinwiddie, mindful of John Brunskill's checkered career, thought it prudent to keep the Welshman Owen, who was too fond of the bottle, away from the pulpit.[75]

This series of events triggered an entirely new direction in the history of the College of William and Mary. It not only brought in a new set of professors with a more secular mindset, but it also changed the nature of the college from that of a British seminary to that of an American institution with a secular foundation. Even with the eventual return of John Camm, the College never reverted to its former state of subservience to the Bishop of London, nor blindly followed the instructions of royal officials.

Small's arrival in Williamsburg brought about a series of changes that transformed the curriculum of the institution, the philosophical direction and intellectual ambitions of his students, and the cooperation and admiration of many of the town's most influential citizens. For most of the two years that Jefferson was officially enrolled at the school, Small was the only professor—teaching all subjects and students.

During the next six years, the college experienced a dramatic change—the method of instruction shifted from the traditional rote and regurgitation to interpretive lectures, discussions, and demonstrations. The focus of interest shifted from a concentration on religion and the classics to an emphasis on science and the examination of new philosophical and literary perspectives. Students were encouraged to pursue intellectual and scientific experimentation outside of the classroom. The catalyst of this innovative approach and the harbinger of the Scottish Enlightenment was the last member of the faculty to be recruited and to arrive—William Small. The two colleagues that proceeded him to the College were remembered more for their colorful activities and dramatic departures that any talents or contributions that they made during their brief stays.

With the departure of William Robinson, John Camm, and Richard Graham, new candidates were sought out and found.

NOTES

1. A. Bailey Cutts, "The Educational Influence of Aberdeen in Seventeenth Century Virginia," *William and Mary Quarterly*, 2nd ser., 15, no. 3 (July 1935): 229.

2. Ibid.

3. Ibid., 231.

4. Robert Polk Thomson, "The Reform of the College of William and Mary," *Proceedings of the American Philosophical Society* 115, no. 3 (June 17, 1971): 188.

5. Cutts, "The Educational Influence of Aberdeen in Seventeenth Century Virginia," 229.

6. Thomson, "The Reform of the College of William and Mary," 188.

7. Cicero, *De Legibus*, 3.8 (London: W. Heinemann, 1928).

8. "Men in both England and Virginia lived relatively short lives (to about fifty in England and to age forty-five in Virginia) and very few survived to boast about grandchildren" (Daniel Blake Smith, "Mortality and Family in the Colonial Chesapeake," *Journal of Interdisciplinary History* 8, no. 3 [Winter 1978]: 426). Colonial women in Virginia also suffered a similar range of mortality, such that men and women often married multiple times, to the extent that special wills were developed and spouses would refer to one another as "now husband" or "now wife" (David Hackett Fischer, *Albion's Seed* [New York: Oxford University Press, 1989], 277; Darrett and Anita Rutman, "Now Wives and Son-in-Laws," *The Chesapeake in the Seventeenth Century*, ed. Thad Tate and David Ammerman [New York: W. W. Norton & Company, 1979], 153–182). The widowed partner would often quickly remarry, and the new spouses would bring into their new marriage the whole range of extended family from the preceding marriage or marriages, thereby creating a system of exponentially ramifying family dynamics. It would be difficult to calculate the consequences of either into an intended slight or a thoughtless offhand remark.

9. Richard L. Morton, *Colonial Virginia* (Chapel Hill: University of North Carolina Press, 1960), 2:761.

10. Ibid., 2:630.

11. Ibid., 2:632.

12. Ibid., 2:628.

13. Ibid., 2:627.

14. John Blair to James Abercrombie, May 30, 1759, in Morton, *Colonial Virginia*, 2:789.

15. Governor Fauquier would later assert that the initial desire of the House of Burgesses to have its own agent "resulted from the desire on the part of the members of the House of Burgesses to have some one to represent them in England in case there should arise in the future a dispute similar to that of Governor Din-widdie's days in reference to the pistole fee. Then a special agent was sent over at great expense to lay before the authorities in England the views of the people of Virginia." H. R. McIlwaine, ed., *Journal of the House of Burgesses, 1758–1761* (Richmond: Colonial Press, 1908), xvii.

16. Morton, *Colonial Virginia*, 2:790. It is a curious circumstance that the wife of Edward Montagu was the elegant Lady Elizabeth Montagu of Bluestocking fame. She was the aunt of Elizabeth Gregory, the wife of John Gregory, William Small's mentor in Aberdeen and likely in London as well.

17. Four Councillors and eight Burgesses composed the first committee of correspondence. The Councillors were Philip Grymes, Peter Randolph, Thomas Nelson, and William Nelson; the Burgesses included Peyton Randolph, Charles Carter, Richard Bland, Landon Carter, Benjamin Waller, George Wythe, and Robert Carter Nicholas. Morton, *Colonial Virginia*, 2:790.

18. McIlwaine, *Journal of the House of Burgesses, 1758–1761*, xvii.

19. E. I. Miller, "The Virginia Committee of Correspondence, 1759–1770," *William and Mary Quarterly*, 1st ser., 22, no.1 (July 1913): 1.

20. Ibid., 13.

21. Ibid., 3.

22. Ibid., 15.

23. Ibid., 99.

24. Privy Council to King George II, July 4, 1759, Virginia Colonial Records Project, Fulham Palace Papers, 72, Library of Virginia. Richmond (hereafter cited as LVA).

25. Andrew Burnaby, *Travels through the Middle Settlements in North-America, in the Years 1759 and 1760* (Dublin: R. Marchbank, 1775), 32.

26. George Reese, ed., *The Official Papers of Francis Fauquier: Lieutenant Governor of Virginia* (Charlottesville: The University Press of Virginia, 1981), 2:552, 145.

27. Morton, *Colonial Virginia*, 2:785n5.

28. Ibid., 2:788.

29. Burnaby. *Travels through the Middle Settlements in North-America*, 32.

30. Minutes of the Council of Virginia, April 21, 1757, Virginia Colonial Records Project, 22, LVA.

31. Francis Fauquier to the Bishop of London, January 5, 1759, in Reese, *Official Papers of Francis Fauquier*, 2:145.

32. In 1715, John Brunskill (Senior) was appointed minister to Virginia, and a bounty of £20 granted to him (Edward Neill. "Virginia Threads for the Future Historian," *William and Mary Quarterly* 1st ser., vol. 1, no. 2 [October 1892]: 80). Complaints were issued against the father not only for dereliction of duties—"A petition by "Benjamin Walker, Gent. ... and many other inhabitants of St. Margaret's parish" that "John Brunskill Clerk Minister of the said Parish hath Neglected to perform Divine Service at the Chapel of Ease built Several Years agoe for the Convenience of a Great Number of Families living remote from the church of the said parish and refusing to preach or Read prayers there by Law he is obliged." (George Carrington Mason, *William and Mary Quarterly*, 2nd ser., vol. 23, no. 4 [October 1943]: 459)— but he also had a reputation for making trouble and for immoral behavior. In 1745, he so provoked one of his parishioners, Hugh Noden, that Noden verbally not only abused him by calling him a "Rogue, Rascal, Villain, Devil, Begger, Scoundrel ... privat Drunkard & Fool" but also "Shook his fist ... & wished for a Sword [and said that] he would beat [Brunskill's] hog's teeth down his throat" (Dawson Papers, June 14, 1745, Archives, Swem Library, College of William and Mary, Williamsburg, Virginia [hereafter cited as Swem Library]). The altercation followed one in which Noden's son, convinced that Brunskill was spreading rumors about his father and that Brunskill's sermon was a personal attack on his father, followed Brunskill after the sermon, and having caught up to him "called him several times old Son of a Bitch (sometimes with the Appellation Damn'd) Old rogue, Old Villain, said several times he had a good mind to pull him from his Horse, and give him a licking, or Drubbing." Dawson Papers, August 7, 1746, Archives, Swem Library.

33. Thomas Dawson to the Bishop of London, July 9, 1757, Virginia Colonial Record Project, Fulham Palace Papers, Microfilm Reel 589 (50), LVA.

34. Governor Dinwwiddie to the Bishop of London., September 12, 1757, in *Historical Collections Relating to the American Colonial Church*, ed. William Perry (New York: AMS Press, 1969), 1:457.

35. Ibid., 456.

36. John Brunskill, April 7, 1757, Brunskill Papers, 22051, Archives, Swem Library.

37. Governor Dinwwiddie to the Bishop of London, September 12, 1757, in Perry, *Historical Collections Relating to the American Colonial Church*, 1:457.

38. Minutes of the Council of Virginia, May 20, 1757, Virginia Colonial Records Project, 22, LVA; Thomas Dawson to the Bishop of London, July 9, 1757, Virginia Colonial Records Project, Fulham Palace Papers, Microfilm Reel 589 (50), LVA. "In the mean Time, the Governor being informed by some of his Majesty's Council, that irregular Clergymen were frequently in Commissary Blair's Time proceeded against before the Governor and the Council; (which I must own had been the Practice) determined to pursue that Method."

39. Robert Dinwiddie to the Vestry of Hamilton Parish, May 20, 1757, Virginia Colonial Records Project, 177, LVA.

40. Thomas Dawson to the Bishop of London, July 9, 1757, Virginia Colonial Records Project, Fulham Palace Papers, Microfilm Reel 589 (50), LVA.

41. Francis Fauquier to the Bishop of London, January 5, 1759, in Reese, *Official Papers of Francis Fauquier*, 2:145.

42. Rhys Isaac, "Religion and Authority: Problems of the Anglican Establishment in Virginia in the Era of the Great Awakening and the Parsons' Cause," *William and Mary Quarterly*, 3rd ser., vol. 30, no. 1 (January 1973): 13.

43. *Report of the Virginia State Library, 1907–1908* (Richmond: Davis Bottom, 1908), 28.

44. Arthur Lyon Cross, *The Anglican Episcopate and the American Colonies* (New York: Longmans, Green and Co., 1902), 137.

45. Despite all the trouble and hardship, Brunskill seemed to have maintained his old propensities for drink, immoral behavior, and agitating his congregation. It was reported that "on one occasion, when the house was full, just before the Revolutionary War, when the whole Colony was incensed against England, Parson Brunskill arose, and, seeing Colonel Archer and one or two other gentlemen dressed in regimentals, called them rebels, and expressed himself indignant to see such indications of a general rebellion, and said he should write immediately to the King and inform against them" (Bishop William Meade, *Old Churches, Ministers and Families of Virginia* [Philadelphia: Lippencott & Co., 1878], 2:20). "Upon which the gentlemen arose and carried their families out of the church, and, on consultation, determined to inflict punishment upon him, which was only prevented by the interference of two of the elder and most influential gentlemen present" (Meade, *Old Churches, Ministers, and Families of Virginia*, 2:21). He was then severely admonished and commanded to "never to repeat such language, or he would receive harsh treatment added to disrespect. He never attempted to preach afterward, but lived a quiet secluded life at the glebe, about five miles

from Grubhill. The Rev John Brunskill was thought to be an amiable man and an indulgent master, but stood very low for piety, and the ruin of the Church here was attributed to him. He died at his glebe, near Amelia Court-House, in 1803 or 1804, in good circumstances, leaving his servants free, and every thing else to a Mr. Richard Booker." Meade, *Old Churches, Ministers and Families of Virginia*, 2:20.

46. Meeting of the Masters of William and Mary College, November 1, 1755. "Mr Emmanel Jones being elected Master of ye Indian School by ye Visitors & Govr did also subscribe his Assent to the 39 Articles [vid p 192] & took ye Oath de fideli Administratione &c. (Meeting of the President & Masters of William and Mary College, November 6. 1755). "Mr James Hubbard is unanimously elected usher of this Grammar School in ye Room of Mr. Em Jones." Although it is said that no degrees were awarded at William and Mary until the 1770s and indeed no documents relating to the granting of degrees have yet surfaced, except an honorary A.M. awarded to Benjamin Franklin in 1755, nevertheless, Emmanuel Jones, who attended only the Grammar School and philosophy school at William and Mary, repeatedly had the designation A.B. follow his name in the faculty minutes at the college (the other members of the faculty were described with an A.M.). See the records for the Meetings of the President & Masters of Wm & Mary College for May 3, 1756, September 17, 1756, September 27, 1756, the session granting an honorary degree to Benjamin Franklin [n.d.], and the session previous to Franklin's degree [n.d.]. Therefore, Franklin's degree was not the first to be conferred at William and Mary. See also Ezra Stiles, *Extracts from the Itineraries and Other Miscellanies of Ezra Stiles*, ed. Franklin Bowditch Dexter (New Haven: Yale University Press, 1916), 158. "31 May 1762. John Whiting of Newport, Esq., just returned from No. Carolina by Land…. He also told me that he was at Williamsburg & visited William & Mary College, when the President, Mr. Yates, told him the Number of Students was seventy five, chiefly Boys & a few about 15 Aet. (Aetas, aetatis – years of age), and that they seldom conferred Degrees." Note that Ezra Stiles relates specifically that the College of William and Mary seldom confer Degrees, not that "they do not confer degrees" nor "that they have never conferred degrees"; *seldom*, at the very least, implies that degrees, and more than one, have been conferred. All of which evokes the tantalizing question—Did William and Mary confer an A.B. on Jefferson as well? Not very likely, but a good tease.

47. Cole Digges was the son of Dudley Digges and Mary Hubard, his wife, and probably a cousin of Matthew and James Hubard, the sons of Matthew Hubard, clerk of York County. "Journal of the Meetings of the President and Masters of William and Mary College," *William and Mary Quarterly*, 1st ser., vol. 2, no. 4 (April 1894): 256.

48. Meeting of the President and Masters of the College of William and Mary, May 3, 1756, Microfilm, Special Collections, Rockefeller Library, Colonial Williamsburg Foundation, Williamsburg, Virginia (hereafter cited as CW).

49. Ibid.

50. William Robinson to the Bishop of London, n.d., Virginia Colonial Records Project, Fulham Palace Papers 13, No. 117, Microfilm, LVA.

51. Robert Dinwiddie to the Bishop of London, September 12, 1757, Special Collections, Swem Library. Original in Clemens Library, University of Michigan. Ann Arbor.

52. Ibid.

53. Ibid.

54. Ibid.

55. Ibid.

56. J. E. Morpurgo, *Their Majesties' Royall College: William and Mary in the Seventeenth and Eighteenth Centuries* (Washington: Hennage Creative Printers, 1976), 122.

57. Meeting of the Visitors and Governors of the College of William and Mary, May 20, 1757, Virginia Colonial Records Project, Fulham Palace Papers, 15 (38), LVA.

58. Thomas Robinson to the Bishop of London, June 30, 1757, Virginia Colonial Records Project, Fulham Palace Papers, 15, No. 37, Microfilm, LVA.

59. Ibid.

60. William Robinson to the Bishop of London, ca. 1761, Virginia Colonial Records Project, Fulham Palace Papers, No. 117, Microfilm, LVA.

61. Ibid.

62. Ibid.

63. Ibid. See also Meeting of the Visitors and Governors of the College of William and Mary, November 4, 1757, Virginia Colonial Records Project, Fulham Palace Papers, 13, No. 178, LVA.

64. "RESOLVED: That the further Consideration of the said Report be referreed to a fuller Meeting, which is agreed to be on Friday 4th Instant at 10 o'Clock in the Morning; and that Notice thereof be given to such of the Members as are not now present" (Meeting of the Visitors and Governors of the College of William and Mary, November 4, 1757, Virginia Colonial Records Project, Fulham Palace Papers, 13, No. 178, LVA). The urgency with which this meeting was called—on the same day at 10 o'clock in the morning, both in terms of the expediency and the need for a quorum, speaks to the desire of the committee members to be rid of all the troublesome professors in one fell swoop.

65. William Robinson to the Bishop of London, ca. 1761, Virginia Colonial Records Project, Fulham Palace Papers, No. 117, Microfilm, LVA. See also Meeting of the Visitors and Governors of the College of William and Mary, November 11, 1757, Virginia Colonial Records Project, Fulham Palace Papers, 13, No. 178, LVA.

66. Ibid.

67. Meeting of the Visitors and Governors of the College of William and Mary, November 11, 1757, Virginia Colonial Records Project, Fulham Palace Papers, 13, No. 178, LVA.

68. William Robinson to the Bishop of London, ca. 1761, Virginia Colonial Records Project, Fulham Palace Papers, No. 117, Microfilm, LVA.

69. Meeting of the Visitors and Governors of the College of William and Mary, December 14, 1757, Virginia Colonial Records Project, Fulham Palace Papers, 13, No. 178, LVA.

70. Thomas Dawson and Emmanuel Jones, "Minutes of the College Faculty, [February 13,] 1758," *William and Mary Quarterly*, 2nd ser., vol. 1, no. 1 (January 1921): 24. For some reason these records were not in the Fulham Palace Papers but were in the Dawson Papers at the Library of Congress, Washington, D.C.

71. Ibid.

72. Thomas Dawson and Emmanuel Jones, "Minutes of the College Faculty, [March 23,] 1758," *William and Mary Quarterly*, 2nd ser., vol. 1, no. 1 (January 1921): 26.

73. Alternatively: Nicolls, Nicholls, Nicols.

74. Robert Dinwiddie to Thomas Dawson, March 14, 1758, MSS 65 PsT D62, Faculty-Alumni Files, Special Collections, Swem Library.

75. Dinwiddie may have been warned by Nichols regarding Goronwy Owen's fondness for spirits. "I am desir'd to recommend him to your friendship, & to ease you of the great trouble in your Parish, may you not Appoint him your Curate or Lecturer." Robert Dinwiddie to Thomas Dawson, March 14, 1758, MSS 65 PsT D62, Faculty-Alumni Files, Special Collections, Swem Library.

CHAPTER 4

The Replacements

The year 1757 was significant both in the history of the colony of Virginia and for the College of William and Mary, ushering in radical changes to the political atmosphere of the Old Dominion and reforms to the instruction and curriculum at the college. Lieutenant Governor Robert Dinwiddie had frequently been at odds with both the members of the House of Burgesses and Visitors of the College of William and Mary and members of the community. Dinwiddie's bristling personality and self-serving policies often initiated disputes, which, even if detached from the institution, had important and negative consequences for the welfare of the College. The changes that came about as a result of his departure may have saved the school.

LIEUTENANT GOVERNOR FRANCIS FAUQUIER

In 1757, Dinwiddie requested that London relieve him of his office "on account of his infirmities" and he was soon replaced by Francis Fauquier.[1] The new lieutenant governor of Virginia had been born in 1704, the son of John Francis Fauquier, a Huguenot physician, who left his native town of Clairac and fled France after the revocation of the Edict of Nantes in 1685.[2] He made his way to England accompanied by his two brothers and two sisters.

In London, Dr. Fauquier found employment in the Royal Mint under Sir Isaac Newton. In 1698, he became a British citizen and married Elizabeth Chamberlayne, the daughter of a country squire. The couple resided in the heart of the financial district of London. Fauquier pater was elected a director of the Bank of England before his death in 1726.

Francis was born in the Lime Street house, and little is known of his early education. He had an early start in the army, for he earned "a pair of colours" at a young age and remained for some time with his unit. Having finished his military duties, Francis married Catherine, the daughter of Sir Charles Dalston. His uncle William, a successful businessman, left both his estate and his connections to Francis after his death in 1747. Francis would become, like his uncle, a Director of the South Sea Company in 1751,[3] and a Fellow of the Royal Society in 1753.

It was during this time that Fauquier became acquainted with his patrons at the South Sea Company, Lord Anson and George Montagu Dunk, Earl of Halifax, President of the Board of Trade. In 1756, encouraged by Lord Anson, Fauquier published an essay, "Ways and Means of Raising Money for the support of the present War without Increasing the Public Debts," in which he enunciated an economic thesis that was well received by Sir James Steuart and became part of the classical doctrine elaborated by Adam Smith and David Ricardo. He asserted that any tax on wages or necessities is always shifted from the laborer to the employer and to ultimately be paid for by the consumer. The first edition, which identified Fauquier only by his initials, was dedicated to Lord Anson; the second edition, however, bore Fauquier's full name, as did a third edition published in 1757.[4]

The Virginian historian and journalist John Burk proposed that Fauquier's election to lieutenant governor of Virginia stemmed from Lord Anson's favorable impression of his character. According to the famous tale, after a night of heavy gambling losses, Fauquier behaved with such grace that Anson felt an obligation to do him a good turn.[5] It was in this way, according to Burk, that Fauquier became the Governor of Virginia. Fauquier's economic essay, however, rather than Burk's gambling anecdote, is a more plausible foundation for his appointment to the post. For Fauquier, in his will, gave credit for the promotion to his other patron, George Montagu Dunk. Robert Dinwiddie indicated that Fauquier also had the support of a substantial community of politically connected merchants of London as well.[6]

Fauquier and his family arrived in Virginia in early June to an official welcome address delivered by the Mayor of Williamsburg on June 10, 1758.[7] The academic replacements for the college appeared shortly after the new lieutenant governor took up residence in the Governor's Palace.

GORONWY OWEN:
MASTER OF THE GRAMMAR SCHOOL

The first of the academic replacements to arrive was Goronwy Owen, known in his homeland of Wales as Gronwy Dhu, or Goronwy the Black. He was born on January 1, 1723, to Owen Gronw[8] in Rhosfawr, Llanfairmathafarn, Eithaf, in the county of Anglesey.[9] His early education included a parish school near his home, a grammar school in Caernarvonshire, followed by the Friar's School in Bangor, at which time he "had reached the limit proposed to me, and gone through the studies of the school."[10] Although he secured a scholarship to Jesus College, Oxford, he only spent about a fortnight there.[11] Owen next served as an usher at a school in Pwllheli from 1742 to 1744, and held a similar post at Denbigh from 1744 to 1745.[12] In 1746, he was able to secure a curacy near his home parish but soon was forced to leave it to make room for the Bishop's relative.

Shortly thereafter, he was appointed a curate at Northolt, a village in Middlesex, and it is likely that he became acquainted with Dr. Samuel Nichols there.[13] The fact that the Bishop of London had formerly been at the Friar's School may account for Nichol's assistance in the matter of his employment in the colony.[14] Negotiations began late in the summer of 1757. Owen was interviewed for the position early in the autumn, and by October, the appointment was all but secured. On October 21, 1757, Goronwy Owen received his bond and his bounty from the Bishop of London. "The said [Goronwy] Owen is by the said Lord Bishop of London Licensed to perform the ministerial office in the province of Virginia in America and hath received his Majesty's bounty of Twenty pounds to defray the Charge of his passage thither."[15]

Owen and his family made preparations for the voyage and anxiously waited for departure. They debarked from Spithead to Virginia in December, 1757. Owen arrived in Virginia early in March, having lost his wife and one son to a highly contagious pox on the ship. Once in Virginia, he quickly settled and commenced his duties on April 5, 1758.[16]

JACOB ROWE:
PROFESSOR OF MORAL PHILOSOPHY

The second replacement was Jacob Rowe and, although later events would make his name notorious, little is known about him before his arrival in Williamsburg. He is said to have been born about 1730,[17] and his bond, issued by the Bishop of London, on February 13, 1758, identified him as "Jacob Rowe Clerk Master of Arts, Late of Trinity College in the University of Cambridge."[18] Curiously, the Bishop of London awarded Rowe a £40 signing bonus, twice the normal bounty.[19] On March 6, 1758, Rowe reported to Spit, England, where Captain Legge transported him to Virginia aboard his ship, the *Chesterfield*.[20] The normal crossing to Virginia was about a ten-week trip. The *Chesterfield*, however, was either delayed in sailing, had several ports of call, encountered turbulent weather, or came across hostile vessels, for Rowe did not appear before a meeting of the President and Masters until the middle of June. On Saturday, June 17, 1758, Jacob Rowe, A.M., was elected Professor of Moral Philosophy by the President and Masters of the College."[21]

Dinwiddie had expressed his hope to Thomas Dawson, William and Mary's President at the time, that this "thorow change will retrieve the Character of the Colledge, & engage the Gentlemen to send their Children to it as formerly, and this must Greatly depend on your Conduct & that of the Professors."[22]

THE FINAL VACANCY

Dinwiddie advised that there was one post left to fill, "Doct' Nicholls Says he will Soon <endeavour to> get a proper person for Professor of Mathamaticks."[23] Although the Visitors had specifically requested that the Bishop of London send over a layman,[24] the first two replacement candidates were men of the cloth. Dinwiddie reported "as soon as the college is properly supplied with (goo)d professors &ct I shall be might (glad to) hear it (su)ceeds & increases with students; & Nicholls has had a great deal of trouble (finding a replacement for the Professor of Mathematicks)."[25]

William Robinson, later the Bishop of London's Commissary, observed that the Visitors desired that all professors be laymen, but wondered how the Bishop could find any "Laymen of Learning and Character to come hither for a hundred sterling a year ... especially when they are to hold this mighty Provision at the Will and Pleasure of twenty Gentlemen, who may dispossess them upon a secret complaint, for imaginary Offenses, is beyond my Comprehension."[26]

AN UNLIKELY CANDIDATE: WILLIAM SMALL

A commission to a post in the colonies was tantamount to academic exile. The candidate would be far away from home and potential opportunities for advancement, the attitude toward professors in the colonies was that of servants rather than as masters, members of the faculty were always carefully scrutinized and often criticized, an extra-academic body routinely dictated terms of academic policies and behavioral mandates, and professors were often burdened with collateral obligations. The privileged life of English academics was a far cry from the expectations at William and Mary, where the internal workings of the college were "exposed to full public view in the capital village and its business and the activities of its faculty and students were the daily concern of the self-conscious local gentry."[27]

Because of the stigma attached to such an assignment, the question that should be asked is: how was the college so fortunate to be able to attract a candidate of William Small's caliber? Indeed, contrary to previous assumptions, it is highly unlikely that William Small hustled down from Scotland to apply for the hard to fill post, but rather that he was actively and aggressively recruited by the Reverend Samuel Nichols in the great metropolis of London.

How Small came to be recruited, and the details of his first days in the colony emerged in an interview that Small gave after he returned to London in 1765. When Small was in London purchasing a scientific apparatus for his classes of Natural Philosophy, he was sought out by a young gentleman named Stephen Hawtrey. Stephen's brother, Edward, had been offered the position as the Grammar School Master at the College of William and Mary. When his brother Stephen learned of Small's presence in the capital, he sought him out for information about the College and advice on his brother's behalf. Although Stephen had twice missed William at his apartment in Sussex Street, he finally caught up with him at Benjamin Franklin's favorite pub, the George and Vulture. The conversation, as related in a letter between the brothers, contains a wealth of information about both Small and the College.

According to Hawtrey's interview, the President of the College wrote to the then Bishop of London in 1758, requesting a person qualified to be a Professor of Mathematicks. "Mr. Small *was applied to* on this occasion, & went over thinking he was in full possession of the office from the time of his nomination by the Bishop. However, upon arrival, [he] found that he was to wait on the Visitors for final approval.—& after taking the oaths, they elected him into that office

& from that time his Salary commenced and not before."[28]Years later, the Rector of the College, Dudley Digges, confirmed Small's account in a letter to the ever-suffering Bishop of London. The rector sarcastically related that Small was disappointed in the "Assurances that Dr. Nicholls gave him ... before he came over."[29]

The date of Small's recruitment may be approximated by evidence from several documents. In a letter dated March 14, 1758, Dinwiddie wrote to Dawson, "Doct". Nichols Says he will Soon <endeavour to> get a proper person for Professor of Mathematicks."[30] Three months later, near the end of June, Dinwiddie again addressed the issue, "Nicholls has had a great deal of trouble [finding a replacement for Professor of Mathematicks]."[31] Assuming that the winds and the weather were not adverse, it was normally a ten-week voyage from London to Hampton, Virginia.[32] Since Small took his oath of office in October 1758, the interview between William Small and Samuel Nichols likely took place between the middle to the end of the month of July.

Small's experience during his voyage to America is reflected in the advice that he gave to young Hawtrey, "Your passage at the outside won't Cost you thirty pounds [to] defray which expense, the Visitors have or will order some Merch[ants in] London to pay you twenty pound, the same as was paid to Mr Sm[all]."[33] In addition, he cautioned against taking provisions "as you will find it troublesome, only agree with the Captain to give him a certain Sum for your passage and board that is breakfast dinner & Supper & Wine twice a day, for [which he] says you won't pay above twenty guineas."[34] It is probable that he embarked from London late in July or early in August and, after tossing about for ten weeks, landed at Yorktown or Hampton late in September or in the early days of October.

Small's educational background was secular rather than religious, and his special passion was for the sciences and medicine. By his education and experience, his genial personality, and with his unusual cultural background, William Small's résumé seemed tailor-made to the specific requests of the Board of Visitors.

However, more complex question may be asked not about the manner in which Small was recruited or when he set sail, but why he accepted such a dicey post in a faraway colony where the entire faculty had been recently sacked and summarily turned out. The answer may lie in youthful enthusiasm, the promise of adventure, the social cachet of the title, and a hope for a new beginning.

The replacements recruited by the Bishop of London's office and confirmed by the Board of Visitors were as diverse in backgrounds as they were in personalities. Small was, in matters of deportment, diligence, and attitude, the polar opposite of his compatriots. Goronwy Owen was the first to be recruited and the first to arrive in Virginia. He was in Williamsburg by the middle of March 1758, just as President Dawson was changing the locks on the Grammar Master's apartments. He took his oaths of office on April 7, 1758.[35] Jacob Rowe, A.M., a recent graduate of Trinity College, Cambridge, followed Owen two months later and took his *de fideli Administratione* on June 17, 1758. William Small was the last to be recruited and the last to arrive; he came early in October, and took his oaths on October 17, 1758.

Faculty Minutes. 17 October 1758
William Small elected Professor
of Natural Philosophy.

O TEMPORA, O MORES

Although Goronwy Owen had a reputation as a hard drinker and carouser in his native Wales, he was also regarded as an excellent classicist and one of the preeminent poets in the Welsh language. By contrast, little is known of Jacob Rowe before he came to America and little after he left, but he had his hour of infamy at the College of William and Mary. It seems that both of these candidates began their careers at the college congenially enough; Rowe attended Fauquier's first soirées at the Governor's Palace without attracting notice, and Owen married President Dawson's sister—who was also the house-keeper for the College—shortly after he arrived.

But the calmness and civility of the two was not to last. Rowe had scarcely been in Williamsburg for three months when, like the ejected professor that he had replaced, he began to remonstrate aggressively against the provisions of the second Two-Penny Act (which extended the provisions of the first Two-Penny Act). No doubt well into his cups while visiting with friends, and not familiar with either the politics or positions of all those who were gathered there, he proclaimed, according to a Burgess who was present, "How many of the House of Burgesses were to be hanged? That every Member who should vote for settling the Parsons Salaries in Money, would be Scoundrels, and that if any Member wanting to receive the Sacrament, was to apply to him, he would refuse to administer it."[36]

The House of Burgesses resolved that Rowe's speech was "scandalous and malicious, highly reflecting on the Honor and Dignity of the House of Burgesses, and that the said Mr *Rowe*, in speaking the same is guilty of an open Violation and Breach of the Privileges of this House."[37] The Sergeant at Arms promptly placed Mr. Rowe in custody. The following day, Rowe offered his most abject apology, saying that he was "sincerely sorry for his Offence, which was committed without any evil Intention," that it had occurred "in a private Conversation at his Friend's House," where he had been "easily and indiscreetly provoked by some rude Expressions used by some of the Company, against that sacred Order to which he belongs," and, finally, that he willingly and "humbly and readily submits himself" to their condign punishment.[38] He was ordered to be discharged—paying fees.

Meanwhile, Goronwy Owen, who had lost his first wife to the pox on the voyage over, was enjoying his new marriage to President Dawson's sister. For a time, it seemed that the rambunctious Welshman had finally settled down. But Mrs. Owen died before the year was out,[39] and Owen soon attached himself to his hard-drinking colleague either through grief or opportunity.

Jacob Rowe and Goronwy Owen were similar in their political leanings and appetites for spirits. They reveled in leading their students into drunken brawls with the youth of the town. When they were first admonished for their behavior in town, the pair clandestinely traveled down to the public houses of Yorktown to escape the surveillance of local monitors, but the Visitors were not deceived. Owen, formerly apolitical, became a firebrand with Rowe urging him on. He, too, made public declarations about the second Two-Penny Act and questioned the motives of the Burgesses.

Their behavior was publicly rebellious and privately debauched. The Visitors assumed that the replacements would be a welcome change from their predecessors, but at least in the case of Owen and Rowe, the cure was worse than the disease. The pair showed, in the most flagrant fashion, their contempt for the Visitors, for President Dawson, for the sensibilities of the town's inhabitants, and for the conventions of the Church. The most-alarming aspect for the townspeople was that these were the very men who were instructing their children and ruining the very institution that they were recruited to save. The remaining master from the former "Society (faculty)," Emmanuel Jones, had learned his lesson about opposing the policies and wishes of the Board of Visitors, and was reticent to comment on their activities.

OWEN, ROWE, AND SMALL:
A STUDY IN CONTRASTS

In contrast, William Small had an entirely different set of interests and inclinations than those of his colleagues at the college. He assiduously avoided dining at the master's table and sometimes took his meals in his room, but more often dined out. Always fond of company, he socialized with the principal gentlemen of the colony and avoided the controversies of his peers. His expenditures at Chowning's and Mrs. Shields's Taverns, payments made for wine to Colonel Tucker and others,[40] reports of the gatherings that he attended at the Governor's Palace, and at the homes of other friends, all suggest that he preferred the company of his students, of their parents, and of the gentlemen of the town to his colleagues at the College.

Small was greeted on his arrival in the autumn of 1758, with all the hospitality and graciousness for which Virginians are so well known. Even one of Small's most vehement detractors, Dudley Digges, admitted to the Bishop of London that Small "being sensible and entertaining in his conversation and of a most winning address, soon ingratiated himself with some of the principal Gentlemen of the Colony."[41] Indeed, Small developed deep and long-lasting associations with many of his Virginia associates and with a number of his students. He voted his conscience on matters dealing with the college, not being influenced or intimidated by the opinions of either the Visitors or the faculty.

Meanwhile, Rowe and Owen were becoming an increasing scandal both to the college and to the town. They spent many evenings in the "publick" houses of Williamsburg and Yorktown, where they were often seen carousing with local girls and cavorting with their students. Their daily discussions turned to dissatisfaction with both the actions of the House of Burgesses and with President Dawson's malleability concerning the designs of the Visitors. Rowe even suggested that the charter of the college should be done away with and a new constitution be written, one that would take control of the college out of the hands of the Visitors and place it where it belonged—with the faculty. Complaints came from all quarters to the Visitors—from merchants, from local families, from the parents of the students, from members of the House of Burgesses, and even from the President himself.

At a meeting of the Visitors on April 26, 1760, the following statement was read into the record: "That the said Mr. Rowe, by a contentious, turbulent, contumacious, and strange Madness of Behavior, has frequently endeavoured to destroy the regular Authority of the President of the College, and to create and keep up Differences and Parties between the President and Masters, to the Destruction of the Ordinary Government of the College ... and that Mr. Owen has been lately guilty of the same Behavior."[42]

Four days later, Rowe appeared before the Visitors to answer the charges. He admitted that occasionally he was "overtaken in Company" and that through "this Infirmity in the Heat of Passion has sometimes been guilty of uttering Oaths" but denied that he "endeavoured to destroy the regular Authority of the President."[43] After the final charge was proved by sworn testimony and letters written by the defendant himself, Rowe pleaded that he had "not stept so far beyond the line which divides Virtue and Vice, as to be unable to draw [my] Foot back again" and that he was "most sincerely sorry for [his] Conduct."[44] The Visitors, "tho' with some difficulty," accepted both his apologies and his promise of better behavior, and agreed that "he may continue in his Office,"[45] but with a warning of the severe consequences for any relapse.

THE BATTLE OF THE CENTURY

For several anxious months, Jacob Rowe adhered to the Visitors' admonitions, but as the cries for his dismissal diminished, the chastised professor became incrementally bolder. Within a short time, Rowe reverted to his old ways and activities. Confident in the

Visitors' lack of resolve, Rowe and Owen incited a confrontation so infamous that a Virginian conducting business in England, Philip Ludwell,[46] soon read about it in the London newspapers and wrote a friend back home, "I have heard many disagreeable things from Virginia; as the Battle of the Scholars, their Regiments laying down their Arms &c."[47]

According to an anonymous *Gazette* contributor, who styled himself Tim Pastime, a mock epic battle occurred in Williamsburg in July 1760. The combatants on one side were the students, led by Jacob Rowe (Orlando Furioso) and Goronwy Owen (Cadwallader); on the other, the apprentices of the town, with publican William Finney commanding. The prelude to the incident had started innocently enough in Bruton Parish Church where the students were accustomed to sit in the loft and the locals in the pews below. During service, some of the townspeople rolled their eyes upward toward the noisy gallery, and the students thought themselves mocked. In revenge, they "collected all the Saliva they could, and stream'd it on the Oppidans (townies) Faces,[48] nay some have asserted that the urinary Conduits were exercis'd on the Occasion."[49] The townsmen took natural exception to this treatment and in an encounter "with some of the Collegians, took some personal Satisfaction of them; and menac'd universal Carnage; if such Indignities were repeated."[50]

When informed of this squabble, Rowe, together with Owen, incited the boys to invite the offending townspeople to a fight—if they were men enough. On the appointed evening, the student troops assembled themselves in the college yard with Owen, decked out "like a Roman Lictor, with a Cutlass in one Hand & a Bunch of Rods worn down to the Stumps in the other, a Tissue of the Punishment the Captives were to receive."[51] Before the townsmen could form ranks, Rowe exhorted his troops "aut cito Mors aut cito Victoria"[52] and fired a pistol to start the charge. The apprentices thinking that the lunatic professors were actually planning to shoot them, took off in a disorganized and frenzied manner.

The collegiate troops captured two of the opposition and the inebriated Owen gave them "35 lashes well laid on,"[53] promising even more the next time. The Attorney General of Virginia and Rector of the Board of Visitors, Peyton Randolph, was passing by at the time and severely admonished Rowe, who responded, "Sir, if you have any thing to say personally to me, know you, that my Name is the Revd. Mr. Jacob Rowe, that I may be met at any Time and Place, when and where soever appointed."[54] The following day Rowe also grossly insulted President Dawson when he came to investigate the incident.

A SIGH OF RELIEF

This was too much for the Visitors, who were likely wishing for the good old days of Camm and Graham and Thomas Robinson. A dismissal trial was instantly arranged; Rowe was summoned to answer the charges. Rowe confessed that they were in part correct; when pressed as to what part was not true "he answered it was in Respect to the President, whom he said he had not ill-used, as he did not deserve any better treatment."[55] The Visitation resolved, "It is the unanimous Opinion of the Visitors and Governors that the said Mr. Rowe be immediately removed and deprived of his Office of Professor in this College."[56] They also warned that if Rowe should offer resistance to being removed, he would be treated in the same manner as the previously evicted professors.

Although the Visitors did not prosecute Owen for his part in the riot, it became clear that his time at the college was drawing to a close. The more lenient treatment accorded to Owen may have had less to do with his diminished guilt than the fact that he had previously been married to President Dawson's sister.[57] It was said about Owen, "Rum which had destroyed more than the sword was his destruction."[58] Whatever the details of the matter, Owen, shortly after Rowe's expulsion, tendered his resignation and, "with a sigh of relief that can still be heard after two centuries,"[59] the Visitors accepted it. He applied for and obtained a position as minister at St. Andrews Parish in Brunswick County, Virginia, where he remained until his death. He married Joan Simmonds, with whom he fathered four more children, and became the owner of a cotton and tobacco plantation.[60]

This series of events left the college with a dipsomaniacal president, an obsequious Master of the Indian School, and William Small. The sad situation counterintuitively resulted in a truly remarkable opportunity, which J. E. Morpurgo so aptly described: "That a polymath of such rare quality [Small] should have appeared at William and Mary at just the right moment to teach the outstanding polymath of them all is one of the happiest coincidences in educational history. That Wythe was available to take over Jefferson from Small is enough to make an agnostic believe in Divine Providence."[61]

The importance of this chronology is the strange confluence of events that put William Small in charge of the entire curriculum of the institution and gave him the ability to exert a personal influence on a number of students at a critical time in the nation's history. This same set of events left President Dawson, so frequently intoxicated that he was unable to hold his cards much less attend to his duties as president of the college. Dawson's personal situation forced Small, by default, to take over the management of the entire collegiate program, initiating substantial changes in teaching methods and curriculum at the College of William and Mary.[62] Many of Small's students were to play important roles in the American Revolution and the founding of the Republic.

NOTES

1. Appointment of Francis Fauquier, January 27, 1757, C.O. 5/1329 f.53, Colonial Williamsburg Foundation, Rockefeller Library, Williamsburg, Virginia (hereafter cited as CW). See also George Reese, ed., *The Official Papers of Francis Fauquier: Lieutenant Governor of Virginia* (Charlottesville: University Press of Virginia, 1980), vol. 1; Commission as Lieutenant Governor to Francis Fauquier,

February 10, 1758; this document marked the beginning of his administration (1) C.O. 324/38, pp. 496–497; Orders in Council delivered to Francis Fauquier, April 1, 1758 (11) C.O. 5/1329 f. 183–184.

2. John Fauquier left France and made his way to England accompanied by his two brothers and two sisters. In London, Dr. Fauquier found employment in the Royal Mint under Sir Isaac Newton. In 1698, he became a British citizen and married Elizabeth Chamberlayne. The couple resided in the picturesque district of Rich's Court in a quaint part of Lime Street, which was in the heart of the financial district of London. Fauquier pater was elected a director of the Bank of England before his death in 1726. Reese, *The Official Papers of Francis Fauquier*, 1:xxxv.

3. Court and City Register. London, 1751, in Notes: A compilation by Edwin Canaan, Professor of Political Economy, University of London, Special Collections, Swem Library, College of William and Mary, Williamsburg, Virginia (hereafter cited as Swem Library).

4. Leslie Stephen, ed., *Dictionary of National Biography* (London: Smith, Elder & Co., 1889), 18:249.

5. "It is stated on evidence sufficiently authentic, that on the return of Anson, from his circumnavigation of the earth, he accidentally fell in with Fauquier, from whom in a single night's play, he won at cards the whole of his patrimony; that afterwards being captivated by the striking graces of this gentleman's person and conversation, he procured for him the government of Virginia." John Burk, *The History of Virginia from Its First Settlement to the Present Day* (Petersburg: Dickson & Pescud, 1805), 3:333.

6. From "Notes: A compilation by Edwin Canaan Professor of Political Economy," University of London, Special Collections, Swem Library.

7. Reese, *Official Papers of Francis Fauquier*, 1:22.

8. "Owen, Goronwy (1723–1769), cleric and poet," Dictionary of Welsh Biography, https://biography.wales/article/s-OWEN-GOR-1723#? c=0&m=0&s=0&cv=0&manifest=https%3A%2F%2Fdamsssl.llgc.org .uk%2Fiiif%2F2.0%2F4393485%2Fmanifest.json&xywh=-854%2C0 %2C4370%2C3771 (accessed July 25, 2021); "Goronwy Owen's Cywydd Hiraeth," The National Library of Wales, https://www.library.wales/discover/digital-gallery /manuscripts/early-modern-period/goronwy-owen/#?c=&m=&s=&cv=&xywh =-455%2C654%2C3422%2C2910 (accessed July 26, 2021).

9. John Jones, "Goronwy Owen's Virginian Adventure," *Botetourt Bibliographical Society*, no. 2 (Williamsburg: College of William and Mary, 1969), 4.

10. Goronwy Owen, *The Letters of Goronwy Owen*, ed. J. H. Davies (Cardiff: William Lewis Printers, 1924), 22.

11. See entry for "Owen, Goronowy (Gronovius). Pleb. Matriculated 3 June 1742, Jesus College, Oxford, aged 19 years," in *Alumni Oxonienses, 1715–1888*, ed. Joseph Foster (Oxford: Parker & Co., 1888), 3:1053.

12. Jones, "Goronwy Owen's Virginian Adventure," 5.

13. Samuel Nichols (ca. 1713–1763), was at the time chaplain to the king, a Prebend of St. Paul's, and Master of the Temple (Francis Fauquier to Samuel Nicolls, July 29, 1761, in Reese, *Official Papers of Francis Fauquier*, 2:522; personal communication from S. J. C. Taylor to Martin Clagett, September 5, 1998). "I think that the explanation for Nichol's involvement (in recruiting and recommending candidates for the College) is fairly simple. Nichols was also chaplain to Thomas Sherlock, the Bishop of London and his successor as Master of the Temple. By the mid-1750s it seems that Nichols was conducting most of Sherlock's correspondence with the colonies—Sherlock was, by this time, old and increasingly disabled. Richard Cumberland wrote in his memoirs that he had visited Sherlock in 1754 and found that he "looks shockingly stupid, is so vastly deaf, and so feeble that he cannot rise from his chair without assistance" (William Carpenter, *Thomas Sherlock, 1678–1761* [London: The Society for the Promotion of Christian Knowledge, 1936], 148). In 1713, Samuel Nichols was born the son of Samuel Nichols, a clerk, in North Somercote, Lincolnshire. In his youth he attended the Haberdashers' School in London and matriculated at St. Magdalene's College, Cambridge, in 1732. He graduated with a BA in 1736, obtained an MA in 1739 and an LLD in 1746. He was named Golden Lecturer, St. Margaret's in Lothbury (1740–1755); Chaplain to the King (1746–1769); Prebend to St. Paul's (1749–1763); Vicar of Northolt, Middlesex (1749–1763); Master of the Temple (1753–1763); and Minister of St. James's, Piccadilly (1759–1763). He died November 11, 1763 (B. Bowen Thomas, "Goronwy Owen and the College of William and Mary, *Y Cymmrodor* [London: Society of Cymmrodorion, 1932], 43:21; Edward Carpenter, *Thomas Sherlock, 1658–1761* [New York: The MacMillan Company, 1936]; "Preferr'd. Rev. Mr. Samuel Nichols, to a Prebend of St. Paul's," *Universal Magazine* 4 [London: John Hinton, 1749]: 191; "Samuel Nichols, L.L.D. promoted by his majesty to the office or place of master of the Temple, in the room of the Bishop of London, who resigned" (*London Magazine* [1753]: 341.) Both Thomas Sherlock and Samuel Nichols were Master of the Temple in Temple Church, London. The first three masters were Templar Knights. *Dublin University Magazine* 86 (July 1875): 568.

14. Thomas Sherlock had been Bishop of Bangor (1727–1734) and was translated from Salisbury to London in 1748. In 1753, his health was seriously affected by a seizure and Nicholls performed most of the Bishop's functions as Chancellor of the College of William and Mary from 1753 until Sherlock's death in 1761. Thomas, "Goronwy Owen and the College of William and Mary," 23.

15. Goronwy Owen, Bond, October 21, 1757, Colonial Records Project, Fulham Palace Papers: Miscellaneous Records, 61.

16. "Friday April 7. Present: The Revd Mr Thomas Dawson President, & Mr Emmanuel Jones Mr of the Indian School. The Revd Mr Gronow Owen being elected by the President and Governors Master of the Grammar School, and having enter'd on the said Office the 5th Instant did this Day subscribe his Assent to the Articles of the Church of England as on Page 19th, and did also take the Oath, *de fideli Administratione* ("Meeting of the President and Masters of the College of William and Mary," Microfilm, CW). The only remaining members of the faculty at the time were the President, Thomas Dawson, and the Master of the Indian School, Emmanuel Jones. The President and the Masters of the College of William and Mary were collectively termed the "Society."

17. Reese, *Official Papers of Francis Fauquier*, 1:393n3.

18. Bond for Jacob Rowe, Colonial Records Project, T31/266, Fulham Palace Papers, "Papers on Church Matters in Virginia," 67, Microfilm, Library of Virginia, Richmond (hereafter cited as LVA); see also Public Records Office, T 60/21, p. 33, and Public Records Office, T 34/82, p. 38, "Treasury General Accounts. Lady Day, 1758."

19. Bond for Jacob Rowe, Colonial Records Project, T31/266, Fulham Palace Papers, "Papers on Church Matters in Virginia," 67, Microfilm, LVA.

20. Virginia Colonial Records Project, Public Record Office, ADM 2/80 (167), Microfilm, LVA.

21. "Meeting of the President and Masters of the College of William and Mary," Saturday, June 17th, 1758, Microfilm, CW.

22. Robert Dinwiddie to Thomas Dawson, March 14, 1758, MSS 65 PsT D62, Special Collections, Swem Library. Original in the Dawson Papers, Library of Congress, Washington D.C. (hereafter cited as LC).

23. Ibid. Note that Thomas Dawson was President of William and Mary from 1755 to 1760; his brother William Dawson had been President from 1743 to 1752.

24. Meeting of the Visitors and Governors of the College of William and Mary, May 20, 1757, Virginia Colonial Records Project, Fulham Palace Papers 15 (38), Microfilm, LVA.

25. Robert Dinwiddie to Thomas Dawson, June 24, 1758, Dawson Papers, Box 3, Folder 9, LC.

26. William Robinson to Bishop of London, n.d., Virginia Colonial Records Project, Microfilm, Fulham Palace Papers 13, No. 117, LVA. Circumstantially the letter was likely written about 1758 and the mention of £100 per annum substantiates Small's claim of salary as opposed to the sum of £80 that Robert Carter

Nicholas asserted—lending credence to Small's claims and making Nicholas's recollection more a memory of convenience and spite than fact.

27. Robert Polk Thomson, "The Reform of the College of William and Mary," *Proceedings of the American Philosophical Society* 115, no. 3 (June 17, 1971): 189.

28. Stephen Hawtrey to Edward Hawtrey, March 26, 1765, Faculty-Alumni Files—Edward Hawtrey, Special Collections, Swem Library.

29. Dudley Digges to the Bishop of London, July 15, 1767, Colonial Records Project, Fulham Palace Papers, 15, Correspondence of the Bishop of London and Miscellaneous Papers, 23; original in Edgehill-Randolph Papers, Alderman Library, University of Virginia, Charlottesville (hereafter cited as UVA). William Robinson to the Bishop of London, ca. 1759, Virginia Colonial Records Project, Fulham Palace Papers, no. 117, Microfilm, LVA.

30. Robert Dinwiddie to Thomas Dawson, March 14, 1758, MSS 65 PsT D62, Special Collections, Swem Library. Original in the Dawson Papers, LC.

31. Robert Dinwiddie to Thomas Dawson, June 24, 1758, Dawson Papers, LC.

32. "And at eight in the evening we came to anchor in the York river, after a tedious and disagreeable voyage of almost ten weeks" (Andrew Burnaby, *Travels Through the Middle Settlements in North-America* [Ithaca: Great Seal Books, 1960], 4, originally published [London: T. Payne, 1775]). "I arrived here the 5th Instant after a Passage of Ten Weeks from London." William Hunter to Mrs. Benjamin Franklin, Williamsburg, Virginia, July 22, 1759, Archives, American Philosophical Society, Philadelphia, Pennsylvania.

33. Stephen Hawtrey to Edward Hawtrey, March 26, 1765, Faculty-Alumni Files—Edward Hawtrey, Special Collections, Swem Library.

34. Ibid.

35. Journal of the Meetings of the President and Masters of William and Mary College, April 7, 1758, Microfilm, CW.

36. H. R. McIlwaine, ed., *Journals of the House of Burgesses of Virginia, 1758–1761* (Richmond: Virginia General Assembly, 1908), 16.

37. Ibid., s.v., "Thursday the 21st of September, 32 Geo II, 1758," 16.

38. Ibid., s.v., "Friday, the 22nd of September, 32 Geo. II," 17.

39. "RESOL: That Mrs. Martha Bryan be appointed House-Keeper to the College in the Place of Mrs. Owen deceas'd.," in the Journal of the Meetings of the President and Masters of William and Mary College, August 28, 1759, Microfilm, CW.

40. College ledgers stated that the college paid out to taverns and local establishments almost half of Small's income derived directly from the college. A great part Small's income, however, may have been from student fees, physician fees,

and perhaps kickbacks from William Hunter's bookstore. "Papers Relating to the College," *William and Mary Quarterly*, 1st ser., vol. 16, no. 3 (January 1908): 164.

41. Dudley Digges to the Bishop of London, July 15, 1767, Colonial Records Project, Fulham Palace Papers, 15, Correspondence of the Bishop of London and Miscellaneous Papers, 23. Original in Edgehill-Randolph Papers, UVA.

42. Journal of the Meetings of the Governors and Board of Visitors of the College of William and Mary, April 26,1760, text copy, CW; originals in the Fulham Palace Papers, Virginia, Box 2, No. 36, LC.

43. Journal of the Meetings of the Governors and Board of Visitors of the College of William and Mary, May 2, 1760, text copy, CW; originals in the Fulham Palace Papers, Virginia, Box 2, No. 36, LC.

44. Ibid.

45. Ibid.

46. Philip Ludwell (1728–1767), was the son of Philip Ludwell and Hannah Harrison and "was educated at William and Mary College, was a member of the Council of Virginia, and like his father and grandfather was a man of much distinction.... He died in England on March 25, 1767, and was buried at Bow Church near Stratford." "The Ludwell Family," *William and Mary Quarterly*, 1st ser., vol. 19, no. 3 (January 1911): 213.

47. Philip Ludwell to Emmanuel Jones, November 8, 1760, Lee Collection, MSS1 651 136, Virginia Museum of History and Culture, Richmond. Originally notated No. 91. According to the information in the letter, Jones had written to him on July 25, 1760, from Virginia, and Ludwell received the letter in London. Evidently Jones had not supplied all of the juicy details. "Your Tenderness suppressed ye Particulars of Mr Rowes abuse which I shoud be glad to know." Some specifics must have reached Ludwell by other means.

48. From the Latin *oppidum* (n): "a provincial town."

49. Tim Pastime to William Hunter, n.d., TR/c 1760, Special Collections, CW.

50. Ibid.

51. Ibid.

52. Ibid. Note: "either swift victory or swift death."

53. Tim Pastime to William Hunter, n.d., TR/c 1760, Special Collections, CW.

54. Ibid.

55. Journal of the Meetings of the Governors and Board of Visitors of the College of William and Mary, August 14, 1760, text copy, CW.

56. Ibid. In a letter from William Robinson to the Bishop of London, Robinson stated, "I was at the meeting which deprived Mr. Rowe, and by looking at the Book of the Visitors since, I was much surprised to find things put down there

as proved against Mr. Rowe, which to my certain knowledge were not proved."
William Robinson to the Bishop of London, ca. 1759, Virginia Colonial Records
Project, Fulham Palace Papers, No. 117, Microfilm, LVA.

57. Mrs. Owen died in August 1759. Not even a year had passed before the
calamitous riot. "That Rowe was not hauled before the Visitors if no proof of his
innocence, for Owen had what Rowe lacked, ... powerful protectors to guard
him from the worse consequences of his own idiocies. When he first arrived in
Virginia he had been a frequent visitor in the Governor's Palace. He had married ...
Mrs. Clayton ... who was President Dawson's sister, ... which also made him ...
if remotely, a member of the powerful Randolph clan." J. E. Morpurgo, *Their
Majesties' Royall Colledge* (Washington: Hennage Creative Printers, 1976), 125.

58. Ibid.

59. Ibid.

60. Jones, "Goronwy Owen's Virginian Adventure," 6.

61. Morpurgo, *Their Majesties' Royall Colledge*, 125.

62. The Statutes of 1758 left it up to the Professor's discretion to choose the
subjects and materials for their classes, and Small, with no seeming opposition,
revolutionized both the curriculum and the teaching methods at the College of
William and Mary and by extension to the other institutions of higher learning
in North America.

CHAPTER 5

The Williamsburg of Small and Jefferson

FIRST IMPRESSIONS

Small's first impression of Virginia was likely similar to that of the Reverend Andrew Burnaby, who visited Williamsburg and the College of William and Mary when Small was in residence. Following his landing in Yorktown, Burnaby described his carriage ride into town: "Having hired a chaise from York, I went to Williamsburg, about twelve miles distant. The road is exceeding pleasant, through some of the finest tobacco plantations in North-America, with a beautiful view of the river and woods of great extent."[1] Another traveler remarked that when Williamsburg first comes into view, "it looks like a large town, but it is far from it."[2] A third noted, "It resembles a good Country town in England."[3] The city was situated on a plain, level piece of land,[4] "between two creeks; one falling into [the] James, the other into [the] York river; and is built nearly due east and west," wrote Burnaby.[5] Originally called Middle Plantation because it sat on higher and healthier ground midway between the York and the James Rivers, Williamsburg had been chosen as a successor to the first capital at Jamestown.[6]

The city was laid out in parallel streets, intersected by others at right angles. The unpaved roads were described as "very dusty ... and "deep in sand."[7] They were, in consequence, "very disagreeable to walk in, especially in the summer."[8] The town's grid resembled a simple cross. Architectural historian Glenn Patton has called it "a diagrammatic layout of simplicity and unified logical order, lucid, rational, and rectilinear."[9] Burnaby depicted the central thoroughfare, Duke of Gloucester Street, as "one of the most spacious in North America, three quarters of a mile in length, and above a hundred feet wide." At its two ends stood the principal institutions of the town—the Capitol at one end and the College of William and Mary at the other.[10] In 1765, an anonymous Frenchman's perspective was that the town was very irregular in that it had only one street that merited the name.[11]

"Upon the whole," Burnaby wrote, Williamsburg was an "agreeable" spot: "There are ten or twelve gentlemen's families constantly residing in it, besides merchants and tradesmen ... and although the houses are of wood, covered with shingles, and but indifferently built, the whole makes a handsome appearance."[12] Reports from visitors twenty years later indicate that there were between one hundred and fifty to three hundred homes.[13] The private residences during these years were mainly painted white and covered with white cypress or cedar shingles.[14]

The Reverend Burnaby calculated that the population of the town "does not contain more than one thousand souls, whites and negroes," except "at the times of the assemblies, and general courts" when the town "is crowded with the gentry of the country."[15] During court sessions, the plantocracy and their families descended on the city, for these were social occasions as well as times of business. An anonymous French visitor noted, "In the Day time people are hurying back and forwards from the Capitoll to the taverns, and at night, Carousing and Drinking In one chamber and box and Dice in another, which continues till morning."[16]

For the more refined, diversions could be found in dress balls, the playhouse, taverns, horse races, and coffeehouses. Gambling, drinking, and eating were the favorite pastimes, and politics and gossip the most frequent topics of conversation. But as soon as public business concluded, the Frenchman noted, Williamsburg's temporary residents "return to their plantations; and the town is in a manner deserted."[17]

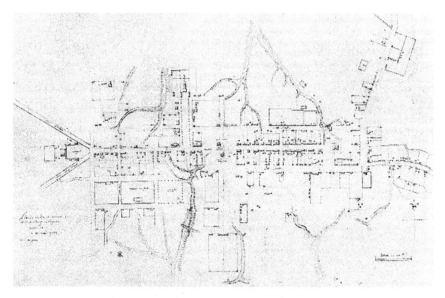

Frenchman's Map of Williamsburg, 1781.
Colonial Williamsburg Foundation.

The Williamsburg that Small and Burnaby knew in the 1760s was both provincial and sophisticated at the same time. The public buildings were constructed of brick. Burnaby stated that the only buildings of any consequence were the Governor's Palace, the Capitol, and the College. The Palace was "one of the best upon the continent," he wrote. It was here that Governor Francis Fauquier held intellectual soirées where the regular attendees included George Wythe, William Small, and Thomas Jefferson. It is said that Small initially brought Jefferson with him to provide fiddle music but that the sophisticated crowd soon found his conversation more stimulating than his recitals. Many of Small's other students also made frequent appearances, but it seems that Thomas Jefferson was the only one to have had a permanent seat. It was during these "Attic nights" that Jefferson secured the tutelage and lifetime friendship of George Wythe.

THE CAPITOL BUILDING

The Capitol building that William Small knew had a radically different appearance from the original model that served as the blueprint for Colonial Williamsburg's modern restoration. The original capital was destroyed by fire in 1747 and was completely rebuilt according to entirely different plan in 1751.

The Old Capitol (1751–1832)[18]

A visitor from France who went to Williamsburg in 1765 described the Capitol as "a very good building in the form of an Each [H]. [T]he Court is held in one wing on the first floor, the assembly room is in the other wing of the Same floor, the Councill and Comitee Chambers are upstairs on the first story."[19] According to Ebenezer Hazard's 1773 description, the Capitol was "surrounded with a Brick Wall; you enter the Court Yard by an elegant Iron Gate. In the Front of the Building is a Portico & Balcony, each supported by

four Pillars; above these the King's Arms (elegantly carved & gilt)....
Upon entering the Capitol you get into a Room in which the Courts
of Justice are held: it is large and convenient; here is a fine whole
Length Picture of Queen Anne by van Dyke."[20]

Thomas Jefferson, viewing the building with the critical and
exacting eye of a budding architect, wrote, "The Capitol is a light
and airy structure, with a portico in front of two orders, the lower
of which, being Doric, is tolerably just in its proportions and orna-
ments,—save only that the intercolonnations are too large. The upper
is Ionic, much too small for that on which it is mounted, its orna-
ments not proper to the order, nor proportioned within themselves.
It is crowned with a pediment, which is too high for its span. Yet,
on the whole, it is the most pleasing piece of architecture we have."[21]
In 1832, the second Capitol, like its predecessor, was consumed by
flames and demolished.

THE GOVERNOR'S PALACE

The Governor's Palace was "situated at the end of an imposing,
tree-lined avenue,"[22] a cubic structure comprised of three floors of
Flemish-bond brickwork topped by a hipped roof that was dotted
with a row of dormer windows and crowned with a flat deck and
an iron balcony. The upper deck was crowned by "a distinctive,
two-stage cupola [that] provided access to this rooftop platform
and, with a pair of massive brick chimneys, served to elaborate the
building's silhouette."[23] Perpendicularly flanking the main building
were two brick dependencies of one and a half stories, complete
with gabled roofs and dormers. The whole was surrounded by a
fence that enclosed several formal gardens, a kitchen, stables, and
other service buildings. Behind the Governor's Palace was an intricate pattern of formal gardens, pathways, and a fine canal built at
the rear expanse.

Governor's Palace. Colonial Williamsburg Foundation

THE COLLEGE OF WILLIAM AND MARY

William and Mary stood at the opposite end of Duke of Gloucester Street. Progressing through the large iron gates, one would have been surrounded by a "formal garden adorned with graveled walks and symmetrically arrayed topiary." The central building, later named for Christopher Wren, was flanked by Brafferton College and the President's House.[24] College historian J. E. Morpurgo locates this nucleus of buildings in an era when "English architecture was fluent, simple . . . practical and aesthetically pleasing."[25]

Up the central stairs of the Wren Building and through its main doors were the classrooms. Natural Philosophy classes were held in the far-left corner of the building, Moral Philosophy in the far-right corner. The Divinity class was supposed to meet in the room next to Natural Philosophy, but during most of Small's tenure, with John Camm in

England, the space would have sat vacant or perhaps been used for storage and penmanship lessons. Jefferson called it the "writing room." Next to the Moral Philosophy room was the Grammar School. The academic classes let out onto a "piazza" or stoa—a covered walkway that gave access to the two wings attached to the rear of the building. To the left, behind Natural Philosophy, was the Chapel, where mandatory services began and ended each day. To the right, behind Moral Philosophy, was the Great Hall. The Convocation Room, the Common Room, the rooms of several professors, and the Gallery occupied the second floor. The third floor held several apartments for the Masters, an infirmary, the housekeeper's quarters, dormitory space for the students, and the college library.[26] The library was said to have contained more than 3,000 volumes at the time of the Revolution.[27] Bookplates indicate that books had been donated by Governors Alexander Spotswood and Robert Dinwiddie. An interesting volume on Natural History by Mark Catesby was given to the college on the condition that it should never go out of the library; the inscription is in Jefferson's hand.[28]

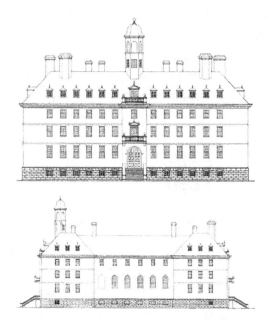

Wren Building, College of William and Mary.

SMALL'S QUARTERS

The professors were entitled to two rooms, one for sitting, reading, and entertaining, the other for sleeping.[29] In a letter to his brother Edward Hawtrey based on information obtained from William Small, Stephen Hawtrey described the master's accommodations: "You have two rooms—by no means elegant tho' equal in goodness to any in the College—unfurnished—& will salute your Eyes in your Entrance with bare plaister Walls." Hawtrey recalled Small telling him he was "very well satisfied with their Appearance tho' at first rather disgusting." Small had urged Hawtrey "not to lay out any money on them." In regard to furniture and bedding, Small informed Hawtrey that the master's "furniture consists of 6 chairs, a table, Grate Bed & Bedstead," which was "as much as you'll want." He cautioned his friend not to transport any furniture with him to Virginia, since colonial "Chairs and Tables [are] rather cheaper than in England." The only things that he would want to bring are "bedding and blankets of which you must carry over."[30] Small's accounts indicate that for at least two years he maintained a servant in his quarters, perhaps an enslaved person lent to him by one of his landowning friends.[31] The servant maintained Small's chambers, tended to his clothes, brought and took away meals, and likely slept in the sitting room.

Most college students lived on the upper floor near their professors, who were meant to serve, like masters in Scottish institutions, in loco parentis. They generally slept three or four to a room. The beds may have been separated by nothing but curtains. Spare chambers not being used by the masters were "let out at moderate rates to the better Sort of the big Boys."[32] Thirteen dormer windows lit each of these barracks-like rooms, with a fireplace at the eastern end providing the only source of heat.[33] It is interesting to speculate who Jefferson's roommates might have been. Possibilities include John Page, Dabney Carr, John Walker, and Benjamin Harrison.

MEALS, TREATS,
AND THE NAUGHTY MRS. COCKE

Members of the faculty took their meals in the Great Hall, or commons.[34] For much of Small's tenure, the meals were prepared by Isabelle Cocke, the housekeeper. She was neither celebrated for her efficiency nor for her belle cuisine. On July 23, 1763, the president and masters ruled that "Mrs. Isabella Cocke has behaved much amiss in her Office of Housekeeper."[35] Among her deficiencies were allowing the servants to neglect their duties, losing the laundry, refusing to darn socks and linens, permitting the slaves to steal from the lauder (larder), not attending properly to the sick, being absent from the college for extended periods, drinking the wine, using the sugar, wood, and candles for her own purposes, playing favorites among the students, ignoring the requests of the faculty to send food to their rooms, lending out college property, and hoarding "rich Cakes, Preserves, etc." for personal use.[36]

The masters were especially concerned about their housekeeper's cooking. The faculty demanded, in no uncertain terms, "that there be always both fresh, and salt meat for dinner; and twice in the Week, as well as on Sunday in particular, that there be either Puddings or Pies besides; that there always be Plenty of Victuals; that Breakfast, Dinner, and Supper, be serv'd up in the cleanest, and neatest manner possible; and for this reason the Society not only allow, but desire you to get a Cook; that the Boys Suppers be not as usual made up of different Scraps, but there be at each Table the same Sort: and when there is cold fresh Meat enough, that it be often hash'd for them.[37]

The masters' other instructions to Cocke revealed additional and latent grievances. They commanded "that a Butcher be agreed with to supply the College regularly, ... that fresh Butter be look'd out for in Time, that the Boys may not be forced to eat salt in Summer." In addition, "Tea & Sugar" were to be served at "Breakfast Only.... Plumbs, Currants, etc. are only to be us'd at the Common Table." The masters told Mrs. Cocke that she was welcome to provide "rich Cakes and Preserves, etc," but they "must be at your own Expence."[38]

Mrs. Cocke's domestic defects and passion for sweets were not the only subjects of faculty attention and admonition. Walter Jones, Jefferson's friend and classmate, wrote to his brother Thomas, "One Bland who you have heard of sufficiently, wrote her a very insolent note & drew an image of a Head upon it & wrote underneath it Venus, which that Woman resenting in a very proper Manner, has made the sly President sett his Witts to work to turn her out of the College & since that is the Case it is to be feared the poor old Lady will be again sent to her Shifts."[39]

Despite Jones's prediction, this incident (in which Cocke appears to have been more the victim rather than the culprit) did not lead to her immediate dismissal, but the faculty did warn her "to have no Boys at Breakfast with you, or to invite particular ones to Tea in the Afternoon, as it causes Disturbances."[40] Apparently Cocke did not conform to these instructions, for she was eventually dismissed. In July 1763, the faculty ordered "that an Advertisement be inserted in the Gazette to desire a Man capable of managing the Housekeeper's Business in the College to apply to the President & Masters."[41] Evidently, the former housekeeper's appetites had gotten the better of her judgment.

The masters ate at tables separate from the students and had finer food in more substantial proportions. As a special privilege, and as a mark of their high regard for him, the Society granted an usher, Mr. Hatton, the right to sit at the masters' table.[42] In February 1763, the faculty voted to allow professors to take their meals in their own quarters if they so desired, and this measure may have been aimed at William Small. He often stood out from his colleagues, taking different positions on politics and religion, and single-handedly opposing measures adopted by the rest of the faculty. He was also intimate friends with several of the Visitors. Perhaps the faculty's decision to allow masters to dine alone in their rooms was meant to encourage his absence from the common table.[43]

Not that Small needed the exclusionary clause, for he dined out frequently. Jefferson recorded both men's weekly presence at the

Governor's Palace, and it is likely that he dined with the Page family at Rosewell, at the home of his "bosom friend" George Wythe, and with Peyton Randolph. The college ledger shows that during his nearly six years at the college, Small earned a total salary of £833. During the same period, the bursar paid out, on Small's behalf, more than £475 to merchants for wine and food,[44] which means he spent more than half of his salary on food and wine consumed off campus, even though he could have had both in the commons for free. The implication is that he spent a substantial portion of his leisure time apart from his colleagues at the college and that he socialized primarily with the gentlemen of the colony and his students.

CLIMATE AND CLOTHES

The Reverend Andrew Burnaby, writing from an Englishman's perspective, described the climate of Virginia as "exceedingly fine," with the autumn and springs being delightful and the winters "so mild and serene (though there are now and then excessively cold days) as scarcely to require a fire." Burnaby's only caveat extended to the excessive heat of the summer, when the thermometer showed "for three months from 85 to 95 degrees high."[45] Small confirmed Burnaby's warnings about the heat and advised Hawtrey that "your Cloathing in Summer must be as thin & light as possible for the heat is beyond your conception.... [Y]our cloth Suit unlined may do for the Month of May, but after that time you must wear the thinnest Stuffs that can be made without Lining." He added, "You must carry with you a Stock of Linnen Waistcoats made very large and loose, that they mayn't stick to your Hide when you perspire. It would have been much better if you had Callico Shirts, as they suck up the Moisture & don't stick to your Skin." In respect to other apparel, Small noted that it was necessary to take over a "handsome full dressed Silk Cloathes" to wear at the Governor's Ball on the King's Birthday, "the only time you will have occasion to appear fine in the whole year" and for "the rest of your Wearing Apparel you may dress as you please for the fashions don't change & you may wear the same Coat (3 years)." Finally, Small advised Hawtrey that his brother might want to carry his own socks and shoes to Virginia, since they were "very dear Articles" there.[46]

Stockings were such an expensive commodity that the masters directed the negligent Mrs. Cocke to find a "proper Stocking-mender" to pay close attention to the notes pinned to the laundry "both at the Delivery and the Return of them," and to make sure that the clothes are "returned clean."[47] Laundry service was not provided gratis; washing was fifty shillings per annum. Small's total laundry fee for his stay was just shy of fifteen pounds.

DIVISION OF COURSES

According to its charter, William and Mary had been founded so "that the church of Virginia may be furnished with a seminary of ministers of the gospel, and that the youth may be piously educated in good letters and manners, and that the Christian faith may be propagated amongst the Western Indians, to the glory of Almighty God; to make, found, and establish a certain place of universal study, or perpetual College of Divinity, Philosophy, Languages, and other good Arts and Sciences."[48]

By the time of Small's arrival, however, the college had begun to adopt a more secular and utilitarian direction, as evidenced by the Divinity School's population of only four students during John Camm's last years, and by the Visitors' request that the ejected masters be replaced by laymen.

The Master of the Indian School was charged with teaching his wards to read, write, and do simple arithmetic. He was also to instruct them in Christianity, the true religion. The Master of the Indian School had the least burdensome position, and in turn, he also received the lowest salary: from £40 to £50 per year. He usually had about eight to ten students and frequently took on other duties to supplement his income. Emmanuel Jones, Master of the Indian School, served for much of his tenure at the college as librarian and as clerk of the Meetings of the President and Masters of the College. He was also allowed to sell schoolbooks.

The Grammar School had the traditional function of preparing the students for work in the collegiate schools. The Master of the Grammar School instructed the students in the "Latin and Greek Tongues" and the "Rudiments and Grammars" of those languages.[49] He was charged with keeping a watchful eye over the habits and morals of the boys. When a Grammar School student completed his coursework, usually about the age of fifteen, he was given an oral examination before the president and master. If he was judged to be satisfactory, he was promoted to the philosophical schools. The Master of the Grammar School was specifically enjoined to "let no Blockhead or lasy Fellow" be allowed to proceed into the college.[50]

The upper schools were divided into the philosophical school and the divinity school. The two Philosophy School masters taught Moral Philosophy and Natural Philosophy. Natural Philosophy encompassed "Physicks, Metaphysicks, and Mathematicks." Moral Philosophy, according to the statutes, consisted of "Rhetorick, Logick, and Ethicks."[51] Students were exercised not only in debate but in declamation. Likewise, The Divinity School had two professors. The first was to teach the "Hebrew Tongue and critically expound the literal Sense of the Holy Scripture," and the second was to explain the "common Places of Divinity, and the Controversies with Hereticks" and conduct Prelections and Disputations on those subjects.[52] During most of Small's time at the college, both of these offices lay fallow.

SALARIES AND PREREQUISITES

The Board of Visitors elected the President of the College. By statute the candidate had to be older than thirty years of age and an Anglican clergyman. His duties included keeping "a watchful Eye" over the rest of the faculty, communicating with the Chancellor when necessary, and giving four lectures on theology during the year. The salaries and other perquisites of the various members of the faculty indicate their relative importance to the Board of Visitors. In the statutes, the highest salary went to the President, who received £200 per annum, along with a handsome house and garden. Many presidents also served as the Bishop of London's Commissary and as the Rector of Bruton Parish, both of which paid substantial salaries.[53] These significant benefits were the legacy of the first President of the College of William and Mary, James Blair, and became such a point of contention that an early professor, Mungo Inglis, resigned over the disparity in wages.[54] As a result, the president was also more dependent on the Board of Visitors and the lieutenant governor than other members of the faculty and often, during disputes, took the side of the Visitors.[55]

The Grammar Master was paid more than the Divinity and Philosophy Professors. Even the Grammar School ushers were paid well—usually £75 plus five shillings entrance fee from each student—almost as much as Professors of the Philosophy School.[56] The unexpectedly generous income may stem from the fact that the ushers were native Virginians who were often related to members of the Board of Visitors.

Next in the pecking order was the Professor of Moral Philosophy and the Professor of Natural Philosophy. As Professor of Natural Philosophy, William Small's salary started at £80 per annum and gradually rose to £150. The professors were allowed other fees as well. Small informed Stephen Hawtrey that "your Salary is £150 Sterling paid as regular as if at the Bank of England—every Boy pays his pistole Entrance Money & 20 Shillings Sterling per annum out of which you pay the first Usher, there being two, at 5 s[hillings]—tho'

I say that every Boy <u>pays</u> this sum, it would be speaking more properly to say—<u>they ought</u> to pay it for they are very irregular in their payment of that, & unless you look sharp after it & insist upon your right you may not stand a Chance of receiving above one fourth."[57] Walter Jones confirmed Small's account regarding the collection of fees in a letter to his brother, Thomas, " I am sorry to acquaint you that I have made no Progress in Mathematics since I saw you; which indeed has not proceeded from any Negligence of mine, but from a Want of Money to pay Mr. Small's Entrance Fee."[58] Like Scottish academics, a professor often made more money from student fees than his official salary from the institution, and this may account for Small's aggressive recruitment of students, his large class sizes and his fraternal relationships with many of the "principal gentlemen of the country." In 1904, Lyon G. Tyler asserted that the faculty the College of William and Mary before the Revolution "were probably better paid than professors at any other college in North America."[59]

When William Small arrived in Williamsburg in 1758, he found himself in an alien landscape. Virginia was a colony of elegant and orderly architecture, deliberately conceived; a country of political and social disorder, verging on revolution; a country of opportunity and opposition, where an unintentional and innocuous aside could stir up a firestorm of controversy and retribution. Above all, however, Virginia was a place where a teacher could have the most profound influence on those he loved and taught.

NOTES

1. Andrew Burnaby, *Travels through the Middle Settlements in North America, in the Years 1759 and 1760: With Observations upon the State of the Colonies* (Dublin: R. Marchbank, 1775), 6.

2. "Journal of a French Traveller in the Colonies, 1765," in Jane Carson, *We Were There, 1699–1859* (Charlottesville: University Press of Virginia, 1965), 19.

3. Lord Adam Gordon, originally in "Journal of an Officer in the West Indies Who Travelled over Part of the West Indies, and of North America, in the Course

of 1764 and 1765," in Newton D. Mereness, ed., *Travels in the American Colonies* (New York: Macmillan Co., 1916), 369–453, and as cited in Carson, *We Were There, 1699–1859*, 18.

4. Abbe Robin in 1781 as cited in Carson, *We Were There, 1699–1859*, 19.

5. Burnaby, *Travels through the Middle Settlements in North America*, 7.

6. John W. Reps, "The Tidewater Colonies: Town Planning in the 17th Century," *Town Planning Review* 34, no. 1 (April 1963): 35.

7. Burnaby, *Travels through the Middle Settlements in North America*, 8.

8. John Ferdinand Dalziel Smyth in 1770 as cited in Carson, *We Were There, 1699–1859*, 25.

9. Glenn Patton, "The College of William and Mary, Williamsburg, and the Enlightenment," *Journal of the Society of Architectural Historians* 29, no. 1 (March 1970): 28.

10. Ibid.

11. From Anonymous, "Journal of a French Traveller in the Colonies, 1765," as cited in Carson, *We Were There, 1699–1859*, 21. Note that the courthouse was not built until 1770. James D. Kornwolf, *Architecture and Town Planning in Colonial North America* (Baltimore: Johns Hopkins University Press, 2002), 2:593.

12. Burnaby, *Travels through the Middle Settlements in North America*, 8.

13. Carson, *We Were There, 1699–1859*.

14. Ibid.; Burnaby, *Travels through the Middle Settlements in North America*, 8.

15. Burnaby, *Travels through the Middle Settlements in North America*, 9.

16. Extract from the Journal of an Anonymous Frenchman as cited in Carson, *We Were There, 1699–1859*, 21.

17. Burnaby, *Travels through the Middle Settlements in North America*, 9.

18. Henry Howe, *Historical Collections of Virginia* (Charleston, S.C.: William Babcock, 1852), 329.

19. Extract from the Journal of an Anonymous Frenchman as cited in Carson, *We Were There, 1699–1859*, 19.

20. Ebenezer Hazard in 1777 as cited in Carson, *We Were There, 1699–1859*, 37.

21. Thomas Jefferson, *Notes on the State of Virginia* (London: John Stockdale, 1787), 254.

22. Mark R. Wenger, "Jefferson's Designs for Remodeling the Governor's Palace," *Winterthur Portfolio* 32, no. 4 (Winter, 1997): 225.

23. Ibid., 226.

24. Mark R. Wenger, "Thomas Jefferson, the College of William and Mary, and the University of Virginia," *Virginia Magazine of History and Biography* 103, no. 3 (July 1995): 342.

25. J. E. Morpurgo, *Their Majesties' Royall Colledge* (Washington D.C.: Hennage Creative Printers, 1976), 76.

26. Wenger, "Thomas Jefferson, the College of William and Mary, and the University of Virginia," 345.

27. Mary Goodwin, *The College of William and Mary: A Brief Sketch of the Main Building of the College* (Williamsburg: Colonial Williamsburg, 1967), 281.

28. Likely Mark Catesby's work *The Natural History of Carolina, Florida, and the Bahama Islands*, first printed in London ca. 1729 for volume one and 1747 for volume two.

29. Lyon G. Tyler, "Early Courses and Professors at William and Mary College," *William and Mary Quarterly*, 1st ser., vol. 14, no. 2 (October 1905): 73.

30. Stephen Hawtrey to Edward Hawtrey, March 26, 1765, Faculty-Alumni Files—Edward Hawtrey, Special Collections, Swem Library, College of William and Mary, Williamsburg, Virginia (hereafter cited as Swem Library).

31. "Papers Relating to the College," *William and Mary Quarterly*, 1st ser., vol. 16, no. 3 (January 1908): 164.

32. Goodwin, *College of William and Mary*, 272.

33. Wenger, "Thomas Jefferson, the College of William and Mary, and the University of Virginia," 344.

34. Edward Hawtrey to the Bishop of London, October 2, 1765, Fulham Palace Papers.

35. Journal of the Meetings of the President and Masters of William and Mary College, July 23, 1763, Fulham Palace Papers.

36. Journal of the Meetings of the President and Masters of William and Mary College, February 9, 1763, Fulham Palace Papers.

37. Ibid.

38. Ibid.

39. Walter Jones to Thomas Jones, n.d., Faculty-Alumni Files, Special Collections, Swem Library. Original in Jones Family Papers, Library of Congress, Washington, D.C. (hereafter cited as LC).

40. Journal of the Meetings of the President and Masters of William and Mary College, February 9, 1763, Fulham Palace Papers.

41. Journal of the Meetings of the President and Masters of William and Mary College, July 23, 1763, Fulham Palace Papers.

42. Journal of the Meetings of the President and Masters of William and Mary College, March 30, 1759, Fulham Palace Papers.

43. Journal of the Meetings of the President and Masters of William and Mary College, February 9, 1763, Fulham Palace Papers.

44. "Papers Relating to the College," 164.

45. Burnaby, *Travels through the Middle Settlements in North America*, 10.

46. Stephen Hawtrey to Edward Hawtrey, March 26, 1765, Faculty-Alumni Files–Edward Hawtrey, Special Collections, Swem Library.

47. Journal of the Meetings of the President and Masters of William and Mary College, February 9, 1763, Fulham Palace Papers.

48. *The Officers, Statutes, and Charter of the College of William and Mary* (Philadelphia: William Fry, 1817), 5.

49. Lyon G. Tyler, *Williamsburg: The Old Colonial Capital* (Richmond: Whittet & Shepperson, 1907), 134.

50. "The Statutes of the College of William and Mary in Virginia," *William and Mary Quarterly*, 1st ser., vol. 16, no. 4 (April 1908): 247.

51. Ibid., 248.

52. Ibid.

53. Lyon G. Tyler, "Bruton Church," *William and Mary Quarterly*, 1st ser., vol. 3, no. 3 (January 1895): 179; Herbert Adams, The College of William and Mary," *A Contribution to the History of Higher Education* (Washington: Government Printing Office, 1887), 18.

54. Tyler, "Early Courses and Professors at William and Mary College," 71.

55. Morpurgo, *Their Majesties' Royall Colledge*, 119.

56. Dudley Digges to the Bishop of London, July 15, 1767, Edgehill-Randolph Papers, Special Collections, Alderman Library, Charlottesville, Virginia.

57. Stephen Hawtrey to Edward Hawtrey, March 26, 1765, Faculty-Alumni Files, Special Collections, Swem Library.

58. Walter Jones to Thomas Jones, June 31, 1762, Faculty-Alumni Files, Special Collections, Swem Library. Original in Jones Family Papers, LC.

59. Tyler, "Early Courses and Professors at William and Mary College," 74.

CHAPTER 6

Friends and Societies

However unpopular Small may have been among his colleagues, he was in equal measure liked by his students and the local gentry. He was certainly more in tune with local political, social, and religious sentiments than his cohorts, and his behavior was considered "unexceptional," even by his most ardent detractors.

A DIVERSE SOCIAL CIRCLE

Small's life in Williamsburg was not confined to the classrooms of the Wren Building, nor were his interactions exclusively with students. He became friends with people of social and political influence in the colony, knew and fraternized with many of the more colorful individuals in town, and formed fast friendships with the enlightened Lieutenant Governor Francis Fauquier, the legal scholar, George Wythe, the Attorney General Peyton Randolph, the proprietor of the Virginia Gazette William Hunter, the famous American sage Benjamin Franklin, and the mysterious and tragic Selim the Algerine. Thomas Jefferson placed Small, Wythe, and Peyton Randolph within a trinity of reason and fine judgment. More than half a century after his college days, he wrote the following to his grandson:

I had the good fortune to become acquainted very early with some
characters of very high standing, and to feel the incessant wish that I
could ever become what they were. Under temptations and difficulties, I would ask myself what would Dr. Small, Mr. Wythe, Peyton
Randolph do in this situation? What course in it will assure me their
approbation? I am certain that this mode of deciding my conduct,
tended more to correctness than any reasoning powers I possessed.
Knowing the even and dignified line they pursued, I could never
doubt for a moment which of the two courses would be in character
for them.[1]

Through his relations with the parents of his students, by his activities in scientific endeavors, and his attendance at many and varied
meetings in the college, in the taverns of the town, and through informal and chance meetings in the streets and shops of Williamsburg,
Small became a familiar and well-liked figure in the colony.

Although the masters took their meals in the dining hall of the
college, Small frequently chose to dine with friends at their homes
or meet with them in local establishments. It was obvious that he
favored the company of his Virginia friends and students than he
did of his colleagues at the college. The meetings, conversations, and
meals that he took at the Governor's Palace are well documented;
his travels to the home of the Page family, Rosewell, and the astronomical observations there were widely reported.[2]

Small frequently walked to the homes of his close friends George
Wythe, Peyton Randolph, and William Hunter (all of whom lived in
close proximity to the Wren Building) for an evening of good food
and philosophical discussion. Although he was congenial and popular
among his students and the inhabitants of the town, Small was especially close to Lieutenant Governor Fauquier and Wythe, with whom
he frequently met for conversations concerning the latest scientific
news and political events. Together, these gentlemen worked to promote plans for philosophical and pragmatic improvements in the
colony.

Francis Fauquier had been made a member of the Royal Society in 1753 on the recommendation of his own brother William and the famous physician, William Heberden.[3] One observer described Fauquier as "A Gentleman of great merit, well versed in Philosophical and Mathematical inquires, and a great promoter of usefull Learning, & the Advancement of Natural Knowledge." In 1758, Fauquier was elected a corresponding member of the Royal Society of Arts, which was established for the encouragement of arts, manufacture, and commerce, and after his arrival in Virginia, he wrote an observation on a hailstorm, which was presented by his brother William before the Royal Society shortly after Fauquier's death.[4]

THE PARTIE QUARREE

If golf and art collecting are the enlightened hobbies of a polished gentleman today, experimental science and intellectual clubs were marks of distinction in the eighteenth century. Fauquier's predecessor, Robert Dinwiddie, was a loyal bureaucrat too distracted by the hostile Indians, encroaching Frenchmen, and bellicose colonists to involve himself deeply in such dilettante distractions. Francis Fauquier, on the other hand, came from a background of intellectual endeavor and profound involvement in the sciences. Fauquier's father placed great value on the concept of human improvement through scientific advances, especially as it related to the British Empire. Small created an intellectual club devoted to practical matters, initiated a scientific society for the encouragement of arts and manufactures, advocated for the building of a mental hospital, and even directed his body be given up for examination if it would serve to accelerate future medical advances.

The purposes of Fauquier's enlightened evenings were manifold. For personal reasons, the sessions provided the governor a chance to meet with educated gentlemen with similar tastes in science, music, and literature and talk over the newest trends while listening to musical interludes. For political reasons, it allowed Fauquier to make allies of men who had been his predecessor's foes, and was an avenue of taking the pulse of the moment's political passions. For domestic purposes, it afforded Fauquier with numerous opportunities to network with disparate individuals, institutions, and endeavors in ways that could be financially beneficial to his friends, encourage economic growth within the colony and make the interests of the home government and the colonists overlap. The surest way to bond with people is to eat with them and the hardest person to dislike is the one who makes you laugh. Through his immediate contact with the College of William and Mary, Fauquier initiated his intellectual gatherings—George Wythe, Peyton Randolph, William Small, and Goronwy Owen were all early invitees.

Small and Fauquier, both newcomers to Virginia in 1758, and sharing an interest in natural philosophy, meteorology, and astronomy in particular,[5] quite naturally became fast friends. Fauquier had been elected a member of the Royal Society in 1753, on the recommendation of his own brother William Fauquier, and the noted London physician, William Heberden.[6] One observer described Francis Fauquier as "a Gentleman of great merit, well versed in Philosophical and Mathematical inquires, and a great promoter of usefull Learning, & the Advancement of Natural Knowledge."[7]

At the beginning of his term as lieutenant governor, Fauquier decided to set up a series of regular gatherings for practical entertainment. Initially, these soirées were initially intended to serve as social events with the local gentry, clergy, and college faculty in attendance but, inasmuch as Fauquier quickly discontinued them, the sessions may have turned into opportunities for requesting favors or voicing discontent rather than serious attempts for improvement.

After a short intermission, Fauquier reinstituted the meetings, but this time, with a more-exclusive guest list and a more defined and serious agenda than before. The regular guests were George Wythe, William Small, and occasionally Peyton Randolph. The social nature of the events was transformed into one of a more intellectual nature, and these dinners were dedicated to discussions of science, philosophy, and an appreciation of music. In the eighteenth century, scientific and academic inquiry was considered an overt expression of informed sociability.

It seems that corresponding, or nonregular, guests were occasionally invited, usually for their expertise in the prescribed subject being discussed. Small, it is said, thought that it would be a good idea to enhance the musical segment of the meetings and brought Jefferson along to play the fiddle. Other student participants may have included John Walker, Walter Jones, James McClurg, Warner Lewis, Robert Carter, John Page, and Dabney Carr. Jefferson recalled that even the governor himself took part in the performances: "The Governor was musical also, and a good performer, and associated me with two or three other amateurs in his weekly concerts."[8]

> They were inseparable friends, and at their frequent dinners with the Governor, (after his family had returned to England,) he admitted me always, to make it a partie quarrae. At those dinners I have heard more good sense, more rational and philosophic conversations, than all my life besides. They were truly Attic societies.[9]

The term "Attic" carries with it an expressed and interesting connotation. The work of Aulus Gellius, *Noctes Atticae*, described the intellectual discussions that passed between his teachers and fellow students at weekly dinners held at the home of his mentor Lucius Calvenus Taurus. These dinners served as symposia where serious subjects and interesting footnotes were intermingled and debated, providing a free-flowing forum in which information and ideas were exchanged and enlarged upon. The curious combination of Wythe, Fauquier, Peyton Randolph, and Small, complemented by the wide-ranging collection of Small's students and ex-students, gives robust but circumstantial support to the theory that William Small and George Wythe may have been providing a type of informal but focused instruction both during and after the exclusive confines of the partie quarrae.[10]

THE VIRGINIA SOCIETY FOR THE ENCOURAGEMENT OF ARTS AND MANUFACTURING

Many of Small's students thought that the most engaging part of Small's classes was his experimental demonstrations. Indeed, many a British scholar turned a tidy profit by going on extended tours of elevated entertainment—namely, lectures and exhibitions for the *hoi polloi*. James Ferguson, Benjamin Franklin's friend and co-author, made a tidy fortune with his iterant shows that dealt primarily with inventions and innovations in astronomy, mechanics, hydraulics, optics, and the ever-popular displays of electrical powers. In eighteenth-century Britain, there was a great demand "for public lectures on scientific subjects both in London and the provinces. Typically, such lectures would be a combination of entertainment and spectacle and serious instruction."[11] Small's classroom illustrations served much the same purpose.

The enthusiastic appraisals of the students must have filtered up to their parents who, knowing Small's reputation for provocative demonstrations, eagerly supported the proposals for a new scientific society promoted by Small and Francis Fauquier. The concept of this society probably originated with Fauquier and began to percolate in his mind even before he arrived in the colony.[12]

Committee meetings were held as early as November 1759, and prominent among the committee members were Fauquier and members of the all-powerful Royal Council—Peyton Randolph, John Blair, Philip Grymes, Lewis Burwell, Charles Carter, George Wythe, Richard Bland, John Robinson, and Benjamin Harrison. They tentatively styled their group the "Society for the Encouragement of Arts and Manufacturing" after the Royal Society in London.[13] On October 30, 1760, an act "to amend the act for encouraging arts and manufactures" was passed "by the Lieutenant-Governor, Council and Burgesses."[14]

Learned societies were all the rage in Europe and in America, stressing the basic tenet of the Enlightenment—improvement. Not only would a society provide intellectual stimulation and entice prospective new members with promises of "praemia" (or rewards) for important proposals and successful experiments, but it also provided opportunities for didactic diversions. In addition to the founders of the society, many other distinguished citizens, including William Nelson, Thomas Nelson, Robert Carter, Lewis Burwell, Archibald Cary, Mann Page, Landon Carter, and George Washington were early subscribers to the society.[15]

Preliminary arrangements were quickly settled with the sister society in London. The statute empowered the trustees to "give and award any sums of money they shall think proper in bounties or premiums, to be issued and paid according to the directions of the said [trustees]."[16] The stated mission of the measure was "more effectively [to] promote the commercial interests of Great Britain and its colonies [and to give] encouragement to the growth, culture and production…of such commodities that either … are consumed in the kingdom … or are essential to its manufacture."[17] Priorities included the enhanced production of wine for which the reward was £500, "the best methods of cultivation, &c… [and]…. A handsome premium for the making of silk … and other such articles as should appear to the committee most advantageous to the colony."[18]

The society inaugurated many of the same projects in which Jefferson would later take such a keen interest as president of the American Philosophical Society. The proposals garnering the greatest attention of the judges were ones that improved the profits of the colony or of the mother country. Thus, the society concentrated on experiments concerning agriculture, by improving production of crops, increasing the production of tobacco, using tobacco refuse as fertilizer, producing potash, using Lupike Vetch to add nutrients to the soil, or introducing new plants to Virginia—cuttings of

Burgundy, Champagne, Claret, Spanish Grapes, and the Zant grape from the Piedmont region of Italy, currant grapes, Spanish nuts, figs and chestnuts, olive trees from Italy, and almonds. In other areas, the society proposed several prizes that would increase the preparedness of the British fleet for war—hemp production for rope, tar, and pitch turpentine to prevent leaks on vessels, production of saltpeter and improved mixtures for gun powder. Other endeavors focused on fish (herring and sturgeon), salt mines, and explosive devices.[19]

Perhaps the most dramatic and entertaining of these experiments to assist the government in its military preparedness involved the use of explosives to minimize the impact of fire onboard his Majesty's ships. Many delighted students from the college were present to observe the presentation of explosions and bursts of fire.[20] In the course of his life, Thomas Jefferson returned to many of the society's ideas and innovations in hopes of improving upon them.[21] It was during this time and for this society that Jefferson constructed his first-documented invention as an entry to a contest—a furnace for turning refuse tobacco into fine potash. The General Assembly awarded him a £100 prize. The London Society, who provided the funding for the rewards, refused the recommendation of the Williamsburg group to supply the prize, apparently because Jefferson had insulted a British official in charge of distributing awards.[22]

The director of the society, Charles Carter wrote to his counterpart at the London Society, asserting, "It [has] given me great Concern that anything should happen to prevent so beneficial [a] Work: whether his imprudent [illegible, illegible] may not exasperate the Ministry so much against him as to lose this Advantage to Great Britain & this Colony, Time can only show."[23] This set of circumstances made clear both Jefferson's scientific abilities and independent spirit at a very early age, foreshadowing a future of scientific experimentation and defiance of authority.

Small's scientific impact was not only considerable among his students, but also on the whole community. The society diminished after Small's departure and shortly thereafter disbanded altogether. It was, however, resurrected by John Page about 1772, and rebranded as the Virginia Society for the Promotion of Useful Knowledge. The mission of the society mirrored that of its predecessor and was set forth as the "Study of Nature, with a View of multiplying the Advantages that may result from this Source of Improvement." One of the members of the resurrected society, writing under the pseudonym Academicus, reported that "in the Commencement of Literature in any Country we are not to expect voluminous and finished Works in History, Philosophy, or the fine Arts; it is rather to be supposed that the first efforts of its Members will appear in detached Facts and Improvements." Many of the founders of this society—John Page, Theodorick Bland, Dabney Carr, John Walker, and James McClurg had been Small's students, Jefferson's friends and classmates, and participants in Small's original science club.[24]

Other members of the Virginia Society for the Promotion of Useful Knowledge included Theodorick Bland, Nathaniel Burwell of Carter's Grove, St. George Tucker, John Clayton, and Professor Samuel Henley.[25] The society expanded and began to recruit corresponding members. In 1774, Benjamin Rush, Benjamin Franklin, David Rittenhouse, Dr. John Morgan, and William Smith were elected as corresponding members. The exigencies of the war, however, caused a decline in the activities of the club, but as late as 1785, John Page was attempting to entice Jefferson to become its president, "I intend shortly to endeavour to revive our Society, and shall recommend you as President and McClurg as Vice President."[26] Despite Page's enthusiasm, the group's activities flagged and then stopped. Nevertheless, its formation and function stand as a tribute to Small.

Small's friend William Hunter was the proprietor and editor of the *Virginia Gazette*, which also served as a post office and bookstore in addition to distributing its publication. Hunter also acted as the publisher for the colony of Virginia and as Benjamin Franklin's Co-Postmaster-General for the American colonies.

As the largest and most well-stocked bookstore in town (and considering Small's personal relationship with Hunter), it is probable that the Gazette Bookstore was the primary source of textbooks for Small's classes. A few hints of what Small may have been teaching are found in what remains of the *Daybooks of the Virginia Gazette*. The entries recorded who bought which books and when, confirmed if a certain person was in town, what that person was reading, and with whom he was corresponding. They allow us to draw interesting, albeit unproven, conclusions. Unfortunately, the account of most of the *Daybooks* has not been located, but several folios from the years 1762 to 1764 are still accessible.

POSTGRADUATE INSTRUCTION

An intriguing possibility exists, if one can extrapolate from *Gazette* records, that Small and Wythe were tutoring and training present and past students from 1762 to 1764. Thomas Jefferson left Williamsburg for the mountains in the spring of 1762 and his final payment for college expenses was entered in the Bursar's Ledger on April 28, 1762.[27] He returned to Shadwell, where he wrote to John Page "I expect to be in Williamsburg by the first of October if not sooner."[28] Jefferson returned at the time specified, writing to Page in the first week of that month, "Affairs at W. and M. are in the greatest confusion. Walker, M'Clurg and Wat Jones are expelled *pro tempore*, or, as Horrox softens it, rusticated for a month. Lewis Burwell, Warner Lewis, and one Thompson have fled to escape flagellation."[29] Furthermore, Jefferson planned for an extended stay as he wrote that he intended to either "rent rooms" or "build … a small house" in town.[30] Local legend reported that Jefferson shared quarters with several of his former classmates in Williamsburg near the college campus during this time.

During his first weeks back in the capital, Jefferson was deeply involved in the study of law. George Wythe instructed Jefferson to observe justice at work and Jefferson pleaded with Page to come to town to visit as "court is now at hand, which I must attend constantly, so that unless you come to town, there is little probability of my meeting with you any where else."[31]

In spite of his rigorous law schedule, it seems that Jefferson likely had time for other academic pursuits, and that he was still under the tutelage of William Small. Records from the *Virginia Gazette* indicate that Jefferson was not only purchasing legal texts such as *Attorney's Companion, Harrison Chancery Practice*, and *Attorney's Companion Pleas*, but also titles of literature (*Death of Abel*), classical studies (*Antonius, Thoughts of Cicero*), belles lettres (*Sheridan on Elocution*), Natural Philosophy (*Dictionary of Arts and Sciences*), and even medical subjects (*Chestdon's Anatomy*).

More intriguing were the volumes that his classmate and close friend Warner Lewis was obtaining at the same time—*Rollin's Ancient History, Locke on Understanding, Virgil Delphi, Homer, Martin's Grammar, Ward's Mathematics*, and *[Dodley's] Preceptor*—all of which appear in the Horrock-Henley catalog, and many of which were in the personal libraries of George Wythe and of Jefferson. They were also standard texts used in Scottish universities.[32] Thus, there is a substantial likelihood that Small continued to tutor not only Jefferson but also many of his classmates far past their official time at the college.

Jefferson's continued connection with Small is known not just through speculation, but also explicitly stated in a letter to John Page in the spring of 1764. "Your friends here would be very glad to see you, particularly Small, and myself," he wrote.[33] But perhaps the most compelling evidence of their strong relationship stems from Small's purchase of a specific volume that conflated "several parts of mathematics" and "Natural Philosophy." This was William Emerson's *Doctrine of Fluxions*, which allowed a man of science to calculate accurately the rate of change in the velocity of a gradient.

In February 1764, William Small purchased two math texts at the Gazette Bookstore; the first was *Stewarts Tracts, Physical and Mathematical, containing, an Explanation of Several Interesting Points in Physical Astronomy and a New Method for Ascertaining the Suns Distance from the Earth, By the Theory of Gravity*, which presented innovative approaches to the proper techniques of celestial and ana-lytic mechanics; the second book was Emerson's *Fluxions* (1743), which expanded on Newton's interpretation of differential calculus. Not only was *Fluxions* one of the books in Jefferson's library more than thirty years later,[34] but he also used the same volume in college as shown in a 1764 letter in which he wrote, "I am much obliged by your letter of yesterday. tho' I possess Emersons Fluxions at home, & it was a book I used at College."[35]

Small's 1764 purchase of *Fluxions* combined with Jefferson's letter to John Page in April of that year makes it probable that Jefferson was in constant contact with Small and, moreover, that Small was still tutoring Jefferson for up to two years after Jefferson had officially left the college.

SELIM THE ALGERINE

Often overlooked when discussing Small's life in Virginia was his connection to Selim the Algerine, one of the most mysterious, exotic, and tragic acquaintances of Small's life. Of Selim, it is known, "One of his greatest pleasures, when in Williamsburg, was to read Greek with Professor Small and President Horrocks, of William and Mary, and at Rosewell, with Mr. Page, and his youngest son, who read Greek and Hebrew at a very early period; but it was always out of doors."[36]

The history of Selim is indeed a fascinating one. He was born about 1740 in Algeria, the son of a Turkish soldier in the service of the Bey of Algers who married the daughter of a local sheik. As a young boy, Selim was sent to a school in Constantinople and received a thorough and classical education. He was instructed not only in the Islamic tradition, but also in Hebrew and Greek. "At 17 years of Age in a Voyage to Phez in Moraocco, where he was to stay with a

Relation there, he was unfortunately taken by a French Ship."[37] The French transported Selim and the other captives to New Orleans where he was sold to a Louisiana planter. The planter cruelly beat and mistreated the unfortunate Selim and sent him up the Mississippi River to "the Mingo Indians & left there a Captive. He spent three years among them, before he made his Escape by the advice of an English man what course to take. He travelled 45 days he says in the woods alone, on herbs, Roots & wild fruit for food, till he was fortunately met by a kind man of Augusta, a frontier County of ours, almost ready to perish his cloths almost torn off."[38]

Samuel Givens and John Graham were among the hunting party that came on Selim near the head steams of the Big Calf Pasture in Augusta County, Virginia. The party came to a clearing with a fallen tree. Hearing rustling in the branches of the tree, Givens pulled out his gun to shoot what he thought was a wild animal, but "Upon coming nearer he found a person in a very pitable condition, being entirely naked excepting a few rags wrapped around his feet and ankles. His body was literally covered with scars and scabs from being scratched by thorns and briers, while he was endeavoring to make his unknown pathless way toward the sunrise.... He was manifestly in extremis from weariness and hunger."[39]

The party nursed him until the danger was past and then placed him on a pack horse, on which he was carried to the home of Capt. John Dickinson. This gentleman was a soul of honor and human kindness. He took in the stranger and treated him like a son for several months. [Selim] was a sprightly educated man and soon learned enough English to make it all plain to the hospitable people who and what he was.[40] At one point in time Captain Dickinson took Selim into Staunton to attend the sessions of the General Court, and it was at that time that Selim spotted the Reverend John Craig, whom he recognized from a dream as his source of salvation. The Reverend Craig, who was the minister of the Old Stone Church near Ft. Defiance, Virginia, agreed to take Selim home and instruct him in the teachings of Christ, "and his efforts were much facilitated by

Selim's proficiency in classic Greek, and thus he was able to read the New Testament in the original. Now instructed in the truths of the Christian religion, Selim renounced Islam, professed his desire to be a disciple of the Lord Jesus. The Reverend Mr. Craig, convinced of Selim's intelligence and sincerity, publicly received him as a communicant in the pale of the Old Stone Church."[41]

After his conversion, Selim determined to return home to spread the good word. "Thus he spent two years in Augusta before he found means to get to this Town, where his good behavior gain'd him a kind reception wth Some."[42] The Reverend Rev. Craig contacted Robert Carter in Williamsburg, who made arrangements for Selim to come to the capital. Upon arrival, "It appeared on Examination he had been learning some Greek & Hebrew which speaks him a Gentleman's Son."[43] Being an exceptional character with an extraordinary history and a pleasing personality, Selim soon became a great favorite of the elite of the town and was passed around from household to household. He was a frequent guest of both the Carters and the Pages.

Finally, in 1768, having been absent from home for almost a decade, Selim convinced John Blair to write to the authorities in London with a plea for assistance "He hopes to meet an Algereen Ambassador at London. Perhaps your Lordship may think fit to take some notice of him & oblige the Dey of Algeers by kindness, contriving him home to his Father & Mother, who no doubt will be greatly pleased to receive their long lost Son, by favours from the English Nation."[44] Blair and the rest of the Council contributed to a fund to send Selim to London, where he met with the Algerian ambassador. He was soon returned to his home country.

According to Selim's account, he had a speedy and safe passage to England, and from there to Africa. He found his parents still alive, but when his father learned of his conversion to Christianity and his refusal to renounce it, he disowned him as his child and turned him out of his house. Selim maintained that his "affection for his parents, grief for their religious prejudices and his own temporal ruin, tormented his tender heart. He was now turned out into the world, without money, without friends, and without any skill by which he could obtain subsistence. He left Algeria, the place where he expected to spend his life, without the most distant prospect of ever seeing it again."[45]

Selim first returned to England, but having no friends there nor prospects of making a livelihood, he decided to return to Virginia. "In his passage to Virginia—while he had probably no pious friend to console him in his distresses nor to encourage and support him under them, and while he had little to do but pore over his wretched situation—he sunk, under the weight of his complicated calamities, into a state of insanity."[46]

In Virginia, Selim relied on the kindness of his friends to sustain him, although his mental state was far from stable. It was said that Selim refused to sleep indoors and wore no clothes except castoff regimentals. As a guest of the Pages at Rosewell, he was a great favorite of the children and was remembered for his kind disposition, cheerful attitude, and pious demeanor. His habitual greeting to the youth was "God Save ye!" Selim also resided with the Carters until one day he wandered away and, having been found in an incoherent state, was remitted to the Williamsburg Lunatic Asylum.[47]

In 1787, John Page took Selim along with him to sessions of the Continental Congress. It was the fashion for those participating in the deliberations to have their portraits painted by Charles Willson Peale. The following is the remembrance of one of the Page family.

Among the pictures that made the deepest impression on me at Rosewell, and which decorated the old hall, was that of Selim. He was painted Indian fashion, with a blanket round his shoulders, a straw hat on his head, tied on with a check handkerchief. This portrait Governor Page had taken in Philadelphia, by Peale; and, when the box arrived at Rosewell, the family and servants were all assembled in the hall to see it opened. Great was their astonishment and disappointment to find, instead of a portrait of their father and master, Selim's picture, which was greeted instantly with his usual salutation, "God save ye."[48]

It is reported by some that Selim left the Continental Congress with a gentleman from South Carolina who promised him a full set of regimentals. Others claim that he died in Williamsburg in a private home.

Although Small's social circle in Williamsburg, which included the inimitable Selim, was distinguished, diverse, entertaining, engaging, and eccentric, the company that he was to find back in England was even more interesting.

BENJAMIN FRANKLIN

It is almost certain that Small and Benjamin Franklin first met in Williamsburg through their mutual acquaintance with William Hunter. One source claimed that Franklin and Small met in Williamsburg at Franklin's degree ceremony in 1756, while another stated that Small journeyed to Philadelphia to meet Franklin. By contrast, many have maintained that the two first met in London in the winter of 1765. Small, however, did not go to America until 1758, and there is no evidence to support that Small traveled outside of Virginia. Therefore, the most logical conclusion is that they came together at the execution of Hunter's will.

The movements of Franklin, a prolific letter writer, can be traced with a fair degree of accuracy by the dates and the places from which he posted the letters. The only time when Franklin and Small can be placed together with a fair degree of certainty was in Williamsburg during the spring of 1763. Franklin was obliged to settle Hunter's estate, and business had kept him from that duty for a long time already. Franklin wrote to Anthony Todd from Philadelphia on April 14, 1763, "I am setting out on a Journey to Virginia to settle the accounts of my late Colleague Mr. Hunter,"[49] and again on April,17, "I am just setting out for Virginia."[50] If Franklin left Philadelphia on April 17, and it was a four-day journey to Williamsburg, he probably arrived in the capital of Williamsburg on April 21, 1763.[51] At that time, Franklin had the opportunity both to settle the estate of William Hunter and to meet his new partner in the post office, John Foxcroft, who served as Francis Fauquier's personal secretary.[52] Franklin wrote to William Strahan on May 9, 1763, "I have been from Philadelphia about 3 weeks on a Journey hither upon the Business of the Post Office, but am now returning home."[53]

Hunter's will and the mutual concern Franklin and Small had in it makes the meeting at this juncture almost a certainty, for Franklin did not return to Williamsburg during Small's remaining time there. Small left Virginia late in September 1764, and with the average winter sailing time being ten weeks, likely arrived in London at the end of November. A central London debarkation station would have placed Small almost on the doorstep of Alexander Small, a Scot physician, who lived in Villiers Street, directly around the corner from Franklin's London residence on Craven Street. Alexander Small quickly notified Franklin of William Small's arrival.

> My namesake [William Small] the Virginia Professor is here; and desires to be most particularly remembered to you. I mentioned to him your Idea, of pulling down by a force applied to a straight Rope. He says it will certainly do, and spoke of it as a new Mechanical Power not attended to by Mathematicians. I told him of your Clock weight. The first thing that made him attend to it was, the practice of Sea Men, who when they have a very great weight to raise, or a great force to exert, do not pull the Rope down, as in common, but pull it to them out of the right line, and thus keeping what they have got, convey the ropes to others who secure it.[54]

Indeed, the letter indicates that Benjamin Franklin and William Small knew one another in America and that they had engaged in scientific discussion and quite possibly scientific experiments when they met in Virginia. William Small, Benjamin Franklin, and Alexander Small would spend a great deal of time together in London during the winter and spring of 1765.

It was rumored, and later documented, that Franklin and Small had cooperated in experimentations with a lamp that became the prototype for the famous Argand Lamp. That prototype had actually been produced by Matthew Boulton in Birmingham after he had employed Small as a scientific advisor. Ami Argand wrote to Matthew Boulton in 1786 that his competitors were attempting to procure a patent on this lamp as "Franklin's cylindrical burner that was brought to [you] from America by Dr. Small—now as our shabby adversaries lay very great stress upon your and Dr. Small's lamps, it is thought by our consel of the utmost consequence that you should come to town as soon as possible so as to consult with you upon the case."[55]

NOTES

1. Thomas Jefferson to Thomas Jefferson Randolph, November 25, 1808, in *The Life and Selected Writings of Thomas Jefferson*, ed. Adrienne Koch and William Peden (New York: Random House, 1944), 540.

2. There are records that favored instructors of the Page family were frequent guests at the Page table; in a response to questions posed by Skelton Jones concerning his history, John Page wrote late in his life, "At College, I lived with the President [Thomas Dawson] who my father had feed (*sic*) handsomely." William Allen, ed., *American Biographical Dictionary* (Baltimore: 1809), s.v., "Letter of Questions Posed to John Page from Skelton Jones," tipped in between pages 464 and 465, originally pages 3–12, Special Collections, Swem Library, College of William and Mary, Williamsburg, Virginia (hereafter cited as Swem Library). There are reports that John Page, Thomas Jefferson, and William Small conducted observations at the Page family home, Rosewell.

3. Heberden co-wrote a pamphlet on smallpox inoculation with Benjamin Franklin in 1759 and consulted with William Small on medical matters 1765–1775.

4. George Reese, ed., *The Official Papers of Francis Fauquier: Lieutenant Governor of Virginia, 1758–1768* (Charlottesville: University of Virginia Press, 1980), 1:xxxvi.

5. In his will Fauquier left behind a telescope, a microscope, a solar microscope, a perambulator, a measuring wheel, a pedometer, a level, a quadrant, a plumb, and other scientific equipment. Reese, *Official Papers of Francis Fauquier*, 1:xliii.

6. Heberden arranged for a post for Small in St. Petersburg in 1765, which Small declined. Dr. Heberden had married the niece of Francis Fauquier in 1760 and had supported Fauquier for membership in the Royal Society. "William Heberden, the London physician, married Mary Fauquier, the niece of the Governor of Virginia, on 19 January 1760," in William Fletcher, *Leichester Pedigrees and Royal Descents* (Leichester: Clark & Hodgson, 1887), 147; Raymond Phineas Stearns, "Colonial Fellows of the Royal Society of London, 1661–1788," *William and Mary Quarterly*, 3rd ser., vol. 3, no. 2 (April 1946): 242.

7. Stearns. "Colonial Fellows of the Royal Society of London, 1661–1788," 242.

8. Thomas Jefferson to L. H. Girardin, January 15, 1815, in *The Writings of Thomas Jefferson*, ed. Albert Bergh (Washington, D.C.: The Thomas Jefferson Memorial Association, 1903), 231.

9. Ibid. Jefferson's memory may be faulty on the date of the return to England of Fauquier's wife and sons. "His [Fauquier's] wife and their elder son, Francis, accompanied him to Virginia, where they stayed until they sailed for England toward the end of May 1766." Reese, *Official Papers of Francis Fauquier*, 1:xxxviii.

10. A reference has already been made to Aulus Gellius and the academic connotations of the term "Attic Nights." This particular and specific phraseology can be no casual reference as Jefferson was, according to the dictates of Common Sense Philosophy and scientific method, very exact in defining his terms. Aulus Gellius was a Roman of the second century AD, who, having finished a normal course of studies in Rome, migrated to the Greek province of Attica in which the city of Athens was located. There he attended several philosophers including Calvenus Taurus (who later mentored Marcus Aurelius) and studied philosophy, history, grammar, and rhetoric. Every week Taurus held elegant dinners at his villa where serious discussions were intermingled with engaging curiosities and casual entertainment; these symposia were, in essence, free-flowing seminars. Coincidentally, a new and expanded edition of Gellius's *Attic Nights* was published in two volumes in 1762 by J. L. Conradi of Leipzig. Jefferson's use of this specific term, however, does not seem to have been by accident. These dinners, where he heard more good sense than in all the rest of his life, were likely extensions of an elevated course of studies.

11. Clive Davenhall, "James Ferguson: A Commemoration," *Journal of Astronomical History and Heritage* 13, no. 3 (2010): 179.

12. In 1758, "shortly before his departure for Virginia, Fauquier was elected a corresponding member of the Society for the Encouragement of Arts, Manufactures, and Commerce, commonly called the Society of Arts (now the Royal Society of Arts) in London; corresponding members were men distinguished in various

ways or men who had rendered service to the society and were usually foreigners or residents abroad. Fauquier had little time to take part in the society's activities before he left England, but in Virginia he promised to forward its patronage of applied science." Reese, *Official Papers of Francis Fauquier*, 1:xxxvi.

13. Fulham Palace Papers, Virginia Colonial Records Project, Microfilm Reel 619, Library of Virginia, Richmond (hereafter cited as LVA).

14. "An Act for the Encouragement of Arts and Manufactures," November 1762, *Statutes at Large, Being a Collection of All the Laws of Virginia*, ed. William Waller Hening (Richmond: Franklin Press, 1820), 7:564.

15. Ibid., 7:568–569.

16. Ibid., 7:563. The original proposal was sent to the House of Burgesses in 1760, giving the following rationale, "It has been long lamented that this colony should pay annually a considerable sum of money for foreign wines, often mean in quality, and at an extravagant price when we have the greatest reason to believe our climate capable of producing as fine wines as any in [the] entire world, were the cultivation of the vineyard properly attended to. We have hitherto wanted something that might employ our young and old, at present a dead charge on the community: the making of silk might probably afford this employment, and yield a large income to the colony. There are many other articles which will in time require our attention: The experiments of wine and silk are attended with little expense; and should either of them fail, the damage cannot he very great."

17. Ibid., 7:564.

18. Ibid.

19. John Fulgham to the London Society for the Promotion of Arts and Encouragement of Manufacturing (Peter Wyche), date unknown, Fulham Palace Papers, Virginia Colonial Records Project, Microfilm Reel 619, LVA; Charles Carter to Peter Wyche, Director of the London Society for the Promotion of Arts and Encouragement of Manufacturing, May 6, 1761, Fulham Palace Papers, Virginia Colonial Records Project, Microfilm Reel 619, LVA.

20. "On the 19th of this month there was a notable Experiment tried by our Society in the presence of the Boys (from William and Mary) [as formerly] and before a prodigious Crowd of Spectators; It was receiving obsolete Chemical Fluid of Mr. Ambrose Godfrey for the [?] Extinction of fires either in Houses or on Board of Ships by Suffocation & Explosions—By order of the Society was this purchase of a House built consisting of three stories & sufficient Quantity of Combustibles was there in Fuel & at a proper time the two under stories was set on Fire at once & blazed Furiously, but an Alarm being made that the Stair-case was on Fire, the order of Extinction was to[o] soon given, however it was

instantly extinguished, afterwards, the Garret all built of wood and Containing likewise other Combustible Matter was ordered to be fired, here the flames more conspicuous to all and the Spectators themselves gave the order of Extinction; Godfrey as before extinguished this likewise in an expeditious Manner to the Great Satisfaction of all present. There will be a Pamphlet wrote on this subject, which as soon as printed shall be sent to you. It is a Thing of the Greatest Consequence to London and the fleet of England, The preserving of Cities & supporting your security." John Fulgham to Peter Wyche, Director of the London Society for the Promotion of Arts and Encouragement of Manufacturing, date unknown, Fulham Palace Papers, Virginia Colonial Records Project, Microfilm Reel 619, LVA.

21. See Martin Clagett, *Scientific Jefferson: Revealed* (Charlottesville: University of Virginia Press, 2009), 1–14.

22. "I have wrote several Letters to him [Mr. Peter Wyche of the London Society for the Encouragement of Arts and Manufactures], wherein I have taken notice of the Particular Articles under the Denomination of Naval Arms, and comply'd with his request for propagating Grapes, with such observations and hitherto made on the Bombeye Worm, which I beg leave to refer to: I must also add that the Refuse or Trash from out Tobacco Crops & the Succors (?) that grow after the Crop is housed, would properly managed, afford a considerable quantity of the first Pot Ash, of which I convinced Mr. Thomas Jefferson some time ago; & his application the Sum of £100 was voted by the General Assembly to [set] a Furnace & process a quantity of Tobacco Ashes in order to his making a publick Experiment, which by some difference with the Ministry he was prevented carrying out & for which he by Letter made an Apology and last Summer came in Person to Excuse himself, and as he was under such difficulties & the great quantity of trash Tobacco saved, made use of before his Return for manure, no Steps are taken according to his Method; and as we have at this time only one Work for making Pot Ashes that I know of." Charles Carter to the London Society for the Promotion of Arts and Encouragement of Manufacturing, ca. 1763, Fulham Palace Papers, Virginia Colonial Records Project, Microfilm Reel 619, LVA.

23. Ibid.

24. Meyer Reinhold, "The Quest for Useful Knowledge in Eighteenth-Century America," *Proceedings of the American Philosophical Society* 119, no. 2 (April 16, 1975): 108–132.

25. Henley was a successor to Small at the College of William and Mary and is reputed to have been in possession of some of the books that Small left behind. Jefferson, on several occasions, tried to purchase those volumes from him. George Wythe may have been the guardian of the remainder of Small's relinquished

possessions (books and scientific equipment) that Wythe may have bequeathed to him. This supposition is not proved.

26. John Page to Thomas Jefferson, April 28, 1785, in *The Papers of Thomas Jefferson*, ed. Julian P. Boyd (Princeton: Princeton University Press, 1953), 8:116.

27. Bursar Record Book, 1745–1770 (43) 1983-122, Archives, Swem Library.

28. Thomas Jefferson to John Page, July 15, 1763, in *The Papers of Thomas Jefferson*, ed. Julian P. Boyd (Princeton: Princeton University Press, 1950), 1:9–11.

29. Thomas Jefferson to John Page, October 7, 1763, in Boyd, *Papers of Thomas Jefferson*, 1:12.

30. Thomas Jefferson to John Page, July 15, 1763, in Boyd, *Papers of Thomas Jefferson*, 1:9.

31. Thomas Jefferson to John Page, October 7, 1763, in Boyd, *Papers of Thomas Jefferson*, 1:12.

32. See *Virginia Gazette* Daybooks, Archives, Harrison Institute, University of Virginia, Charlottesville, Virginia; *The Henley-Horrocks Inventory* (Williamsburg: Botetourt Productions, 1968); Millicent Sowerby, comp., *Catalogue of the Library of Thomas Jefferson* (Charlottesville: University Press of Virginia, 1983).

33. Thomas Jefferson to John Page, April 9, 1764, in Boyd, *Papers of Thomas Jefferson*, 1:17.

34. James Gilreath and Douglas Wilson, eds., *Thomas Jefferson: A Catalog with the Entries in His Own Order* (Washington: Library of Congress, 2001), Chapter 25: "Mathematics. Pure. Arithmetic," 14. *Emerson's Fluxions*, 8°. Dabney Carr, another of Small's students and Jefferson's classmate and brother-in-law had a number of editions of Scottish authors among his collection of books: Lord Kaim's (Kames) Law Tracts, Hutcheson's *Enquiry*, *Beattie on Truth*, Robertson's *History of Scotland*, and *Charles the 5th, Buchanan's History*; as well as texts commonly found in the libraries of Scottish universities: *Works of Puffindarious* (Puffendorf), *Rollin's Letters*, Vattel's *Law of Nations*, and *Yorreck's (Yorrick's) Sermons*. Two editions that are of particular interest in Dabney Carr's library may well be reflective of Small's influence and even direction. The first is *Watt's Logick*, which was considered the standard text along with Duncan's *Elements of Logick* during Small's days in Aberdeen, and also two volumes of Dodsley's *Preceptor*, which included Duncan's influential *Elements of Logick*. In "Errata: Errata: Virginia Troops in French and Indian Wars," *Virginia Magazine of History and Biography* 2, no. 2 (October 1894): 226.

35. Thomas Jefferson, *The Papers of Thomas Jefferson*, ed. Barbara Oberg (Princeton: Princeton University Press, 2003), 30:234; It is also interesting to note that Jefferson wrote a letter to "unknown" on July 26,1764, in which he affirmed the unknown's proposal "of keeping up an epistolary correspondence on subjects

of some importance." Jefferson stated that "at present" he did not have any direct questions dealing with "natural philosophy." Jefferson further suggested that since that he might be discussing a sensitive subject that "were they to come to light, might do injustice to a man's moral principles in the eyes of persons of narrow and confined views it will be proper to take great care of our letters. I propose as one mean of doing it to put no name or place to the top or bottom of the letter, and to inclose it in a false cover which may be burned as soon as opened." He closed his letter with a reminder of an astronomical event to take place the next day: "Orion is 3 Hours—40' west of the sun and of consequence goes down and rises that much before him. So you must rise early in the morning to see him. The upper star in his belt is exactly in the Æquinoctial" (Thomas Jefferson to unknown, July 26, 1764, in *The Papers of Thomas Jefferson*, ed. John Caranzariti [Princeton: Princeton University Press, 1997], 27:665). Although purely speculative, the recipient—because of the closeness in date to Small's departure, because of the content relating to matters of natural philosophy, physical anatomy, mathematics, and astronomical observances, and because of the fact that the only letter that Jefferson is known to have sent to Small arrived after Small's death—most likely to have been Small himself.

36. Bishop William Meade, "ARTICLE XXIX. *Gloucester.*—No. 3. *History of Selim, the Algerine Convert,*" in *Old Churches, Ministers and Families of Virginia* (Philadelphia, J. B. Lippincott Company, 1891), 338.

37. John Blair to Lord Hillsborough, July 12, 1768, PRO: CO 5/1346, Microfilm, Colonial Records Project, Letters to the Secretary of State and Others from Governors Francis Fauquier and Lord Botetourt, and Mr. President Blair, with enclosures and replies, ff. 84–85, LVA.

38. Ibid.

39. William T Price. "Selim the Algerine," *West Virginia Historical Magazine* 4, no. 1 (January–October 1904): 57.

40. Ibid., 58.

41. Ibid., 60. "When I was in my distress, I once in my sleep dreamed that I was in my own country, and saw in my dream the largest assembly of men my eyes had ever beheld, collected in a wide plain, all dressed in uniform and drawn up in military order. At the farther side of the plain, and almost at an immense distance, I saw a person whom I understood to be one of great distinction; but, by reason of the vast distance he was from me, I could not discern what sort of a person he was. I only knew him to be a person of great eminence. I saw every now and then one or two of this large assembly attempting to go across the plain to this distinguished personage; but when they had got about half-way over, they suddenly dropped into a hole in the earth, and I saw them no more. I also imagined that I saw an old

man standing by himself, at a distance from this large assembly, and one or two of the multitude applied to him for direction how to cross the plain in safety; and all who received and followed it got safe across. As soon as I saw you," added Selim, "I knew you to be the man who gave these directions; and this has convinced me that it is the mind of God that I should apply to you for instructions in religion. It is for this reason I desire to go home with you. When I was among the French, they endeavoured to prevail on me to embrace the Christian religion. But, as I observed they made use of images in their religious worship, I looked on Christianity with abhorrence; such worship being, in my opinion, idolatrous." Meade, "ARTICLE XXIX. *Gloucester.*—No. 3. *History of Selim, the Algerine Convert,*" in *Old Churches, Ministers and Families of Virginia,* 344. St. George Tucker wrote a poem entitled "The Dream of Selim" based on this story.

42. John Blair to Lord Hillsborough, July 12, 1768, PRO: CO 5/1346, Microfilm, Colonial Records Project, Letters to the Secretary of State and Others from Governors Francis Fauquier and Lord Botetourt, and Mr. President Blair, with enclosures and replies, ff. 84–85, LVA.

43. Ibid.

44. Ibid.

45. Meade, "ARTICLE XXIX. *Gloucester.*—No. 3. *History of Selim, the Algerine Convert,*" in *Old Churches, Ministers and Families of Virginia,* 346.

46. Ibid.

47. Price. "Selim the Algerine," 61.

48. Meade, "ARTICLE XXIX. *Gloucester.*—No. 3. *History of Selim, the Algerine Convert,*" in *Old Churches, Ministers and Families of Virginia,* 348. The portrait at the time Bishop Meade wrote this report in 1857 was still to be seen in the library in the home of Robert Saunders, the President of William and Mary, who had married Governor Page's youngest daughter, Lucy Burwell Page. It was carried away by Northern troops during the Civil War and likely by a collector of letters, documents, and artwork, Samuel Putnam, of Worcester, Massachusetts. It has not been found and may well be in an attic, a parlor, or an antique shop of the area. See also Hezekiah Butterworth, *In the Days of Jefferson* (New York: Appleton, 1900); "Selim the Algerine and the People of Bath," *Times Past* (April 17, 1997): 17; *West Virginia Historical Encyclopedia* (Richwood: Jim Comstock, 1976), 4282–4283; and, Robert Doares, "But for the Savior, I could not bear it," *Colonial Williamsburg Magazine* (Summer 2002).

49. Benjamin Franklin to Anthony Todd, April 14, 1763, *The Papers of Benjamin Franklin, Volume 10: January 1, 1762 through December 31, 1763,* ed. Leonard W. Labaree (New Haven: Yale University Press, 1966), 10:252.

50. Benjamin Franklin to Richard Jackson, April 17, 1763, in Labaree, *Papers of Benjamin Franklin*, 10:254.

51. "Being but four days from Philadelphia to Col. Hunter's [William Hunter's brother]," Benjamin Franklin to Deborah Franklin, March 30, 1756, in *The Writings of Benjamin Franklin*, ed. Albert Smyth (New York: MacMillan Co., 1907), 10:332–333.

52. Reese, *Official Papers of Francis Fauquier*, 2:673n. "Foxcroft has been identified as Fauquier's secretary, on the grounds of a letter from Franklin to Lord Hillsborough ... which mentioned an application from Fauquier to have his secretary appointed Hunter's successor and a notice in the *Pennsylvania Gazette* on 7 January 1762 (no. 1724) that Mr. Foxcroft, secretary to Governor Fauquier, of Williamsburg, was appointed as Franklin's colleague."

53. Benjamin Franklin to William Strahan, May 9, 1763, in Labaree, *Papers of Benjamin Franklin*, 10:254.

54. Alexander Small to Benjamin Franklin, December 1, 1764, Franklin Papers, 1/110, Archives of the American Philosophical Society, Philadelphia, Pennsylvania.

55. Ami Argand to Matthew Boulton, February 13, 1786 (London), BCL MS 3782/12/31/21, Archives, Birmingham Central Library, Birmingham, England.

CHAPTER 7

Small and Instruction
at William and Mary

The underpinning of Small's instruction at the College of William and Mary was the influence of the Scottish Enlightenment, which was the foundation of his own education. It was in this tradition that Thomas Jefferson first encountered the expansion of science and the system of things in which we are placed.

THE COURSES

Small's first year at Marischal College was devoted to the Greek language and literature, which was taught by the Principal of Marischal, Thomas Blackwell.[1] Greek was considered the basis of all knowledge and was usually left in the hands of the most experienced professor.

In his second year Small attended Francis Skene who taught a new course which encompassed "History, Geography, Chronology, and Natural History, commonly called special physics, and ... students of this class shall attend the lessons of the Professor of Mathematics."[2] The special physics portion of this course investigated the rise and fall of nations, the evolution of society, and the nature of governments. This course grounded students in the theories of social evolution, constitutions of the ancient world, comparative economics, and what we might today describe as psychology.

In Small's third year William Duncan, Small's tertian professor, taught natural and experimental philosophy, criticism and belles lettres, and mathematics. Natural and experimental philosophy included mechanics, hydrostatics, pneumatics, optics, astronomy, magnetism, and electricity. The mathematical component probably was devoted to trigonometry, geometry, and algebra.

The final year was spent in the abstract sciences, moral philosophy, logic, ethics, and "the philosophy of the human mind and the sciences that depend on it—which include politics and law, and what we would now call psychology."[3]

The two major foundations of the Scottish Enlightenment included the scientific methodology of Bacon and Newton and the mission of the advancement of the state of mankind through changes in society, science, and economic means—in short, improvement.

THE PROFESSORS

In addition to his duties as the Greek Professor, Thomas Blackwell was selected principal in 1748. In 1750, Blackwell introduced a new course for the instruction of the students in ancient history, geography and chronology, which informed students about the principles of natural bodies and about "the rise and fall of states, and of the great revolutions that have happen'd in the world"[4]

Francis Skene, Small's semi-bejan professor, had tutored Lord Monboddo before he taught at Marischal College and was the first to teach the new course of civics and natural history designed by Principal Blackwell.

William Duncan, Small's tertian professor, taught natural and experimental philosophy, criticism and belles lettres, and mathematics. Natural and experimental philosophy included mechanics, hydrostatics, pneumatics, optics, astronomy, magnetism, and electricity. The mathematical component probably was devoted to trigonometry, geometry, and algebra. Duncan was Aberdeen borne, he attended the grammar school in Aberdeen and graduated from Marischal in 1737. After graduation he migrated to London where he was an author of several well received translations of Caesar and Cicero. His most famous work, however, and the one that is most likely to have made an impression on the young William Small was published in Dodsley's *Preceptor* in 1748. Its full title was *Elements of Logick... Designed... for Young Gentlemen at the University and to prepare the Way of the Study of Philosophy and the Mathematicks."* Samuel Johnson in the preface to *The Preceptor* advised the student to advance to Isaac Watt's *Logick: or, the Right Use of Reason in the Enquiry After Truth* after mastering Duncan's *Elements of Logick*. Samuel Johnson considered William Duncan and Isaac Watts as the two most important rhetorical theorists of the age, and John Collard, in his *The Essentials of Logic* published in 1796, calls Watts and Duncan "the two logical writers in the highest esteem at our universities."[5] William Duncan put forth a set of rules, or *regulae*, that acted as a touchstone of utilitarian precepts in his work *The Elements of Logick*. Many of these principles were incorporated into a metaphysical tradition known as the "School of Common Sense." Several authors maintain that Thomas Jefferson was heavily influenced by the works of William Duncan and that the Declaration of Independence resonates both its sentiments, its logical arrangement, and its very words.

Small's senior or Magistrand Professor was Alexander Gerard. From 1750 to 1752 he substituted for Dr. Fordyce, Professor of Natural Philosophy at Marischal. When Dr. Fordyce drowned off the coast of Holland, Gerard was appointed professor of logic and moral philosophy.[6] Although a junior member of the faculty, he was chiefly responsible for the changes that took place at Marischal College in 1753.[7] In 1756, Gerard, an early promoter of the study of belles lettres, was awarded a prize by the Edinburgh Society for the Encouragement of Arts for his *Essay on Taste*.[8] Jefferson noted that at William and Mary, and indeed in British America, Small "was the first who ever gave regular lectures in Ethics, Rhetoric &

Belles letters" and Small's expertise in this field, no doubt, derived from Gerrard's instruction.

Thus, records at Marischal College suggest that William Small's professors were Thomas Blackwell, Francis Skene, William Duncan, and Alexander Gerard. John Gregory, who taught at King's College, was co-founder of the Aberdeen Philosophical Society, and was Thomas Reid's cousin has long been consider Small's mentor in Aberdeen. Although at King's while Small was at Marischal, there were institutional and collegial bonds which conjoined the institutions. In a letter to James Watt in 1773, Small referred to Gregory "as a dear friend whom I have loved for 21 years"—Small's first year at Marischal. From Virginia, Small later sent students and recommended to his colonial friends that they should send their sons to Edinburgh for a medical education, and the inspiration and foundation of Small's medical career began with Gregory's encouragement and instruction.

Thus, records at Marischal College suggest that William Small's professors were Thomas Blackwell, Francis Skene, William Duncan, and Alexander Gerard. John Gregory, who taught at King's College, was co-founder of the Aberdeen Philosophical Society, and was Thomas Reid's cousin has long been consider Small's mentor in Aberdeen. Although teaching at King's College while Small was attending Marischal College, there were institutional and collegial bonds which conjoined the institutions. In a letter to James Watt in 1773, Small referred to Gregory "as a dear friend whom I have loved for 21 years"—Small's first year at Marischal. From Virginia, Small later sent students and recommended to his colonial friends that they should send their sons to Edinburgh for a medical education, and the inspiration and foundation of Small's medical career began with Gregory's encouragement and instruction.

The importance of Small's adherence to the philosophical tenets of Common Sense Philosophy was that it was based on what is real, not imagined; on what is practical, not pedantic; and on what is useful in pragmatic application rather than sophistic in argumentation. These regulae permeated all areas of instruction, personal interactions, and the foundations of argumentation and demonstration. When Small departed for Virginia in August 1758, he brought along a solid foundation for philosophical exchange based on Common Sense and a wealth of specialized knowledge.

ACADEMIC STRUCTURE OF
THE COLLEGE OF WILLIAM AND MARY

The College of William and Mary was the admixture of two British educational models—it followed the English model of ceremonial traditions with the mission of producing scholarly gentlemen. It mimicked the Scottish model in its administrative structure and charter. William and Mary operated on a tri-semester schedule during colonial times. The first semester, or Hillary Term, began the first Monday after Epiphany, January the sixth, and lasted until the week before Palm Sunday, late in March or early in April. The second semester, Easter Term, began a week and a day after Easter, usually in mid-April, and lasted until Whit Sunday, late in May or early in June. The third semester, Trinity Term, began the day after Trinity Sunday, late in August, and lasted until the sixteenth of December. During Trinity Term, the school granted students a week-long vacation in mid-October between St. Luke's Day and St. James' Day.[9] The length of terms varied; Hillary Term lasted approximately thirteen weeks, Easter Term about seven weeks, and Trinity Term almost twenty weeks. Small was formally inducted into the faculty, or "Society," on October 18, 1758, likely in the middle of the Trinity vacation.

The William and Mary Charter of 1727 established four schools for the College—the Indian School, the Grammar School, the Philosophical School (which was divided into Natural Philosophy and Moral Philosophy), and the Divinity School (which largely lay fallow during Small's tenure in Williamsburg). The Indian School was an endowed institution to train select Native Americans in the rudiments of English and religion. The Master of the Grammar School was to instruct his charges in the rudiments of Latin and Greek and prepare them for the collegiate schools.

The Master of the Indian School was charged with teaching his wards to read, write, and do simple arithmetic. He was also to instruct them in Christianity, the true religion. The Master of the Indian School had the least burdensome position, and in turn, he also received the lowest salary: from £40 to £50 per year. He usually had about eight to ten students, frequently taking on other duties to supplement his income. Emmanuel Jones, Master of the Indian School, served for much of his tenure at the college as librarian and as clerk of the Meetings of the President and Masters of the College. He was also allowed to sell schoolbooks.

The upper schools were divided into the philosophical school and the divinity school. The two Philosophy School masters taught Moral Philosophy and Natural Philosophy. Natural Philosophy encompassed "Physicks, Metaphysicks, and Mathematicks." Moral Philosophy, according to the statutes, consisted of "Rhetorick, Logick, and Ethicks."[10] Students were exercised not only in debate but in declamation. Likewise, The Divinity School had two professors. The first was to teach the "Hebrew Tongue and critically expound the literal Sense of the Holy Scripture," and the second was to explain the "common Places of Divinity, and the Controversies with Hereticks" and conduct Prelections and Disputations on those subjects.[11] During most of Small's time at the college, both of these offices were left vacant.

The Grammar School had the traditional function of preparing the students for work in the collegiate schools. The Master of the Grammar School instructed the students in the "Latin and Greek Tongues" and the "Rudiments and Grammars" of those languages.[12] He was charged with keeping a watchful eye over the habits and morals of the boys. When a Grammar School student completed his coursework, usually around the age of fifteen, he was given an oral examination before the president and master. If he was judged to be satisfactory, he was promoted to the philosophical schools. The Master of the Grammar School was specifically enjoined to "let no Blockhead or lasy Fellow" be allowed to proceed into the college.[13]

Classes met six days a week, with each day devoted to a certain set of lectures. According to Robert P. Thomson, "Each week college students received two days' instruction in mathematics, one in natural philosophy, and three in the various phases of rhetoric, logic, and moral philosophy."[14] At William and Mary, students were not grouped into classes or given yearly examinations, but instead "attended lectures and pursued studies as far as their abilities and diligence permitted."[15] Although instruction seems to have been linear and sequential, a specific sequence or set of subjects does not seem to have been mandated, nor did students actively seek degrees, and "professors did not seem to have encouraged them to do so."[16] No diplomas (except an honorary one to Benjamin Franklin) were awarded during the colonial period. The first marks of academic accomplishments were the Botetourt Medals first issued in 1772, with one being presented to the top student in Natural Philosophy and a second one for Moral Philosophy. Only eight were awarded between 1772 and 1775.

NATURAL PHILOSOPHY—INNOVATIONS, EXPERIMENTATION AND DEMONSTRATION

In the eighteenth century, Natural Philosophy was synonymous with the study of science, but it actually embraced so much more. Small taught the substance and in the style that he had experienced back in Scotland. At Marischal College, Natural Philosophy included both theoretical and practical branches. The theoretical subjects, which were taught in the second year, included: "Classics, Natural and Civic History, Geography, Chronology, Arithmetic, Algebra, Geometry, and plain Trigonometry."[17] According to an article in the

Scots Magazine, the practical branch included Natural Philosophy, General Physics, Mechanics, Pneumatics,[18] Optics, and Astronomy.[19] Subjects specified in the Minutes of the Aberdeen Philosophical Society included: Spherical Trigonometry, Spherical Geometry, Higher Algebra, Quadrature of Curves, Fluxions, and Newton's Principals of Philosophy.[20]

According to Robert Polk Thomson, a student's progression in mathematics was carefully articulated into four courses. The following description was taken from a letter written by Thomas Gwatney, Professor of Mathematics, to the *Gazette* in 1770. Gwatney, who succeeded Small at William and Mary, adopted Small's formula of instruction as well. The schedule and rotation below are, in general, the same routine that was used in course descriptions at Marischal College and seem to have been set out in Williamsburg along similar lines.

> First the student worked through the six books of Euclid, hearing propositions explained on one day and demonstrating them at the next meeting. Then he studied plane trigonometry, including work in surveying and the use of logarithms; next came algebra. The third course stressed the properties of mechanical powers and the use of globes.[21] It involved those aspects of physics that could be comprehended without a previous knowledge of solid geometry, conics, the elements of fractions and physical astronomy.[22]

Small introduced changes that revolutionized pedagogical practice in at least three areas at William and Mary. He introduced the lecture system rather than rote learning; he introduced the study of belles lettres; and he introduced scientific experiments, demonstrations, and observations. During his career in Williamsburg, Small adhered closely to the philosophical tenets and lines of inquiry that he had pursued in Aberdeen. The underlying foundation for all studies was systematic and logical sequencing.

Judging from both circumstantial evidence and documented sources, Small instructed in the following areas: in Natural Philosophy, he taught and demonstrated concepts in Mathematics, Science, Biology, Zoology, Chemistry, Agriculture, Astronomy, Meteorology, History, Geography, and related subjects; in Moral Philosophy, he lectured on Ethics, Rhetoric, Belles Lettres, Law, Logic, and Metaphysics. In addition, both during the time he was the sole collegiate professor at the college and even after the return of Richard Graham and John Camm, he taught Classical studies, various branches of Mathematics, and those subjects "most usefull in life."

The primary evidence of the subjects and methods employed by Small in Williamsburg comes from the testimony of his students, the books they studied, the lectures they heard, and the interests that they developed as a result of their education.

As Professor of Mathematics and Natural Philosophy, Small addressed the mathematical aspects in class in a widespread and ramified way. John Page, in the year before he died, recalled that "under the illustrious Professor of Mathematics, Wm. Small ... natural and experimental Philosophy, Mechanics, and, in short, every branch of the Mathematics, particularly Algebra, and Geometry, warmly engaged my attention, till they led me on to Astronomy"[23] Walter Jones wrote his brother and guardian, Thomas, "I can with the greatest Satisfaction Acquaint you that I have been under Mr Small's Tuition ever since I saw you, without losing any considerable Time by whose Methods & my own Diligence I have made tolerable Progress in Algebra."[24]

In addition to the statements of his former students, there is also evidence of the books that were purchased by both Small and those who attended his lectures. Walter Jones informed his brother that "nor are [there] any other Books which I have purchased [since], only such as Mr Small said there was an immediate Necessity of getting immediately."[25] Warner Lewis, another Small student, is recorded having bought a copy of John Ward's time-tested text *The Young*

Mathematician's Guide, Colin MacLauren's Treatise on Algebra, and Samuel Cunn's edition of *Euclid's Elements of Geometry.*[26]

Major topics of pure mathematics taught in Small's classes included basic mathematics, algebra, geometry, calculus, and the study of fluxions.[27] Both texts suggest that Small was lecturing in Natural Philosophy up until the time he returned to England, which in turn may imply that he continued to instruct in that area and was intending to return to the college and use the experimental apparatus he had bought in London for demonstrations in his classes.

The testimony of the students and the evidence of the books purchased from the *Virginia Gazette* bookstore by Small's students indicate that there was a concatenation of math, science, medicine, and astronomy present in the professor's classroom. Indeed, Page and Jefferson performed parallel observations of the most-celebrated astronomic event of the late eighteenth century—the Transit of Venus—on June 24, 1778, which was communicated to the American Philosophical Society.[28] Small and several of his students made a tradition of conducting intermittent celestial observations from the cupola on the roof of Rosewell, the family home of John Page.

There were more than several titles that indicate Small's acumen in the subject of astronomy and that he transmitted his enthusiasm both to his students and his personal friends in Williamsburg on this head. The best evidence is a book that Small left behind that was later returned to the college library. Although the identification of the owner on the frontispiece is not in Small's handwriting, the internal corrections in the marginalia are certainly in his hand. The name of the work is *The Description and Use of Globes and the Orrery,* which addressed topics related to making appropriate astronomical calculations and the proper usages of globes. It describes multiple mathematical calculations used to make astronomical predictions.[29]

Warner Lewis, Jefferson's friend and classmate, purchased both Richard Helsham's *Lectures on Natural Philosophy* and James

Ferguson's *Astronomy Explained upon Sir Isaac Newton's Principles* on September 5, 1764, at the Gazette store shortly before Small departed for England.[30] Helsham's volume expounded on pure mathematics, mechanics, gravity, optics and optical instruments.

In a curious postscript to John Walker, Jefferson wrote, "Celeberrimus ille Ferguson, qui scripsit de astronomia venturus est, ut fertur, ad. Coll. Gul. et Mar. Successor dignus dignissimi Parvi," which translates as "that most celebrated Ferguson, who wrote about astronomy, as it is reported, is intending to come to the College of William and Mary. A worthy successor of the most worthy Small."[31] Within this context, it is interesting to note that Benjamin Franklin collaborated with Ferguson on his book, *Tables and Tracts, Relative to Several Arts and Sciences*, which was published in London by A. Millar, in 1767, about the same time that he was working with Small on a number of scientific matters, including the development of a working steam engine.[32]

Jefferson attested to Small's abilities as a math and science teacher half a century later, writing, "I have been for some time rubbing up my mathematics from the rust contracted by fifty years' pursuits of a different kind. And thanks to the good foundation laid at college by my old master and friend Small, I am doing it with a delight and success beyond my expectation."[33]

Classical languages, although technically within the realm of Moral Philosophy, were integrated among all disciplines. Ancient authors, both Greek and Latin, were interspersed across the curriculum and students honed their knowledge of these authors, as well as logic and rhetorical skills in "debates" and "declamations." In these exercises, students demonstrated their abilities in logical persuasion, voice inflection, facial expression, and gesticulation. Their constant exposure to classical literature endowed the students with a firm sense of logical and argumentative progression, a sense of style and cadence, and an elegance of expression that is found in no other discipline.

BOTH A GENERALIST AND A SPECIALIST

The revolution in pedagogical methodology that occurred at Marischal College (at the very time that Small was in attendance) allowed Small both to be a generalist (in that he could teach everything) and a specialist (in that he had advanced knowledge about specific subject matter) at the same time. This fortuitous turn of events took on great importance after the departure of Jacob Rowe, which left Small the sole professor of all academic subjects just at the moment when Thomas Jefferson was arriving at the college.

One area of study that transcended all branches of academia at the college was the study of classical languages. Inasmuch as Jacob Rowe left the college in August 1760 and admitted to having no students at the time of his appearance before the Board of Visitors, it is certain that Small had already been conducting instruction in Latin and Greek.

Even after the reinstatement of Professor Richard Graham, it is likely that many students attended Small's lectures in classical languages. Walter Jones reported to his brother, "As to the Languages I must depend on myself for all improvement I shall make hereafter in them, As Mr. Graham is altogether unqualified to instruct in either. I still continue to read Homer by myself but do not perform with sufficient correctness, without the assistance of Pope's Translation & Notes, with a classis Homerica which I have [used] since I wrote you last, nor are [there] any other <Books> which I have purchased [since], only such as Mr Small said there was an immediate Necessity of getting immediately."[34]

Jones's progress in the classics must have improved substantially, for after studying with Small he wrote, "I proceeded about six o'clock to the College where I found my Task to be a Latin Theme two sides of Paper in length. [A set] of twelve hexameters and pentameter verses & forty Lines to get in Juvenal by heart which the rest of the class did with great difficulty."[35]

The classical authors that Jones purchased in 1760 included Martial's *Epigrams*, Caesar's *Commentarii de Bello Gallico*, and *Graeciae Sententiae*. In 1761, he bought Cicero, Anacreon, and Xenophon (*Anabasis*).[36] Warner Lewis is recorded as having purchased Virgil and Homer (as Jones had mentioned).[37] Jefferson made repeated references to Cicero throughout his life and mentioned Aulus Gellius in his autobiography.[38] Jefferson's Commonplace Book includes citations from Homer, Euripides, Virgil, Horace, Ovid, and Seneca, and his purchases at the *Virginia Gazette* bookstore included *Thoughts of Cicero* and *Antonius* (Plutarch).

MORAL PHILOSOPHY

In 1760, by circumstance and fiat, Small also subsumed the classes of moral philosophy, which consisted of "Rhetorick, Logick, and Ethicks." Lyon Tyler, who later became President of William and Mary, stated that the term "ethics" covered "natural and civil law," and that the students were exercised not only in debate but also in declamation.[39]

After he had taken over Rowe's classes, Small became an academic springboard for exploring the philosophical foundations of ethical and scientific considerations. Moral philosophy generally covered ethics, rhetoric, logic, criticism, and belles lettres, and "the philosophy of the human mind and the sciences that depend on it— which included politics and law, and what we now call psychology."[40] Jefferson wrote that Small was the first professor at the college who gave college regular lectures on ethics, rhetoric, and belles lettres.[41]

Belles lettres was a relatively new subject area at the time, a nebulous concept that combined an interest in style, taste, and criticism in the areas of rhetoric, poetry, history, art, philology, and literature. The belletristic tradition concerned itself mainly with the art of speaking and writing well, and with the study of the faculties of the human mind by which nature was perceived. The founders of the belletristic tradition were Hugh Blair, whose work *Lectures on Rhetoric and Belles-Lettres* had a major impact on eighteenth-century intellectual life, and Alexander Gerard, whose "Essay on Taste" won a major award in 1756. At the very time that he won the award, Gerard was also lecturing Small in Moral Philosophy at Marischal College. Blair and Gerard were colleagues and friends, and both were disciples of the tenets of Common Sense Philosophy.

Central themes in the studies of belles lettres and Common Sense Philosophy were investigations of the human mind and the means by which it perceived truth and beauty. Moreover, the study of belles lettres was also concerned with the ways in which an appreciation of literature and the arts improved the social fiber and moral imperatives of mankind.

In teaching Logic to his Williamsburg charges, Small surely based a substantial part of the course on either the notes that he had taken in Duncan's class or his celebrated book *The Elements of Logick*, first published in 1748, as part of Dodley's influential compendium *The Preceptor*. Records indicate that it was in the *Gazette* bookstore as early as 1752. Tellingly, Warner Lewis purchased the work in 1764,[42] and a volume was also found in the library of Dabney Carr, Jefferson's brother-in-law and student of Small.[43]

In his study of the influence of logic on the Declaration of Independence, Wilber Howell wrote, "We may be sure that Small, when forced to add logic, rhetoric, and ethics to his teachings at William and Mary during Jefferson's first college year, would naturally remember the famous *Logick* that his own master had published in 1748, and would naturally recommend that work to young Jefferson, his daily companion and close friend."[44] The tenets of the scientific method, the mission of improvement, and the concept of utilitarianism inherent both in the *Elements of Logick* and character of the Scottish Enlightenment would guide many of Small's students throughout their lives. Carr, who died in 1773 at the age of thirty, left behind many of the Scottish Enlightenment writers' most important works including Hutchinson's *Enquiry*, Beattie's *On Truth*, Robertson's *History of Scotland*, and Dodley's *Preceptor*.[45]

THE STUDY OF MEDICINE

Small also practiced medicine in Virginia, and counted William Hunter, Franklin's Co-Postmaster-General and proprietor of the *Virginia Gazette* bookstore, among his clients. Although there is no direct testimony, it is interesting that a number of Small's students ended up in the medical profession, and that four—George Gilmer, John Galt, Walter Jones, and James McClurg—not only studied medicine at the University of Edinburgh, but also attended the classes of Small's college mentor, John Gregory.[46] Jefferson, although he never took up the mantle, seems to have considered the option.

As there were few medical schools in the colonies before the Revolution, those who wished to become physicians either apprenticed at home with a local practitioner or went to Britain for a formal education—the most popular medical school for Americans became the University of Edinburgh. In the late eighteenth century, Virginia supplied the majority of the American medical students at Edinburgh, followed by Pennsylvania.[47] Indeed, the number of Virginians at the school was so large that a group of these ex-patriots formed the Virginia Club in 1761.[48]

Evidence of the cachet brought by a medical degree from Edinburgh was that even in an age when diplomas were not required nor expected, coursework was demanding and the expenses of formal foreign training were almost prohibitive; the second half of the eighteenth century saw sixty-five Virginians obtain an Edinburgh M.D. and many more took classes without bearing the cost of laureation.[49] While an English education was preferred for the legal profession and for social reasons, Edinburgh was recognized as an academically superior institution for medicine and other universities in Scotland had high reputation for their instruction in Moral and

Natural Philosophy. In terms of a medical education, the advantages of a Scottish education were so overwhelming that between 1750 and 1850 only 500 doctors graduated from English universities in that field while more than 10,000 obtained their M.D. degrees in Scotland.[50]

The disproportionate number of American students who came from either Virginia or Pennsylvania may be an indication of encouragement at home; those from Pennsylvania may have been directed to Scotland by Benjamin Franklin and many from Virginia may have come on the recommendation of William Small.[51] Former students of William Small who became Edinburgh graduates included George Gilmer, John Galt, Walter Jones, and James McClurg.[52] By way of friends or relatives, Small may have also pointed the way for Theodorick Bland, James Blair, John Ravenscroft, George Steptoe, and Thomas Tudor Tucker. Small taught Theodorick Bland's younger brothers, James Blair attended William and Mary, John Ravencroft's father was a member of the Williamsburg Science Society, George Steptoe was Arthur Bland's cousin, and Thomas Tucker was the brother of St. George Tucker. Although Gilmer, Galt, McClurg, and Walter Jones were the most illustrious of this select fraternity, all of Small's medical students had distinguished careers.

In 1764, Jefferson purchased *New Dispensatory: The Theory and Practice of Pharmacy* and *Cheston's [Cheseldon's] Anatomy* from the *Gazette* bookstore.[53] Although he never seriously considered taking up the "practice of physick," nevertheless, he promoted advances in medicine throughout his life. He was one of the first of his college crowd to embrace the cause of inoculation. In 1766, Warner Lewis wrote to his old classmate Watt Jones (who was studying Medica Materia at the University of Edinburgh with Small's old mentor, John Gregory), "Jefferson at this Time is under Inoculation in Maryland."[54] It has been reported previously that Jefferson took the inoculation in Philadelphia with John Morgan at a later date.[55] Jefferson sought solutions not only to the scourge of smallpox, but also for the origin and prevention of yellow fever, which led him to advocate for prophylactic architecture and urban planning.[56]

THE STUDY OF NATURE

Natural Philosophy, however, was Small's greatest passion, and his devotion to the subject is apparent by his innovations. The topics that most engaged him, which were the subjects of his lectures and the kinds of experimental demonstrations that he performed, are evident by the apparatus that he procured for the college on his return to England and that he likely intended to use in his own classes upon his return.

The apparatus came from the most well-regarded instrument makers in London—Peter Dolland, Edward Nairne, and the shop of Francis Hauksbee the Younger. Dolland was especially known for his fine optical instruments, achromatic lenses, sidereal and terrestrial telescopes. Nairne was a pioneer in developing instruments for experimentation in the new areas of electricity and magnetism. He focused on electricity because of its potential for the medical arts. Nairne's shop was also famous for the quality of its barometers, magnets, and telescopes. Small may have also obtained some of the instruments developed by Francis Hauksbee the Younger, whose shop in Crane's Court (one of Benjamin Franklin's favorite haunts) sold high-quality air pumps, hydrostatic balances, and reflecting telescopes. Benjamin Franklin was a great fan, friend, and client of these instrument makers, and years later Thomas Jefferson made purchases of scientific instruments from the very same vendors.

A partial inventory of the apparatus that Small bought for the College of William and Mary on his return to England included instruments for use in astronomy—a pendulum to swing in vacuo, a dipping needle compass 9 inches in diameter with needles for the dip, 5 platonic bodies, an acromatic telescope with a triple-object glass, two eye tubes for astronomy and one for day objects, a 12-inch concave mirror, a flat mirror, and a mahogany inclined-plane that sets to any angle with a scale and nest of weights. For experiments in optics and chromatics, Small bought 2 best prisms, a water prism, a reflecting mirror, a true parallel glass (also important for navigational measurements), and a best double-microscope. For meteorological studies: the fountain experiment in vacuo in open air with a bason, a lung's glass (for barometric measurements), a wire cage for breaking glasses with 6 brass caps with valves (for atmospheric pressure), a standard barometer, and 6 plates for attraction & cohesion (which were also used for medical demonstrations). For the pragmatic sciences and mechanics: a set of glasses for the air pumps (used by Hauksbee and Smeaton for experiments involving pumps and steam engines), a horizontal needle with a center pin work for it to stand on for the variation (surveying), a machine for the resistance of the air according to Mr. Robinson, Dr. Barker's mill (both of which demonstrated principles of efficient water power for mills), and machines for demonstrations involving the properties and usages of electricity and magnetism. Further, he purchased an electrical machine of Edward Nairne's design, and 17 capillary tubes (which were employed both in electrical properties and for medical experimentation).[57] There was also an apparatus to be used for enlightened entertainment, such as the solar microscope, which included a reflecting mirror and a true parallel glass (which acted like a camera obscura for revealing objects in perspective).[58]

The scientific equipment that Small purchased for the college indicates that Small was observing, experimenting, or demonstrating in specific areas of optics, statics, Newton's Laws of physics, hydrostatics, pneumatics, astronomy, meteorology, electricity, and new medical techniques. His interest in electrical experimentation may derive from his association with Benjamin Franklin, and his demonstrations may have been some of the first performed at an American college.

ALL IS EXPERIMENT AND DEMONSTRATION

Before Small, rote learning was universally employed in colonial institutions. It was the process by which the master gave notes to the students to copy and required them to regurgitate the information. By contrast, the lecture system employed a more-engaging methodology—informed lectures and clear examples, followed by a session of questions and answers delivered in a Socratic fashion.

In the classroom, Small used the pedagogical scheduling that he himself had experienced at Marischal College, structuring the daily routine of his classes according to Bacon's instruction. He typically began class, as was the custom in his days at Marischal, with a lecture complete with examples to demonstrate specific points. Next, he structured an interactive session to categorize those facts and draw conclusions from them, and not infrequently he conducted an experimental demonstration to confirm or disprove the hypotheses formed in the second stage. The interactive portion of the class followed the tradition of a question-and-answer session and was frequently capped by an experimental demonstration or a sophistic contest in declamation. Part of the class would advocate for one side of an issue and the remaining part of the class the other side. The two groups would then switch positions. The following class often started with a review and discussion of lessons learned in the previous session. The substance of the lectures would either be new information that came to Small by way of friends or associates, or was patterned after his Scottish instruction, where professors would use the same set of lectures verbatim for generations.

Two outgrowths of his popular lecture style and demonstrations were the admission of several of his students to the exclusive intellectual club known as the Partie Quarree and the more inclusive Virginia Society for the Encouragement of Arts and Manufacturing in addition to these stimulating activities, George Wythe and Small held informal and extramural forums for current and past pupils outside of regular instruction. Wythe held mock courts, Peyton

Randolph held sessions discussing politics, and Small held sway with free-ranging discussions of science, literature, and philosophy. The symposia were so "unconscious" and "elastic" that they had neither formal rules nor an established place of meeting. This was perhaps a common practice in Scottish universities.[59] James Madison had the same experience and remained at Princeton after graduation for extra instruction under the supervision of John Witherspoon—another Scottish academic trained at the University of Edinburgh. Madison has been called the first graduate student in the colonies, but Small had already departed from Virginia before Witherspoon arrived in New Jersey.

NOTES

1. The specific courses are listed in H. Lewis Ulman's work *The Minutes of the Aberdeen Philosophical Society, 1758–1773* (Aberdeen: Aberdeen University Press, 1990), 22. First year—Classics; second year—Classics, Natural and Civic History, Geography, Chronology, Arithmetic, Algebra, and Plain Geometry; third year—Criticism and Belles Lettres, Natural and Experimental Philosophy, Spherical Trigonometry, Spherical Geometry, and Higher Algebra; fourth year—Logic, Metaphysics, Pneumatology, Natural Theology, Moral Philosophy, Higher Algebra, Quadrature of Curves, Fluxions, and Newton's Principles of Philosophy.

2. Ibid.

3. Jennifer Carter and Colin McLaren, *Crown and Gown: An Illustrated History of the University of Aberdeen* (Aberdeen: Aberdeen University Press, 1995), 59.

4. Paul Woods, "Science and the Aberdeen Enlightenment" in *Philosophy and Science in the Scottish Enlightenment*, ed. Peter Jones (Edinburgh: John Donald Publishers, 1988), 46.

5. Steven Lynn, "Johnson's Rambler and Eighteenth-Century Rhetoric," *Eighteenth-Century Studies* 19, no.4 (Summer 1986): 466.

6. Ulman, *Minutes of the Aberdeen Philosophical Society, 1758–1773*, 35.

7. In 1755, his *Plan of Education in the Marischal College and University of Aberdeen, with the reasons of it*, which advocated a change from the regenting system to the professorial system, was printed by order of the faculty. *Fasti Academicae Mariscallanae Aberdonensis*, ed. P .J. Anderson (Aberdeen: New Spalding Club, 1898), 2:45.

8. Ulman, *Minutes of the Aberdeen Philosophical Society, 1758–1773*, 35.

9. "The Statutes of the College of William and Mary in Virginia," *William and Mary Quarterly*, 1st ser., vol. 16, no. 4 (April 1908): 254.

10. Ibid.

11. Ibid., 248.

12. Lyon G. Tyler, *Williamsburg: The Old Colonial Capital* (Richmond: Whittet & Shepperson, 1907), 134.

13. "The Statutes of the College of William and Mary in Virginia," 247.

14. Robert Polk Thomson, "The Reform of the College of William and Mary, 1763–1780," *Proceedings of the American Philosophical Society* 115, no. 3 (June 17, 1971): 202.

15. Ibid.

16. Ibid. With the exception of an honorary degree to Benjamin Franklin in 1756, there is no documented evidence of degrees being awarded until 1770 when the Botetourt Medals were awarded. According to Thad Tate, co-author of *The History of William and Mary* and former history professor at the college, "The hoop-la that surrounded the ceremony awarding the medals suggest that this was the first time degrees had been granted." In 1769 the Board of Visitors had appropriated money for the casting of the medals. Personal communication, Thad Tate to Martin Clagett, September 5, 2002.

17. Ulman, *Minutes of the Aberdeen Philosophical Society*, 22.

18. Jefferson described Pneumatics as "the theory of air, its weight, motion, condensation, rarefaction, &c." "Report of the Commissioners for the University of Virginia," August 4, 1818, in *The Writings of Thomas Jefferson*, ed. Merrill Peterson (New York: Literary Classics of the United States, 1984), 463.

19. *Scots Magazine* 14 (December 1753): 606.

20. Ulman, *Minutes of the Aberdeen Philosophical Society*, 22.

21. One errant book belonging to William Small was left behind at William and Mary; it was entitled *The Description and Use of Globes and the Orrery*, ed. J. Harris (London: Wright & Cushee, 1731), marginalia corrections in Small's hand.

22. Thomson, "The Reform of the College of William and Mary, 1763–1780," 202.

23. William Allen, ed., *American Biographical Dictionary* (Baltimore, 1809), s.v., "Letter of Questions Posed to John Page from Skelton Jones," tipped in between pages 464 and 465 (originally from another book), Special Collections, Swem Library, College of William and Mary, Williamsburg, Virginia (hereafter cited as Swem Library). Courtesy of Miss Margaret Cook.

24. Walter Jones to Thomas Jones, n.d., Jones Family Papers, Library of Congress, Washington, D.C. (hereafter cited as LC).

25. Ibid.

26. *Virginia Gazette* Daybooks, Special Collections, Small Library, University of Virginia, Charlottesville (hereafter cited as UVA).

27. Carter and McLaren, *Crown and Gown, 1495–1995*, 59; see also *Scots Magazine* (Edinburgh: Sands, Brymer, Murray & Cochran, 1753): 14:606.

28. John Page to Thomas Jefferson, August 19, 1778, Thomas Jefferson Papers, LC.

29. Harris, *The Description and Use of Globes and the Orrery*.

30. *Virginia Gazette* Daybooks, September 5, 1764, Special Collections, Small Library, UVA.

31. Thomas Jefferson to John Walker, September 3, 1769, in *The Papers of Thomas Jefferson*, ed. Julian P. Boyd (Princeton: Princeton University Press, 1950), 1:32.

32. Personal communication, Thomas Baughan to Martin Clagett, June 5, 2017.

33. Thomas Jefferson to Bishop Madison, December 29, 1811, in *The Writings of Thomas Jefferson*, ed. Albert Bergh (Washington: Thomas Jefferson Memorial Association, 1907), 19:183.

34. Walter Jones to Thomas Jones, June 7, 1762, Special Collections, Faculty-Alumni Records, Swem Library.

35. Ibid.

36. Bills for Books, Jones Family Papers, LC. William Duncan, Small's Professor, famously translated *Caesar's Commentaries* (London: J. and R. Tonson, 1753).

37. *Virginia Gazette* Daybooks, April 7, 1764, Special Collections, Small Library, UVA.

38. Aulus Gellius, *Noctium Atticarum* (Leiden: Ludgini Batvorum, 1706). See also E. Millicent Sowerby, *Catalogue of the Library of Thomas Jefferson* (Washington: Library of Congress, 1952), 5:161.

39. Lyon G. Tyler, "The Statutes of the College of William and Mary," *William and Mary Quarterly*, 1st ser., vol. 14, no. 2 (October 1905): 72.

40. Carter and McLaren, *Crown and Gown*, 59.

41. Thomas Jefferson, *The Writings of Thomas Jefferson, Autobiography* (New York: Literary Classics of the United States, 1984), 4.

42. *Virginia Gazette* Daybooks, September 5, 1764, Special Collections, Small Library, UVA.

43. "Errata: Errata: Virginia Troops in French and Indian Wars," *Virginia Magazine of History and Biography* 2, no. 2 (October 1894): 226.

44. Wilber Samuel Howell, "The Declaration of Independence and Eighteenth-Century Logic," *William and Mary Quarterly*, 3rd series, vol. 18, no. 4 (October 1961): 472.

45. "Errata: Errata: Virginia Troops in French and Indian Wars," 226.

46. Whitfield J. Bell, Jr., "Some American Students of That Shining Oracle of Physic, Dr. William Cullen of Edinburgh, 1755–1766," *Proceedings of the American Philosophical Society* 94, no. 3 (June 1950): 280.

47. R. H. Girdwood, "The Influence of Scotland on North American Medicine," in *The Influence of Scottish Medicine*, ed. Derek Dow (London: Butler & Tanner, 1988), 36.

48. Ibid., 38.

49. Ibid., 36. The attestation of a mentoring physician was often more-highly regarded than an actual diploma and cap and gown exercises that were prohibitively expensive.

50. Ibid., 39.

51. Benjamin Franklin's letter of introduction of [Benjamin] Rush and [Jonathon] Potts to [Dr. William] Cullen and Sir Alexander Dick was written several months later. Franklin noted that "they are at Edinburgh to improve themselves in the Study of Physic, and from the character they bear of Ingenuity, Industry and good Morals, I am persuaded they will improve greatly under your learned Lectures and do Honour to your medical school." Benjamin Franklin to William Cullen, December 20, 1766, in *Science and Society in Early America* (Philadelphia: American Philosophical Society, 1986), 120.

52. "I wrote you a letter with the Bills by the way of Whitehaven, in which I informed you of all the news I then had. Nothing important has since occurred, only that Drs Gregory, Cullen & Black are the professors, for the first season, of Practice, Institutes & chemistry and exceed, each in Their several Departments, the great Expectations the public had formed of them." Walter Jones to Thomas Jones, Edinburgh, November 29, 1766, Jones Family Papers, LC.

53. *Virginia Gazette* Daybooks, August 3, 1764, Special Collections, Small Library, UVA. See also William Lewis, *The New Dispensatory: Containing the Theory and Practice of Pharmacy* (London: J. Nourse, 1753), multiple editions; likely William Cheseldon, *The Anatomy of the Human Body* (London: Hitch and Dodsley, 1750), multiple editions.

54. Warner Lewis to Walter Jones, July 8, 1766, Edrington Family Papers, Mss., MSS1Ed274a437, Virginia Museum of History and Culture, Richmond.

55. Thomas Jefferson to John Page, May 25, 1766, in Boyd, *Papers of Thomas Jefferson*, 1:18.

56. See Martin Clagett, *Scientific Jefferson: Revealed* (Charlottesville: University of Virginia Press, 2009), 53–69.

57. "Papers Relating to the College," *William and Mary Quarterly*, 1st ser., vol. 16, no. 3 (January 1908): 162–173.

58. Ibid.

59. "It was not unusual for a student to remain at college even after his normal course of study. There could be any number of reasons for this—having a tutor's post, having yet to satisfy the presbytery regulations for license, expecting or hoping for some particular post etc., etc. ... It was by no means uncommon for some divinity students to stick around after completing their normal courses." Personal communication from Robert Smart, Archivist Emeritus to the University of St. Andrews, to Martin Clagett, May 18, 2007.

CHAPTER 8

William Small and Thomas Jefferson

SMALL AND JEFFERSON

It is easy to forget that when Thomas Jefferson went to Williamsburg, he was still a boy whose attentions were focused on horses, tricks on his friends, and, above all, on the young ladies. Jefferson is often depicted as riding out of the mists of the mountains, into the relative sophistication of Williamsburg, a man—but also an impressionable and vulnerable child of seventeen, who had only recently lost his father.

The strange confluence of circumstances that put William Small in charge of William and Mary's curriculum allowed him to exert a personal influence on a number of students who would be instrumental in the conception, birth, and development of the United States of America. It also enabled Small, who had been left in charge of the institution, by default, to initiate substantial changes in teaching methods and foci of learning at the College of William and Mary at a critical juncture in the history of the country.[1] Many of Small's students, having been indoctrinated into the pragmaticism of the Scottish Enlightenment, employed the inherent doctrines to guide them during a period of turbulent and often confusing change in social, scientific, and political matters. Jefferson, more than any other, would take the knowledge he acquired in Small's classroom to the forefront of the American Revolution, cementing his place in history with the birth of a new republic.

Jefferson acknowledged William Small's impact on his life, to "his enlightened and affectionate guidance of my studies while at college I am indebted for everything."[2] Nor was he exaggerating, for the linear and logical schemata that undergirded Jefferson's choices and decisions throughout his life, the cool and precise scientific methodology that was the framework of his decision-making processes, the openness to exploring questions of religion, moral philosophy, and politics, the elegance and refinement of his writing, his diction, and his scholarship derived from his study of classical literature and the tenets of Common Sense Philosophy under the guidance of William Small.

Writing in his autobiography many years later, Jefferson gave an elegant and informationally rich description of the man who had been his mentor and had had a lasting impression on him.

> It was my great good Fortune, and what probably fixed the destinies of my life that Dr. Wm. Small of Scotland was then professor of Mathematics, a man profound in the most useful branches of science, with a happy talent of communication, correct and gentlemanly manners, & an enlarged & liberal mind. He most happily for me, became soon attached to me & made me his daily companion when not engaged in school; and from his conversations I got my first views of the expansion of science & of the system of things in which we are placed. Fortunately the Philosophical chair became vacant soon after my arrival at college, and he was appointed to fill it per interim: and he was the first who ever gave regular lectures in Ethics, Rhetoric & Belles letters.[3]

Small's importance to Jefferson and his other students was not restricted to classroom instruction; he also served as a road sign to the future, as a template of philosophical and intellectual ambition, and, most important, as a friend and confidant. After the passage of almost half a century, Jefferson confided to Louis Hue Girardin that, "Dr. Small was … to me as a father."[4] Jefferson recalled the important role that his three mentors had played in his youth and the salutary effect they had, collectively and individually, exerted on the formation of his character and the path that he determined to take in life. He wrote to his grandson and namesake—Thomas Jefferson Randolph:

> I had the good fortune to become acquainted very early with some characters of very high standing, and to feel the incessant wish that I could ever become what they were. Under temptations and difficulties, I would ask myself what would Dr. Small, Mr. Wythe, Peyton Randolph do in this situation? What course in it will assure me their approbation? I am certain that this mode of deciding my conduct, tended more to correctness than any reasoning powers I possessed. Knowing the even and dignified line they pursued, I could never doubt for a moment which of the two courses would be in character for them. Whereas, seeking the same object through a process of moral reasoning, and with the jaundiced eye of youth, I should have often erred. From the circumstances of my position, I was often thrown into the society of horse racers, card players, fox hunters, scientific and professional men, and of dignified men; and many a time have I asked myself, in the enthusiastic moment of the death of a fox, the victory of a favorite horse, the issue of a question eloquently argued at the bar, or in the great council of the nation, well, which kinds of reputation should I prefer? That of a horse jockey? A fox hunter? An orator? Or an honest advocate of my country's rights. Be assured, my dear Jefferson, that these little returns into ourselves, this self-catechising habit, is not trifling or useless, but leads to prudent selection and a steady pursuit of what is right.[5]

THE IMPACT OF THE SCOTTISH
ENLIGHTENMENT ON JEFFERSON

Jefferson was born into a century already steeped with change and discovery. The way in which man viewed himself, his relationship with God, and his own position in "the system in which we are placed" evolved as radically and rapidly as in any period before. This era of systematic and scientific progress is generally referred to as the Enlightenment. Although variations on the Enlightenment manifested themselves in different societies, all versions shared the common belief in the supremacy of reason and the betterment of the human condition. Scottish Enlightenment philosophy, and, in particular, the "Common Sense School of Philosophy," was a brand of reasoning, centered around concrete methods of improvement and the overall well-being of a nation's citizenry.

William Small brought many facets of the Common Sense Philosophy to Virginia. Two of the most important focused on science and democracy. If one were to be judged by his intellect, integrity, and industry, it would surely open up a society based on merit and establish an aristocracy of intellect, one based on reason and honesty, not dogma, superstition, or disinformation. While pragmatic subjects were of primary interest, Jefferson took the conventional view concerning the subject of moral philosophy. He thought that "it lost time to attend lectures in this branch."[6] With distilled echoes of Thomas Reid,[7] Jefferson expressed the essence of the Common Sense moral philosophy and his adherence to it in a letter to his grandson:

> Moral philosophy. I think it lost time to attend lectures in this branch. He who made us would have been a pitiful bungler if he had made the rules of our moral conduct a matter of science.... [Man] was endowed with a sense of right and wrong merely relative to this. This sense is as much a part of his nature as the sense of hearing, seeing, feeling; it is the true foundation of morality, and not the truth, &c., as fanciful writers have imagined. The moral sense, or

conscience, is as much a part of man as his leg or arm. It is given to all human beings in a stronger or weaker degree, as force of members is given them in a greater or less degree. It may be strengthened by exercise, as may any particular limb of the body. This sense is submitted indeed in some degree to the guidance of reason; but it is a small stock which is required for this: even a less one than what we call Common sense. State a moral case to a ploughman and a professor. The former will decide it as well, and often better than the latter, because he has not been led astray by artificial rules.[8]

Jefferson's most-famous scientific work, *Notes on the State of Virginia*, is in many ways a reflection of the statistical surveys completed by early Scottish Enlightenment thinkers, often assisted in data collection by local clergymen. *Notes* is primarily a compendium of observations and data collections, marshaled in such a way as to make the information useful and applicable. Jefferson's objectives in the volume were not only to answer questions and make utile compilations, but also to support his own political and social theories with scientific evidence. This same exacting process is seen in Jefferson's formation of the University of Virginia. The efficacious arrangement of subjects to be taught, the educational methodology to be employed, the professors to be hired, and even the architectural positioning of buildings on the Grounds were manifestations of Jefferson's philosophical worldview.

Jefferson's *Notes* may be regarded as a political document as well as a scientific one, in that he repudiated the assertions of George-Louis Leclerc, Count of Buffon, that the North American continent, having recently emerged from the broiling oceans, produced a degenerative effect on the physical, mental, and moral natures of man and beast. Buffon asserted that native American animals and humans were smaller and less robust than their European counterparts, having been compromised by the nature of the fetid and gaseous conditions of the continent. In addition, Buffon also proposed that once transported to America, both man and beast would generationally diminish in size and strength and that their intellect and moral fortitude would incrementally grow frailer until the inhabitants were reduced to shadows of their former selves. To refute the absurdities of the notion, Jefferson employed the technique that served as the primary instrument of the improvement efforts of the leaders of the Scottish Enlightenment—data collection, surveys scientifically ordered and organized, and considered and reasoned analysis.

Jefferson and others were often demonized for the atheistic tendencies attributed to the scientifically inclined. As discussed, however, Scottish clergymen were at the forefront of the Enlightenment movement in their country, and among the most vocal advocates of the Newtonian precepts. Instead of seeing science as a tool to diminish the relevance of God and the intercession of the Church, they saw a cosmos ordered on scientific principles as an affirmation of the existence and power of God. Throughout his life, Jefferson promoted science, utility, and improvement using the hallmarks of the Common Sense Philosophy. In everything he did, he sought something that led to the betterment of the lives of his fellow citizens, accomplished by reasoned and useful means, following scientific principles.

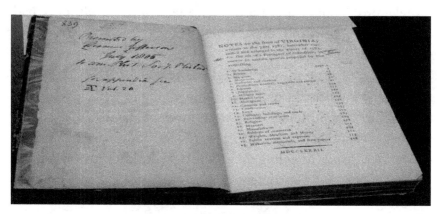

Jefferson's Presentation Copy of *Notes on the State of Virginia*.
American Philosophical Society

THE DECLARATION OF INDEPENDENCE

In 1837, George Tucker, a cousin of St. George Tucker, wrote the first comprehensive biography of Thomas Jefferson. Jefferson had long been a friend to various members of the Tucker family and St. George had, like Jefferson, studied law with George Wythe. Jefferson strongly encouraged the Board of Visitors at the University of Virginia to hire George Tucker as the Professor of Moral Philosophy and on March 9, 1825, he wrote Tucker that the Board had "unanimously appointed you Professor of the school of Moral Philosophy."[9]

Tucker emigrated from Bermuda to Williamsburg in 1795 to study law at the College of William and Mary with George Wythe. While in town he lived at the home of his cousin St. George Tucker. St. George not only had links to Thomas Jefferson through the common instruction of Wythe but also through mutual friendships—especially with Governor John Page and his wife, Margaret Lowther Page.

Governor Page was residing in Richmond at the time of his death and after his passing Mrs. Page returned first to the family estate, Rosewell, and finding it too isolated, she moved into Williamsburg to stay at the home of St. George Tucker, taking along not only her luggage and her husband's papers, but also, presumably, many of the papers that Thomas Jefferson had left with him. Therefore, beside his relationship and conversations with Jefferson himself, Page had access to a rich trove of Jefferson's letters and papers from the earlier part of Jefferson's life.[10]

It is of special significance to take note both of the proximity of time of the publication of Tucker's biography to Jefferson's death, the closeness and intimacy of their personal and family connections, and the access that Tucker had to both Jefferson's papers and his perspectives, when assessing the accuracy of the information and the validity of Jefferson's sentiments.

George Tucker wrote in respect to the impact of Small, "The value of such a friend and preceptor is scarcely to be estimated. But for the incidents of so varied a course of instruction, it may be fairly presumed that Mr. Jefferson would not have been the author of the papers which gave him reputation…; he would not have been placed on the committee that drew the Declaration of Independence; or, if we can believe that he would nevertheless have been in the first place…, we may safely say that the Declaration, as well as other papers drawn by him, would have been far less worthy of their elevated purposes, and less an object of pride to the nation, and of honour to their author."[11]

The influence of Scottish Enlightenment philosophy on Jefferson is, as Tucker implied, quite apparent when analyzing the Declaration of Independence. William Duncan, Small's former Professor of Natural Philosophy, wrote *The Elements of Logick*, which was popular in the colonies and had been available in the *Gazette* Bookstore for almost a decade before Small arrived in Virginia. In addition, Small certainly would have used his notes and directions from Duncan's class in Natural Philosophy to instruct his own charges at the College of William and Mary. Small's lectures and Duncan's logic were essential foundations of Jefferson's philosophy, which would form the propositions of the Declaration.

Some authors have ascribed Jefferson's inspiration for the philosophical underpinnings of the Declaration to the French philosophes, others to the writings of John Locke. Carl Becker's interpretations as represented in *The Declaration of Independence*, first printed in 1922, fortified that perception. Hans Eichols commented on the variety of theories concerning the likely fountainheads of inspiration as having included "the Lockean reading (most widely accepted), the Scottish moral sense reading, the democratic egalitarian thesis, and even a religious deistic perspective."[12]

Controversy surrounding the Declaration's philosophic provenance extends back almost to the time of Declaration's writing. John Adams once expressed the opinion that Virginians garnered all the plum positions, including the composition of the Declaration of Independence, and Jefferson may have just been the first on the list of that committee, or that it may have fallen to him by default. Some later asserted that Jefferson had plagiarized the Declaration, to which

Jefferson calmly replied in a letter to James Madison, "Pickering's observations, and Mr. Adams' in addition, that it contained no new ideas, that it is a commonplace compilation, its sentiments hacknied in Congress for two years before and it's essence contained in Otis' pamphlet, may all be true. Of that I am not to be the judge. Richard H. Lee charged it as copied from Locke's treatise on Government. Otis' pamphlet I never saw, & whether I had gathered my ideas from reading or reflection I do not know. I know only that I turned to neither book nor pamphlet while writing it. I did not consider it as any part of my charge to invent new ideas altogether & to offer no sentiment which had ever been expressed before."[13]

In short, the substance and style of the Declaration had been drawn from Jefferson's experience and education. In a very polite and gentle rebuff, Jefferson wrote to Henry Lee, towards the end of his life in regard to Lee's allegation that the content and ideas were lifted from Locke.

> When forced, therefore, to resort to arms for redress, an appeal to the tribunal of the world was deemed proper for our justification. This was the object of the Declaration of Independence. Not to find out new principles, or new arguments, never before thought of, not merely to say things which had never been said before; but to place before mankind the *common sense* of the subject, in terms so plain and firm as to command their assent, and to justify ourselves in the independent stand we are compelled to take. Neither aiming at originality of principle or sentiment, nor yet copied from any particular and previous writing, it was intended to be an expression of the American mind, and to give to that expression the proper tone and spirit called for by the occasion. All its authority rests then on the harmonizing sentiments of the day, whether expressed in conversation, in letters, printed essays, or in the elementary books of public right, as Aristotle, Cicero, Locke, Sidney, etc.[14]

Jefferson may have not paid strict attention to the details of attribution, but even in his letter to Lee it is curious to see the term "common sense." His reply to Lee also affirms his conformation (perhaps unconsciously) to the precepts of the Scottish Enlightenment through the philosophy of Duncan, Reid, and Small.

Garry Wills argued with elegance and logic that Jefferson had not been persuaded by the philosophes of France (as earlier scholars had asserted) but rather by the persuasive arguments and optimistic conclusions of a collective group of virtuosi, informed clergymen and progressive patrons, and pragmatic professors from the remote regions of Scotland. The alarm that Wills provoked with his rebuke of the Declaration's French origins may have risen to the level of exasperation that Jefferson's *Notes on Virginia* caused to the devotees of Count Buffon and his theories of degeneration of flora and fauna in the New World. Wills succinctly concluded his arguments for the Common Sense origin of the Declaration as follows:

> The ideas expressed by Jefferson in 1776 were first introduced to him, and examined by him, in the prior decade of intense reading and discussion that formed his mind. These same ideas went into his major philosophic work, the *Notes on the State of Virginia*, composed five years after the Declaration, when Jefferson had made only a few short journeys outside of Virginia. Those ideas were not derived primarily from Philadelphia or Paris, but from Aberdeen, Edinburgh and Glasgow. We have enough evidence of his reading, and of his conclusions from that reading to establish that the real lost world of Thomas Jefferson was the world of William Small, the invigorating realm of the Scottish Enlightenment at its zenith.[15]

STRUCTURAL PARALLELS: THE ELEMENTS OF LOGICK *AND* THE DECLARATION OF INDEPENDENCE

While the content of the Declaration was likely a fortuitous confluence of multiple metaphysical authorities of various ages, nations, and philosophical precepts, the structure of the document directly and precisely reflects the axioms of William Duncan. In terms of logical argumentation and progression, the steps laid out by Jefferson strictly adhere to those advocated in *The Elements of Logick*.

Duncan explained that an important element in establishing a self-evident truth is to state first one's definitions of the words used in an initial statement. He used the most unambiguous example— mathematicians, who proceed along lines that can be commonly understood, no matter what language one may speak, and deal with matters that are inherently objective. But, even to mathematicians, Duncan interjected the following caveat.

> First, then, it is to be observed, that (mathematicians) have been very careful in ascertaining their ideas, and fixing the significations of their terms. For this purpose they begin with definitions, in which the meaning of their words is so distinctly explained, that they cannot fail to excite in the mind of an attentive reader the very same ideas as are annexed to them by the writer.[16]

Duncan then instructed, once definitions are determined, that it is necessary to articulate the general matter in a clear and concise way and the "next care is, to lay down some self-evident truths, which may serve as a foundation for their future reasonings. And here, indeed, they proceed with remarkable circumspection, admitting no principles but what flow immediately from their definitions, and necessarily force themselves upon a mind in any degree attentive to its perceptions."[17]

Finally, the conclusion, will be undeniable if "by a clear series of proofs, we can make out the truth proposed, insomuch that self-evidence shall accompany every step of the procedure, we are then able to demonstrate what we assert ... whoever understands the terms made use of, perceives, at first glance, the truth of what is asserted; nor can he, by any efforts, bring himself to believe the contrary. The proposition therefore is *self-evident*, and such that it is impossible by reasoning to make it plainer; because there is no truth more obvious."[18]

Garry Wills was not the only scholar to detect the influence of the Scottish Enlightenment in the Declaration. Wilbur Howell noted, "It is difficult to believe that the word 'self-evident' appears at this point in the Declaration by mere chance. Jefferson is laying down the major premise ... that constitutes the whole demonstrative strategy of the Declaration ... to ... compel the assent of mankind."[19] Howell persuasively maintained that "if we may consider that the beginning words of Jefferson's immortal document have the effect of a logical definition, so far as they bring his present purposes into relation with a specific series of disruptive events, on the one hand, and with the generalized 'respect of the opinions of mankind,' on the other, then it is obvious that the Declaration as a whole fits Duncan's recommended plan for a demonstrative proof. For after that opening, almost as if Duncan were looking over his shoulder, Jefferson next undertook to 'lay down some self-evident Truths,' which served as the foundation of his future reasonings."[20]

In the Declaration of Independence, Jefferson follows Duncan's sequential instructions for setting out the definition of intent in a clear and coherent fashion.

> When in the Course of human events, it becomes necessary for one people to dissolve the political bands which have connected them with another, and to assume among the powers of the earth, the separate and equal station to which the Laws of Nature and of Nature's God entitle them, a decent respect to the opinions of mankind requires that they should declare the causes which impel them to the separation.[21]

Jefferson next follows Duncan's instruction "to lay down some self-evident truths, which may serve as a foundation for their future reasonings," in the most explicit terms.

We hold these truths to be self-evident, that all men are created
equal, that they are endowed by their Creator with certain unalien-
able Rights, that among these are Life, Liberty and the pursuit of
Happiness. That to secure these rights, Governments are instituted
among Men, deriving their just powers from the consent of the governed, That whenever any Form of Government becomes destructive
of these ends, it is the Right of the People to alter or to abolish it,
and to institute new Government, laying its foundation on such
principles and organizing its powers in such form, as to them shall
seem most likely to effect their Safety and Happiness. Prudence,
indeed, will dictate that Governments long established should not
be changed for light and transient causes; and accordingly all experience hath shewn, that mankind are more disposed to suffer, while
evils are sufferable, than to right themselves by abolishing the forms
to which they are accustomed. But when a long train of abuses and
usurpations, pursuing invariably the same Object evinces a design
to reduce them under absolute Despotism, it is their right, it is their
duty, to throw off such Government, and to provide new Guards for
their future security. Such has been the patient sufferance of these
Colonies; and such is now the necessity which constrains them to
alter their former Systems of Government. The history of the present
King of Great Britain is a history of repeated injuries and usurpations, all having in direct object the establishment of an absolute
Tyranny over these States. To prove this, let Facts be submitted to
a candid world.[22]

Duncan's subsequent dictum involves laying out demonstrated
proofs or corollaries that proceed "with remarkable circumspection, admitting no principles but what flow immediately from their
definitions, and necessarily force themselves upon a mind in any
degree attentive to its perceptions." Jefferson detailed very explicit
charges against King George III to convince his audience that the
king indeed was the very definition of a tyrant, that the rebellion had
not taken place for "light and transient causes," and that it had only
been considered after "a long train of abuses and usurpations" meant
to reduce the colonies "under absolute Despotism." Jefferson made

certain that "by a clear series of proofs" the audience could "make out the truth proposed" and that "self-evidence had accompanied every step of the procedure" by which he was "able to demonstrate" what he had put forth. Indeed, whoever understood the terms, would perceive, at first glance, the truth of what was asserted. Nor could the reader, "by any efforts, bring himself to believe the contrary." Jefferson added the justification for the break not only with the British king but also with the British nation in the last of the list of charges.

> We have warned them from time to time of attempts by their legislature to extend an unwarrantable jurisdiction over us. We have reminded them of the circumstances of our emigration and settlement here. We have appealed to their native justice and magnanimity, and we have conjured them by the ties of our common kindred to disavow these usurpations, which, would inevitably interrupt our connections and correspondence. They too must have been deaf to the voice of justice and of consanguinity.[23]

Having set forth the statement of the case, the self-evident truths, and the propositions stemming from those first principles, in a logical and linear order, Jefferson followed Duncan's last rule of argumentation that stated, when "all the previous propositions of a demonstration, [are] manifestly true, the last conclusion, or proposition to be demonstrated, must be so too."

> WE, THEREFORE, THE REPRESENTATIVES OF THE UNITED STATES OF AMERICA, in General Congress, Assembled, appealing to the Supreme Judge of the world for the rectitude of our intentions, do, in the Name, and by authority of the good People of these Colonies, solemnly publish and declare, That, these United Colonies are, and of, Right ought to be FREE AND INDEPENDENT STATES; that they are Absolved from all Allegiance to the British Crown, and that all political connection between them and the State of Great Britain, is and ought to be totally dissolved; and that as Free and Independent States, they have full Power to levy War, conclude Peace, contract

Alliances, establish Commerce, and to do all other Acts and Things which Independent States may of right do. And for the support of this Declaration, with a firm reliance on the protection of Divine Providence, we mutually pledge to each other our Lives, our Fortunes and our sacred Honor.[24]

Whether Jefferson was deliberately adhering to the formal sequencing of rhetorical argumentation or unconsciously drawing on his college experiences, the points of connection between the logical construction in the Declaration and the instructions of the *Elements of Logick* are, according to Duncan's definition, *self-evident*. Likewise, it is difficult to believe that the exhaustive nature of data collection, the intentional and efficacious organization, and the calculated presentation of both the details of the investigation and rationale of its conclusions expressed in the *Notes of the State of Virginia* are not explicitly modified from a typical Scottish survey model to fit the political, social, and scientific needs of a study in natural history.

SCIENCE AND MATHEMATICS

While Small had an unparalleled influence on Jefferson's political philosophy, he also was responsible for Jefferson's "canine" interest of science and mathematics. These subjects were so inherently ingrained in Jefferson's nature that they permeated every sector of his life. In his first extant letter, he used mathematics to rationalize his desire to attend the College of William and Mary, "as I stay in the Mountains the Loss of one fourth of my Time is inevitable."[25] At the funeral of his childhood friend and brother-in-law, Dabney Carr, a time of intense grief, Jefferson calculated, by what he observed, how long it would take the gravediggers to dig up an acre of land.[26] He also planned a more extended education for his daughter than was customary because "the chance that in marriage she will draw a blockhead I calculate at about fourteen to one, and of course the education of her family will probably rest on her own ideas and direction without assistance."[27]

Jefferson's innate mental agility was sharpened and reimagined by his studies with Small, who introduced him to the finer points of geometry, algebra, fluxions, and their interrelationship with surveying, astronomy, meteorology, metrics, physics, and measurements. Jefferson expressed his debt to Small's instruction, and his qualities as a math and science teacher, writing, "I have been for some time rubbing up my mathematics from the rust contracted by fifty years' pursuits of a different kind. And thanks to the good foundation laid at college by my old master and friend Small, I am doing it with a delight and success beyond my expectation."[28]

Moreover, Jefferson applied the mathematical and scientific skills learned in the classrooms of Wren Hall throughout his life. He developed the Mouldboard of Least Resistance (a plow), set up decimal coinage for the United States in 1784,[29] acted as the first director and arbitrator of the Patent Office of the United States,[30] promoted the oldest scientific bureau in the United States government—the Coast Survey[31]—and supported and directed one of the greatest scientific surveys ever attempted, the Lewis and Clark expedition. There is even an interesting note in Jefferson's *Memorandum Books* in which he referenced a scheme, with explicit directions on how to develop a water mill on Small's plan.[32] His other contributions to science and math are almost too numerous to recount, many of which he initiated in his later years.

Jefferson's interest in electricity was likely initiated in Small's classroom demonstration, or in conversations at the Governor's Palace. Indeed, Small had purchased an "electrical machine" for use at the college from Edward Nairne in London. It is certain that the primary source for his philosophical and scientific inclinations was William Small, from whom, Jefferson affirmed, "I got my first views of the expansion of science & of the system of things in which we are placed."

NOTES

1. The Statutes of 1758 left it up to the professor's discretion to choose the subjects and materials for their classes and Small, with no seeming opposition, revolutionized both the curriculum and the teaching methods at the College of William and Mary and by extension the other institutions of higher learning in North America.

2. Thomas Jefferson to L. H. Girardin, January 15, 1815, Thomas Jefferson Papers, General Correspondence, Library of Congress, Washington, D.C. (hereafter cited as LC).

3. Thomas Jefferson, *The Writings of Thomas Jefferson: Autobiography*, ed. Merrill Peterson (New York: Literary Classics of the United States, 1984), 4.

4. Thomas Jefferson to L. H. Girardin, January 15, 1815, Thomas Jefferson Papers, General Correspondence, LC.

5. Thomas Jefferson to Thomas Jefferson Randolph, November 25, 1808, in *The Life and Selected Writings of Thomas Jefferson*, ed. Adrienne Koch and William Peden (New York: Random House, 1944), 540–541.

6. Thomas Jefferson to Peter Carr, August 10, 1787, Thomas Jefferson Papers, LC.

7. Compare with Thomas Reid: "Perception whether original or acquired, implies no exercise of reason; and is common to men, children, idiots, and brutes" (Thomas Reid, *An Inquiry into the Human Mind on the Principles of Common Sense,* ed. Derek Brooks [Edinburgh: Edinburgh University Press, 1997], 173). "The five external senses ... claim to be the first considered in an analysis" (Reid, *Inquiry,* 24). "When I look at the Moon, I perceive her to be sometimes circular, sometimes horned, and sometimes gibbous. This is a simple perception, and is the same in a philosopher, and in the clown" (Reid, *Inquiry,* 172). "It is genius, not the want of it, that adulterates philosophy, and fills it with error and false theory. A creative imagination distains the mean offices of digging for a foundation, of removing rubbish, and of carrying materials; leaving the servile employments to the drudges in science, it plans a design, raises a fabric. Invention supplies materials where they are wanting, and fancy adds colouring, and every befitting ornament. The work pleases the eye, and wants nothing but solidity and a good foundation" (Reid, *Inquiry,* 15). Like Jefferson's composition of the Declaration, this statement seems to be an unconscious amalgamation and distillation of concepts and precepts that he has gathered and put away in the storehouse of his mind like the notes written on scraps of paper from his youth that he retrieved for use in the *Notes on the State of Virginia.*

8. Thomas Jefferson to Peter Carr, August 10, 1787, *The Papers of Thomas Jefferson*, ed. Julian P. Boyd (Princeton: Princeton University Press, 1955), 12:14–19.

9. Thomas Jefferson to George Tucker, March 9, 1825, Founders Online, National Archives and Records Administration, Washington, D.C., https://founders .archives.gov/about/Jefferson (accessed July 29, 2021).

10. "From John Page, Esq., he has received the letters that give a history of Mr. Jefferson's college life, of which there is probably no other memorial extant." George Tucker, *The Life of Thomas Jefferson* (London: Charles Knight and Co., 1837), 1:x.

11. Tucker, *Life of Thomas Jefferson*, 1:22.

12. Hans L. Eichols, *Harmonizing Sentiments* (New York: Peter Lang, 2001), 102.

13. Thomas Jefferson to James Madison, August 30, 1823, Thomas Jefferson Papers, LC.

14. Thomas Jefferson to Henry Lee, May 8, 1825, *The Writings of Thomas Jefferson*, ed. Albert Bergh (Washington: The Thomas Jefferson Memorial Association, 1904), 16:117.

15. Garry Wills, "Or Was Jefferson More Influenced by Scottish Thinkers?" *What Did the Declaration Declare?* (Boston: Bedford/St. Martin's, 1999), 77.

16. William Duncan, *The Elements of Logick* (Albany: E. F. Backus, 1814), 133.

17. Ibid., 135.

18. Ibid., 131.

19. Wilbur Samuel Howell, "The Declaration of Independence and Eighteenth-Century Logic," *William and Mary Quarterly*, 3rd series, vol. 18, no. 4 (October 1961): 478.

20. Ibid., 479.

21. *The Declaration of Independence, 1776: Literal Print* (Washington: Department of State, 1911), 3.

22. Ibid.

23. Ibid., 7.

24. Ibid.

25. Thomas Jefferson to John Harvie, January 14, 1760, in Boyd, *Papers of Thomas Jefferson*, 1:3.

26. "May.22: 2 hands grubbed the Grave yard 80.f.sq = 1/7 of an acre in 3 ½ hours so that one would have done it in 7. Hours, and would grub an acre in 49.hours = 4. Days." Thomas Jefferson. *Thomas Jefferson's Garden Book, 1766–1824*, ed. E. Morris Betts (Charlottesville: Thomas Jefferson Memorial Foundation, 1999), 40.

27. Thomas Jefferson to Duc de Marbois, December 5, 1783, in Boyd, *Papers of Thomas Jefferson*, 6:374.

28. Thomas Jefferson to Bishop Madison, December 29, 1811, in Bergh, *Writings of Thomas Jefferson*, 19:183.

29. Silvio Bedini, *Thomas Jefferson: Statesman of Science* (New York: Macmillan Publishing Company, 1990), 206.

30. Lawrence Kingsland, "The United States Patent Office," *Law and Contemporary Problems* 13, no. 2 (Spring 1948): 356.

31. G. T. Rude, "The Survey of the Continental Shelf," *Scientific Monthly* 34, no. 6 (June 1932): 547.

32. "To make a water mill on Small's plan," Thomas Jefferson, *Jefferson's Memorandum Books*, ed. James Bear and Lucia Stanton (Princeton: Princeton University Press, 1997), 1:282.

CHAPTER 9

Leaving Virginia

As reflected by the growth of the scientific society, the accolades of his students, and his concerns for a set of more advanced and sophisticated scientific instrumentation, William Small's innovations made an enormous impact at the College of William and Mary. Small's time at William and Mary was transformative, but not indefinite. As was often the case in his life, he would make a life-altering decision that changed both his environment and the direction of his life.

THE RETURN OF RICHARD GRAHAM

For almost two years, Small enjoyed relative tranquility at the college. Meanwhile, back in London, John Camm had been doggedly campaigning for both himself and Richard Graham to be reinstated to their former posts. After the Reverend Andrew Burnaby refused the position that was vacated by Jacob Rowe, it was reluctantly offered to Richard Graham.[1] In spite of his frequent complaints about the college,[2] Graham readily accepted and was reinstated as Professor of Moral Philosophy instead of his previous place in Natural Philosophy.

In the same year that the Reverend Graham reappeared in Williamsburg, Small began to advocate for a return to England in order to purchase new scientific apparatus for his classes. In December 1762, the House of Burgesses appropriated £450 for the purpose of purchasing "a proper Apparatus for the Instruction of the Students of the College in Natural and Experimental Philosophy."[3] This was a considerable sum, and the evidence suggests that it was because of Small's insistence and with Governor Francis Fauquier's support that the House of Burgesses agreed to allocate the funds.[4]

SCIENTIFIC APPARATUS

The Burgesses may well have been encouraged by the enthusiasm of their sons for Small's classroom demonstrations and exercises in experimental philosophy, and some Burgesses both were subscribers to and participated in the scientific club. Small quickly volunteered to select the equipment and applied to the Board of Visitors for a leave of absence, but was refused. A member of the Board of Visitors later wrote:

> Our Assembly some Years ago gave the Visitors £450 sterl. To purchase an Apparatus for the use of the College; Mr Small, judging this a favourable Opportunity, proposed to the Visitors to go to England to purchase it, and presuming upon his Interest with them, informed the Visitors that he had a Prospect of doing Some thing advantageous for himself; if he succeeded, he should remain in England, and would desire Nothing for his Trouble in buying this Apparatus, but if not, he expected a Continuance of his Salary, til his Return, his Absence we were given to understand would not exceed eighteen Months.[5]

Either because the Visitors considered eighteen months to be too long a period for Small to be gone, or because they lacked confidence in Richard Graham—a professor who was in the process of litigating against the Board of Visitors and whose academic reputation was judged to be anemic, they denied Small's request. Undeterred,

Small again approached the Board with a written petition, and again came away with the same result. Dudley Digges, one of Small's most intractable enemies on the Board of Visitors, complained to the Bishop of London:

> This Gentleman much displeased that we did not close with his Proposal, at a succeeding Visitation regarding the Application in a written Paper, pen'd more with an Air of Remonstrance than any Thing else, and taxing us with Ingratitude and Inattention to his past Services. The Matter concluded as before.[6]

BENJAMIN FRANKLIN: FRIEND, MENTOR, COLLABORATOR

It was during this unwelcomed hiatus that Small and Benjamin Franklin met and became fast friends in Williamsburg. In his final days, Franklin's Co-Postmaster-General, William Hunter, was under William Small's medical care. Small provided such diligent and compassionate attention to Hunter during his illness that he was named as a beneficiary in Hunter's will—Franklin was the executor. It was when Franklin went to Williamsburg to execute Hunter's will that he and Small became friends and collaborators.[7]

Franklin also met Hunter's replacement, John Foxcroft, and wrote to his colleague Anthony Todd:

> In my last of April 14. I acquainted you that I was then just setting out for Virginia, in order to settle Accounts with Mr. Hunter's Executors who reside there…. In Virginia I met my new Colleague Mr. Foxcroft, and we had many Consultations concerning the Virginia Office.[8]

Foxcroft was Fauquier's personal secretary during the early part of his administration and received his new post with Franklin on Fauquier's recommendation.[9] It is not only possible but even likely that Franklin met conjointly with Fauquier and Small, and it is certain that Franklin and Small developed a friendship during this time for Franklin acted as a colleague and mentor to Small from this time onward and played an active role in providing opportunities and promoting Small to his friends in England. The two men continued their symbiotic relationship until Small's death in 1775.[10]

Interestingly and unremarked on until this time, Franklin and Small collaborated on a new scientific project during the short time Franklin was in Virginia and improved on it in England. It was during this period, in 1763, in Williamsburg, that Small and Franklin began work on an original type of lamp with a cylindrical burner. They continued their refinement of this device once in London, and it was later taken to Birmingham to be produced by Small's employer and friend, Matthew Boulton. Some years later, Ami Argand contacted Boulton about the lamp that was "brought from America by Dr. Small."[11]

It is also likely that during this same visit to Williamsburg that the ever-alert Franklin, seeing the potential in Small, began to entice him to go to England where there might be greater opportunities for pursuing his scientific interests. Franklin may, at this time, have also played a pivotal role in showing Small how his natural abilities and inclinations could be used not only to advance scientific knowledge but also to add to his own financial security. The seeds planted by Franklin may well have been fertilized by the return of that old and constant fly in the ointment—the Reverend John Camm.

CAMM RETURNS—SMALL DEPARTS

By January 1764, John Camm had returned from England with an order from the Privy Council stating, "The Revd Mr. Graham and the Revd: Mr. Camm to be reinstated in their former Professorships."[12] Camm had been Professor of Religion when he was ejected by the Board of Visitors; Graham had been Professor of Natural Philosophy (aka – Professor of Mathematicks). At Graham's initial reinstatement he assumed the post of the much-disgraced and quickly replaced Jacob Rowe, Professor of Moral Philosophy. The order of the Privy Council now commanded the Board of Visitors to reinstate Graham as Professor of Natural Philosophy and to move Small from Natural Philosophy to Moral Philosophy. The incandescent Small, however, asserted that the position of Natural Philosophy was the only office for which he could have been persuaded to go to Virginia.[13]

The Visitors moved Small collaterally to the professorship of Moral Philosophy and increased his salary, thinking that he would be satisfied with more money and less work. Despite the adjustments made by the Privy Council's orders, Small continued to style himself as the Professor of Mathematics (synonymous with Professor of Natural Philosophy) and even signed receipts for his wages in that manner.[14] Since students could choose whichever professor's lectures they wished to attend, Small continued as the de facto Mathematics professor until his departure and, indeed, he and Wythe continued to hold their regular forums and discussions with both current and former students.

Camm's return and the restoration of Graham to the post of Professor of Natural Philosophy compounded Small's increasing unhappiness with his circumstances in the college, which began with the Board of Visitors' continuous denial of his request to visit England.

Small's persistence and, according to Robert Carter Nicholas, his subterfuge, finally paid off.[15] It took almost eighteen months to work out the details of the arrangement and there was a complex set of negotiations between Small and the Visitors, in which Small promised to return to the college within eighteen months but refused to sign a "statute" proposed by the Visitors that acknowledged the authority of the board over the governance of the college. Nevertheless, Small, having obtained the Visitors' blessings and, according to social conventions in the colony, advertised his pending departure in the *Virginia Gazette* in August 1764.[16]

THOMAS JEFFERSON'S
LETTER TO "UNKNOWN"

Several weeks before before Small's announcement made its appearance in the *Gazette* and while Small was still making final arrangements for his imminent departure, Thomas Jefferson sent a letter to a friend whom he cautiously, curiously, intriguingly addressed only as "unknown." The contents and the timing, although not definitive, have all the markings that his old professor was the intended recipient. It reads:

Wmsburgh July 26th 1764

I like your proposal of keeping up an epistolary correspondence on subjects of some importance. I do not at present recollect any difficult question in natural philosophy, but shall be glad to have your opinion on a subject much more interesting. what that is I will tell you. in perusing a magazine some time ago I met with an account of a person who had been drowned. he had continued under water 24 hours, and upon being properly treated when taken out he was restored to life. the fact is undoubted, and upon enquiry I have found that there have been many other instances of the same kind. Physicians say that when the parts of the body are restrained from performing their functions by any gentle cause which does not in any manner maim or injure any particular part, that to restore life in such a case nothing is requisite but to give the vital warmth to the whole body by gentle degrees, and to put the blood in motion by inflating the lungs. but the doubts which arose in my mind on reading the story were of another nature. we are generally taught that the <u>soul</u> leaves the body at the instant of death, that is, at the instant in which the organs of the body cease totally to perform their functions. but does not this story contradict this opinion? when then does the <u>soul</u> take it's departure? let me have your opinion candidly <and at length> on this subject. and as these are doubts which, were they to come to light, might do injustice to a man's moral principles in the eyes of persons of narrow and confined views it will be proper to take great care of our letters. I propose as one mean of doing it to put no name <or place> to the top or bottom of the letter, and to inclose it in a false cover which may be burned as soon as opened. No news in town only that Sir John Cockler has given Knox £450 for his house and lots here. Orion is 3 Hours—40′ west of the sun and of consequence goes down and rises that much before him. So you must rise early in the morning to see him. the upper star in his belt is exactly in the Æquinoctial.[17]

The cover of the copy letter retained Jefferson's name, the date, and a title *De Anima* (Concerning the Soul) but was not written in Jefferson's hand.[18] This letter was not publicly known until a sale at Sotheby's in 1994 (Sotheby's Catalogue No. 6553, May 3, 1994, Lot 60). The descriptor of the item in the catalog stated that the document had come from a branch of the Page family and, thus, the recipient had likely been John Page. There are, however, many factors that argue against that conclusion.

Thomas Jefferson to Unknown.
July 26, 1764. Gilder-Lehrman Foundation.

From the standpoint of provenance, there are a myriad of families in Virginia with deep roots who are related to the Pages in one degree or another, and the direct relationship of the letter to John Page is not robust. As a matter of fact, the content, context, and style of the letter not only argues against John Page as being the recipient, but rather, seems better to fit a profile for William Small.

Small's advertisement of his imminent departure in the *Gazette* (August 4, 1764) was intended to serve as a notice to all people to whom he may either have owed a debt or from whom he was due an obligation. The date of Jefferson's letter to "unknown" provides the first clue. July 26 was a little more than a week before the ad in the *Gazette* and Small's impending departure must have been heavy on Jefferson's mind. The other evidence pointing to Small is found both in both the context and stylistics.

In the first line, Jefferson states, "I like your proposal of keeping up an epistolary correspondence," with the implication that the recipient had initially proposed uninterrupted communications during a period of absence and that a prolonged journey was likely on the horizon. In the same line Jefferson writes that, pro tempore, he does not "recollect any difficult question in natural philosophy." Small, of course, was Jefferson's professor of natural philosophy and, undoubtedly, he would have been Jefferson's first and primary resource for questions of that nature.

Jefferson asks a question of "unknown" that is central to the conflict that exists between the objective and external knowledge of science and the internal and subjective knowledge of faith. Jefferson related that "in perusing a magazine some time ago I met with an account of a person who had been drowned. he had continued under water 24 hours, and upon being properly treated when taken out he was restored to life. the fact is undoubted, and upon enquiry I have found that there have been many other instances of the same kind."

Jefferson then remarked that physicians agree (and Small, even at this time, was recognized as a doctor with extensive medical training) that if a body is "restrained from performing their functions by any gentle cause which does not in any manner maim or injure any particular part, that to restore life in such a case nothing is requisite but to give the vital warmth to the whole body by gentle degrees, and to put the blood in motion by inflating the lungs." He confessed, however, that doubts had arisen in his mind because "we are generally taught that the <u>soul</u> leaves the body at the instant of death, that is, at the instant in which the organs of the body cease totally to perform their functions." In short, if the man died when his organs ceased to function, the soul must have departed from the body. If departed, how did it return? In other words, does the soul exist and what should Jefferson believe—the physical and logical or the metaphysical and the intuitive? How does one reconcile the two, and is it possible to maintain two incompatible concepts at once? These things seem to be more a question for a mentor than a chum.

In light of the serious censure that would have occurred should this discussion or others of like nature became known, Jefferson suggested, "As these are doubts which, were they to come to light, might do injustice to a man's moral principles in the eyes of persons of narrow and confined views it will be proper to take great care of our letters. I propose as one mean of doing it to put no name or place to the top or bottom of the letter, and to inclose it in a false cover which may be burned as soon as opened." While Page was fascinated (even obsessed) by scientific matters, he was completely conventional in matters of metaphysics and religion and the response required a knowledge far beyond the limits of his scientific knowledge, medical training, and likely, in Jefferson's estimation, philosophical capacity. It seems unlikely that Page (considering his consistent and traditional set of religious beliefs) ever considered the possibility of the nonexistence of the soul—or that Jefferson would pose such a blasphemous question to him.

Furthermore, Page and Jefferson maintained a continuous and open correspondence throughout Page's life. In fact, Jefferson corresponded with Page so frequently that less than a decade after the letter to unknown was written, he chided Page for not responding to his letters, "Am I never to have a letter from you? Why the devil don't you write? But I suppose that you are always on the moon, or some of the planetary regions ... if your spirit is too elevated to advert to sublunary subjects, depute my friend Mrs. Page to support your correspondencies."[19] Thus, the central purpose of Jefferson's admonition does not seem to apply to John Page at all. Indeed, (except for a single letter that came to Birmingham after Small's death), no other letter (or copy letter) from Jefferson to Small or from Small to Jefferson is known to have existed.

Finally, if one compares this letter to other messages that Jefferson sent to Page, it is easy to note a distinct difference in style and content. Jefferson's letters to Page, particularly in their youth, almost always contained gossip, social news, joy, and angst. It was to Page that Jefferson conveyed his most intimate and immediate thoughts and feelings—a colonial stream of consciousness. This letter is totally unlike the others that Jefferson wrote to Page, as it centers on a question of metaphysics and is devoid of adolescent chitchat. The style is formal and academic, and it approaches the subject in a straightforward and detached manner, looking for guidance in a complicated area.

A DEATH, AN ATTEMPT, AND A DEBARKATION

After Small's August notification in the *Gazette*, his preparations became more hurried and urgent. He apparently concluded his agreements with the Board of Visitors, consulted others, made the lists for the scientific apparatus he wished to purchase, packed his belongings for the voyage, and stored his books for his eventual return. That same month, President William Yates's health took a turn for the worst, and he enlisted Small as both a scribe and a signatory of his last will and testament on September 5, 1764.[20]

Late in September or early in October, while Small was in the port of Hampton waiting to board his ship home, a report came announcing President Yates's death. As soon as the news reached Small, he hurried back to Williamsburg to gather and solicit support for his candidacy for the office of president. Small, however, was disappointed when he learned that the college's charter held that a candidate's status as an Anglican minister was a nonnegotiable prerequisite for the post.

Perhaps Small believed that because of Yates's possible acquiescence, the increasingly secular nature of the institution, and anticlerical feeling among the population at large, his close relationships with many of the Visitors, the efficient manner in which he had single-handedly and successfully managed the college for almost two years, or the lack of any other acceptable candidate on the horizon, he would be able to overcome this tiny detail in the charter.[21]

Certainly, Richard Graham and, particularly, John Camm had made themselves obnoxious to the Visitors. Although James Horrocks was deemed by the Visitors to be an adequate Grammar School Master; he was thought to have had few abilities beyond that capacity. Nevertheless, the foundational requirements of the charter quickly narrowed the choice down to the unripe Horrocks. Whatever Small's influential friends may have thought of the situation, it was quickly concluded that the constitutional impediment could not be overcome and Small embarked for England.

Small's unrelenting nemesis, Dudley Digges, confirmed the details of this narrative in a letter to the Bishop of London:

In the Fall of 1764, Mr. Small being determined on a Voyage to England, and resolved, as it appeared afterwards, to make it on the very Terms he had proposed in the Visitation, tho' there rejected, he applied separately to such of the Visitors as were convenient, we suppose a Majority, informed them that his Presence was immediately

necessary in England, and desired Leave to be absent for eight
Months, promising to return at the End of that Time, or near it
as might be; the Visitors to whom he applied, not doubting his
Assurances, and as there were no Students in the Philosophy-School
just then, gave their Consent, though some of us soon afterwards
were convinced from his own Declarations to a few of his Intimates,
that he left the College in full Hopes that he would never return to
it again; at any Rate he was resolved to secure the Place he was in,
if he miscarried in his other Views. Just before he embarked, Mr.
Yates died; from Hampton where he proposed to take shipping,
he wrote circular Letters to the Visitors, desiring to succeed to the
Presidency, he knew that a Statute coeval with the College, and
which was intended by the Founders as the corner Stone and Pillar
of her Orthodoxy, stood in his Way; we mean that Statute which
declares that the President should be a Minister of the Church of
England; but this he had the Confidence to hope might be repealed.[22]

Small left the sureties of Virginia for the promise of London late in
September 1764. Perhaps buoyed by the prospects of a brighter future
and a longing to return to his native land, Small was enthusiastic about
the journey. While he left behind the petty jealousies of colleagues and
unappreciative employers, he also left a host of amiable friends, devoted
students, and the certainty of a comfortable life. Across the ocean lay
potential wealth and the promise of unfulfilled ambition; Small was
an accomplished gentleman of thirty years at this point.

NOTES

1. "Meeting of the President and Masters of William & Mary College,"
June 26, 1761, Fulham Palace Papers, Microfilm, Colonial Williamsburg Foun-
dation, Rockefeller Library, Williamsburg, Virginia (hereafter cited as CW). "The
Rev[d]. Mr. Graham has at a Meeting of the Visitors & Governors of the College,
held the 12th Inst. Having been elected as Professor of Morality in the Room of
Rev.[d] M[r]. Andrew Burnaby, who declin'd the Place did this Day subscribe his
Assent to the 39 Articles of the Church of England."

2. Richard Graham expressed his animosity toward the College of William and Mary in pointed terms—he advised the authorities at Queen's College, Oxford, in 1760, "Pray send no more of your young gentlemen into this wretched land of Tyrants & Slaves." He also informed the authorities of the death of Thomas Robinson, the dismissed professor who had originally brought the charges against Digges and Hubard, and attributed his death to the harsh treatment he had received at the hands of the Board of Visitors. "I am sorry to inform you of the death of poor Mr. Robinson, who died in the 4th instant...; it is generally thought that he died of a broken heart. The treatment he received at the hands of the Board of Visitors was truly savage." Richard Graham to the Bursars of Queen's College, Oxford, September 16, 1760, Faculty-Alumni Collection, Box 3, Folder 17, Archives, Swem Library, College of William and Mary, Williamsburg, Virginia (hereafter cited as Swem Library).

3. H. R. McIlwaine, ed., *The Journals of the House of Burgesses of Virginia, 1761–1765* (Richmond: The Colonial Press, E. Waddey Co., 1908), 151.

4. See Susan Godson, Ludwell Johnson, Richard Sherman, Thad Tate, and Helen Walker, *The College of William and Mary* (Williamsburg: King and Queen Press, 1998), 100; J. E. Morpurgo, *Their Majesties' Royall Colledge: The College of William and Mary in the Seventeenth and Eighteenth Centuries* (Washington, D.C.: Hennage Creative Printers, 1976), 138.

5. Dudley Digges to the Bishop of London, July 15, 1767, Fulham Palace Papers, Box 2, No. 23, Lambeth Palace Library, London, England (hereafter cited as London).

6. Ibid.

7. "I am setting out on a Journey to Virginia to settle the accounts of my late Colleague Mr. Hunter." Benjamin Franklin to Anthony Todd, April 14, 1763, *The Papers of Benjamin Franklin, Volume 10: January 1, 1762 through December 31, 1763*, ed. Leonard W. Labaree (New Haven: Yale University Press, 1966), 10:252.

8. Benjamin Franklin to Anthony Todd, June 1, 1763, in Labaree, *Papers of Benjamin Franklin*, 10:270.

9. George Reese, ed., *The Official Papers of Francis Fauquier: Lieutenant Governor of Virginia* (Charlottesville: University of Virginia Press, 1981), 2:673n4.

10. William Small to Benjamin Franklin, August 10, 1771, in *The Papers of Benjamin Franklin, Volume 18: January 1, 1771 through December 31, 1771*, ed. William B. Willcox (New Haven: Yale University Press, 1968), 18:197–199.

11. Ami Argand to Matthew Boulton, February 13, 1786, MS 3782/12/31/21, Archives, Birmingham Central Library, Birmingham, England.

12. "Meeting of the President and Masters of William & Mary College," January 20, 1762, Fulham Palace Papers, Microfilm, Rockefeller Library, CW.

13. "You seem to arrogate some Merit to yourself for being inclined to give as Little Trouble as possible by accepting the first vacant Professorship <tho' not agreeable to you> which presented [itself] after you had lost the only one [Professorship] which you say would originally have brought you from England." Dudley Digges [in the handwriting of Robert Carter Nicholas] to William Small, June 25, 1767, Edgehill-Randolph Collection, Harrison Institute, University of Virginia, Charlottesville (hereafter cited as UVA).

14. "Feb. 7, 1764, had of the treasurer of the College Thirty Seven Pounds current money to the acct of my salary as Professor of Mathematics—W. Small." 1983.122, Bursar Book, 1743–1779, p. 99, Archives, Swem Library.

15. "It was very well known at the very Time that you had no Design of returning if you could fall into any other Way more agreeable; thus you obtain'd the End proposed in your fruitless Applications to the Visitation, by a Piece of Art which every honest Man would despise; you gain'd an Opportunity of seeking your Fortune in England & if nothing better turn'd up poor William & Mary was once more to be bless'd with your Company." Robert Carter Nicholas to William Small, June 25, 1767, Edgehill-Randolph Collection, Archives, Alderman Library, UVA.

16. "William Small—Adv[ertisement] of Departure," in the *Virginia Gazette* Daybooks, August 1764, Harrison Institute, UVA.

17. Thomas Jefferson to Unknown, July 26, 1764, GLC04366, Gilder Lehrman Collection, Gilder Lehrman Institute, on deposit at the Morgan Library & Museum, New York City. Compliments of Endrina Tay, ICJS, Monticello, Virginia.

18. The modern version of the medial "s" suggests that it may have been inserted at a later date and was written in pencil.

19. Thomas Jefferson to John Page, February 21, 1771, in *The Papers of Thomas Jefferson*, ed. Julian P. Boyd (Princeton: Princeton University Press, 1950), 1:35.

20. William Yates, Will, September 5, 1764, Accession 26024, Personal Papers Collection, The Library of Virginia, Richmond. Both the text of the document and the signature of Small appear to be in his hand. It is interesting that the witnesses included William Small, Emmanuel Jones, and Susanna Meriton, but not James Horrocks, John Camm, or Richard Graham. It may be that Yates, despite their intermittent disagreements, anointed Small as his successor at this meeting.

21. Robert Carter Nicholas later wrote bitterly to Small, "Upon the Death of Mr. Yates, just before you embarked for England you solicited the Presidentship. But one thing stood in the way of this desire, namely the Statute co-eval with the College, & which seem'd to be regarded by its Founders as the chief Pillar of her Constitution, the President is to be an Orthodox Clergyman of the Church of

England; this you seem'd to hope might be either dispensed with or repeal'd for your Sake, & it's more than probable that you might have presumed that other Alterations would as easily have follow'd." Robert Carter Nicholas to William Small, June 25, 1767, Edgehill-Randolph Collection, Harrison Institute, UVA.

22. Dudley Digges to the Bishop of London, July 15, 1767, Fulham Palace Papers, Box 2, No. 23, Lambeth Palace Library, London.

CHAPTER 10

Small and London and Franklin

From the perspective of American researchers, when Small sailed away from the Chesapeake Bay, he left behind his former life and disappeared like a scurrying cloud over the horizon. According to the British version, he appeared magically on the steps of Hungerford Wharf, and, like a furtive émigré, quickly sloughed off his amorphous past. All in all, he arrived in London after an uneventful eight-week voyage.

We know that Small was in England before the end of November because of a letter that Alexander Small (Franklin's old friend and perhaps a distant relative of William Small) posted to Benjamin Franklin from London on December 1, 1764. Alexander Small wrote. "My namesake the Virginian Professor is here; and desires to be most particularly remembered to you."[1] Small evidently made the short trek from his ship to the home of Alexander Small in Villiers Street,[2] which was conveniently located near the Adelphi Wharfs, the Hungerford Stairs, the York Building Stairs, and Charing Cross.

The letter to Benjamin Franklin immediately after William Small's arrival suggests an established relationship between all three men, and implies Franklin's foreknowledge and involvement in Small's appearance at Alexander Small's home. The proximity of the three men's residences to each other in London hints at an

Alexander Small lived in Villiers St., Franklin in Craven St. and
Small on Suffolk St. next to the Mews and Charing Cross.
The Hungerford Stairs were located between Villiers and Craven Streets.

agenda that predated William Small's departure from America. He resided at Mr. Banner's, Suffolk Street,[3] Alexander Small dwelled on Villiers Street, and Benjamin Franklin lived on Craven Street, all three within shouting distance of Charing Cross.

NETWORKING IN LONDON

Franklin arrived in London on Monday, December 10, 1764[4] and what a memorable Christmas and New Year it must have been for Small. For the next several months, Small clung to Franklin's flapping coattails in a social, political, and intellectual whirlwind about the great metropolis. Small was a guest of Franklin at the Royal Society on January 9th, 1765,[5] was overheard discussing medical advances at St. Paul's Coffee Shop, and was observed with fellow Scots at the British Coffee House on Cockspur Street. Franklin, the ultimate networker, scientific investigator, and social butterfly, happily brought along his protégé Small on incessant jaunts throughout the omphalos[6] (hub) of the British Empire. Franklin wrote to his old friend Hugh Roberts, "For my own part, I find I love the Company, Chat, a Laugh, a Glass, and even a Song, as well as ever; and at the same Time relish better than I us'd to do, the grave Observations and wise Sentences of old Men's Conversation."[7]

Franklin's favorite clubs and meetings included the Royal Society, the Monday Club, the Honest Whigs Society,[8] and the Thursday Dinner Club. Other stops along Franklin's social and intellectual circuit were the Philosophical Club, the New England Coffee House, the Pennsylvania Coffee House, the London Coffee House Club, the Old Slaughter Coffee House, and closer to Craven Street, the British Coffee House (frequented by Scots) on Cockspur Street, which was right around the corner from Small's apartment on Suffolk Street and close by Charing Cross.[9]

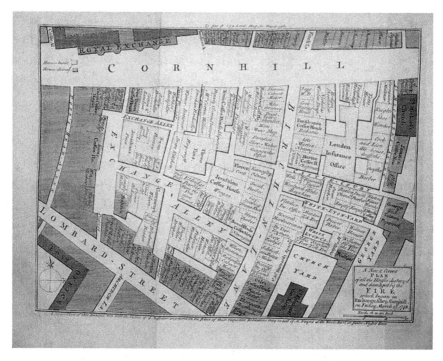

Bryant Lillywhite. *London Coffee Houses.*[10]

Social clubs included meetings of the Royal Society in Crane Court, the Society of Arts in Denmark Court, and Dr. Brays Society (which promoted the education of enslaved children). There were frequent Sunday night dinners at the residence of William Strahan, Franklin's publisher. Impromptu gatherings and informal lunches, experimental demonstrations, and scientific lectures were scattered throughout a frequently changing itinerary during these phrenetic and halcyon days.

While Franklin certainly enjoyed the company, there were also utilitarian aspects to his conviviality. His multiple societies and coteries provided political and economic inroads as well as informal access to cutting-edge scientific knowledge, access to insider trading, and the ability to promote and control his image in the most positive light. Franklin's social and scientific connections in London provided a vortex of activity and advancement for Small during those exhilarating months.[11] The associations made during this period in various clubs, pubs and private homes allowed Small to network with the some of the most influential movers in social, political, scientific, and economic circles of the capital. The friendships nurtured at this time formed a firm foundation from which Small was able to launch numerous initiatives and bring together men of ideas and imaginations who transcended national boundaries and political agendas.

In March 1765, Stephen Hawtrey, hoping to obtain information for his brother Edward about the College of William and Mary, sought out Small. After several missed opportunities, Hawtrey caught up with Small at the Virginia Coffee Shop,[12] located two doors down from the George and Vulture, the home of one of Franklin's favorite societies, the Honest Whigs Club.[13] During this interview, Small informed Hawtrey that he would "be gone these three weeks."[14] During this interval, Small journeyed to Scotland to obtain his M.D. from Marischal College. The most common method of obtaining a medical degree at that time was by the attestation of two physicians;[15] Small's recommenders were his old mentor, John Gregory, Mediciner at the University of Edinburgh, and John Elliot, the king's physician in Scotland and senior physician at Greenwich Hospital.[16]

MEDICAL DEGREE FROM MARISCHAL COLLEGE

Medical Degree Attestations.
University of Aberdeen Archives. MS M 28 f-20.

Some scholars have asserted that Small merely purchased his degree for a trivial sum, as was often the case in the eighteenth century, but several factors seem to indicate otherwise. First, his experience and reputation as a doctor in Virginia denotes an advanced degree of education and training. Second, his first Recommender and mentor, John Gregory, was in the vanguard of those physicians calling for the standardization of the medical profession. Gregory had specifically advocated for a prescribed course of studies and collegiate training as a prerequisite to qualify for a medical degree. In 1757, Gregory and Francis Skene (Small's bejan professor) attempted to establish a professional medical school at Aberdeen with a "proper dissecting room and laboratory."[17]

His second Attester was John Elliot, a prominent London physician who would become the king's personal physician in England (John Gregory was the king's physician in Scotland) and Senior Physician at Greenwich Hospital.[18] Neither of these gentlemen would have likely issued bogus recommendations for Small.[19] Furthermore, while visiting medical classes at the University of Edinburgh, in the course of obtaining his attestation from Gregory, Small so impressed the students there with his knowledge of medicine and surgery that several followed him back to London and begged him to conduct medical seminars there.[20]

A fellow Scot, John Elliot was born in Edinburgh in 1736, and after some training there went to London to become an apothecary's assistant. Once in London he was enticed and induced by the lure of adventure and booty and so signed on to be the saw-bones for a privateer's ship; he returned home from his adventures with many tales and a handsome premium. It was at this point that he decided to turn physician, took a medical degree, and established himself in the fashionable Cecil Street in London.

In 1771, Eliot married the extraordinarily beautiful Grace Dalrymple, the seventeen-year-old daughter of Hugh Dalrymple, a prosperous Edinburgh barrister, and took her back to London. In London, Grace soon discovered the pleasures of the flesh and after many and well-known dalliances, ran off to Paris with Lord Valentia in 1773.[21]

Grace Dalrymple Elliot.
By Thomas Gainsborough.

Humiliated, Eliot obtained a divorce and £12,000 in compensation from Grace's father. Having been tracked down and returned
to Scotland, Grace was then placed by her brother in a nunnery in
France from which Valentia again rescued her. Back in England,
she became the mistress of the Prince of Wales, and bore him a
daughter (Georgiana). Ironically, her erstwhile spouse, John Eliot
was to become the future king's physician in 1778 and was knighted
for his services to his Royal Highness. He was listed in the *Medical
Register of 1779* as Senior Physician at Greenwich Hospital. Dr. Judith
Curthoys, archivist at Christ Church College, Oxford University,
advised that Sir John Eliot of Greenwich Hospital should not be
confused with a second John Elliot, also a London physician of the
same era, who died insane in Newgate Prison.[22]

Small had obtained his sophisticated medical skills by acting as an
apprentice to John Gregory and his brother in Aberdeen, attending
the lectures of distinguished surgeons, and observing the operations

of Sir John Pringle and William Hunter (not in the primitive hospitals of remote Aberdeen, but in the cutting-edge clinics of London). Small was so well regarded in London that after his return from Virginia, the celebrated physician and author William Heberden obtained a post for him (which he refused) in the Court of the Empress Catherine in 1765.

MEDICAL CONNECTIONS IN LONDON

Small had practiced medicine in Virginia, and became well known to a number of prominent doctors in London. Small likely knew some of the physicians from his days of "walking the wards" at St. George's Hospital or was introduced to them by Franklin or Alexander Small in London. It was during this time that Small became acquainted with the celebrated physician William Heberden who had co-written a pamphlet with Benjamin Franklin in 1759 promoting smallpox vaccinations.[23] It is also likely that during this time Small joined a society formed by George Fordyce and John Hunter (both Scots), in 1771, for Hunter and Fordyce sent a letter to Small signed "your brethren in the medical society."[24]

In all likelihood, Small's sudden and pressing desire for a medical degree from a university came at Franklin's urging. Franklin, after Small's return from Aberdeen and Edinburgh, sent him quickly to Birmingham to meet Matthew Boulton, knowing that Franklin's wealthy industrial friend was in need of a personal physician and scientific adviser.

Small indirectly benefited by observing Franklin's infectious ways of attracting friends and directly through Franklin's introductions to new acquaintances and entries into prestigious societies and institutions—all of which would be instrumental to Small in pursuing his personal ambitions, enlarging his own circle of friends and colleagues, and accessing the corridors of power, influence, and knowledge. He would use these connections to become a potent recruiter for Boulton in Birmingham and ultimately as a lobbyist for James Watts's effort to obtain from Parliament a monopoly for his improved steam engine.

Just as his close association with professors and mentors in Aberdeen had been the impetus for spreading the sentiments of the School of Common Sense in Virginia, the influence of Franklin had opened his eyes to new possibilities and endless horizons of opportunity in an era of rapid scientific expansion and gave him a new perspective on the system of things in which we are placed. His connection to Franklin endowed him with a certain aura of gravitas and auctoritas. Important people began to take notice and seek his company, his collaboration, and his advice. Franklin's intercession and assistance led him to Birmingham and to his old and wealthy friend, Matthew Boulton. Boulton, a man of great industry and plans, who, in turn, opened up for Small a whole new vista of connections, areas of interest, and opportunities for advancement.

NOTES

1. "My namesake the Virginian Professor is here; and desires to be most particularly remembered to you." Alexander Small to Benjamin Franklin, December 1, 1764, Franklin Papers, I/110, American Philosophical Society, Philadelphia, Pennsylvania.

2. "Alexander Small," *European Magazine* (January 1799): 20–21. See also "Obituary of remarkable Persons; with Biographical Anecdotes," *Gentleman's Magazine* 44 (September 6, 1794): 864–865. Alexander and William Small may have been related. Both branches of the Small family were from the contiguous counties in Scotland—William's family was from Angus and Alexander's from Perthshire. Alexander's father, Patrick Small, may have been a cousin of William.

3. Stephen Hawtrey (London) to Edward Hawtrey, March 26, 1765, Ganter Collection, Box 3, Folder 21, Archives, Swem Library, College of William and Mary, Williamsburg, Virginia (hereafter cited as Swem Library). Courtesy of Miss Margaret Cook, Archivist. Suffolk St. was located across the Strand from Craven St. and in between the Royal Mews and St. Martin-in-the-Fields.

4. Benjamin Franklin to Deborah Franklin, December 9, 1764, *The Papers of Benjamin Franklin, January 1, 1764, through December 31, 1764*, ed. Leonard

W. Labaree, Helen C. Boatfield, and James H. Hutson (New Haven: Yale University Press, 1967), 11:516.

5. Journal Book of the Royal Society, 1763–1766, Archives, Royal Society of London, England, 25:416, 426.

6. Martin Clagett to Emily Salmon, Personal communication, August 8, 2021. "At the ancient temple at Delphi (for Apollo - the god of intellect and light) the priestess (the Pythia) sat over a crack of the floor of the holy cave from which emanated vapors which she inhaled then pronounced (in dactylic hexameter) omens that always turned out true (if you could interpret them correctly). She was there for over 2000 years and in her last prediction she was asked (during the reign of Julian the Apostate) if the old gods yet reigned. After huffing in the illuminating vapors (thought to have been enhanced by fresh bay leaves - sacred to Apollo) she pronounced "The old gods are dead and Christ is triumphant." - that was her last prediction and she was the last Pythoness. The crack over which she sat was known as the omphalos - Greek for bellybutton - or center of the enlightened universe. Hence London = omphalos.

7. Benjamin Franklin to Hugh Roberts, February 26, 1761, *The Papers of Benjamin Franklin, January 1, 1761, through December 21, 1761*, ed. Leonard Labaree (New Haven: Yale University Press, 1966), 9:279.

8. It is not unlikely that Small became acquainted with Joseph Priestley about this time as he was both a correspondent and an acquaintance of Franklin and a friend of Richard Price (a member of the Honest Whig's Club) who brought Joseph Priestley as a guest to the Royal Society.

9. Benjamin Franklin to Hugh Roberts, February 26, 1761, in Labaree, *Papers of Benjamin Franklin*, 9:279.

10. The George and Vulture, Corner of George Yard and Castle Street; Pennsylvania Coffee House on Birchin Lane; Strahan's Bookbinders on Cornwall Hill.

11. The Royal Society held dinners every fortnight, on Mondays, at the Mitre Tavern on Fleet Street, ("In Mitre Court near St. Dunstan's Church Fleet Street … between Mitre Court and Ram-Alley over against Fetter-Lane. Mentioned as early as 1603 and in the eighteenth century was the meeting place not only of the Royal Society [1746–1780] but also of the Society of Antiquaries [1730s–1777] and often used for Masonic meetings in the 1760s. Besides Franklin, Samuel Johnson, and James Boswell were frequent visitors. Bryant Lillywhite, *London Coffee Houses* [London: Allen & Unwin, 1964], 370), where there was to be found an ample menu, good drink and scientific conversations; between 1757 and 1775, Franklin attended 60 percent of the time and for several years was the most frequent guest for several years running. Franklin also religiously attended his Monday Club at

the George and Vulture in St. Michael's Lane near the Royal Exchange, where his friend John Ellicot, the clever clockmaker, held court. Franklin and Ellicot had like interests in promoting public health—Franklin encouraged a public hospital in Philadelphia and Ellicot was a governor at the Foundling Hospital in London, a position once held by Francis Fauquier. ("The George and Vulture was located at the northeast corner of George Yard, Lombard Street. The yard itself surviving from one of the oldest and most interesting Inns of London known as the George, which adjoined the east side of the Church of St. Edmund the King. The George is listed in 1479 as the Jorge in Lumbard Strete." [In Lillywhite, *London Coffee Houses*, 699.] Rumors circulated that the George and Vulture was one of the local establishments from which the notorious Lord Dashwood recruited prostitutes dressed as nuns for his Hellfire Club—which implies that Franklin's activities may have been as physical as intellectual. Alternative Thursday evenings were often devoted to the Honest Whigs Club, which convened in St. Paul's Coffeehouse (which stood at the corner of the archway of Doctor's Commons adjacent to St. Paul's Churchyard). James Boswell related on September 21, 1769, "I went to a club to which I belong. It meets every other Thursday at St. Paul's Coffee House. It consists of clergymen, physicians and several other professions. There are of it: Dr. Franklin, Rose of Chiswich, Burgh of Newington Green, Mr. Price who writes on morals, Mr. Jeffries, a keen Supporter of the Bill of Rights, and a good many more. Some of us smoke a pipe, conversation goes on pretty formally, sometimes sensibly sometimes furiously. At nine a side-board with Welsh rabbits and apple puffs, porter and beer. Our reckoning is about 18d a head." [In Lillywhite. *London Coffee Houses*, 508.] Despite the name, the meetings avoided political subjects; among the group were a number of dissenting ministers and graduates from Scottish universities. Franklin's friend and the leader of the society was John Canton, born a weaver's son, who continued in that occupation but also expanded into scientific inquiries and journalism, writing for the *Gentleman's Magazine*. He was interested in both the effects of magnetism and the properties of electricity and was the first in England to promote Franklin's work on electricity. Some Honest Whigs also belonged to the scientific club (the Lunar Circle) established in Birmingham by Matthew Boulton and William Small. Prominent among them were Joseph Priestley, John Whitehurst, Thomas Day, Dr. Daniel Solander, Rudolph Eric Raspe, and Josiah Wedgwood. Small is reported to have witnessed Sir John Pringle perform an operation when he was "walking the wards" at St. George's Hospital before he departed for the colonies. It also appears that there were connections with the Royal Society and "the discussions at this club were, in part, continuous with those at the Royal Society and the Royal Society Club." [Lillywhite. *London Coffee*

Houses, 217.] Thursdays might also find Franklin at the Thursday Dinner Club at Dog Tavern on Garlick Hill. (No. 23 Holywell St. In the 1830s the Old Dog was advertised to have been established in the same place for more than 200 years and was situated over the ancient well that gave the street its name. [Lillywhite, *London Coffee Houses*, 193]. Other stops along Franklin's social and intellectual circuit were the Philosophical Club on Mitre Street, the New England Coffee House in Threadneedle Street (No. 61 Threadneedle St.—"right behind the Royal Exchange." [Lillywhite, *London Coffee Houses*, 217], Pennsylvania Coffee House in Birchin Lane (No. 25 Birchin Lane "intermixt premises of the Marine Coffee House and the London Assurance House." [Lillywhite, *London Coffee Houses*, 444], the London Coffee House Club (24 Ludgate Street next to St. Martin's Church, established ca. 1731, where besides coffee the tavern offered a punch made from "the finest old Arrack, Rum and French Brandy." Frequently used for Masonic meetings, it became the place for convening the Thursday club, which formerly met in St. Paul's Coffee House and consisted of physicians, dissenting ministers, and masters of academies. [Lillywhite, *London Coffee Houses*, 339], the Old Slaughter Coffee House located at 77 St. Martin's Lane (Old Slaughter's was established in 1692 and was considered an artist's hangout in the mid-eighteenth century. It was a particular favorite of Hogarth but also hosted medical societies as well. John Hunter was known to hold meetings there. [Lillywhite, *London Coffee Houses*, 423]. Closer to Craven Street was the Star and Garter on Pall Mall. [Lillywhite, *London Coffee Houses*, 325], and the British Coffee House (27 Cockspur St. "over against King's Mews near Charing Cross opposite Suffolk St. Another center for Masonic meeting favored by the Scots and actors and right around the corner from Small's apartments on Suffolk St." [Lillywhite, *London Coffee Houses*, 133]. Social clubs included meetings of the Royal Society in Crane Court, the Strand; the Society of Arts, in Denmark Court, also in the Strand; Dr. Brays Society, which promoted the education of slave children, at Mr. Bird's Bookshop in Ave Mary Street. And there were always the Sunday night dinners and conversations at the home of Franklin's friend and publisher William Strahan. There were impromptu gatherings and informal lunches; demonstrations and the like were also on the itinerary during these phrenetic days as well. Indeed, Small probably reconnected with his old acquaintances in the medical field. It may be during this time that Small met William Heberden, who had co-written a pamphlet in 1756 with Franklin on smallpox inoculation. Heberden later obtained a post for Small at the Court of St. Petersburg in 1765, which Small declined.

12. The Virginia Coffee House was early identified as being in Threadneedle Street but evidently moved after the Great Fire and by 1761 was in Birchin Street,

Cornhill [Lillywhite, *London Coffee Houses*, 623]. The Virginia Coffee House was convenient to the Pennsylvania Coffee House, the George and Vulture, and Strahan's bookbinding shop—all places that Franklin frequented. Coffeehouses in London often catered to colonials and carried news and newspapers from their homes. Frequently these coffeehouses carried newspapers from the colonies whose names they carried, as well as shipping news, and served as a drop-off location for mail brought over by individuals; hence, one of Franklin's frequent stops was the Pennsylvania Coffee House.

13. Vernon Crane, "The Honest Whig Society," *William and Mary Quarterly*, 3rd Series, vol. 23, no. 2, (April 1966): 210–233.

14. Stephen Hawtrey (London) to Edward Hawtrey, March 26, 1765, Ganter Collection, Box 3, Folder 21, Archives, Swem Library.

15. MS M 28 f-20, Archives, University of Aberdeen, Aberdeen, Scotland.

16. Elliot or Eliot, depending on the source.

17. Paul Wood, ed., *The Aberdeen Enlightenment* (Aberdeen: Aberdeen University Press, 1993), 71.

18. P. J. Wallis and R. V. Wallis, *Eighteenth-Century Medics* (Newcastle upon Tyne: Project for Historic Bibliography, 1988), 178.

19. That John Gregory was King's Physician in Scotland and John Elliot was King's Physician in England is not only a fascinating fact but also attests to the elevated level of Small's medical training. John Elliot (Eliot) was born in Edinburgh in 1736 and left for London at a young age to train as an apothecary's assistant. Enticed by the lure of adventure and booty, Elliot signed on to a privateer's ship and returned home with a substantial premium. He then determined to become a physician, graduated from Christ College, Oxford, and established himself in Cecil Street, London. In 1771, he married the seventeen-year-old daughter of the wealthy Edinburgh barrister, Hugh Dalrymple. The elder Elliot took his beautiful and bewitching young wife, Grace Dalrymple, back to London, where she became a great favorite of the fashionable crowd. She was such a renowned beauty that Gainsborough painted six portraits of her. In London, she was soon tempted and willingly succumbed to the advances of several royal courtiers. In 1773, she ran off with the elegant but debauched Lord Valentia. Elliot divorced his flagrantly unfaithful wife and received £ 12,000 in compensation from her father. Grace's brother retrieved his errant sister and transported her to a convent near Paris, from which she was gallantly rescued by Lord Cholmondeley and taken back to London. Following her triumphant return, she had an affair with the Prince of Wales resulting in a beautiful daughter, but eventually she eloped to France with the Duke of Orleans. Her former husband, John Elliot, later became the

physician to the father of her child, King George IV. Elliot was a talented doctor and was listed as Senior Physician at Greenwich Hospital in 1779. He died in 1786. (*Dictionary of National Biography* [courtesy of Dr. Judith Curthoys, Christ Church College, Oxford University]. J. R. Partington and Douglas McKie, "Sir John Eliot and John Elliot," *Annals of Science* 6 [1948–1950]: 262–267). The *Dictionary of National Biography* gives mixed information concerning John Eliot with part of the information from one John Eliot living in Cecil Street and the other in Great Marlborough Street; Wallis & Wallis in *Eighteenth Century Medics* also commingle the biographies of two into one.

20. "Before I settled at Birmingham, I was asked at London on this account by many students in Medicine who had left Edin[bu]r[gh] to give lectures on those parts of Physics that most immediately concern Doctors & Surgeons, & truly it is easy to perceive that most of them very much wanted instruction." William Small to James Watt, October 27, 1773, MS 3782/12/76/151, Archives, Birmingham Central Library, Birmingham, England.

21. See James W. Singer, "Painting of the Week: Thomas Gainsborough, Grace Dalrymple Elliott," July 19, 2020, https://www.dailyartmagazine.com/grace -dalrymple-elliott/ (accessed July 27, 2021).

22. Wallis and Wallis, *Eighteenth-Century Medics*, 178; personal correspondence, Michelle Gait (Archivist, University of Aberdeen) to Martin Clagett, June 26, 2002. "However, as I emailed you yesterday, the index to the printed *Records of Marischal College* (whose entries are transcribed from the original register), which I have copied and enclosed, gives a few more details, *Eliot, Sir John, kt. M.D. London.*" *National Biography* gives mixed information concerning John Eliot, some of the information fits Sir John Eliot and some seems to be derived from a second John Elliot in London living in Great Marlborough Street, Wallis & Wallis in *Eighteenth Century Medics* provides information for both John Elliots—one Sir John Eliot and the second John Eliot; Partington and McKie, "Sir John Eliot and John Elliot," *Annals of Science*, 262–267. Courtesy Dr. Judith Curthoys, Archivist, Christ Church College, Oxford University.

23. William Heberden and Benjamin Franklin, *Some Account of the Success of Inoculation for the Small-Pox in England and America* (London: William Strahan, 1759).

24. Small received a letter from Fordyce and Hunter signed "your brethren in the medical society" dated April 5, 1771 (Matthew Boulton Papers, MS 3783/12/199, Archives, Birmingham Public Library. Birmingham, England). John Hunter (1728–1793), began his medical career as an assistant in dissections to his elder brother, William Hunter, in 1749, became Assistant Surgeon at St. George's in 1756, and

surgeon in 1768. George Fordyce (1736–1802) was born in Foveran (Small family ancestral home) and was educated at Marischal. He studied at Leyden under Albinus, was elected physician at St. Thomas' Hospital, and lectured on *Materia Medica* and Chemistry. He also became a member of the Royal Society and the Royal College of Physicians. Personal communication from Simon Chaplin, October 26, 2008. "The cases are recorded in the Pringle papers at the Royal College of Physicians in Edinburgh, RCPE Pringle 1/4/f.157 (c.1757) and RCPE Pringle 1/8/f.188 (1769)." Both of these dates agree with the timeframe that Small and Hunter were present in London.

Chapter 11

Boulton, Birmingham,
and the Lunar Society

Small had the same capacity as Franklin for mobilizing people of similar tastes, personalities, and interests. Franklin correctly calculated that Small was precisely the person that Matthew Boulton was seeking to intercede in his personal and professional ventures. For just as William Small had unconventionally answered the needs of the Board of Visitors at the College of William and Mary, he also had the very set of skills, background, interests, and personality that Boulton had in mind for a family physician and scientific adviser.

The urgent desire for Small to receive a medical diploma was at Franklin's exhortations, for Franklin, immediately after Small's return to from Scotland, sent him directly to Birmingham and to Matthew Boulton with a proper letter of introduction in hand. Franklin was aware of the potential for a mutually beneficial relationship, agreeable to both his scientific friend Small and his industrialist friend Matthew Boulton. Boulton, utilizing technological and scientific advancements to his own advantage, was already influential and wealthy. He surrounded himself with men of talent and knowledge and, as it so happens, was at this moment looking for someone who could attend to his ailing daughter and act as a scientific advisor

From their first meeting, it was clear to Boulton that Franklin was as insightful in his recommendation as he was resourceful in scientific matters. Boulton immediately took to Small and recognized that he had all the requisite talent and ability that he was seeking. At that moment a partnership, and, more important, a friendship began.

FRANKLIN'S INTRODUCTION

Franklin's introduction read, "I beg leave to introduce my Friend Dr Small to your Acquaintance, and to recommend him to your Civilities. I would not take this Freedom, if I was not sure it would be agreeable to you, and that you will thank me for adding to the Number of those who from their Knowledge of you must respect you, one who is both an ingenious Philosopher & a most worthy honest Man. Introducing the Bearer Dr Wm: Small."[1]

By the time Small arrived in Birmingham, Boulton had already maintained a longstanding relationship with Erasmus Darwin as a consulting physician and scientific advisor. But Darwin was too busy with his own expanding medical practice and scientific initiatives to give Boulton all the time and attention that Boulton required. Franklin's reputation, and his relationship with Boulton made the recommendation of Small all the more compelling. Franklin's letter was later complemented by one from a London associate of Boulton, a silversmith of some merit, Nathaniel Jeffreys, who confirmed not only Franklin's opinion but also added new detail.

> Dr Wm Small who has been settled some years at Virginia as a Phisician, and with great success & was the same time proffesser of Mathematicks in the Colledge of Williamsburgh, but came home on acct. of his health & some buissiness. & prefers a settlement at home to returning to Virginia as he never kept his health there—he is recommdd to me by some of my best friends here, as a Gentm. of great Worth, Integrity & Honour, & in the way of his profession has the best recommendations of our most Eminent Phisicians here—who are the best judges of his Merit as a Physician.[2]

CIVIC DUTIES AND THE MEDICAL PRACTICE

Small quickly established himself in Birmingham. After a successful operation on Boulton's daughter and impressive results to several other "dangerous cases," he became a highly sought-out figure in medical circles. Within six months of his arrival in Birmingham, Small had established a medical practice and opened a clinic at 9 Temple Row (just opposite St. Philip's Church)[3] with John Ash, the most well-respected doctor in the region.[4]

Dr. John Ash. Courtesy of Professor Robert Arnott.
University of Birmingham.

Small became a valued addition to the community as well as an asset to Boulton and the medical interest of the town. Dr. John Ash co-opted Small for a hospital project, and Boulton seems to have encouraged both the hospital and Small's participation. Small, Ash, and Boulton were among the twelve original trustees who purchased land for the hospital on May 16, 1766.[5] In addition, to this endeavor, Small acted as a town commissioner in 1769, for the purpose of "widening ... passages within the town of Birmingham ... and for the cleaning and lighting of streets ... and removing and preventing nuisances and obstructions therein."[6] In 1774, Small and Boulton were among the investors who established the New Street Theatre— an alternative to the deteriorating King Street Playhouse.[7]

By the end of his first year in Birmingham, Small had already become an indispensable part of Boulton's family. It came as a shock, then, when Boulton heard the rumor that Dr. William Heberden was attempting to lure Small away to take a post at the Court of Catherine the Great, the Empress of Russia. In a panic, Boulton turned to his printer and friend John Baskerville to inquire into the matter.

Baskerville allayed Boulton's angst and reported that Small was so satisfied with his new friends and the extent of his medical practice that he had rejected the idea of going to Russia, but added that he thought it only proper to go to London to thank Heberden for his interest.[8] Moreover, "from 1765 until Small's death ... Boulton did very little, particularly in scientific matters, without Small's advice."[9]

Because of their conjoined business concerns, mutual and multiple scientific interests and personal regard for one another, Boulton and Small began to meet at Soho for working dinners. These informal repasts developed into semiregular "philosophical feasts," centered on the practical application of technological advances. In February 1766, Boulton wrote to Franklin, "The addition you have made to my happiness in being the cause of my acquaintance with the amiable and ingenious Dr. Small deserves more than thanks," and mentioned several of the scientific subjects that he and Small had been discussing.

SMALL AND BOULTON'S FIRST STEAM ENGINE

In the same letter to Franklin, Boulton mentioned that he had conducted an experiment for a prototype steam engine and "open'd it in the presence of Dr. Small."[10] Although Boulton minimized Small's role to an observer in the execution of this model, it is more plausible that it was Small who had done the majority of devising, testing, and construction of the model rather than Boulton—in fact, five years later, Boulton confessed his limited knowledge of mechanics when he wrote to Watt, "I do not intend turning engineer."[11]

After receiving the steam engine model from Boulton, Franklin was so impressed with its promise that he put in on public display in London, where the model drew great attention from many quarters. Shortly after hearing of the exhibition, Boulton hastily requested Franklin to send it back. "I Should be much oblig'd to you if you would Let the Servant order a Corker to neal [nail] up the model of the Engine in the box again, and take it to the Birmingham Carrier at the Bell in smithfield."[12]

A week later, Franklin sent his suggestions for improvements along with the assurance that "I sent the Model last Week, with your Papers in it, which I hope got safe to hand."[13] The exhibition in London must have caused great excitement, for Erasmus Darwin wrote to Boulton (even before Franklin's package had arrived), "Your model of a Steam Engine I am told gain'd so much approbation in London, that I can not but congratulate you on the mechanical Fame you have acquired by it."[14]

Darwin, who had been fascinated by the concept of steam engines for some time was agog with anticipation and likely a little jealous at not having been part of the initial collaboration,[15] he continued, "This Model I am so impatient to see, and to hear any Observations you have made or heard on this Subject, that I am determined to spend a Day with you, the first vacant Day that occurs to me: and shall trust to the Stars for meeting with you at Home."[16]

Darwin was so eager to see the model, and knowing that Boulton was frequently away from home on business, he suggested "if the Stars do not shine on me, pray contrive, that, in your Absence, Mrs. Boulton may have it in her Power to shew me this celebrated Model."[17] Darwin, wishing to insinuate himself into their confidence, even had concerned advice for Small. "Yesterday I was informed another Physician was arrived in Birmingham, but hope this gives no uneasiness to our ingenious Friend Dr Small, from whom and you, when I was last in Birmingham, I received Ideas, That for many

Days occurred to me at the Interval of the common Business of Life, with inexpressible Pleasure."[18]

Darwin also urged Boulton and Small to participate in a potentially profitable canal scheme in Birmingham. It seems significant that he appealed to Boulton and Small conjointly. "I am undone to know what Observations Dr Franklin supply'd you with about your steam-Engine... And I wish yourself and our ingenious Friend Dr Small will communicate to me your joint Opinion on this Head." Darwin also offered some advice of his own, writing, "I hope you will give this Scheme your assistance.... I desire you & Dr Small will take this Infection, as you have given me ye Infection of steam-enginry."[19]

It has been suggested that Darwin was an original member of the Birmingham club from the start, but it is difficult to imagine that Darwin would have been so eager to see the Small-Boulton engine (already praised and paraded by Franklin) or to be so impatient to join in their conversations if he had already been participating in the brainstorming sessions and experiments. In addition, Darwin even at this time was referring to the Small and Boulton collaboration as the Birmingham Philosophers, not a thing he would have likely done were he already a part of the group.

There are a total of six reasons why Darwin's flurry of correspondence in the early months of 1766 warrants attention. First, Small and Boulton were having a series of detailed discussions about the prospect of a viable steam engine and had actually constructed a model and sent it to Franklin in London for assessment. Second, Franklin thought that it showed so much promise he put it on public display in the business and academic circles of London. Third, the model received so much praise that news of it very quickly reached Darwin in rural Lichfield. Fourth, Darwin was not participating in Small and Boulton's philosophical dinners and experimental trials at Soho but hinted in his letter to Boulton that he would like to be a part of the continuing process. Fifth, Small likely suggested that Boulton should invite Darwin to join the conversations. Lastly, Boulton and Small, and indeed Darwin, had not just a strong interest, but also some practical and successful experience in the subject of "steam enginry" long before a then-unknown Scottish inventor—James Watt—appeared in Birmingham at the doors of the Soho Factory for a visit and with hopes of meeting the celebrated Matthew Boulton.

In short, Small and Boulton formed the nucleus of what would later become the Birmingham Lunar Society, and it seems that the evolution of this society happened much in the same way as the Partie Quarree had developed in Williamsburg. First, there was an exclusive and intimate group of friends, which, bit by bit, became more extended in its membership, interests, and accomplishments. It is likely that Small was eager to add Darwin to the symposia much in the same way as he had wanted to include Jefferson and his students into Governor's Palace discussions. Small achieved many of the same results through his efforts to bring new thinkers into the club, but this time in a grander and more expansive way than was the case in Williamsburg. In addition, the group not only changed its composition from the private gathering of Boulton and Small, but also changed the direction of its mission. Despite the conjectures about its inception, Robert Schofield maintained, "The story of the Lunar Society essentially begins in 1765 with the arrival in Birmingham of Dr. William Small."[20]

THE BIRMINGHAM LUNAR SOCIETY

Eric Robinson had suggested that the probable initiator of the Lunar Circle was Erasmus Darwin.[21] It was Small, however, who encouraged Boulton to include Darwin in their regular dinners and then expanded the circle to include a wide range of similarly minded individuals.[22] Richard Lovell Edgeworth noted that "Dr. Small formed a link which combined Mr. Boulton, Mr. Watt, Dr. Darwin, Mr. Wedgwood, Mr. Day and myself together—men of very different character but all devoted to literature and science."[23] Biographer Samuel Smiles concurred, describing the inception of the group:

From an early period the idea of a society ... seems to have been entertained by Boulton. It was probably suggested by his friend Dr. Small. The object of the proposed Society was to be at the same time friendly and scientific. The members were to exchange views with each other on topics relating to literature, art, and science; each contributing his quota of entertainment and instruction.[24]

SMALL AND THE FOUNDING OF THE LUNAR SOCIETY

Several other factors point to Small as the true catalyst for this group. Even though Darwin and Boulton had associated with each other for several years before Small's arrival, it was not until after Small came to Birmingham that the informal circle began to meet.[25] Jenny Uglow called Small the "linchpin of their circle,"[26] but he was also its genesis. As early as December 1765, Darwin was writing to Boulton and Small suggesting his idea for constructing a boiler for a steam engine and asking if "you Birmingham Philosophers" (Boulton and Small) agreed with his viewpoint. The content and context of the message suggested that Boulton and Small were already a cohesive and recognized association in Darwin's eyes.[27]

Of special concern to Boulton was the development of the Soho Manufactory, which he had established in 1761. Boulton transformed the method of production at his factory so radically that within a year of Small's arrival in 1765, the old building was replaced by a new and greatly enlarged structure. Boulton also embraced the new theory of an integrated system of production, with the manufacturing and assembly of parts taking place under a single roof, each element of the whole crafted to exact specifications by a mechanic trained in that specific assembly, and each piece fitted together with others on a precise and calculated construction. The result was more rapid production, executed with more exacting detail, and with greater ability for flexible modification, at lower costs and higher profits. The expansion and transformation of the industry was the product of Boulton's genius in adapting and refining the concept of mass production, uniformity of design, and the principle of line assembly.

In the process of innovating, there were several areas that required special attention. Inasmuch as Boulton's plans for change included power generated by water wheels, the steam engine became a matter of compelling importance to him.

Samuel Smiles pointed out that "want of water was one of the great defects of Soho as a manufacturing establishment." A reservoir supplied the water mill, which kept the factory's machines operating. However, the reservoir all but dried up in the summer, which caused great trouble and anxiety. Boulton had initially used horses as a method of conveying water back into the reservoir, but doing so was both costly and frequently inefficient. He next considered constructing a pumping engine based on the Savery or Newcomen's design, "for the purpose of raising the water from the mill-stream and returning it back into the reservoir—thereby maintaining a head of water sufficient to supply the water-wheel and keep the mill in regular work."[28] While the horse team was expensive and only intermittently successful, the Newcomen pumping system was deemed totally unreliable.

By February, Boulton was eager to find a solution before summer began to create vexing problems. He wrote to Benjamin Franklin, "My engagements Since xmas have not permitt'd me to make any further progress, with my Fire Enguine but as the Thirsty Season is approaching apace, Necessity will oblige me to set about it in good Ernest."[29] He informed Franklin that he and Small had been working on a new design and had actually progressed to the point of constructing a model engine, which he had boxed up and sent to Franklin in London to inspect. He implored Franklin to use his "fertile Genius" to evaluate the results of his experiment and to let him know those things "which you think may be usefull or preserve me from Error in the Execution of this Engine."[30]

As valuable as Franklin's guidance was, Boulton thought it might be best to cast wider nets and he himself and Darwin and Small started to pursue alternative resources by seeking out a broader group of individuals with diverse sets of knowledge and experience. Small, like Franklin, was by nature and personality a born extrovert and networker and with his "winning way of speaking" was a magnet for people from all walks of life. The new adventure called for someone of his character to draw in not only the scientists and intellectuals but also mechanics, workmen, and craftsmen with fresh insights. In short, Small, through his gregarious personality, became the default recruiter for the scientific club to come.

CHARACTERISTICS OF THE LUNAR SOCIETY

As the fields of investigation became more wide-ranging, the invitees from different fields of research broadened. Schofield characterized the importance of the Lunar Society to both England and the world as follows:

> More than any other single group, the Lunar Society of Birmingham represented the forces of change in late-eighteenth-century England, for the Lunar Society was a brilliant microcosm of that scattered community of provincial manufacturers and professional men who found England a rural society with an agricultural economy and left it urban and industrial…. Together they comprised a clearing-house for the ideas which transformed their country materially, socially, and culturally within a generation. They were men of broad interests and their discussions ranged widely, but their major mutual interest was the sciences, pure and applied—particularly as applied to the problems of industry.[31]

Schofield's description makes several important distinctions between the Lunar Society and other intellectual clubs of the times. These differences include the provincial rather than urban nature of the group; the professional span of regular, semiregular, and corresponding members—scientists, academics, and mechanics; the wide-ranging impact it had on Britain and the rest of the world; and the diversity of scientific, philosophical, and industrial interests. The Birmingham Lunar Society was an anomaly—it was inclusive rather than exclusive, and its only rituals were a good meal and stimulating conversation. It was, in many ways, a mixture of Small's enthusiasm and Boulton's generous nature. According to Schofield, the official name of Lunar Society did not even come into being until the year after Small's death. "The first recorded use of the name 'Lunar' does not appear before 1776," he writes, and "the characteristic pattern of time and place of meeting was not finally fixed until 1780."[32]

The initial meetings of the group took place at Soho House, Boulton's home on Handsworth Heath. Small, Boulton, and Darwin attended the unscripted and ad-hoc sessions. These early meetings were so informal that Eric Robinson characterized them as "unconscious." As new affiliates joined in, it became a moveable feast. Sometimes there would be a meeting at Boulton's home (also known as l'hôtel de amitié sur Handsworth Heath), sometimes at Darwin's house in Lichfield, and sometimes in the residences of other members. Although initially the date and location of the meetings varied, the group always came to meet on the Sunday nearest to the full moon so that members could more easily find their respective ways home by "fair Cynthia's rays," hence the name Lunar Society. The meetings normally began about two o'clock in the afternoon and typically ended around eight. But there were no circumscribed records or rules, and after a meal, discussions, demonstrations, and lectures, group experimentations took place. Soho, Boulton's house, was the favorite destination because of its central location, his affable character, and his generous table.

Soon, the group's original focus on steam engines diversified into other branches of science. Friends and associates of the three original members were encouraged to attend. The greatest joy for participants came with the acquisition of knowledge and that "the tracing of an idea or process to its conclusion became the most entertaining of games. The introduction of a new topic, whether for profit motives or not, by one member was a signal for the rest to add their contribution, sometimes learned, more often not, but always with enthusiasm."[33] The word of their investigations soon spread, and the number of those wishing to contribute or profit by the meetings increased. With the expanding exposure came a greater number of interested and mechanically minded individuals with amplified stores of specialized knowledge.

DISCUSSIONS AND DEMONSTRATIONS

Specific topics, talks, demonstrations, and experiments were probably prearranged for the "philosophical repasts," but the collective whole (and Boulton in particular) encouraged deviation from the prescribed subject matter and gloried in the spontaneity of experimentation. Talks that began with the technical aspects of clock making could easily segue into discussions of alkalis and clay. Hypotheses on the variations of the composition of different alkali could transition into impromptu lectures on Roman pottery. If the benefits of canals to the transport of goods began the dialogue, the discourse could suddenly switch to hydraulics, barometers, or the intricacies of raising and lowering barges by a lock system. The fine points of making pottery glaze might evolve into chemistry or the discoveries of "fossil shells and other curiosities" uncovered in group outings to the caverns of Derbyshire that might, in turn, lead to discussions of the formation of the earth and the concept of evolution.

In many ways, the Lunar Circle dinners combined the prearrangement and seriousness of the Wise Club of Aberdeen with the didactic camaraderie and nimbleness of Governor Fauquier's Williamsburg soirées—and added a dash of eccentricity to the mix. Within the former groups there was a consistent homogeny of caste and academic background, but in Birmingham, the profiles of the individuals involved in the society were widely divergent. As the society proved, the most innovative ideas often find their foundations in the diversity of backgrounds and experiences.

MEMBERSHIP AND CONTRIBUTIONS

From intimate beginnings, the Lunar Society quickly became the most prominent and influential of the provincial intellectual clubs. In order to attend a meeting of this distinguished group, it was not necessary to present oneself for inspection with a letter of recommendation in hand, but only to express an interest in the subject being discussed and either come with one of the members or be invited by them. Scientists, chemists, geologists, botanists, electricians, opticians, physicians, astronomers, poets, horologists, educators, mechanics, and men of the cloth, and, in short, anyone with a recognized expertise in any field being discussed, might be invited to contribute to the conversation.

Communication was maintained through correspondence, personal relationships, and the multiple club memberships that many associates of the circle maintained. Eric Robinson wrote, "All the world came to Soho, to meet Boulton, Watt, or Small, who were acquainted with the leading men of science throughout Europe and America."[34] Schofield remarked, "The network of connexions, by friendship or self-interest, between Lunar members and other persons with scientific or technological leanings" from an early date was "already extensive" and guests "were always welcomed…. Indeed, few persons" that the Lunars "set out to charm were ever wholly to escape their influence for the rest of their lives."[35] Robinson's statement and Schofield's characterization points out the convivial nature of the group, but also the far-reaching consequences of its actions and the importance of its role in the trans-Atlantic intellectual and scientific community and so-called Republic of Letters—which transcended politics, personalities, caste, or national identities.

The Lunar Society hosted individuals ranging from the exalted— Princess Dashkova of Russia, Benjamin Franklin, John Smeaton, Hugh Blair, James Ferguson, James Hutton, Daniel Solander, and Adam Afzelius, to the infamous and shadowy—Eric Raspe, the suspected jewel thief, and John Collins, the American rebel. Its inherent democratic sociability meant that anyone might be invited to attend its meetings and any area of science, religion, education, or politics might become the topic of the evening with the twist of a phrase or a provocative comment. Although little is known about what went on during the group's meetings, Robinson emphasized, "Its indirect significance in the cross fertilization of ideas is testified to by its long life and by the esteem in which it was held not only by those who were a part of it, but by a wide circle of distinguished contemporaries."[36]

In an age and in a country saturated by intellectual clubs, with the preeminent societies being situated in London, the Birmingham Lunar Society was exceptional. If Small was the spark for this intellectual conflagration, Boulton was the fuel supply, in that he contributed his genius for innovation, personality, resources, and connections. Potential access to Boulton's wealth and generosity may have been an incentive to a few—nevertheless, it was more often Boulton who benefited from the discussions.[37]

Questions have arisen among scholars concerning the membership of the Birmingham Lunar Society. It appears that the Lunar Society was not limited to Schofield's list of fourteen,[38] to Robinson's more expanded version,[39] or even to the generous assessment of R. V. Wells.[40] In fact, the group was far more elastic in its parameters than these estimates. Particularly in its early years, the Lunar Society was a living, breathing organism, expanding or contracting depending on circumstances, convenience, or necessity.

Because of crowded schedules and extended distances, few associates were available to attend on a consistent basis. In the period before the death of Small, a variety of philosophers, artists, political figures, and those with specific mechanical or scientific expertise wandered in and out of meetings with nonchalant regularity. Eric Robinson wrote of the society, "The most that can be said with certainty is that there was always a nucleus of regulars and a fairly constant flow of visitors to Lunar Society meetings. Since the transition from a member to an occasional visitor or vice versa cannot be determined accurately it is better not to dogmatize about it."[41]

PROSOPOGRAPHICAL PROFILES

The background and conventions of the attendees of the society were as varied as their interests. Religious beliefs ranged the gamut of conservative and conventional to radical and heretical. The Reverend Joseph Berrington, a friend of Samuel Galton, was a Catholic priest, James Keir and Matthew Boulton were conventional Anglicans, Joseph Priestley a Unitarian, Erasmus Darwin a Deist, Samuel Galton a Quaker, and John Baskerville an atheist. As a whole, the group tended to be politically radical. Some (like Boulton) were steadfastly Tory and traditional in sentiment, some supported the American opposition, most were in favor of democratizing the British government, and Priestley was so extreme in his support of the French Revolution that a conservative crowd burned down his house in Birmingham and chased him out of the county.

The "Lunatics," as they were sometimes called, were innovators in areas outside of science as well: Day promoted theories of equality and freedom; Priestley advocated political radicalism; Darwin championed female education; and Edgeworth proposed a child-centered pedagogy with a varied curriculum, and use of a didactic approach, foreshadowing Frederick Froebel and Johann Pestalozzi, the progenitors of progressive education. Edgeworth and Day were so taken with the philosophy of Jean-Jacques Rousseau that they raised their children according to his precepts, which led to some disastrous outcomes.[42]

ACCOMPLISHMENTS AND INNOVATIONS

The accomplishments of various associates of the Lunar Circle (later styled the Lunar Society) are breathtaking, but because there was so much exchange and brainstorming among the various members of the Lunar Society, the credit for specific inventions, improvements, or theories is often blurry and as historian Eric Robinson noted, "It is not always possible to separate the work being done by the Lunar Society members as individuals, from work being done by them as members of the society."[43]

The following is a partial listing of contributions made by members or associates of the Lunar Society: Among the inventions were clocks, engines, steam engines, horizontal windmills, barometers, pyrometers, magnets, micrometers, thermometers, chronometers, lightning conductors, speaking machines (automatons), powered vehicles, telegraphs, electrical machines, copying machines, coin presses, and hydraulic rams. Contributions to chemistry included the discoveries of oxygen, hydrogen, nitrous oxide, carbon dioxide, the use of alkalis, and carbonated water. Interest in scientific classification and investigation by members of the Lunar Society led to discoveries in mineralogy, botany, geology, paleontology, hygiene, anatomy, and medicine.

The participants considered all sources, advice, and variance of opinion. Suggestions were offered without a need for recognition. Determination of credit for theories, inventions, and discoveries was not only separated from Birmingham by distance, but also by time.

In an age of shameless self-advertisement, Small exhibited almost no interest in promoting himself. As Boulton was best at adapting the theoretical concepts of others into practical and profitable application, Small was at his best coaxing the potential out of others.

Boulton's area of expertise was industrial application; James Keir was the point man for chemistry; Josiah Wedgwood specialized in ceramic chemistry and dabbled in geology and clays; John Whitehurst was an expert mechanic and instrument maker; Erasmus Darwin experimented with botany, physics, and zoology; Joseph Priestley was interested in the properties of fixed air and chemistry (and was communicating with Small and Boulton as early as 1773); James Watt was a prodigy in the subjects of geology, mechanics, and instrument making (he and Small collaborated on clocks, quadrants, telescopes, drawing machines, and the steam engine); Richard Lovell Edgeworth was accomplished in mechanics, magnetism, and surveying; and

Thomas Day's passion was educational innovation. Small, in his own right, was a master of chemistry, metallurgy, instrument making, surveying, agriculture, astronomy, optics, pharmacology, and surgery, and by his wide range of knowledge often provided insightful links among the different fields to others.

NOT ALWAYS BUSINESS:
UNUSUAL THEORIES AND ECCENTRIC BETS

Not all discussions and demonstrations were of a truly serious nature and some proposals and experiments were suggested in a frivolous manner or conducted as the result of a bet. Small proposed to Watt that it had been his observance that "the frozen space of the Globe is annually increasing at the rate of about 300 part of a degree of latitude at the modicum <or more>. So that after a certain number of Years, all Europe, & finally the whole surface of this earth will be frozen, as the Moon is now, & has long been" and, therefore, it would be "exceedingly" proper for him to write the "Emperors and Empresses of Constantinople, Germany and Austria [and] the Kings of France, Spain, Britain & Prussia" a circular letter requesting enough gunpowder (for certainly they had wastefully used more in the last 20 years) to blow up the icebergs and tow them down to the 'torrid zones,'" thereby preserving the world from another ice age and "producing a perpetual Summer."[44] While this seems on the face of it nonsense, a like project was recently being proposed to alleviate water shortages in South Africa.[45]

With a rumor circulating about a automaton that had been invented in France, Darwin asked Franklin if he knew of such a machine, "I have heard of somebody that attempted to make a speaking machine, pray was there any Truth in any such reports."[46] It seems that Darwin brought the matter to Matthew Boulton's attention and evidently because of the ribbing that Boulton directed at him, Darwin wagered that he himself could construct such a device. Boulton called his bluff.

I promise to pay to Dr. Darwin, of Lichfield, one thousand pounds upon his delivering to me (within two years of the date hereto) an instrument called an organ that is capable of pronouncing the Lord's Prayer, the Creed, and the Ten Commandments in the vulgar tongue, and his ceding to me, and only me, the property of said invention with all the advantages thereunto appertaining.[47]

Darwin was evidently successful in this endeavor and described his automaton in his work *Temple of Nature*.

Many years ago, I contrived a wooden mouth with lips of soft leather, and with a valve over the back part of the nostrils, both which could be quickly opened or closed by the pressure of the fingers, the vocality was given by a silk ribbon ... between two bit of smooth wood a little hollowed; so that when a gentle current of air from bellows was blown on the ribbon, it gave an agreeable tone, as it vibrated between the wooden sides, much like a human voice. This head pronounced the p, b, m, and the a, with so great nicety as to deceive all who had heard it unseen, when it pronounced mama, papa, map and pam; it had a most plaintive tone, when the lips were gradually closed.[48]

Whether or not Boulton concluded that Darwin had sufficiently met the terms of the agreement is not known but his friend and fellow Lunar club member Richard Lovell Edgeworth wrote to Darwin many years later reporting, "The speaking machine, which is just announced from France, does not say so many words as yours did many years ago.... I placed one of yours in a room near some people ... who actually thought I had a child with me calling mama and papa."[49]

RESULTS AND RAMIFICATIONS

The exchange of useful knowledge in the eighteenth century was a transfer that tended to be more circular than linear, and the need for individual recognition was less acute than the desire to improve the situation of society—or in the case of industrialist tycoons—to make a significant profit. Rather than proceeding in a direct line from problem to solution, often theories, innovations, and improvements came about through intellectual curiosity and very frequently by accident. Particularly as it relates to the Lunar Society, the freewheeling nature of the society led to discoveries in areas that were sometimes tangent, but sometimes totally unrelated to the original subject of the conversation; often discoveries that were made in one sphere had applications in other areas. The steam engine was originally conceived of as a way to pump flooded copper mines free of water; it then expanded to an application to convey water to water mills, and then to power rotative motors and move trains—circular rather than linear—much like the meetings of the Lunar Society itself.

What distinguished the Lunar Society from many other intellectual clubs of the times was its explicit request to more industrial and commercial members to take the results of intellectual inquisitiveness and find a way to utilize them in commercial enterprises, thus enhancing their potential for profit, expanding the corridors for collateral applications, and ensuring that the innovations and new concepts did not die aborning.

Soho Factory   Etruria Factory

Boulton, Keir, and Wedgwood used the Lunar Society's discoveries and scientific methods to their own economic advantages. Boulton's Soho Factory adapted mechanical power and assembly line processes to manufacture goods and engines swiftly and inexpensively; Wedgwood's Etruria Factory combined botany, chemistry, and new industrial processes to turn out the finest pottery, and Keir's Tipton Works comingled chemistry and medical theory to produce a million pounds of soap a year. All three employed scientific methodology, division of labor, and the standardization of parts to make their factories function ergonomically. Both the process and the progress were the incipient steps of the Industrial Revolution.

The great advantage of being a part of this group was that it was a nexus of ideas about advancements in industry, science, literature, and commerce. Through their collective influence, projects that might not have been undertaken were done, theories that might have gone unexplored were refined and published, and patents that might have gone begging received approval and were put into use. The filiations spawned by the multiple memberships maintained by friends and associates of the Lunar Society crossed all manner of social, political, religious, and geographic boundaries.

Some accomplishments of Lunar Society members are more evident than others. The collaborations accomplished during these years were not restricted to the narrow boundaries of the Midlands and across England, but throughout the Western world, and were always on the cutting edge of technology. In addition to the discoveries made in Birmingham, members of the society cross-fertilized their concepts, theories, and inventions by their memberships in other organizations. Eleven members of the Lunar Society were also members of the Royal Society; others were participants in multiple medical societies, literary clubs, and political organizations, The extent and impact of the pollination of ideas crossed religious, social, and political lines—even oceans.

MATTHEW BOULTON'S CENTRAL
ROLE IN THE LUNAR SOCIETY

Matthew Boulton.
European Magazine.

Matthew Boulton was a born promoter. He never saw a business without conceiving ways of improving it; he never spent a year without attempting to expand and improve his own. Throughout his life, he jumped from one project to another, often before the first was completed and frequently before it was apparent whether it could successfully be completed. Although he possessed a quick mind, he worked best at the elaboration of other people's ideas.[50]

In addition to being a congenial manipulator, Boulton was also a kind and generous benefactor, willing to use his resources or influence to help friends and employees. Boulton also considered the Lunar Society as a vehicle to advance his industrial designs. Meetings often followed the track of his most current business interest, and Small and Darwin often appeared instrumental in recruiting people of potential value to his projects. Boulton (and indeed Josiah Wedgwood) were always anxious to pursue a new venture or an improvement, sometimes taking inspiration from something as innocuous as a stray comment uttered during a Lunar Society meeting.

When Boulton was concentrating on "selling what the world most wanted—power," many of the meetings focused on "steam-enginry." When Boulton and Josiah Wedgwood wanted to make a fortune in the pottery and vase business, aspects of the use of alkalis, clays, and ormolu were the foci of discussions and experimentation. Since many of the regular attendees had invested in canal projects, inland navigation often became a topic of conversation and debate. Not all meetings were exclusively subordinated to Boulton's economic purposes, however, and subjects totally unrelated to Boulton's immediate concerns were frequently discussed. Boulton was always open to new opportunities; when archaeological excavations created hyperbolic headlines, Boulton and Wedgwood turned their intellectual curiosity into a good money-getting scheme, reproducing copies of the ancient urns, thereby capitalizing the excitement about archaeological finds into profitable reproductions in the pottery business.[51]

SOHO FACTORY

Another way in which Boulton was a precursor to the Industrial Revolution was in systematic operation of his manufactories. His factory, Soho, was of an entirely new design. It was built for utility, flexibility, and mass production. While there have been suggestions that Boulton followed Adam Smith's prescription with regard to the division of labor, Smith's *Wealth of Nations* was not published until 1776, more than a decade after the establishment of Boulton's factory—a historical hysteron-proteron. In 1774, Soho was described in *Swinney's Birmingham Directory* as follows:

> This place is situated in the Parish of Handsworth, in the County of Stafford, two Miles distant from Birmingham. The building consists of four Squares, with Shops, Warehouses, &c., for a Thousand Workmen, who, in a great variety of Branches, excel in their several Departments; not only in the fabrication of Buttons, Buckles, Boxes, Trinkets, &c., in Gold, Silver, and a variety of Compositions.... And

it is by the Natives hereof, or of the parts adjacent, (whose emulation and taste the Proprietors have spared no Care or Expense to excite and improve), that it is brought to its present flourishing State. The number of ingenious mechanical Contrivances they avail themselves of, by the means of Water Mills, much facilitate their Work, and saves a great portion of Time and Labour.[52]

The novelty and ingenuity of Boulton's plan at Soho and especially its reputation for producing fine products in a swift and economic way spread the fame of the factory and its architect across the land. Many ambitious mechanics, industrialists, men of science, philosophers, writers of fact and fiction, lawyers, politicians, and those seeking advancement soon made their way to the doors of Soho. Boulton's reputation for geniality and graciousness acted as an incentive for the yet uninitiated.

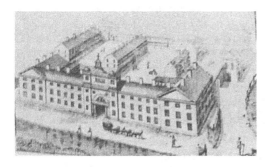
Soho Factory—Front

Soho Factory—Rear

The already-celebrated work and reputations of Small, Boulton, and the Lunar Society were about to advance exponentially with the arrival of a little-known and unheralded instrument repairman from Glasgow—James Watt.

NOTES

1. Benjamin Franklin to Matthew Boulton, May 22, 1765, *The Papers of Benjamin Franklin, Volume 12, January 1, 1765 through December 31, 1765*, ed. Leonard W. Labaree, Helen C. Boatfield, and James H. Hutson (New Haven: Yale University Press, 1968), 12:140.

2. Nathaniel Jeffreys to Matthew Boulton, July 5, 1765, MS 3782/12/23/79, Archives, Birmingham Public Library, Birmingham, England (hereafter cited as Birmingham). The date in the Birmingham Inventory is October 5, 1766, but it is in error as the date on the letter reads July 5, 1766.

3. "Birmingham Hospital," *Aris's Birmingham Gazette*, December 30, 1765, Ganter Collection, Archives, Swem Library, College of William and Mary, Williamsburg, Virginia (hereafter cited as Swem Library); see also: J. A. Langford, *A Century of Birmingham Life* (Birmingham: E. C. Osborne, 1868), 1:157.

4. "Birmingham Hospital," *Aris's Birmingham Gazette*, December 30, 1765, Ganter Collection, Archives, Swem Library.

5. Robert Schofield, *The Lunar Society of Birmingham* (Oxford: Clarendon Press, 1963), 36. Boulton's skilled workers from Soho were treated by Small at the hospital—making his factory one of the first to offer compulsory health care to its employees.

6. Schofield, *The Lunar Society of Birmingham*, 88; see also original articles of agreement between William Small, M.B., and others, of Birmingham, of the one part, and Richard Yates of London, gent., of the other, "for the erection and establishment of a Theatre or Play House in New Street," September 10, 1773, MS 3069/Acc1920-020/288216, Birmingham Central Library, Birmingham; see also Langford, *A Century of Birmingham Life*, 1:190.

7. John Money, *Experience and Identity: Birmingham and the West Midlands* (Manchester: Manchester University Press, 1977), 88.

8. "I have the Pleasure to inform You, that Dr Small's affairs are become greatly more extended then when we left Bir. & some dangerous Cases have offered, this greatly increased his reputation, so that I took the Liberty of saying what You had told me in Confidence in Relation to Russia; he replied he had altered his Mind, as his Practice (nearly) was as Much as his Wish, but that he Must go to London to thank Doctor Heberden for his kind Intention, which he could not well do (or at least so respectfully) by Writing." John Baskerville to Matthew Boulton, December 9, 1765, MS 3782/12/219/201, Archives, Birmingham Central Library, Birmingham.

9. Schofield, *The Lunar Society of Birmingham*, 35.

10. Matthew Boulton to Benjamin Franklin, February 22, 1766, MS 3782 /12/1/2, Archives, Birmingham Central Library, Birmingham. See also Benjamin Franklin, *The Papers of Benjamin Franklin, Volume 13, January 1, 1766 through December 31, 1766*, ed. Leonard W. Labaree (New Haven: Yale University Press, 1969), 13:166.

11. Matthew Boulton to James Watt, February 7, 1769, in James P. Muirhead, *The Origin and Process of the Mechanical Inventions of James Watt* (London: John Murray, 1856), 2:41–42.

12. Matthew Boulton to Benjamin Franklin, February 22, 1766, MS 3782 /12/1/2, Archives, Birmingham Central Library, Birmingham; Benjamin Franklin, in Labaree, *Papers of Benjamin Franklin*, 13:166.

13. Benjamin Franklin, in Labaree, *Papers of Benjamin Franklin*, 13:196.

14. Erasmus Darwin to Matthew Boulton, March 11, 1766, Erasmus Darwin Commonplace Book, Erasmus Darwin Centre, Lichfield, England. See also Samuel Smiles, *Lives of the Engineers: Boulton and Watt* (London: John Murray, 1904), 149.

15. "As I was riding Home yesterday, I concider'd a Scheme of the fiery Chariot, and the longer I contemplated this favourite Idea, the [more] practicable it appeared to me. I shall lay my Thoughts before you, crude and indigested as they occur'd to me." Erasmus Darwin to Matthew Boulton, June 6, 1764, MS 3782/13/53/40, Archives, Birmingham Central Library, Birmingham.

16. Erasmus Darwin to Matthew Boulton, March 11, 1766, Erasmus Darwin Commonplace Book, Erasmus Darwin Centre, Lichfield, England. See also Smiles, *Lives of the Engineers: Boulton and Watt*, 149.

17. Ibid.

18. Ibid.

19. Schofield, *The Lunar Society of Birmingham*, 41.

20. Robert Schofield, "The Lunar Society of Birmingham: A Bicentenary Appraisal," *Notes and Records of the Royal Society of London* 21, no. 2 (December 1966): 146.

21. Eric Robinson, "The Lunar Society: Its Membership and Organization" (London: Newcomen Society Lecture, 1963), 154. Courtesy of Dr. Richard Hills.

22. "Dr. Small formed a link which combined Mr. Boulton, Mr. Watt, Dr. Darwin, Mr. Wedgwood, Mr. Day, and myself together." Robinson, "The Lunar Society: Its Membership and Organization," 156.

23. Schofield, *The Lunar Society of Birmingham*, 36.

24. Samuel Smiles, *Lives of the Engineers: The Steam Engine, Boulton and Watt* (London: John Murray, 1878), 4:293.

25. "The beginnings of that group were already at hand in Matthew Boulton, a native of Birmingham who had recently expanded the modest buckle factory inherited from his father into what was ultimately to be the most extensive manufactory in England, the Soho Works; in Erasmus Darwin, physician of nearby Lichfield after medical study in the University of Edinburgh, with John Hunter in London, and at St. John's College, Cambridge; and in John Whitehurst, clock and scientific instrument-maker and itinerant builder of Derby. Boulton, Darwin, and Whitehurst had known one another for about ten years when Small appeared; they had together or in pairs entertained Franklin during his tours into the Midlands, and already begun some of those investigations into instrumentation, electricity, meteorology, and geology which later were to be so persistent a concern of Lunar Society members. The scant remaining correspondence from this early period does not, however, reveal much of the sense of group cohesion nor any of the centripetal tendency drawing others into the group which soon becomes apparent after Small's arrival." Schofield, "The Lunar Society of Birmingham: A Bicentenary Appraisal," 147.

26. Jenny Uglow, *The Lunar Men* (New York: Farrar, Straus, and Giroux, 2002), 81.

27. Erasmus Darwin to Matthew Boulton, December 12, 1765, MS 3782/13/53/30, Birmingham Archives and Heritage, Birmingham Central Library, Birmingham. Courtesy of Saley Ahmed.

28. Smiles, *Lives of the Engineers: Boulton and Watt*, 147.

29. Matthew Boulton to Benjamin Franklin, February 22, 1766, MS 3782 /12/1/2, Archives, Birmingham Central Library, Birmingham. See also Labaree, *Papers of Benjamin Franklin*, 13:166.

30. Ibid.

31. Schofield, *The Lunar Society of Birmingham*, 12.

32. Ibid., 17.

33. Ibid., 89.

34. Robinson, "The Lunar Society: Its Membership and Organization," 160.

35. Schofield, *The Lunar Society of Birmingham*, 112.

36. Robinson, "The Lunar Society: Its Membership and Organization," 160.

37. Ibid., 18.

38. Ibid., 82. Schofield listed Matthew Boulton, Erasmus Darwin, Thomas Day, Richard Lovell Edgeworth, Samuel Galton Jr., Robert Augustus Johnson, James Keir, Joseph Priestley, William Small, Jonathon Stokes, James Watt, Josiah Wedgwood, John Whitehurst, and William Withering.

39. Robinson, "The Lunar Society: Its Membership and Organization," *ad passim*.

40. R. V. Wells, "The Lunar Society," *School Science Magazine* 33, no. 119 (1951–1952): 13–14.

41. Robinson, "The Lunar Society: Its Membership and Organization," 157.

42. Ibid., 160.

43. Ibid., 157.

44. Ibid., 102.

45. Tim Smedley, "The outrageous plan to haul icebergs to Africa," BBC News, September 21, 2018, https://www.bbc.com/future/article/20180918-the-outrageous-plan-to-haul-icebergs-to-africa (accessed August 1, 2021).

46. Erasmus Darwin to Benjamin Franklin, July 18, 1772, quoted in L. Hussakof, *Benjamin Franklin and Erasmus Darwin*, 774, cited in Schofield, *The Lunar Society of Birmingham*, 109.

47. Schofield, *The Lunar Society of Birmingham*, 109.

48. Erasmus Darwin, *Temple of Nature* (Baltimore: John W. Butler, and Bonsal and Niles, 1804), 138–139, cited in Schofield, *The Lunar Society of Birmingham*, 110.

49. Schofield, *The Lunar Society of Birmingham*, 109.

50. Ibid., 18.

51. See Barbara Fogarty, "Matthew Boulton and Francis Eginton's Mechanical Painting" (Ph.D. diss., 2010, University of Birmingham), Archives, University of Birmingham, Birmingham.

52. Quoted in Samuel Timmins, "The Industrial History of Birmingham," ed. Samuel Timmins, *Birmingham and the Midland Hardware* (1866; New York: Routledge, 1967), 218.

CHAPTER 12

William Small and James Watt

In his early years, before visiting Birmingham, James Watt had been a repairman and maker of optic, astronomical, mathematical, nautical, and musical instruments. He had apprenticed at constructing and repairing scientific and musical instruments in London and Dublin, and when he returned to Scotland, became a technical assistant to several faculty members at the University of Glasgow.

WATT AND SMALL'S FIRST MEETING

"In 1767, however, on his [Watt's] return from London, after attending the Committee of the House of Commons on the Forth and Clyde Canal Bill, he visited Soho, being introduced by Dr. William Small, who along with Mr Fothergill, a partner of Mr. Boulton, showed him the works. Mr Boulton being absent from home, the future friends and associates did not meet at that time."[1]

During the tour, the two—Small and Watt—struck up a conversation about "steam-enginry," a subject that had been the frequent topic of interest between Small, Boulton, Franklin, and Erasmus Darwin. Watt, in his capacity as a mechanic for the professors of Natural History at the University of Glasgow, had repaired a model of a Newcomen steam engine. In the course of the repairs, he reimagined alternative concepts to create a design that could make the instrument more efficient, both in terms of improved operation and of productive outcomes. Small immediately recognized the ingenuity of the construction and implications for the future applications of Watt's ideas; he actively promoted both the inventor and the invention to Boulton.

It was not until 1768 on his return from London—where he had been taking the necessary steps for obtaining a patent for his improved steam engine—that Watt was introduced to Boulton. "With whom," Watt recalled, "I had much conversation on the subject of the Soho manufactures. He explained to me many things of which I had been before ignorant. On my part, I explained to him my invention of the steam-engine, and several other schemes of which my head was then full, in the success of which he expressed a friendly interest. My stay at Birmingham at that time was short, but I afterwards kept up a correspondence with Mr. B. through our mutual friend Dr Small."[2]

THE COLLABORATION BEGINS

The fortuitous meeting between Small and James Watt set in motion a series of events that would result in the world's first practical steam engine. Small was pivotal in recognizing the value of Watt's concept for modifying the design of the Newcomen steam engine; he was essential in influencing Boulton to employ Watt, a critical advisor in freeing Watt from his financial obligations, central in collaborating with Watt to fine-tune his invention, and indispensable in finding political backing for the Act of Parliament that made the steam engine a monopoly for the firm of Boulton and Watt.[3]

From the time of their first meeting, Small unrelentingly harangued Boulton to come to Watt's support and make capital from his ideas. The straightforwardness of this prospect, however, was already compromised by Watt's obligations to Dr. John Roebuck.[4]

During a time of desperation and setbacks, Watt had sold a portion of his patent to the former Birmingham doctor, but subsequently regretted this decision. Small and Watt, like secret sorority sisters, furtively and conspiratorially wrote back and forth, seeking a way around this impediment. Small always bolstered Watt's flagging spirits with reports of Boulton's interest in his invention and predicted that better times would come.

Boulton, intrigued by Watt's concepts, was not yet ready to commit to taking on the obligations and expenses of the funding such a risky project. At last, nagged by Small and seduced by thoughts of the potential profits and benefits to his own operations such an invention might generate, Boulton wrote to Watt in the winter of 1769. He claimed that having been motivated by "love of you, and love of a money-getting, ingenious project," he was willing to act as a midwife to "ease your Burthen" and "introduce your Brat into the World."[5] The snag in this plan, however, was the necessity of coming to an understanding with Dr. Roebuck.

NEGOTIATIONS WITH DR. ROEBUCK

The major impetus and reason for Dr. Roebuck's initial interest in Watt's design of the steam engine were the mines that he owned at Prestonpans, near Edinburgh, which flooded with intermittent regularity—the design of Watt's engine showed great promise for resolving the recurring and increasing threat. Roebuck, although convinced that Watt's design would be the answer to his problem, had encountered an unrelenting series of financial reversals. Alarmed by the exigencies and the dire circumstances at Prestonpans, Roebuck's creditors were anxious to be repaid their long overdue loans and threatened litigation. Strapped for cash and looking for reprieve and a possible partner, Roebuck approached Boulton with a proposal for a limited partnership. Boulton informed Watt that while Roebuck's overture was appreciated it did not meet his expectations.

I note what you say in respect to your connection with Doctor Roebuck, from whom I received a letter, dated the 12th December, offering me a share of his property in your engine, as far as respects the counties of Warwick, Stafford, and Derby. I am obliged to you and him thinking of me as a partner in any degree; but the plan proposed to me is so very different from that which I conceived at the time I talked with you upon that subject, that I cannot think it a proper one for me to meddle with, as I do not intend turning engineer…. It would not be worth my while to make for three counties only; but I find it very well worth my while to make for the whole world.[6]

There was a great deal of back and forth between Boulton and Roebuck, the negotiations becoming tenuous and prolonged. Within a short time, however, Roebuck's situation declined even further, and his financial position began to become more and more precarious. In the autumn of 1769, the mines once again flooded and the receivers were more fiercely howling for the immediate payment of the debts. He made a second and more enticing offer to Boulton—proposing that in return for the sum of £1,000 he was willing to become equal partners in the steam engine patent (for the whole world this time).

Whereas Mr. James Watt has assigned me two-thirds of the property of the patent of the steam-engine, which he took out some time in the course of the last winter, I hereby offer you one-half of the above two-thirds, or one-third of the whole patent, on condition that you pay to me such a sum, not less than one thousand pounds, as you, after experiments of the engine shall be completed, shall think just and reasonable; and twelve months from this date you are to take your final resolution. I oblige myself to procure Mr. Watt's assent to this agreement.[7]

Boulton once again rejected the offer. As zealous as Small was about the prospects for the steam engine, Boulton was still not won over. If he decided to engage in a business venture, he wanted control. A one-third proposition did not inspire him. Negotiations sputtered on for several years. Roebuck's financial situation was becoming more and more unstable as time went by, familiar troubles were recurring, new disasters were impending, the outcry of the creditors became ever more strident, and dire consequences were at hand. It was at this juncture that Watt secretly wrote to Small pleading Roebuck's financial and psychological state. "The Doctor is on the contrary too sanguine & always thinks things easier than they are, his present exigencies may also attempt him to insist on higher terms for his property than it is really worth."[8] In the same letter he pressed Small to convince Boulton to offer the best terms possible.

Excruciating reversals of fortune and dunning creditors finally forced Roebuck's hand.[9] In April 1773, Roebuck's creditors held a meeting to discuss his position and, as his mines at Boroughstoness (Bo'ness) were once again flooded and his hopes of financial recovery were dashed. Boulton appointed Watt to act as his agent at this meeting and agreed to abide by whatever resolution that Watt might consider reasonable. Inasmuch as the creditors did not think Watt's patent to be worth "a farthing," Watt was able to procure rights to the patent at a reasonable price, the agreement was settled with Roebuck and his creditors, and the already-rusting engine was soon dismantled in Scotland and sent in pieces to Birmingham.[10]

SURVEYING IN SCOTLAND

Until Watt moved to Birmingham, intricate details about the steam engine were communicated to Small through the post. Watt often indiscreetly revealed important specifications about the engine— Small responded in a more-reserved fashion. In an age in which industrial spies, inefficient postal carriers, and plain nosey-parkers were ubiquitous, both Boulton and Small were concerned about revealing explicit directions and details of improvements by way of the mail. Small was most concerned about furtive London scoundrels; Boulton was anxious of Continental operatives, particularly the French. Some archivists have suggested, from the nature of the extant correspondence between Watt and Small it is likely that Boulton instructed Small to preserve their correspondence so that it might be used as evidence in the eventuality of patent litigation. In order to avoid such a forensic inconvenience, Small gave precise instructions to Watt for writing up patent information:

> You should neither give drawings nor descriptions of any particular machinery (if such omissions would be allowed at the office), but specify in the clearest manner you can that you have discovered some principles, and thought of new applications of others, by means of which, joined together, you intend to construct steam-engines of much greater powers, and applicable to a much greater number of useful purposes, than any which hitherto have been constructed; that to effect each particular purpose, you design to employ particular machinery.[11]

At the time of the Boulton-Roebuck agreement, Watt was still in Scotland completing a survey of canals between Loch Oich and Loch Lochy, and during the process he had developed new surveying devices, including an improved micrometer and a quadrant to enhance the accuracy of surveying techniques. His value to Boulton, in addition to his steam engine, now included an advanced knowledge and expertise in naval surveying and canal construction, which was increasingly becoming a new avenue of investment and innovation that was enriching those getting in on the ground floor—including Boulton, Small, Wedgwood, other members of the Lunar Society, and several of their aristocratic patrons. It would soon serve as an invaluable resource to advance their commercial plans.

THE CANAL SCHEME

A plausible and welcome alternative to poor roads—impassable during times of bad weather, full of potholes, plagued by delays, and haunted by highwaymen—was the concept of an integrated canal system that would connect English cities and industries with London. It was a particularly enticing opportunity for industrial concerns in the Midlands. Boulton and Wedgwood were especially keen about the prospect of a canal system in that it would both allow for raw materials to be brought in and manufactured wares to be taken out of the city in an expedited and inexpensive fashion with a minimum of breakage or loss.

Small wrote to James Watt with regard to the expertise and experience that he could bring to such a project, "Your survey would be the first, and as things now stand, both you and it could be warmly commended to Lord Dartmouth, who is the head of the Council of Trade, to Lord Sandwich, the first Lord of the Admiralty, and to Lord North."[12]

The powerful Lord Dartmouth was an acquaintance of Boulton and Small as a fellow subscriber to the Birmingham Public Hospital and a member of the Birmingham Navigation Committee. Watt's presence in Birmingham meant not only that the progress on the engine could be supervised in a more efficient manner, but also that Watt (because of his experience in this area) could wisely advise and contribute to the advancements of the canal scheme. In an attempt to lure him more quickly to Birmingham, Small wrote to Watt in the spring of 1773 that he and Darwin "were trying to persuade the Coventry Canal Company to hire" him as their chief engineer.[13]

In spite of the lack of economic and scientific opportunities in Scotland, Watt refused to leave the country because of the failing health of his wife Peggy. Watt informed Small that she died on September 24, 1773, and, with her death, his only reason for remaining in Scotland had evaporated. Watt completed the survey between Inverness and Fort William, dismantled the rusting machine, and followed the steam engine to Birmingham. Boulton arranged rooms for Watt in his own former quarters at Newhall Walk.[14]

WATT MOVES TO BIRMINGHAM

With Boulton, Watt, and Small now in immediate communication with each other and with the advice of Darwin and Edgeworth close at hand, progress on the steam engine continued apace. Small and Watt, at last, were able to discuss the details for correcting defects and making improvements in perfect freedom. At the same time, they would have the ability to the spontaneous brainstorming that was not possible in written communications. In addition, the Soho Factory was available for new or necessary parts and improvisations, there was also the immediate access to technical advice and experienced mechanics, and the overseeing and anxious eye of Matthew Boulton left no room for melancholy and inertia, but provided a stream of fresh energy and inspiration for alternative applications. Small's ability to spot and fix the flaws in design and construction proved critical to Watt's success. At meetings of the Lunar Circle, members suggested and created new improvements to the already-existing details and provided new avenues for modification.

A third area in which Small was indispensable to the success of Watt's steam engine was his behind-the-scenes lobbying to obtain a government-sanctioned monopoly for the firm of Boulton, Watt, and Small.[15] At issue was the authority, only to be procured by an Act of Parliament, to extend a monopoly on Watt's improved steam engine for twenty-five years. This monopoly would eventually put Boulton in control of the manufacture and distribution of steam engines and this authorization was central to the profitability of the enterprise.

LOBBYING FOR THE PATENT

Small, Boulton, and other members of their philosophical circle were crucial in successfully obtaining this Act of Parliament. Josiah Wedgwood had important connections with the London Board of Merchants, Matthew Boulton enjoyed the confidence of many members of Parliament, and other members of the Lunar Circle had connections with prominent scientists, politicians, men of society, finance, and industry. Even so, the efforts to obtain a monopoly were difficult and seemed, at times, impossible. Boulton, Watt, and Small made frequent trips to London to advocate for their project. Darwin, Franklin, and Wedgwood also used their considerable and combined influence to persuade certain members of Parliament to support and encourage the passage of the bill.[16]

Yet there was still much groundwork to be done. Various individuals and factions worked in Watt's interest, but, even so, the efforts were exhausting and expensive, the support was vacillating, and the outcome uncertain. Some prominent politicians railed against the bill as a vehicle to stifle competition, others predicted that the act would promote useful inventions and increases in domestic output of goods, and some appealed to the national pride of House of Commons members.

Finally, in February, matters came to a head. On February 23, 1775, the bill to extend Watt's patent for twenty-five years was drawn up with Small's help and presented to the House of Commons. On March 9, 1775, the bill was read before the House of Commons for the first time and was violently opposed by Edmund Burke and others resistant to monopolies of any kind. After considerable wrangling and extensive compromise, the bill passed all its stages and received the Royal Assent on May 22, 1775. "The Act (15 Geo. III, cap. LXI, p. 1587) extended the patent for twenty-five years from that date and expanded the boundaries of its jurisdiction to include Scotland."[17] The complex web of interconnectivity created by the activities, friendships, and loyalties of Boulton, Watt, and Small, as well as the constant and unwavering support of the other members of the Lunar Society made the success of the bill attainable.

THE DEATH OF WILLIAM SMALL

"Early in 1775 [Small] was seized with the symptoms of the ague to which he had previously been subject, and which did not at first appear to threaten an illness of more than common severity."[18] The son of Erasmus Darwin wrote about Small's final illness, "About three weeks before his Death [25 February 1775], when already poorly, Small had to travel to Tamworth, when called by a Patient for whom he had a great Regard. He vomited most of the Way in the Chaise and when he arrived there he was so feeble that he was obliged to lye down as he prescribed. On his return he went to bed and was delirious above half his Illness which was a nervous fever attended with great Feebleness."[19]

When he finally returned to his home at 9 Temple Row, Small was immediately put to bed. At first, his illness did not seem dangerous, but he suffered several relapses. Nevertheless, he continued to believe in his own recovery. As it became apparent that his illness was more serious than originally thought, a number of Small's friends, colleagues, and acquaintances were consulted. John Ash was watching over Small. Mrs. Boulton and Mrs. Fothergill acted as nurse attendants.[20]

In response to Boulton's desperate pleas for additional medical assistance, John Fothergill tried to convince Dr. Heberden and Sir John Pringle to come to Birmingham. William Heberden wrote that he could not come but thought that Small's symptoms indicated "Jail or Putrid Fever." Alexander Small wrote that he was unable to travel to Birmingham because of complications of the gout and agreed with Dr. Heberden that it was difficult to prescribe anything with propriety.[21]

Nevertheless, William remained optimistic about his recovery and on February 22 Boulton reported to Watt that "the Dr. was apparently much better yesterday, he lay upon the sofa in his own room some hours, & had a very good night, so that we all began to sing hollalujas that morning." Boulton became crazed by the vacillating states of Small's health—which quickly went from sure recovery to certain death—and wrote a desperate letter to Watt imploring him to dispatch Heberden immediately down to attend to Small."[22] Snatched from the hopes of a remarkable recovery, Small's final day was excruciating for his friends. Sweating profusely from a high fever, he became delusional, confused, nauseated, and finally fell into a coma and died. On his last day, still confident to the end that he would recover, Small was surrounded by his surrogate family, Matthew Boulton, James Keir, Erasmus Darwin, Mrs. Boulton, and Mrs. Fothergill.[23] Boulton painfully informed Watt, who was in London:

> Lo the scene is changd despair is return & sadness sits on every brow.... His pulse is very feeble & beats 136 pr minute. He sinks below his load & every vital power seems to give way. Dr. Ash expresses greater doubts than ever. I have recv. A line from Mr. [Alexander] Small today but cant answer it to night the last hour being almost come; but you may inform [him] that we are worse. The minutes of Life are few, bestow two of them in the indulgence of an affectionate Sigh for our dear Friend & then bussle.[24]

CAUSES OF DEATH

Small was only forty-one at the time of his passing, and there has been much speculation as to the cause of his death. It has been proposed by some that he became ill in Virginia. Nathaniel Jeffreys's letter of introduction for Small to Boulton, in part, read, "[Small] came home on acct. of his health & some [business] & prefers a settlement at home to returning to Virginia as he never kept his health there."[25]

Indeed, there were certain symptoms that could support that conclusion. His activities in Williamsburg, however, tell a different story. In Virginia, Small had led an active life—teaching all the collegiate courses at the college and directing the curriculum, practicing medicine in distant parts of the colony, attending convivial meetings at the Governor's Palace, organizing and conducting a scientific society, presiding at symposia for his former students, and also engaging in a such an active social life that he spent nearly half his salary from the college on wine or in taverns. It was said that he had a less hectic schedule in Birmingham, and, according to Erasmus Darwin, "he lived a quiet a recluse studious life."[26]

In spite of his "reported" quiet domestic habits, Small was not inert; he sat on various committees, acted as a town councilman; helped to establish a local theater; opened a clinic with Dr. Ash; participated in local forums to promote the canal business; organized and encouraged the meetings that would metamorphosize into the Birmingham Lunar Society; served on local committees and acted as a public servant; provided free medical assistance to the poor; encouraged, assisted, and brainstormed with a frequently despondent Watt; oversaw mechanical activities at Soho; traveled to London to attend the gatherings of various scientific and medical societies and to advocate for an extension of Watt's patent. In between this whirlwind of activities, he would collaborate with others on their inventions, work on his own, and consult with physicians both locally and in London.

Yet, he wrote to Watt that "*ennui mortel* has totally ruined me for an experimental philosopher. I have now about ten capital points in philosophy, original, important, unthought of, all capable of procuring fame, and two of procuring fortune, and yet I cannot resolve to prosecute them. I flatter myself that I shall soon be 'pulvis et umbra,' and fold my arms to sleep. Who will call me projector now?"[27]

Small seems to have been intermittently plagued by bouts of depression, or ennui, and it is difficult to determine whether this derived from a medical condition or state of mind. It seems to have been a malaise of spirit that primarily incapacitated him. On one occasion, Small wrote to Watt that his medical practice exhausted him, that it paid him "but indifferently," and that he felt fine as long as he was making progress in his work, "but if I am absolutely puzzled, and see no clue, my head turns me around, and I speedily become more tired than a galley slave."[28]

When Watt's wife was dying Small had advised him that letting himself slip away into despair would not help his wife and would be a great detriment to his own future; that the best answer to the sadness was to throw himself into his work—Watt took Small's advice on this head not only in regard to his wife but also in regard to Small. Small also recommended that Watt take baths in "decoctions" of herbs to relieve the conditions and claimed that nausea often accompanied the ennui. In 1773, he described his own symptoms to Watt.

> However, in spite of all sects of philosophers and of all their doctrines, one maxim is infallible—life must either be spent in labour or ennui. Which is best or which is worst of the two—I cannot easily discern. Unfortunately, in my case, labour seldom alleviates and often increaseth the ennui, and almost always disorders my stomach.[29]

He wrote to Watt in 1773, "I have done nothing of la[bour], Ennui and hypocondrison plague me perpe[tu]ally."[30] Small's complaints of fatigue, malaise, and depression reached such a state that Boulton called on his friend Alexander Small to confer with Sir John Pringle and William Heberden concerning Small's case.

When Thomas Day learned the severity of Small's illness, he hurried back from Brussels, but he arrived too late and his mind "was long in recovering."[31] James Watt was in London on crucial engine business. William Small's brother, Robert Small wrote to Boulton that their mother had just passed away and that the family could not immediately come down. "We were not without some fears for this week past about our brother imagining he was sick as we had written him of his mother's death about 4 weeks ago and received no answer. But weak as we knew his constitution to be we dreamt not of his death."[32]

The night Small died, an extremely distraught Boulton dashed off two letters to Watt, both reflecting the extent of his anguish. Boulton's grief was palpable:

> You have just lost a friend, so have I. Take him all in all we shall ne'er see his like again. My Loss is as inexpressible as it is irreparable. I am ready to burst.
>   Your inconsolable and affection Friend,
>   Mattw Boulton
>   Acquaint Dr Roebuck, I can't[33]

OBITUARIES AND RECOLLECTIONS

Two days after Small's death, a notice was placed in the local paper, *Aris's Birmingham Gazette*, that read:

> On Saturday Morning last died of a Fever, after a short Illness, William Small, M.D. His extensive Knowledge and great Abilities procured him universal Admiration; his eminent Virtues gained him the Esteem and Affection of all his Acquaintances. By his Death, the Poor are deprived of a most humane and disinterested Physician, and his Friends have suffered an irreparable Loss.[34]

More important to his family and his friends in Birmingham were Small's reputation and legacy. In a letter to Boulton shortly after his brother's funeral, Robert Small wrote, "Our opinion of the poor Doctors qualifications both of head and heart was very high and nothing be more acceptable to us than to find his other friends as sensible of them as we."[35] The statements and testimonials left behind by Small's friends in Birmingham perhaps give the most complete picture of his character and the legacy of his life. It is interesting to see how closely these tributes parallel the statements of Thomas Jefferson and John Page.

A regular member of the Birmingham Lunar Society, Richard Lovell Edgeworth recalled:

> By means of Mr. Keir I became acquainted with Dr. Small of Birmingham, a man esteemed by all who knew him, and by all who were admitted to his friendship beloved with, no common enthusiasm. Dr. Small formed a link which combined Mr. Boulton, Mr. Watt, Dr. Darwin, Mr. Wedgwood, Mr. Day, and myself together men of very different characters, but all devoted to literature and science. This mutual intimacy has never been broken but by death, nor have any of the number failed to distinguish themselves in science or literature.[36]

James Keir, the chemist, who attended to Small in his last days, wrote:

> [A]lthough [Small] possessed of various and eminent talents to instruct mankind, [he] has left behind no trace of all that store of knowledge and observation which he had acquired, and from which his friends never left him without drawing fresh information...He lives only in the memory of those friends who knew his worth and of the poor, whom his humane skill was ever ready to rescue form disease and pain.[37]

Thomas Day described Small as a "physician in Birmingham, who, to the most extensive, various, and accurate knowledge, in the sciences, and in life, joined engaging manners, a most exact conduct, and an enlightened humanity. Being a great master in the exact sciences, he seemed to carry their regularity and precision into his reasonings and opinions on all other subjects.[38]

It is remarkable to note that Thomas Day's characterization of Small matched almost word for word the description written by Jefferson in his *Autobiography*, in Jefferson's version, "a man profound in the most useful branches of science, with a happy talent of communication, correct and gentlemanly manners, & an enlarged & liberal mind."[39]

The last tribute to Small came from his old protégé from Virginia. A little more than two months after Small's death (the typical span of time for a commercial vessel to cross from America to London), a package and a letter arrived from Thomas Jefferson. Not knowing Small's fate and hoping that the bonds that they had forged in peace would not be broken apart by the events of the impending conflict, Jefferson gathered up a store of fine Madeira wine that he had purchased three years after Small departed from Virginia, carefully packed the wine in crates, and sat down and wrote what was to be his final letter to his old friend. He sent the bundle off by way of Captain Aselby of the *True-Patriot*. Jefferson was unaware that Small had already died before he shipped off his gift and an expression of his wishes. He closed his letter with the following:

> But I am getting into politics tho' I sat down only to ask your acceptance of the wine, and express my constant wishes for your happiness. This however seems secured by your philosophy and peaceful vocation. I shall still hope that amidst public dissension private friendship may be preserved inviolate, and among the warmest you can ever possess is that of Your obliged humble servant. Th: Jefferson

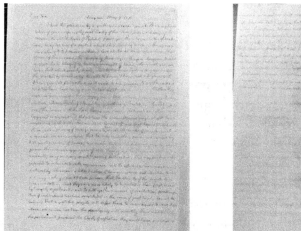

Thomas Jefferson to William Small. 7 May 1775.
Archives, Birmingham Central Library, Birmingham, England.[40]

It is intriguing to find that this is the only letter found from Jefferson to Small, and that it remarkably matches the suggestions and instruction that were expressed in the letter from Jefferson to Unknown (July 26, 1764). The hand that addressed the envelope to "Dr Small, Physician in Birmingham" did not belong to Jefferson and that neither the name of the author nor the recipient was mentioned in the text of the letter—which gives rise to the possibility that there may have been other correspondence from Jefferson that Small destroyed or letters from Small to Jefferson that may also have been discarded.

SCENE: 9 TEMPLE ROW; DATE: FEBRUARY 25, 1775

On the night of Small's death, Boulton lamented, "If there were not a few remaining objects yet remaining for me to settle my affections upon, I should wish also to take up my lodgings in the mansions of the dead."[41]

But Boulton was not the only one writing on that fateful evening—Erasmus Darwin composed an astonishing letter to his friend, William Withering:

> A person at Birmingham desired I would acquaint you with Dr. Small's death as soon as I could, but would not permit his name to be mentioned lest he might disoblige some he did not wish to disoblige. I saw by Dr. Small's papers that he had gained about £500 a year at average, taking the whole time he had been at Birmingham, and above £600 on the last year's.[42]

Darwin noted that Small had lived rather frugally and made a considerable income both from his medical practice and "by some other circumstance of manufacture or schemes." He encouraged Withering to apply to Matthew Boulton at Soho as soon as possible, and that the chances for procuring this position, "the most eligible of any country situation," were good only for a person who has "some philosophical acquirements, as well as medical." Darwin also cautioned Withering not to mention the letter to anyone and advised him to "please put <u>private</u> on the internal cover."[43] It is not known what happened to the papers of Small that Darwin mentioned in the letter. The most likely candidate to have asked Darwin to approach Withering is Dr. John Ash, but this is pure speculation.

It was several weeks after his death before Small was buried on March 15, 1775, in the graveyard at St. Philip's Cathedral, directly opposite from Small's residence and office at 9 Temple Row. The long delay for the interment may have been caused by the efforts of Matthew Boulton and James Keir to get appropriate instructions from William Small's brother, Robert Small, and wait for his arrival. After some delay, Robert Small wrote to Boulton:

> Mr Kier wrote me in your name and his own for directions about the internment and I beg leave to refer you on this subject to what I have said to him. It is in Substance that you and he do everything as if he were a brother of your own: for it is impossible that my other brother or I can be present.[44]

Boulton informed Watt that he had communicated with Robert Small, "shewing him the impropriety, nay the impossibility of settleing the Drs affairs which cannot be done by anyone but such as takes out letters of administration & therefore I have pressed him and his brothers to come down."[45] On March 9, 1775, Boulton wrote to Watt, "None of the Smalls are arrived nor any Letter w[ch] surprises me."[46]

The brothers Small departed from Dundee about March 22, 1775, and arrived in Birmingham on March 30. They had missed the funeral but immediately went to Soho, and not finding Boulton, proceeded to Darwin's house, where they engaged a Mr. Howard to write to London for the letters of administration.

The management of Small's estate and his funeral fell to Boulton's discretion. Boulton in turn seems to have delegated many of the details to his associate and William Small's good friend James Keir. To a great extent, what happened to Small's possessions—his furniture, books, paintings, papers, apparatus, and clothes—remains a mystery. Keir arranged for Small's friends to stop by Temple Row and gather up a few mementos—they likely took or bought the majority of his books and scientific apparatus, and it seems that Darwin or Ash may have ended up with his papers. Boulton made plans for his family to inherit whatever stocks and moneys that were left behind (but did not include them in the proposed partnership—which will be detailed later).

Boulton, Watt, and other friends, however, decided to set up a memorial for Small in the celebrated gardens of a nearby estate. Boulton later recalled:

> [I] wish to fix in my mind ... the remembrance of my dear departed friend ... in the prettiest and most obscure part of my garden...; tis a sepulchred grove, in which is adapted for contemplation; from one of its windows ... the church in which he was interred...; it is a sarcophagus standing upon a pedestal, on which is written: M:S: Gulielmi Small, M.D. Ob. Feb. xxv, MDCCCLXXV.[47]

The site of the memorial was located in William Shenstone's "tomb infested gardens at the Leasowes."[48] It is intriguing to note that on their trip to England in 1789, two future American presidents John Adams and Thomas Jefferson visited this very estate.[49]

THE MYSTERY OF SMALL'S PAPERS
AND POSSESSIONS

Boulton or Keir arranged for a local auctioneer, T. Warren, to conduct an estate sale of the remainder of Small's possessions.[50] These consisted of Small's books, scientific equipment, domestic items, and many of his personal effects. Marie Edgeworth wrote about some items her father, Richard Lovell Edgeworth, had inherited through Thomas Day:

When Dr. Small died, Day made some purchases from Small's estate, including a set of the *Memoires de l'Academie Royale des Sciences* and a Papin's digester. According to Marie Edgeworth, her father received some mathematical instruments from Day's estate which "were valuable ... to him, from recollections of former times.[51]

One additional item of great interest was an oil portrait of Small, painted by Tilly Kettle and purchased by local Birmingham artist James Millar. On July 23, 1779, Millar sold the painting to William Withering for four pounds and four shillings. By many twists and turns, the portrait landed at an obscure auction house in Maine, and was sold to the College of William and Mary, where it now hangs above the fireplace in the President's Office in Bafferton Hall.[52]

THE SLINGS AND ARROWS OF OUTRAGEOUS FORTUNE

The timing of Small's passing was ironic. In a final twist of fate, death snatched Small away on the cusp of wealth, a life of luxury, extended opportunities, and great fame. Small would undoubtedly have lived a life of celebrity, wealth, and opportunities had he survived.

It had been intended to include Small in the steam engine partnership on the renewal of the patent. He had been consulted in all stages of the proceedings, and one of the last things that he did was to draw up Watt's petition for the bill. No settled arrangement had yet been made—not even between Boulton and Watt. Everything depended on the success of the application for the extension of the patent.[53]

Recent information has come to light that Small was indeed an equal partner in the steam engine firm. Matthew Boulton recorded an account of this arrangement in the following document:

As I have not been instrumental in Bringing upon Boulton & Fothergill's house any risk of loss by carrying into execution of Mr Watt's invention of the fire engines I have originally agreed with

Mr Watt and Dr. Roebuck for two thirds of the patent right, the term of which I have extended by obtaining an Act of Parliament, and although I agreed with Watt and Dr Roebuck for two thirds yet at the same time I agreed with Dr Small that he should take one half of my purchase.[54]

Several particulars ought to be noted from the above description: 1) The date of the statement was after the passage of the Act of Parliament, and thus, also after the death of Small; 2) the original purchase of the patent was divided between Watt and Boulton with Boulton having a two-thirds share, and 3) therefore, Small's portion was to be one-third—an equal partnership among the three. William Small's brothers, Robert and James Small, however, received very little in material goods or financial resources after Small's death. There are several letters between Boulton and Robert Small that indicate that Boulton was paying William's brother Robert dividends from the stock that Small had bought in the Canal corporation (63 shares) and Boulton made a final settlement of the remaining funds to Robert Small and his daughter in 1803.[55] Boulton made no mention, however, of the partnership agreement to Small's relatives. The central question remaining regards the importance of being Small and the legacy that he left behind.

NOTES

1. James P. Muirhead, *The Origin and Progress of the Mechanical Inventions of James Watt* (London: John Murray, 1854), 1:cxlvii.

2. Ibid.

3. "It had been intended to include Small in the steam-engine partnership on the renewal of the patent. He had been consulted in all the stages of the proceedings, and one of the last things he did was to draw up Watt's petition for the Bill. No settled arrangement had yet been made not even between Boulton and Watt. Everything depended upon the success of the application for the extension of the patent. Samuel Smiles, *Lives of Boulton and Watt* (London: John Murray, 1865), 209.

4. James Watt to Matthew Boulton, October 20, 1768, MS 3782/12/76/1, Archives, Birmingham Central Library, Birmingham, England (hereafter cited as Birmingham). "Doctor Roebuck agreed to take my debts upon him & to lay out whatever more money was necessary either for Experiments or securing the Invention for which cause I made over to him two thirds of the property of the Invention the debt, & expences are now about £1200."

5. Matthew Boulton to James Watt, February 7, 1769, in Muirhead, *The Origin and Process of the Mechanical Inventions of James Watt*, 2:41–42.

6. Ibid.

7. John Roebuck to William Small and Matthew Boulton, November 28, 1769, in Muirhead, *The Origin and Process of the Mechanical Inventions of James Watt*, 2:82.

8. Muirhead, *The Origin and Process of the Mechanical Inventions of James Watt*, 2:25.

9. "Roebuck owed Boulton and John Fothergill, his partner, £1,200. Boulton hesitated in taking over Roebuck's shares in the patent for fear of the other creditors' opinions of him. Boulton was concerned that if he offered too little to rectify the doctor's accounts that he would appear to be taking advantage of the Roebuck's desperate situation; and, if he were too generous that he would appear overanxious and stimulate competition for the engine patent. However, the other creditors did not think the patent worth 'a farthing,' and Boulton was able to get it from the receivers into his hands." Boulton's own partner, John Fothergill, agreed with the other creditors and considered the patent of little use and took his share of the £1,200 debt in cash rather than any stake in the steam engine. Afterward, when the engine became a success, this led to much acrimony on Fothergill's part although entirely without justification.

10. James Watt to William Small, May 20, 1773, in Muirhead, *The Origin and Process of the Mechanical Inventions of James Watt*, 2:49; MS 3782/12/76/180, Archives, Birmingham Central Library, Birmingham.

11. William Small to James Watt, February 13, 1769, MS 3782/12/76/123, Archives, Birmingham Central Library, Birmingham.

12. William Small to James Watt, June 2, 1773, in Muirhead, *The Origin and Process of the Mechanical Inventions of James Watt*, 2:51.

13. Robert Schofield, *The Lunar Society of Birmingham* (Oxford: Clarendon Press, 1963), 43.

14. H. W. Dickinson, *Matthew Boulton* (Cambridge: University Press, 1937), 84.

15. Samuel Smiles, *Lives of the Engineers: The Steam Engine, Boulton and Watt*, Vol. 4 (London: John Murray, 1878).

16. J. P. Muirhead, *The Life of James Watt: With Selections from His Correspondence* (London: John Murray, 1858), 186.

17. Dickinson, *Matthew Boulton*, 85.

18. Muirhead, *The Life of James Watt*, 251.

19. Erasmus Darwin Jr. to Unknown Friend, March 9, 1775, Darwin Papers, 227. 7: 21, University Library, Cambridge, Cambridge, England. Courtesy of Marion Roberts.

20. Robert Small to Matthew Boulton, March 5, 1775, MS 3782/12/24/26, Archives, Birmingham Central Library, Birmingham.

21. Alexander Small to Matthew Boulton, February 21, 1775, MS 3728 /12/24/23, Archives, Birmingham Central Library, Birmingham. "Mr. [Alexander] Small offered to go down with Dr Hebberden ... & said he could be of no service as he conceived of the disease being one of the stomach & incurable." James Watt (London) to Matthew Boulton (Soho), February 27, 1775, MS 3782/12/76/9, Archives, Birmingham Central Library, Birmingham.

22. Matthew Boulton to James Watt, February 24, 1775, MS 3219/4/66/9, Archives, Birmingham Central Library, Birmingham.

23. Robert Small to Matthew Boulton, March 5, 1775, MS 3782/12/24/26, Archives, Birmingham Central Library, Birmingham.

24. Matthew Boulton (Temple Row) to James Watt (London), February 23, 1775, MS 3219/4/66/7, Archives, Birmingham Central Library, Birmingham.

25. Nathaniel Jeffreys to Matthew Boulton, July 5, 1765, MS 3782/12/23/79, Archives, Birmingham Central Library, Birmingham. Note: The Archives resources list gives the date as October 5, 1765, but the date on the letter actually reads July 5, 1765.

26. Erasmus Darwin to William Withering, February 25, 1775, in *The Letters of Erasmus Darwin*, ed. Desmond King-Hele (New York: Cambridge University Press, 1981), 68; Erasmus Darwin to William Withering, February 25, 1775, in Joseph Hill, "Dr. Small and His Friends," *Birmingham Evening Post* (August 26, 1899), 6; T. Whitmore Peck and K. Douglas Wilkinson, *William Withering of Birmingham* (Bristol: John Wright & Sons Ltd., 1950), 1.

27. William Small to James Watt, December 3, 1773, in Muirhead, *The Origin and Progress of the Mechanical Inventions of James Watt*, 2:36.

28. William Small to James Watt, October 5, 1770, in James P. Muirhead, *The Life of Watt* (London: John Murray, 1858), 223.

29. William Small to James Watt, October 16, 1773, in Muirhead, *The Origin and Progress of the Mechanical Inventions of James Watt*, 2:64. See also MS/ 3782 /12/76/151, Archives, Birmingham Central Library, Birmingham.

30. William Small to James Watt, March 15, 1773, MS 3782/12/76/173, Archives, Birmingham Central Library, Birmingham. Note: hypochondriasis: *Path.* A disorder of the nervous system, generally accompanied by indigestion, but chiefly characterized by a patient's unfounded belief that he is suffering from some serious bodily disease (OED).

31. Muirhead, *The Life of Watt*, clvi.

32. Robert Small to Matthew Boulton, March 5, 1775, MS 3782/12/24/26, Archives, Birmingham Central Library, Birmingham.

33. Matthew Boulton to James Watt, February 25, 1775, MS 3219/4/66/10, Archives, Birmingham Central Library, Birmingham.

34. *Aris's Birmingham Gazette*, February 27, 1775, Archives, Birmingham Central Library, Birmingham.

35. Robert Small to Matthew Boulton, March 22, 1775, MS 3782/12/24/29 (Old -340/50), Archives, Birmingham Central Library, Birmingham.

36. Smiles, *Lives of Boulton and Watt*, 202.

37. Muirhead, *The Life of James Watt*, 252.

38. James Keir, *An Account of the Life and Writings of Thomas Day* (London: John Stockdale, 1791), 29.

39. Thomas Jefferson, *The Writings of Thomas Jefferson: Autobiography*, ed. Merrill Peterson (New York: Literary Classics of the United States, 1984), 4.

40. Thomas Jefferson to William Small, May 7, 1775, MS 3782/12/76/189, Archives, Birmingham Central Library, Birmingham.

41. Muirhead, *The Origin and Progress of the Mechanical Inventions of James Watt*, 2:81.

42. This and next paragraph from Erasmus Darwin to William Withering, February 25, 1775, in Hill, "Dr. Small and His Friends," 6. Several interesting points arise from this letter; rigor mortis had not even set in to stiffen Small's features when Darwin wrote furtively to William Withering to come and take Small's position; Darwin had immediately gone through Small's papers to obtain information and seemingly had an accomplice in these matters. Even if the interests of the Lunar Society and Boulton may have prompted Darwin's haste to arrange for a replacement, his actions still seem insensitive and callous at best. From this letter, it also appears that Small did have a cache of papers and books that have yet to come to light. The unmentioned person who may have enlisted Darwin's aid in this mission may have been Dr. John Ash, who shared the Temple Row house with Small and may have been seeking a replacement in the clinic and as a roommate on Temple Row. See Peck and Wilkinson, *William Withering of Birmingham*, 1.

43. Peck and Wilkinson, *William Withering of Birmingham*, 1.

44. Robert Small to Matthew Boulton, March 5, 1775, MS 3782/12/24/26, Archives, Birmingham Central Library, Birmingham.

45. Matthew Boulton to James Watt, March 11, 1775, MS 3219/4/12, Archives, Birmingham Central Library, Birmingham.

46. Matthew Boulton to James Watt, March 9, 1775, MS 3219/4/66/11, Archives, Birmingham Central Library, Birmingham.

47. Muirhead, *The Origin and Progress of the Mechanical Inventions of James Watt*, 1:clv.

48. "He [Boulton] would have been familiar with William Shenstone's tomb-infested gardens at the Leasowes and when, in 1775, Small, his family doctor and closest confidant, passed away he had a monument to his memory erected in his garden." Peter Jones, "Matthew Boulton, Birmingham and the Enlightenment," in *Matthew Boulton: Enterprising Industrialist of the Enlightenment*, ed. Kenneth Quickenden, Sally Baggott, and Malcolm Dick (Farnham, Surrey: Ashgate, 2013), 28.

49. "7 April 1786—Leasowes (Shenstone's, now Horne's)." Thomas Jefferson, *Jefferson Memorandum Books: Accounts, with Legal Records and Miscellany (1767–1826)*, ed. James Bear and Lucia Stanton (Princeton: Princeton University Press, 1997), 1:619.

50. Thomas Day wrote to Boulton on March 17, 1775, "Should Mr. Small, return that Set of the *Mémoires de L'acédémie*, I will trouble you to take care of them for me: and Should the Drs. Books & goods be sold, to purchase for me the præceding Volumes, together with a Pepin's Digester which I remember the Dr. had" (Thomas Day to Matthew Boulton, March 17, 1775, MS 3782/12/81/84, Archives, Birmingham Central Library, Birmingham). Therefore, Small's brothers must have gone to his apartments and taken what personal possessions that they wished, and (Day is hinting—and he did end up with the Papin's Digester) that a sale would follow. Finally, the leftovers were sold at a garage-type sale (Bill. T. Warren to John Scale, April 18, 1775, MS 3782/16/3/183, Birmingham Central Library, Birmingham. Courtesy of Archivist Fiona Tait). "Items purchased at Dr. Small's sale: a cotton counterpane (15s.); Cushee's terrestrial globe (£1 13s.); seven white teacups and saucers, a sugar dish, cover, and pint bason (6s. 6d.) (Receipted by J. S. Warren for his father, same day.) What happened to Small's papers is not known for certain; Darwin, however, reviewed them on the night of Small's death and Withering knew the details of Small's hospital work.

51. Schofield, *The Lunar Society of Birmingham*, 54.

52. See Martin Clagett, "The Portrait of William Small," Privately Printed for Presentation at the Meeting of Eighteenth-Century Scottish Studies Conference (2005), Funded by the Earhart Foundation. The monograph follows the history

of the portrait from 1766 until its purchase by the College of William and Mary in 2005.

53. Samuel Smiles, *Lives of the Engineers: The Steam Engine, Boulton and Watt* (London: John Murray, 1874), 155. "To Matthew Boulton, he was invaluable and when he died … it had been finally arranged for him to become a partner." Joseph Hill, *The Book Makers of Old Birmingham* (Birmingham: Shakespeare Press, 1907), 61.

54. J. E. Cule, "The Financial History of Matthew Boulton, 1759–1800" (Master of Commerce thesis, University of Birmingham, 1935), 65, Diss C1, B35, C8. Paraphrased from information in a booklet written by Boulton and sent to J. H. Ebbinghaus entitled "Case between Boulton & Fothergill." Booklet entitled "Case between Boulton & Fothergill," from Matthew Boulton to John Herman Ebbinghaus, October 24, 1772, Matthew Boulton Papers, MS/3782/12/2/59, Birmingham Central Library, Birmingham.

55. Matthew Boulton to Robert Small, August 28, 1781, MS 3782/12/5/143, Archives, Birmingham Central Library, Birmingham.

CHAPTER 13

Conclusion:
The Importance of Being Small

When presented with even a brief synopsis of the life of William Small, the observations that occur immediately to most are twofold. First, how did a seemingly ordinary and unremarkable minister's son from a rural hamlet come to live such an extraordinary and consequential life? Second, how could the significance of his life have been so long overlooked?

Small was a gentleman who, through his life's twists and turns, had an astonishing effect, not only in his own century, but also far past his own time on earth. William Small was an accidental apostle of the Scottish Enlightenment—he brought its methods and philosophical foundations to a nation being born; he helped transform the abstractions of Newtonianism into an early manifestation of logical positivism, and he was also an active agent in transforming Britain from an agrarian society into an industrial one by means of intellectual, scientific, and collegial engagement. Through these actions, Small was a part of an international cooperation in philosophy and literature known as the Republic of Letters.

Small had a profound impact on a young Thomas Jefferson, shaping his scientific and philosophical worldviews and, by extension, Jefferson's contributions to science, politics, and governance. He would later encounter a brilliant but despondent James Watt, a man buffeted by a series of misfortunes and unlucky turns of timing, helping him to develop his unfinished design for an improved steam engine. The most notable consequences of these intersections of time, place, and personality resulted in enduring and profound relationships with two men of consequence and impact, the first, Thomas Jefferson, who would revolutionize government with his Declaration of Independence, and the second, James Watt, whose invention of the practical steam engine would transform the world from an agrarian into an industrial society with all the implications—good and bad—that that metamorphosis would entail.

For Small to have been a player in such seemingly disparate events seems remarkable; for him to have had such a central role in the fates and fortunes of both men (who in turn had such extraordinary impacts on the course of history) stretches credulity. Thus, it is with a fear of disbelief and a concern that the facts presented will smack of overstatement, hero worship, or an element of supernatural intervention shrouded in a patina of predestination that the story of Small has been laid out with an especial detail in documentation. For however unlikely, however unbelievable, however counterintuitive the interconnections and impacts may seem, they represent the facts of his life.

But it ought to be remembered that a number of Small's closest friends and associates also came from unremarkable backgrounds—Jefferson was the son of a frontier squire who was raised in "the backwoods of America"; George Wythe was born on a rural plantation on the brackish shores of Tidewater Virginia and had an informal education provided by his Quaker-raised mother; Benjamin Franklin was the last son of a Boston soap-maker whose formal education ended at age ten; James Watt was born to a Scottish shipwright, had a sickly youth, was apprenticed to a Dublin musical instrument maker, and worked as a mechanical repairman in Glasgow before he took it into his head to visit the fabled Soho Factory where he, quite by chance, met William Small.

For the associations between Small and all these prominent individuals, for the common factors and correlations of these momentous events (both independent and intertwined) that conjoined these men together, for the impact of Small on Jefferson and Boulton and Watt and their signal accomplishments to have been little remarked on and frequently minimized or ignored altogether is, perhaps, the only thing more amazing than the lack of investigation into his life.

CHARISMA AND CHARACTER

Questions of Small's importance revolve around his personal characteristics, mental acuity, and boundless curiosity. The areas in which these elements are most evident are in his roles as a teacher and mentor, as a founder and organizer of societies that were in the vanguard of science and philosophy, and as a messenger between men of different perspectives, fields of knowledge, and national identities.

Having been raised in the precepts of the Scottish Enlightenment, in that "hotbed of genius," Small had been introduced to new perspectives in science, philosophy and medicine at an early age. The new and creative approaches to science, philosophy, and pedagogy that took place during his years at Marischal College informed his performance as a teacher, as a mentor, as a scientist, and as an inventor.

In Aberdeen, he absorbed the principles of Newton and Bacon—scientific methodology and its interpretation as seen through the lens and the precepts of the School of Common Sense. In short, Small synthesized the scientific with the philosophical by interlocking the process of gathering facts, assorting them into logical and sequential order, making and testing hypotheses with the philosophical mandate of the Scottish Enlightenment—the improvement of mankind through society to produce a better world. This approach was foundational for Small, who enthusiastically distilled its beneficial doctrine to students, friends, associates, and colleagues throughout his life. The people he influenced, in turn, not only employed his perspectives and methodologies but also added their own aspirations and permutations and eagerly shared them with others in an ever-widening circle.

ACADEMIC IMPORT

Small's training both at Dundee Grammar School, Marischal College, and in the corridors and operating rooms of London hospitals prepared him to become not only someone with a catholic sense of curiosity in a multiplicity of arenas but also a person possessing precise and informed expertise in a variety of subjects—a Renaissance man—but in an age that had an expanded base of knowledge to master. This unique combination of talents was the lucky happenstance of a rigorous foundation in Dundee, the transition in curriculum and systems of instruction at Marischal, and the diverse mastery of scientific knowledge required of a physician in the rapidly and ever-expanding knowledge base needed to be at the forefront of the medical profession in the sophisticated surroundings of London.

In Williamsburg, Small utilized his training to widen the curriculum, and to invigorate and to resurrect intellectual fervor among a community of students and long accustomed to low expectations and rote instruction. And while Small's impact was significant among the denizens of Williamsburg in general, it took on a more important and incisive impact and long-lasting influence among his students and friends in the distant and forlorn colony. Most conspicuously was the future author of the *Notes on the State of Virginia*, the Virginia Statute for Religious Freedom, and Declaration of Independence; the initiator of the Lewis and Clark Expedition, the founder of the U.S. Patent Office, the president of the American Philosophical Society and of the United States, and the father of the University of Virginia—Thomas Jefferson.

Small became not only Jefferson's only professor at the College of William and Mary, but also his trusted advisor, and from his instruction in scientific methodology, with his inculcation of the utilitarian dictates of Common Sense Philosophy, and by the example of his own all-consuming curiosity about the expansion of science and the system in which we are placed, he not only acted as a mentor but also as a signpost for Jefferson's philosophical predispositions and his insatiable scientific curiosity.

The consequences of these influences are well known to an American audience, which included the most-distinguished scientific work by an American in the eighteenth century, *Notes on the State of Virginia*; the widest and most comprehensive scientific excursion up to that time, the Lewis and Clark Expedition; and the most-famous political manifesto in American history, the Declaration of Independence, which resonates with the cadence of Cicero's orations and follows the logical dictates of William Duncan's *Elements of Logick*. Although Jefferson was the most celebrated of Small's charges at the college, other of Small's Williamsburg charges led significant and distinguished lives to the benefit of their country.

Until the recent past, many scholars asserted that the source of Jefferson's philosophical viewpoints were derived almost exclusively from John Locke and the French philosophes. One of the most compelling and cogent arguments for the importance of the Scottish Enlightenment in general and William Small in particular was first articulated by Garry Wills in his controversial book, *Inventing America: Jefferson's Declaration of Independence*. Wills argued with persuasion, facts, and logic that the real source of Jefferson's philosophical and scientific inclinations did not derive from "Philadelphia or Paris, but from Aberdeen and Edinburgh and Glasgow [and] was the world of William Small."[1]

SMALL THE PROJECTOR AND TALENT AGENT

Small's second great talent was that of a projector—a person who could identify individuals of ability, or could refine or improve on the theories of others, or, more important, be able to recruit individuals to collaborate and feed on the wisdom of one another. A projector could persuade, inspire, propose, and design schemes, and develop strategies of his own. Small was, in the terms of Samuel Johnson, "clubbable," and by his kind and engaging nature, his charismatic personality, and his humility he was able to draw people of different backgrounds, interests, political loyalties, and social statuses to work together on projects of mutual interests. His genius was in drawing out the latent talents in others, encouraging and collaborating in their development, and effecting connections and synergies among people of like interests and ambitions.

Even Dudley Digges, Small's most vehement detractor, reluctantly admitted, because of Small's unexceptional behavior and winning address, that after Small's arrival in Williamsburg, he won the favor of some of the principal gentlemen of the colony. Among these were Governor Francis Fauquier, Attorney General Peyton Randolph, and the town's most-celebrated legal scholar, George Wythe with whom he met weekly for informed conversations, light entertainment, and a good meal.

SOCIETIES, SYMPOSIA, AND CLUBS

Small also introduced some of his other students into this intimate and exclusive coterie. This approach not only of permitting but also of encouraging intermittent and transient membership to an inner court of permanent members of a society, which made the experience doubly valuable to all—first, by introducing his students to the practice of deliberate and illuminating debate informed by those experienced and conversant in the subject matter and the corresponding methodologies, and second by infusing the sometimes stodgy discussions with fresh perspectives and jolting the tenets of established theory and by going down pathways that ran counter to established conventions and ways of thinking. Small would later employ this same modus operandi in the founding of the Birmingham Lunar Circle (Society) by establishing a core group of founders for the society and, then by inviting disparate and diverse corresponding members (in a very democratic fashion) to join in and contribute in the areas of their expertise to great advantage. Small's penchant for recruiting and gathering together people of divergent backgrounds and talents was his second great ability and a major part of the reason for his important place in history.

In the eighteenth century, many scholars and scientists made a healthy living by means of itinerate lectures and demonstrations. Boulton's acquaintance, Franklin's co-author and Small's rumored replacement at William and Mary, James Ferguson, gave anticipated performances throughout Scotland and England; coffeehouses and intellectual (or improvement) societies as convenient venues for discussion, which were institutions that generated many of the advances taking place in the political, scientific, and intellectual world. Both activities were considered enlightened entertainment that promoted cultivated sociability and progress in the arts and sciences, or, in a word—improvement.

In addition to being a part of the governor's circle of discussion, Small, Fauquier, and Wythe collaborated to promote a scientific society in Virginia as early as 1759. It was decided to build on the popularity of Small's classroom exhibitions and expand the concept into an enterprise with the more universal appeal of combining scientific entertainment with the spirit of competition and the prospect of cash prizes. It served the dual purpose of useful civic engagement and as symposia of practical application for Small's students and at the same time popularized the public's appetite for intellectual stimulation. The trustees tentatively styled their group the "Society for the Encouragement of Arts and Manufacturing" after the Royal Society in London, which would act as their patron and parent.

The originators, the first subscribers to the society, pledged themselves and their heirs, executors and administrators, to contribute annually for the perpetuation of the organization. The initial supporters included the governor, the Council, and the most prominent citizens of the area. In addition to the private initiative, the society also received the approval and support of the Virginia General Assembly to form the group; to hold competitions for the most valuable concepts, products, and invention; and to determine the winners of the contests.

Small later replicated his Williamsburg experience in the more celebrated alliance that he formed once he returned to Britain. Having been employed by the wealthy and energetic industrialist Matthew Boulton, the two began to meet for informal dinners and conversations concerning solutions to perplexing problems at the Boulton factory. One of the first and most urgent mechanical necessities was to devise a program by which the factory's water mill could be replenished by a constant stream of water during the dry season of the summer. After several failures, Boulton and Small hit on the idea of constructing a steam engine by which a fresh quantity of water could be drawn up from the nearby pond and supply the requisite amount of water necessary for the operation of the mills. Having developed such an engine, Small and Boulton sent it off to London for inspection by Dr. Franklin. Franklin, being impressed, displayed the machine in a public forum where it quickly drew the attention of the press. Reports went out and reached Erasmus Darwin in Lichfield almost before Boulton knew of the celebrity of the invention himself.

Darwin immediately and urgently wrote to Boulton with a request to join in the talks and experiments. Small advocated that Boulton include him in subsequent meetings and, thus, began the nucleus of the Birmingham Lunar Society. The news of these discussions became common knowledge and local parties began to ask to be included. In many ways this was of great advantage to Boulton's industrial agenda in that he, and the other attendees, were able to draw on a wide range of capabilities and also use the meetings as an opportunity to merge together skills and business interests.

THE BIRMINGHAM LUNAR SOCIETY

Small was able to draw together, in the most congenial way, an ever-widening group of talented and able craftsmen, mechanics, physicians, philosophers, and men of science. Boulton encouraged these gentlemen—by his persuasive nature, his generous table, and his genius for turning an academic problem into an industrial solution—to join in, to contribute to the conversation, to assist one another selflessly, and to create a provincial clearinghouse of technical and scientific knowledge that rivaled any society in London.

The irregular and almost "unconscious" gatherings quickly gained attention and their local club, the Birmingham Lunar Circle, or Birmingham Lunar Society, grew in numbers, multiple and many-sided collaborations, and tangential accomplishments. As the reports of its ingenuity and sociability became more widespread, the number of corresponding members flowed in—first from nearby towns and London, then from northern England, from Edinburgh and Glasgow, and finally from all over Europe and even America. "All the world came to Soho to meet Boulton, Watt or Small, who were acquainted with the leading men of Science throughout Europe and America. Its essential sociability meant that any might be invited to attend its meetings."[2]

Small was often the spark that started a successful conflagration; he selected, he recruited, he corralled, and he convinced individuals with the advanced knowledge and talent to come to the meetings and to initiate promising projects. Often, he was the calming and cajoling voice that encouraged others to bring their stalled and abandoned experiments to fruitful outcomes. Although Jenny Uglow called Small the "linchpin of their circle,"[3] more than that, he was also, almost certainly, the genesis.

The meetings at the Governor's Palace provided an inseminator and incubator for progressive perspectives; the Williamsburg society sparked an interest in science and innovation while providing a venue for Thomas Jefferson's first invention; and later the Birmingham Lunar Society gained universal recognition and has often been credited with changing Britain from an agrarian society into an industrial one.

Jenny Uglow rightly cautions us that while the Lunar Society was said to have "kick started the Industrial Revolution," nevertheless, "no individual or group can be said to change society in such a way" and it can easily be pointed out "that if they hadn't invented or discovered something, someone else would have done it." She added, however:

> This small group of friends really was at the cutting edge of almost every movement of its time in science, in industry and the arts, even in agriculture. They were the pioneers of the turnpikes and canals and of the new factory system. They were the group who brought efficient steam power to the nation. They were the white heat of the drive to catalogue and name plants, to study minerals, to detect and work out the history of the formation of the earth. The philosophers among them were keenly concerned with the nature of human knowledge itself, and the process of learning, and beyond this with enquiring into the origin and evolution of all organic life…. They formed a constellation of extraordinary individuals, a tangle of friendships and dependencies and loyalties…. They were colourful, strong, idiosyncratic…. They felt the greatness of the cosmos and its limitless possibilities, and the beauty of the infinitely small.[4]

SMALL: SINE QUA NON – THE ESSENTIAL ELEMENT

The importance of Small's role in the Partie Quarree, the Society for the Advancement of Arts and Manufactures, and the Birmingham Lunar Circle has already been established by the events surrounding their inceptions and their activities. The most defining proof, however, of Small's impact on these associations is not so much about how his personal presence brought into existence the aforementioned institutions but how quickly his absence brought about their decline and eventual dissolution.

In 1766, after Small had returned to England from Virginia, Arthur Lee went back to Williamsburg from London and attempted to revive the society but with little success.[5] On November 20, 1772, former students and friends of Small, erstwhile members of the Society for the Advancement of Arts and Manufactures, determined to resurrect Small's science club. Among the group was George Wythe, John

Page, Mann Page, Dabney Carr, John Walker, and James McClurg, and its mission was much the same as the former affiliation. Page even enlisted David Rittenhouse as a corresponding member and attempted to lure Jefferson back into the fold by a promise of the presidency of the society.[6] Jefferson demurred.

In the end, these organizations faltered and fell after the departure of Small. The same was true of the more celebrated club—the Birmingham Lunar Society—which Small inspired and helped to institute with the collaboration of Matthew Boulton. From the group's beginning in 1765 until Small's death in February 1775, the society had no formal name, it had no rules or regulations, it kept no records or books, but it was a spontaneity of enthusiasm, mutual admiration, and boundless innovation in a burgeoning expansion of investigation and scientific interest. The society was exceptional in its the absence of infighting and intrigue and for the collective support that all members extended to each other, who were not concerned about which individual received credit for a new discovery or invention.

The proof of Small's centrality to the enterprise emerged at the moment of his death. Rigor mortis had not even set in when Erasmus Darwin frantically wrote to William Withering to come and take Small's place as local physician, as a replacement in the Lunar Circle, and as a substitute in Boulton's heart. "Withering did not, however, fill the scientific place of Small. He was not a mathematician; after Small's death there was to be no mathematical member of the Lunar group.... Withering did not have Small's interest in clocks, or optics, or astronomy and these subjects soon disappeared from serious Lunar Society investigations."[7]

By 1775, the "Birmingham Philosophers" had become a group, one "brought together in friendship" and "tied together by mutual interest in science." All "had shown themselves to be successful in some endeavor useful or interesting to others; all were prepared to experiment themselves and to try the ideas of others."[8] It was quickly recognized, even by Boulton, that after the death of Small, "who had provided the nucleus for their social gatherings ... if social intercourse were to continue," if the society were to survive, "something had to be provided to replace his influence."[9]

"The first reference to a meeting of the Lunar group, after the death of Small, comes in a letter from Darwin to Withering of 13 May 1775, "there was no mention of a 'lunar' connexion, but this was definitely to be a meeting of the Lunar group, whatever they called themselves."[10] This letter was in transit just as Withering was moving his furniture to Mr. Wheeler's on the Square (directly next door to Dr. Ash's house),[11] just as Thomas Jefferson's letter and Madeira wine were arriving in town, and shortly after Robert Small had appeared in Birmingham to attend to his brother's estate.[12]

The earliest formal meeting, more regulated than earlier sessions, "is dated within three months of Small's death."[13] Only Withering was new to the group, and he had just settled into his home on the Square; "the only other circumstance involved in this meeting of philosophers was the absence of Small [that] provides justification for the suggestion that the formality of semi-organized meetings was a consequence of Small's death."[14] Despite the introduction of rules and procedures, the regularity, the spontaneity, the willingness to attend and participate became "inconsistent" and "from 1776 to 1780 the pattern of meetings changes from regular to irregular to infrequent."[15]

After 1777, Boulton, Watt, or both, were frequently away from Birmingham to attend to the expanding steam-engine business, which made scheduled meetings of the society (usually held at Soho) more unsustainable. The meetings "at once romantic and pragmatic, gave the group its identity ... but the society became famous" because of the individual efforts of its members rather than any "immediate product" of a gathering."[16] Moreover, "the accomplishments were, in large measure, made possible by the co-operation of the members, and the most frequent occasions for that co-operation were outside of Lunar Society meetings."[17]

The Lunar Society thus changed from a brotherhood to a corporate model. Members profited individually rather than collectively and competition between members incrementally crept into the society's interactions (even Darwin and Withering fought over the discovery of digitalis). The investigations, the experimentations, and the multiple and interactive brainstorming sessions became less frequent and more self-involved. Even the advent of Priestley could not bring back the camaraderie and conviviality of the early meetings.

Small was the essence that defined and held together the Partie Quarree, the Society for the Advancement of Arts and Manufacturing, and the Birmingham Lunar Society by way of his example of self-lessness and humble charisma. Without his presence, it all changed.

WIDESPREAD INFLUENCE

Small's importance also lies in the reverberations of his influence across a wide spectrum of individuals and on society, from the most local sense of the word to its widest application. In a time of limited mobility, Small bounced back and forth between towns, nations, and continents with great frequency and regularity. In an age of struc-tured social interaction, he flitted from one social class to another without judgment or prejudice. In an era of restraining ideologies, he embraced new concepts and visions of what could be. More than this, he was of such an incisive mind and of such an unassuming affect that he was embraced by people from all persuasions, and by means of his disinterested intent, he enlisted the support and involvement of those with whom he came into contact. The sheer number and diversity of his deliberate or random friends and colleagues defy all expectation.

In an age of shameless self-promotion, Small exhibited almost no interest in advancing himself into the public consciousness. While Boulton was at his best when he adapted the theoretical concepts of others and transformed them into practical and profitable realities, Small was at his best coaxing the potential out of others. Francis Galton, Samuel Galton's son, was likely thinking of Small when he wrote, "Some eminently scientific men have shown their original power by little more than a continuous flow of helpful suggestions and criticisms, individually of little importance, but in their aggregate, a notable aid towards progress."[18]

Small's impact on Jefferson, Boulton, and Watt has been demonstrated; his complex and symbiotic relationship with Franklin has been noted; the synergy that his physical presence generated in Williamsburg, in London, and in Birmingham can be extrapolated from the diminution of cohesion and activity within the associated intellectual communities after his passing. Eric Robinson asserted that although little is known about what went on in the Birmingham meetings, "its indirect significance in the cross[-]fertilization of ideas is testified to by its long life and by the esteem in which it was held not only by those who were a part of it, but by a wide circle of distinguished contemporaries."[19]

IN FINE

The final aspect of Small's importance is really an amalgamation of the elements of his philosophical outlook, his catholic sense of curiosity, and his infinite desire to help. By training he was a philosopher and a scientist, by personality a source of encouragement and quiet determination, by inclination a magnet that recruited individuals of varying desires and ambitions into his invisible orbit and by charisma and gravitational pull kept them there. Thus, in the end, he encouraged the organic, elastic, and symbiotic zeitgeist that allowed men of different nations, political persuasions, and religious outlooks to support and nurture one another in that eighteenth-century phenomenon known as the Republic of Letters.

That Small's life was so peripatetic and multifaceted is somewhat surprising; that Small's story was so full of incidental and accidental affiliations is counterintuitive; that Small's interests and influence extended through such a wide array of sciences is inspiring; that he embraced nontraditional values and philosophical perspectives is unexpected; that his impact seamlessly spread across cities, nations, and

oceans is amazing; and the fact that—having accomplished so much—
he died at the age of forty-one is almost incomprehensible. Imagine.

NOTES

1. Garry Wills. "Or Was Jefferson More Influenced by Scottish Thinkers?," in *What Did the Declaration Declare?*, ed. Joseph Ellis (Boston: Bedford/St Martin's, 1999), 77.

2. Eric Robinson, "The Lunar Society: Its Membership and Organization," *Transactions of the Newcomen Society* 35, no. 1 (1962): 160.

3. Jenny Uglow, *The Lunar Men* (New York: Farrar, Straus, and Giroux, 2002), 81.

4. Ibid., 501.

5. Robert Dores, "The Virginia Society for the Promotion of Usefull Knowledge," *Colonial Williamsburg Journal* (Autumn 2003).

6. Ibid.

7. Robert Schofield, *The Lunar Society of Birmingham* (Oxford: Clarendon Press, 1963), 125.

8. Ibid., 141.

9. Ibid.

10. Ibid.

11. Erasmus Darwin to William Withering, May 14, 1775, MS 0014, Archives, Mt. Holyoke College, Mt. Holyoke, Massachusetts. Courtesy Miss Micha Broadnax.

12. Robert Small to Matthew Boulton, April 1, 1775, MS 3782/12/24/30, Archives, Birmingham Central Library, Birmingham, England.

13. Schofield, *The Lunar Society of Birmingham*, 144.

14. Ibid.

15. Ibid., 145.

16. Ibid.

17. Ibid.

18. Ibid., 36.

19. Robinson, "The Lunar Society: Its Membership and Organization" (London: Newcomen Society Lecture, 1963), 160. Courtesy of Dr. Richard Hills.

CHAPTER 14

Post Scripta—Doctor Small

William Small is best known for his influence on Thomas Jefferson and James Watt, his importance in establishing both the organization and character of various philosophical and scientific societies on both sides of the Atlantic, and his role as a transforming agent of change, both as an apostle of the Scottish Enlightenment and as catalyst for the post-Revolutionary Republic of Letters. A substantial part of his life, however, has been almost entirely overlooked—his career as a physician.

His contemporaries and friends first identified Small, not by his contributions to industry or to political philosophy, not by his importance to Jefferson, not by his founding of the Birmingham Lunar Society, not by his clever inventions, not by his civic service, not as a liaison between men of science throughout the world, not by his critical intercession in the life and successes of James Watt, but by his capacity as a compassionate caregiver.

Therefore, although much of the information about this part of his life and character has been scattered about the narrative of Small's story in a partial and willy-nilly manner, for those who have an interest in his medical career and achievements—it is both convenient and important to concentrate solely on his medical career in one place. Because of the emphasis placed on his impact on and intimacy with men of great fame, the facts of his medical career have been difficult to uncover and display. Thus, although the information here provided is certain to be incomplete and lacking—it is the most the author could find. For the present.

DR. WILLIAM SMALL: PHYSICIAN

Two days after his passing, the local Birmingham journal noted that "by his Death, the Poor are deprived of a most humane and disinterested Physician."[1] His friend Thomas Day described him as "physician in Birmingham, who, to the most extensive, various, and accurate knowledge, in the sciences, and in life, joined engaging manners, a most exact conduct, and an enlightened humanity."[2] Captain James Keir remembered Small as a man who lived "in the memory of those friends who knew his worth and of the poor, whom his humane skill was ever ready to rescue form disease and pain."[3]

TRAINING

Small was first introduced to the medical field as an apprentice to John Gregory and his brother James Gregory during his time at Marischal College in Aberdeen.[4] In 1755, John Gregory took a position as a physician in training at St. George's Hospital in London.[5] Small followed his old mentor to the center of the British empire to learn the medical trade as well. In the papers of John Pringle there are references to Small, which place him at dissections attended by Pringle and performed by John Hunter, two of the most-distinguished British surgeons of the era. The first recorded observation in which Small's presence was mentioned took place in 1757 at St. George's Hospital, where he observed a dissection performed by John Hunter, one of the most-notable British physicians of the era.[6]

WILLIAMSBURG:
SMALL DECIDED TO COMMENCE PHYSICIAN

When Small arrived in Williamsburg, he found that there was a desperate need for his services as a physician as well as a teacher. Small's greatest detractor and a member of the Board of Visitors at the college, Robert Carter Nicholas wrote to the Bishop of London that sometime after his arrival, Small "took it into his Head to commence Physician, and not only practiced in the City of Williamsburgh, but also in many distant Parts of the Country; how consistent this was with his Duty, your Lordship may judge."[7] Shortly thereafter, Nicholas wrote another letter—but this time to Small himself—complaining of his duplicity and ingratitude. Nicholas again castigated Small, "Things then seem'd to go on very cleverly & peaceably with you; but you were at this Time only Mr. Small & had not assumed the Title of Dr. which soon after magnified your Importance, chiefly in your own Eyes."[8]

Small, however, had already become acquainted with some prominent citizens in the town. One of them was the proprietor of the *Virginia Gazette* Bookstore and Benjamin Franklin's Co-Postmaster-General, William Hunter. Hunter had taken a long journey to Britain and returned ill. Small attended to Hunter during his protracted sickness and must have served him well, for Hunter remembered him especially in his will. Small and Franklin (who was Hunter's executor and guardian of his son) were the only two people outside of Hunter's immediate family to receive a cash settlement, the bequest noted that Hunter expressed a desire that his executors should pay William Small £100 in "Current Money" as a token of friendship and the esteem, "Which Directions were given by the Said [to] William Hunter during his last Sickness."[9]

MEDICAL DEGREE

In the autumn of 1764, Small returned to England to purchase scientific apparatus for the college and arrived in London at the home of "his namesake" Alexander Small on December 1, 1764. Franklin followed shortly thereafter on the 13th. After a season of meetings, conviviality, and networking, Franklin dispatched Small up to Aberdeen to obtain his medical degree, for Franklin's friend, the wealthy industrialist, Matthew Boulton, was in the market for a family physician with scientific tastes.

Small told Stephen Hawtrey in May 1765 that that he would be gone from London for three weeks to obtain his diploma. Small may have first obtained a recommendation from John Elliot, who had a successful practice in London, and then proceeded to Edinburgh, where his old mentor John Gregory was teaching, for his second attestation. From Edinburgh and Gregory, Small made his way to his old alma mater, Marischal College, and there procured his medical degree.[10]

MS M 28: Registration of MD Degrees Conferred by
Marischal College (1755) Aberdeen

Some scholars maintain that Small merely purchased his degree for a trivial sum, but several factors seem to indicate otherwise. First, his experience and reputation in Virginia denote an advanced level of education and training. Second, his recommender and mentor, John Gregory was in the vanguard of those physicians who were calling for the standardization of the medical profession, and he specifically advocated for a prescribed course of studies and collegiate training as a prerequisite to qualifying for a medical degree. John Elliot, his other attestor, was Senior Physician at Greenwich Hospital. Later, Gregory would be appointed King's Physician for Scotland and Elliot, King's Physician for England.

LONDON CONNECTIONS AND COMMUNITIES

Returning to London for a brief interval after his trip to Scotland, Small completed his apparatus shopping spree and continued to meet with Franklin and associates, develop ties with the medical and scientific communities, and investigate new advances in instrument making. He was also toying with the idea of conducting scientific and medical classes in the capital. Evidently, while visiting Gregory in Edinburgh, he gave lectures or demonstrations to classes there. Many students were impressed:

> Before I settled at Birmingham, I was asked at London on this account by many students in Medicine who had left Edinr to give lectures on those parts of Physics that most immediately concern Doctors & Surgeons, & truly it is easy to perceive that most of them very much wanted instruction.[11]

Events and evidence also point to his extended networking among the medical community: the doctors with whom he consulted over the years, the shared information and techniques, and the new pharmaceutical applications that he explored on a semiregular basis. The most frequent correspondents and colleagues included John Hunter, Alexander Small, William Heberden, Sir John Pringle, John Elliot, and George Fordyce—some of the most celebrated and sought-after doctors and surgeons in London.

It was also at this time that Small was likely inducted into various medical clubs and societies. He had not only attended many of Franklin's clubs but also developed ties of his own. In 1771, George Fordyce and John Hunter, consulting on a medical matter, concluded a letter to Small, "We remain your brethren of the Phil. Society, G. Fordyce, J. Hunter."[12] The particular society mentioned was likely the Society of Licentiate Physicians—an organization that advocated for the rights of Scots to be included in the London College of Physicians, which up to that time had only accepted candidates who had graduated from Oxford or Cambridge. In the mid-eighteenth century many Scots, who obtained their medical degrees at home, did not qualify for the prestigious but parochial society. In 1767, William Hunter and George Fordyce collaborated to establish the Society of Licentiate Physicians in order to campaign for the rights of Scottish licentiates in the college.[13]

SMALL'S MEDICAL CAREER IN BIRMINGHAM

After his return to London for a short period, Small made his way to Birmingham with a letter of recommendation from Franklin. A second letter of endorsement arrived by way of a friend of Matthew Boulton, Nathaniel Jeffreys, which confirmed several of the details Small's Virginia practice and his reputation in London, "Dr Wm Small who has been settled some years at Virginia as a Phisician, and with great success & was the same time proffesser of Mathematicks in the Colledge of Williamsburgh ... & in the way of his profession has the best recommendations of our most Eminent Phisicians here— who are the best judges of his Merit as a Physician."[14]

Matthew Boulton's primary medical concern was for his daughter who suffered from a deformity of the hip. Small consulted for some time with Doctors Darwin, Fordyce, and Hunter in this matter.[15] His success in her case increased his reputation greatly in the town, word of his competence quickly spread, and soon he shared a practice and a residence with the town's leading physician, John Ash.

By the following autumn, alarming rumors reached Boulton that Small was planning to take a position at the court of Catherine the Great; uneasy that the reports might have merit, he sent his friend John Baskerville to sound Small out on the matter. Baskerville swiftly sent him a reassuring letter, "I have the Pleasure to inform You, that Dr Small's affairs are become greatly more extended then when we left Bir. & some dangerous Cases have offered, this greatly increased his reputation, so that I took the Liberty of saying what You had told me in Confidence in Relation to Russia; he replied he had altered his Mind, as his Practice (nearly) was as Much as his Wish, but that he Must go to London to thank Doctor Heberden for his kind Intention, which he could not well do (or at least so respectfully) by Writing."[16]

Small's practice continued to grow but by 1767 he was devoting more of his time and efforts to scientific and industrial inquiries and orchestrating the activities of the Birmingham Lunar Society than previously. Inasmuch as he found his involvement with the Lunar Society more stimulating and rewarding, he began to complain about his extended medical obligations.

He wrote Watt, "The practice of medicine is worse than a gaol."[17] He also groused that his medical practice exhausted him and it paid him "but indifferently" and although he felt fine as long as he making progress in his work, "if I am absolutely puzzled, and see no clue, my head turns me around, and I speedily become more tired than a galley slave."[18] Whether Small's early malaise was from a physical or psychological origin is a matter of some guesswork, but he fell into fugues of melancholy as often as Watt. His medical practice had already greatly extended when he and Boulton and Ash promoted the establishment of the Birmingham General Hospital.

BIRMINGHAM GENERAL HOSPITAL

In December 1765, a committee was established for the purpose of "erecting a GENERAL HOSPITAL, for the relief of the sick and the lame."[19] Ash, Boulton, and Small were foundational supporters and all were members of the original Board of Trustees.[20] Small was named one of the first physicians and attended to the workers of Soho Factory in particular. Inasmuch as the actual building was several years in coming together, during this interval Small and Ash likely saw clients at their clinic at 9 Temple Row in town, and Small may have also used a house close to Temple Row for consultations and experimentations as well—Mr. Wheelers, 10 the Square.[21]

The Birmingham Hospital transformed Small's general practice from a private and elite clientele into a larger and more socially diverse group. The list of his patients grew exponentially. Small's replacement in Birmingham, William Withering, gave an approximation of the number of people that Small would see on a regular basis.

> My worthy predecessor in this place, the very humane and ingenious Dr. Small, had made it a practice to give his advice to the poor during one hour in a day. This practice, which I continued until we had an Hospital opened for the reception of the sick poor, gave me an opportunity of putting my ideas into execution in a variety of cases; for the number of poor who thus applied for advice, amounted to between two and three thousand annually.[22]

According to Withering's calculations, if Small advised between 2,000 and 3,000 pro bono clients per annum and he was practicing in Birmingham between 1765 and 1775, he could have potentially had 20,000 to 30,000 consultations during his time in practice there with this separate set of clients alone. The surprisingly large number of individuals that he was seeing on a daily basis may have been the result of an innovative program that he and Boulton had implemented at the Soho Factory.

BOULTON AND SMALL: CORPORATE
AND COMPULSORY HEALTH INSURANCE.

Boulton believed that the success of his new factory model at Soho depended on an integrated workforce, an assembly-line arrangement, interchangeable parts, an effective distribution system, and a highly qualified and motivated workforce. He sought out or trained expert mechanics, artisans, and assembly-line workmen; he paid them a premium salary for the time, and, in order to keep them in good health (so that they would not change employers and he could avoid the expense of retraining new recruits) he and Small initiated one of the earliest health-insurance policies.

David Schmidtz noted that "Boulton's innovation consisted in pioneering the use of interchangeable parts and a better integrated factory model. He also developed a form of disability insurance for his worker."[23] Medical historian Joan Lane reported:

> The [friendly] society founded by Boulton and Watt at their Soho factory near Birmingham began as a compulsory insurance organization for all employees ... the Soho society must have been established ... soon after the factory was built in 1764.[24]

Michael Zmolek, a scholar of the Industrial Revolution provided more-explicit details about the program that Boulton and Small established:

> [At Soho Factory] An insurance Society was established for the workers, offering sickness and funeral benefits. Rule III of the rule-book reads 'Each member shall pay to the treasure box agreeable to the table following, which is divided into eight parts, viz. the member who is set down at two shillings and sixpence a week, shall pay one halfpenny per week: five shillings, one penny ... etc.[25]

The innovative program probably accounts for Small's exhaustion with the practice of "physick" and how it came to be a fate worse than "gaol." It should be remembered that in addition to his duties at the factory, Small also had a substantial and profitable private practice, oversaw and advised on new mechanical and scientific projects and experiments, performed his duties as a councilman, maintained his position on the Canal Committee, designed and wrote specifications for the steam engine patent, lobbied for the patent in London, and paid especial attention to his pet project—the Birmingham Lunar Society. With Withering's assessment that Small saw 2,000 to 3,000 pro bono clients annually, it is not a surprise that Small was often exhausted and depleted. Ironically and it seems inaccurately, Darwin submitted that Small lived a "quiet and reclusive life."

COLLABORATIONS AND CONSULTATIONS

Another facet of Small's medical profession was the mutual coop-eration with others in his field. He consulted on a regular basis with Alexander Small, his old friend and namesake, and also with Sir John Pringle, the noted physician. In 1767, William thanked Alexander Small for a formula of hemlock suggested by Pringle for treating a cancer patient. William Small noted the positive outcome of Pringle's remedy, "Hemlock well tolerated, pain subsided, tumour began to shrink."[26] In that same year William Small again wrote to Alexander Small concerning the successful treatment of chronic skin diseases by a "Tincture of White Hellibore."[27] And in the summer of 1768, Alexander Small wrote to Pringle, "Dr. [William] Small has written to state that all clinical evidence of breast cancer has now disappeared."[28]

Even after his death, evidence of his pharmaceutical skills remained in his office at Mr. Wheeler's house (Withering temporarily took up quarters there after his arrival in Birmingham) and just before Withering was to move in, he received a note from his old friend Erasmus Darwin with the following request, "Dr. Small made a grey Powder which was composed of the flowers of Tea (?) & teotacea [if] a Powder looking like such a Drug should be found in the House, I should be obliged to you to send or save it."[29]

Small routinely instructed Watt to take a bath in a "decoction of herbs" for his ennui, but, evidently, did not follow his own advice. He did, however, continue to consult and advise others in his field on both infusions of herbs and mixtures of medical compounds. Responding to a series of questions from Benjamin Franklin about the origins and cures of various ailments, Small referred Franklin to Aulus Celsus, who proscribed that a patient should avoid over-eating, the sun, and the cold if the problem was a sore. He also advised taking a long sea voyage for stomachaches. Zenophon and Plato thought excess and indulgence were the source of the common cold, and Hippocrates maintained that eating and drinking sparingly helped with diseases related to moisture; but, in the end "nemo mortalium fere est sine catarrhis"—Almost no one of mortal men is without colds.[30]

The extensive use of herbs and concoctions that Small employed might indicate that Small studied with an apothecary. His abilities in this field might also have derived from either his early associa-tion with John Gregory or the influence of Erasmus Darwin, a pio-neer in the study of botany and the use of plants in modern medical treatments.

Several of Small's alumni (James McClurg, Walter Jones, George Gilmer, and John Galt), after studying with Small at William and Mary, proceeded to the University of Edinburgh to study under John Gregory. Gilmer and Galt, when they returned to Williamsburg from their studies in Scotland, opened up an apothecary shop in Williamsburg. During the Revolution, McClurg and Jones were both appointed Physician Generals to the Continental army and McClurg was also named the Director of the Asylum in Williamsburg, where he concocted medications and cures for his patients.

In spite of his incessant complaints about the practice of medicine and his preference for intricacies of scientific explorations, it is obvi-ous that Small devoted an extended portion of his time (maybe the greatest part of his professional life) to consulting with fellow physicians, developing new surgical procedures, researching, and experimenting with botanical combinations, and examining and treating patients in an effort to improve life for those around him.

Small's training and early level of expertise in the medical field are apparent from his ability to act as a physician while he was in Virginia, the regard in which he was held among the most-prominent doctors in Britain, his reputation and medical successes in Birmingham, and the stunning number of patients that he saw (gratis) at the hospital or at his clinic. This evidence is accompanied by the number of prominent people who sought his medical advice and the glowing medical tributes that he received postmortem. These testimonials serve as robust confirmation that the medical profession was a major part of Small's life's work and one that has been persistently overlooked.

NOTES

1. *Aris's Birmingham Gazette*, February 27, 1775, Archives, Birmingham Central Library, Birmingham, England (hereafter cited as Birmingham).

2. James Keir, *An Account of the Life and Writings of Thomas Day* (London: John Stockdale, 1791), 29.

3. James P. Muirhead, *The Life of James Watt: With Selections from His Correspondence* (London: John Murray, 1858), 252.

4. Gillian Hull, "William Small, 1734–1775: No Publications, Much Influence," *Journal of the Royal Society of Medicine* 30 (February 1997): 102.

5. Elizabeth Gregory to Elizabeth Montagu, June 28, 1756, MS 1063, Archives, Huntington Library, San Marino, California. Courtesy of Mary Robertson.

6. Personal correspondence, August 26, 2008, courtesy of Simon Chaplin, Director of Museums and Special Collections. Citation from the Pringle papers at the Royal College of Physicians in Edinburgh, Scotland. Pringle 1/4/f.157(ca. 1757). Courtesy of Mrs. Estela Dukan and Iain Milne of the RCPE Special Collections.

7. Dudley Digges to the Bishop of London, July 15, 1767, Fulham Palace Papers, Box 2, No. 23, Lambeth Palace Library, London. Note that the letter was signed "Rector." Dudley Digges was the rector at the time, but the handwriting belongs to Robert Carter Nicholas.

8. Robert Carter Nicholas to William Small, June 25, 1767, Edgehill-Randolph Collection, Archives, Alderman Library, University of Virginia, Charlottesville. It is not known how this letter ended up at the University of Virginia, although Randolph is a family with familial ties to Thomas Jefferson.

9. William Hunter's Will, August 17, 1761, York County Records, Wills, and Inventories, 21:79–82, Library of Virginia, Richmond. See also Mary Godwin, "The Printing Shop: Block 18, Colonial Lot #48" (Williamsburg: Colonial Williamsburg Foundation, 1952), 24.

10. MS M 28 f-20, Archives, University of Aberdeen, Aberdeen, Scotland; see also Procuratory Accounts of Marischal College, MS M 27, Archives, University of Aberdeen.

11. William Small to James Watt, October 27, 1773, MS 3782/12/76/151, Archives, Birmingham Central Library, Birmingham.

12. George Fordyce and John Hunter to William Small, April 5, 1771, MS 3782 /12/23/199, Archives, Birmingham Central Library, Birmingham.

13. F. Clifford Rose, *The Neurobiology of Painting: International Review of Neurobiology* (Oxford: Elsevier Press, 2006), 74:19. Other prominent clubs in which Hunter and Fordyce were also likely members were the "Medical Society of London," which was founded in 1773 and met in Crane Court and Fleet Street. In 1782, Hunter and Fordyce founded the Society for the Improvement of Medical and Chirurgical Knowledge. In addition, in 1785, they also founded the Lyceum Medicum Londinense. There, of course, may be other clubs. These other societies, however, postdated the 1771 letter and the natural interest that Small may have had in the Licentiate group strongly points to that organization. *Medical Times and Gazette* 18 (March 1859): 278.

14. Nathaniel Jeffreys (Jeffries) to Matthew Boulton, October 5, 1766, MS 3782 /12/23/79, Archives, Birmingham Central Library, Birmingham.

15. "Mr. Boulton having consulted us on his daughter's case and desired us to communicate our opinion to you that we may also have your sentiments with regard to it." George Fordyce and John Hunter to William Small, April 5, 1771, MS 3782/12/23/199, Archives, Birmingham Central Library, Birmingham; see also Erasmus Darwin to Matthew Boulton, June 6, 1769, MS 3782/12/53/40, Archives, Birmingham Central Library, Birmingham.

16. John Baskerville to Matthew Boulton, December 9, 1765, MS 3782 /12/23/54, Archives, Birmingham Central Library, Birmingham.

17. William Small to James Watt, May 1, 1773, MS 3782/12/76/145, Archives, Birmingham Central Library, Birmingham.

18. William Small to James Watt, October 5, 1770, in Muirhead *The Life of James Watt*, 223.

19. "Birmingham Hospital," *Aris's Birmingham Gazette*, December 30, 1765, Ganter Collection, Archives, Swem Library, College of William and Mary, Williamsburg, Virginia.

20. J. A. Langford, *A Century of Birmingham Life* (Birmingham: E. C. Osborne, 1868), 1:157. For a brief history of the General Hospital, see ibid., 153–174.

21. Erasmus Darwin to William Withering, May 14, 1775, MS 0014, Archives, Mt. Holyoke College, Mt. Holyoke, Massachusetts (hereafter cited as Mt. Holyoke). Courtesy of Miss Micha Broadnax.

22. William Withering, *An Account of the Foxglove and Some of its Medical Uses* (Birmingham: M. Sweeny, 1785), 2.

23. David Schmidtz and Jason Brennan, *A Brief History of Liberty* (Chichester, U.K., and Malden, Mass.: Wiley-Blackwell, 2010), 1904.

24. Joan Lane, *A Social History of Medicine* (London: Routledge, 2001), 74.

25. Michael Zmolek, *Rethinking the Industrial Revolution* (Boston: Brill Publishing, 2013), 177.

26. William Small to Alexander Small, August 18, 1767, in Sir John Pringle, Medical Annotations (unpublished notebooks), Royal College of Physicians of Edinburgh, Scotland. Courtesy of Dr. Andrew Doig.

27. William Small to Alexander Small, October 7, 1767, in ibid.

28. Alexander Small to Sir John Pringle, June 27, 1768, in ibid.

29. Erasmus Darwin to William Withering, May 14, 1775, MS 0014, Archives, Mt. Holyoke College, Mt. Holyoke. Courtesy of Miss Micha Broadnax.

30. William Small to Benjamin Franklin, August 10, 1771, original at the Library of Congress, Washington, D.C. https://franklinpapers.org/framedNames.jsp (accessed August 4, 2021; see under "Small, William").

William Small Timeline

October 13, 1734	William Small born in Carmylie, Scotland.
1743–1750	William and his elder brother Robert attend Dundee Grammar School.
1750–1755	William attends Marischal College, Aberdeen, and has internship with John Gregory.
1755–1758	Small works at hospitals in London.
July–August 1758	Small interviews with the Reverend Dr. Samuel Nichols (Nicholls) for the position of Professor of Mathematicks at the College of William and Mary. Sets sail for the colonies late in July or early in August.
October 18, 1758	Small takes his Oath of Office and is sworn in at the College of William and Mary.
1760	William Small co-founds and leads the Virginia Society for the Encouragement of Arts and Manufacturing, a scientific club in Williamsburg.
1760	In the spring of 1760, Jacob Rowe, who was the only other collegiate professor at William and Mary, is put on trial before the Board of Visitors on numerous charges and claims that he has "few or no students." In August, after leading a student riot, he is dismissed, leaving William Small in sole charge of the classes and curriculum at the college.

1760–1761	William Small is the only collegiate professor at the College of William and Mary at the very same time when Thomas Jefferson was a student. During this time Small introduced Jefferson to George Wythe and into the intellectual society, the "partie quaree," where he became a regular member. Richard Graham is reinstated by the Privy Council late in 1761.
1762–1764	The dismissed professors, Richard Graham and John Camm, reinstated to the professorships from which they had been ousted. Small practices medicine and meets and becomes a friend and collaborator of Benjamin Franklin. He receives permission from the Board of Visitors to return to England to purchase scientific apparatus.
April 1763	Benjamin Franklin goes to Williamsburg to settle the estate of his old friend and colleague William Hunter. It was at this time that Small and Franklin met, became friends, and collaborated on a prototype of the Argand lamp.
October 1764	Small departs from Hampton, Virginia, for London.
December 1, 1764	Small arrives in London at the home of Alexander Small, Benjamin Franklin's close friend and prominent London surgeon.
Winter 1765	Small becomes Franklin's protégé in London. Franklin introduces Small to his social, financial, and philosophical friends, and takes him along to his literary and scientific clubs and societies. Small makes new friendships and reestablishes old ties among London's elite medical professionals.
March 1765	Small journeys to Aberdeen and Edinburgh to obtain the requisite recommendations for his M.D.
May 1765	Small arrives at the home of industrialist Matthew Boulton to interview for the position of physician and scientific advisor with a letter of introduction from Benjamin Franklin.

1765	Small and Boulton begin to have working dinners to discuss technological innovations connected with Soho Factory. Small and Boulton construct a working model of a steam engine and send it to Franklin in London, where he exhibits it to great applause.
1765	Erasmus Darwin is included in the "philosophical repasts" of Small and Boulton to form the nucleus of the soon-to-be philosophical society. The club grows in size and diversity of membership and topics discussed.
1765–1775	In addition to acting as a physician and scientific advisor to Matthew Boulton, 1) Small joins a private medical practice, 2) is a founding sponsor of the Birmingham Hospital, 3) becomes a town councilman, 4) is a member of the council to establish a canal system for transport of goods, 5) devotes pro bono services to the poor, 6) recruits for and orchestrates the meetings of the nascent Birmingham Lunar Society, 7) consults and collaborates with James Watt on refining technical aspects of the steam engine, and 8) lobbies London friends on the passage of an Act of Parliament granting a monopoly to the firm of Boulton, Watt & Small for the improved steam engine.
Spring 1767	James Watt comes to Birmingham and first meets with William Small. From this time, Small urges Boulton to invest in Watt's concept for a new and improved steam engine.
1769–1775	Small collaborates with Watt to correct and refine deficiencies in his design of the steam engine, and Small lobbies influential members of Parliament to grant a monopoly to the firm of Boulton and Watt.
1773	Matthew Boulton obtains Dr. Roebuck's interest in Watts's patent and Watt moves to Birmingham. From 1773 to 1775, Small and Watt work closely together improving Watts's invention.

February 23, 1775   A bill is successfully introduced in
                                       Parliament to extend a monopoly for the
                                       steam engine for twenty-five years to the
                                       firm of Boulton and Watt.

February 25, 1775   William Small, ill from a fever, falls into a
                                       coma and dies at the age of forty-one.

Dramatis Personae (1734–1758)

SCOTLAND AND LONDON

Family

George Small (ca. 1600–1660)
William Small's great-great-grandfather. A weaver from Foveran, a hamlet near Aberdeen.

Thomas Small (ca. 1620–1687)
William Small's great-grandfather, son of George Small. He graduated from the University of St. Andrews, MA (1640) and became a schoolmaster at Meigle; he was translated (was transferred) to the parish of Lintrathen (1650); he married the daughter of the powerful Earl of Airlie, Susanna Ogilvie (1650); they had two sons, James and David.

James Small (1652–1729)
Granduncle to William Small; son of Thomas Small, he followed in his father's footsteps as an Episcopalian minister; he graduated from the University of St. Andrews, MA (1670); he was the minister of Cortachy (1679); he was "driven from his church without so much as a shadow of a cause" (1716) likely because he refused to renounce his Episcopal allegiance and swear an oath to the Presbyterian synod; died 1729.

David Small (ca 1664–ca. 1749)

William's grandfather was indentured to Henry Crawford, merchant of Dundee in 1676; he became a successful burgess in the town and established a home at Westhouse, in Leuchars, near St. Andrews in Fife; he married Margaret Lindsay and the couple had six children and at least four sons: John, James, Andrew, and Alexander.

James Small (1689–1771)

William's father, James, likely attended Forgan parish school (the local church in Leuchars), and then Dundee Grammar School. He obtained his first bursar post at the University of St. Andrews in 1706 and received his BA in 1709. Next, he applied for a second bursar's post, was awarded the post, and graduated with an MA in 1710. In 1712, he was granted bursar's status a third time and entered the Divinity School of St. Mary's College (a division of St. Andrews). In 1718, he was appointed keeper of the university library. In 1719, he took his trials for the ministry. In 1720, having passed his trials, he represented Forgan Church at the General Assembly of the Presbyterian Church and was soon transferred to the parish of Carmylie, Angus. In 1723, he married Lillias Scott of Montrose and the couple had five children. James Small remained the minister at Carmylie until the time of his death in 1771.

Robert Small (1732–1808)

Elder brother to William, Robert and William attended Dundee Grammar School. Robert received his MA from the University of St. Andrews and was licensed by the Presbytery in 1759. He was awarded his DD from St. Andrews in 1778, the same year he was appointed Chaplin to the Royal Highlanders Infantry. In 1782, he co-founded a medical dispensary for the poor, which was eventually transformed into the Dundee Royal Infirmary. He married Jean Yeaman, daughter of the Provost of Dundee in 1764. Among his publications were *An Account of the Astronomical Discoveries of Kepler*, *Demonstrations of Some of Dr. Matthew Stewart's General Theorems*, and an *Account of the Town and Parish of Dundee*. He was the Minister of St. Mary's Church in Dundee until his death.

SMALL'S MASTERS AT
DUNDEE GRAMMAR SCHOOL

George Blair (1707–1773)

Tutor in the home of Colonel Ogilvie and ordained in 1729. He was appointed the minister of Abernyte in 1733. He resigned this post to take up the position as Master of Dundee Grammar School (1738–1749). He introduced many changes to the rigor, character, and curriculum of the school. He was called back to Abernyte in 1749 and remained there until his death in 1773. Blair was the Rector of Dundee Grammar School while the Smalls were in attendance and may have been responsible for bursaries for both William and Robert Small.

William Lauder (1680–1771)

May have taught both Robert and William Small. He was a noted poet who obtained a post as a Master at Dundee Grammar School (1743–1745). He had an eccentric character and a checkered life. Later he was dismissed from his post at Dundee Grammar School and immigrated to Barbados where he died a drunk.

Gilbert Lundie (dates unknown)

William's first teacher at Dundee Grammar School (1743–1747). After a dispute with the Rector over wages, he was dismissed from the staff.

John Mearns (1715–1786?)

William's and Robert's teacher; he was the Master of the Latin school at Dundee (1741–1756) and later moved to the Latin School at Dunkold.

PROFESSORS AND COLLEAGUES AT MARISCHAL COLLEGE

Thomas Blackwell (1701-1757)

Principal of Marischal College and Professor of Greek. He was born in 1701; he attended Aberdeen Grammar School and received an MA from Marischal in 1718. In 1723, he appointed to the Regius Chair of Greek at Marischal; in 1748, he was elected the Principal of Marischal College. Under his administration the college underwent substantive changes, both in teaching methodology and curriculum, developing a more progressive and scientific program. He was Small's Professor of Greek in his first year at Marischal.

Francis Skene (ca. 1721–1775)

The son of George Skene and a regent at Marischal College from 1734 to1775. Skene was Small's second year, or bejan, professor. He was the first to teach the new course of Civil and Natural History.

William Duncan (1717–1760)

Born in Aberdeen and received his early education at Foveran Grammar School. He studied at Marischal College under Thomas Blackwell. In 1748, his work, *The Elements of Logick* (considered one of the most influential books of the times on the subject), was published in *Dodley's Preceptor*. Duncan instructed Small as Professor of Natural Philosophy in his third year. Duncan's instruction served as a model and template for Small's teaching at the College of William and Mary.

Alexander Gerard (1728–1795)

The son of the Reverend Gilbert Gerard, an Aberdeen minister. He attended Foveran Grammar School and studied Divinity at Marischal College and King's College and was licensed to preach in 1748. In 1750, he served as a temporary replacement for Professor David Fordyce. After Fordyce's death, Gerard was elected Professor of Moral Philosophy at Marischal (1752–1759), as Professor of Divinity (1759–1773), and as Professor of Divinity at King's College, Aberdeen (1773). Best known for his plan to revise the teaching methodology and curriculum at Marischal (1753), his "Essay on Taste" (1759), and his "Essay on Genius" (1774). Gerard was Small's senior (magistrand) professor who taught logic, ethics, and metaphysics, and was a pioneering proponent of belles lettres.

John Gregory (1724-1773)

Small's mentor, John Gregory, was born into a celebrated family of scholars and physicians in Aberdeen, he studied at the University of Edinburgh (1741) under Monro, Sinclair, and Rutherford. He then proceeded to the University of Leyden (1745–1746) in Holland, known for its progressive medical instruction. While at Leyden, he received an unsolicited degree in medicine from King's College, Aberdeen. He returned to Scotland in 1746 and lectured at King's College for three years in mathematics and moral and natural philosophy. In 1749, he resigned his position at King's and began to practice medicine in Aberdeen with his brother, James Gregory. In 1752, he married Elizabeth Forbes, daughter of Lord Forbes and niece of Elizabeth Montagu of "bluestocking club" fame. In 1754, Gregory moved to London to begin a career at St. George's Hospital. During this period, he and his wife lived with her aunt Elizabeth Montagu. After the death of his brother, James Gregory, John Gregory was offered his position as Mediciner to King's College. He accepted but did not return until 1756. After returning to Aberdeen in 1758, Gregory co-founded the Aberdeen Philosophical Society with his cousin Thomas Reid. In 1764, Gregory published a book entitled *A Comparative View of the State and Faculties of Man*, the same year in which Reid published his *Inquiries into the Human Mind on the Principles of Common Sense*. In 1766, Gregory was named the King's physician in Scotland and left his post at Aberdeen for a position at the University of Edinburgh, where he taught the practice of medicine and related subjects until his death in 1773.

James MacPherson (1738–1796)

A classmate of William Small. He was educated at Marischal College and taught school in Ruthven for several years after graduating. In 1761, MacPherson published a work called *The Highlander* that contained ancient poems written in Gaelic or Erse that he translated. In 1762, he published his other finds, the story of Fingal, an ancient Scot hero who fought against the Romans, supposedly composed by Fingal's son Ossian. It received wide acclaim and Thomas Jefferson declared the poems by Ossian to be as sublime as Homer. In 1763, MacPherson became a British tax collector in Florida and in 1775 wrote a vitriolic pamphlet against the rebelling Americans.

MEMBERS OF THE ABERDEEN PHILOSOPHICAL SOCIETY

In addition to those members below, John Gregory and Alexander Gerard are listed above. The majority of the members were, at the time Small departed for London in 1755, professors at either Kings College or Marischal College, and it is likely that Small would have known many of them personally.

Thomas Reid (1710–1796)

Related to John Gregory on his distaff side. He attended Aberdeen Grammar School and Marischal College and graduated in 1731. He was licensed by the Church and served at Kincardine until named librarian at Marischal College in 1733. In 1737, he became minister at New Marchar Church, near Aberdeen. In 1751, he was elected regent at King's College. In 1762, he received an honorary doctor of divinity degree from Marischal College. He was elected to succeed Adam Smith as Professor of Moral Philosophy at the University of Glasgow in 1764. He published his immensely influential work *Inquiry into the Human Mind on the Principles of Common Sense* in 1764. In addition to his teaching duties, Reid published two volumes based on his lectures at Glasgow: *Essays on the Intellectual Powers of Man* (1785) and *Essays on the Active Powers of Man* (1788). Reid's precepts became known as the School of Common Sense Philosophy and had a profound impact not only in Scotland but also in the American colonies.

Robert Traill (1720–1775)

The son of William Traill, Minister of Benholm, and a cousin of William Trail (see below). He was licensed to preach at Brechin (1744), then at Kettins (1745), and finally at Banff. He received a doctor of divinity degree from St. Andrews in 1760 and was appointed Professor of Oriental Languages at the University of Glasgow in 1761. He was later transferred to the post of Professor of Divinity.

David Skene (1731–1770)

The son of Andrew Skene. He graduated from Marischal College in 1748 and received his M.D. in 1753. After graduating, he interned in his father's medical practice in Aberdeen for several years, then continued his studies in Edinburgh and, like Gregory, studied under Alexander Monro primus, and John Rutherford, before training in midwifery with William Smellie. He finished his education in Paris before returning to Aberdeen. He was a medical colleague to John Gregory; the two attempted to establish a medical school in Aberdeen. He was also a founding member of the Aberdeen Philosophical Society.

William Trail (1746–1831)

The son of the Reverend William Trail, Minister of St. Moran and also a nephew of the Robert Trail, who was one of the original members of the Aberdeen Philosophical Society. He graduated from Marischal College MA in 1766 and in the autumn of 1766 was appointed Professor of Mathematics at that institution and admitted as a member of the Wise Club (Aberdeen Philosophical

Society). While a member of the Society, he published the *Elements of Algebra* (1770) and in 1774, he received an LLD from Marischal. He then resigned his professorship and took orders in the Church of England. He was thereupon appointed to a position at Carncastle and later took a post with his uncle the Bishop of Down and Connor in Ireland. The Bishop was also associated with the Aberdeen Philosophical Society.

James Traill (1725–1783)

Raised in Angus, near Forfar, he earned his MA from Marischal in 1745, and doctor of divinity in 1760. His father, Robert Traill, was the minister at Panbride who baptized William Small. James Traill was educated at Marischal College, took an MA at Cambridge, and was tutor to the Marquis of Hereford. In 1762, he became the Rector of St. John's at Horsleydown and became Chaplain to the English Ambassador, then Chaplain to the Lord Lieutenant of Ireland. He was consecrated as Bishop of Down and Connor in 1765 where he served until his death in 1783. He was an honorary member of the Aberdeen Philosophical Society.

LONDON PHYSICIANS

John Elliot (1736–1786)

Born in Edinburgh, he attended Christ Church, Oxford. After an adventurous stint as the sawbones on a pirate ship, he established a practice in Cecil Street, London, and eventually became King's Physician and Senior Physician at Greenwich Hospital. He and John Gregory were the two physicians who attested to Small's medical skills for his M.D. from Marischal College.

George Fordyce (1736–1802)

Born in Aberdeen and attended school in nearby Foveran. He matriculated at Marischal College, where he obtained his MA at the age of fourteen. He next apprenticed with his uncle John Fordyce and continued his education at the University of Edinburgh in 1758, where he studied under William Cullen and wrote his dissertation on catarrh, or the common cold. Fordyce did postgraduate work at the University of Leyden where he studied anatomy. In 1759, he returned to London where he set up a medical practice and conducted lectures on chemistry, materia medica, and the practice of physic. In London, he was a physician at St. Thomas' Hospital, was chosen a member of the Literary Club, a Fellow of the Royal Society, and a Fellow of the Royal College of Physicians. He and John Hunter formed a society of distinguished surgeons and physicians.

William Heberden (1710–1801)

Born in London, he was educated at Cambridge, where he received his M.D. in 1739. He remained at Cambridge teaching materia medica for some years, and was elected a member of the Royal College of Physicians in 1746, and a fellow of the Royal Society in 1748. In 1759, he co-authored a pamphlet "Some Account of the Success of the Inoculation for the Small-Pox in England and America" with Benjamin Franklin. Heberden recommended Small to serve as a physician at the Royal Court of Russia.

John Hunter (1728–1793)

A Scottish surgeon who studied anatomy with his brother William Hunter in London. He was an army doctor who set up his own school of anatomy in London and collaborated with Edward Jenner on the smallpox vaccine. In 1756, he became an assistant surgeon at St. George's Hospital at the same time Small was walking the wards at the same institution. In 1767, he was made a Fellow of the Royal Society of London and shortly after this he "induced a number of his friends and associates in forming a club." The name of the club was the Society of Licentiate Physicians; its main purpose was to campaign for medical licenses for those applicants who were unfairly denied a medical license. "Many of the founders were Scots who did not qualify because they lacked a medical degree from Oxford or Cambridge."[1]

Sir John Pringle (1707–1782)

Educated at St. Andrews, Pringle was a physician at Edinburgh (also Professor of Moral Philosophy there). He was a leading voice in the study of military diseases, jail fever, and the use of antiseptics. He was acquainted with Small from his early days in London and it was even mentioned that he and Small attended surgeries performed by John Hunter at St. George's Hospital in London. Small often consulted with him after arriving in Birmingham.

Alexander Small (1710–1791)

Born in Perthshire, near Angus, Alexander Small was a possible relative of William Small—in a letter to Franklin, he calls William "his namesake." He was a close friend of Benjamin Franklin and an expert on infectious diseases who advocated for proper ventilation in hospitals to prevent the spread of infection. He was also summoned to diagnose William Small in his last days and concluded that his critical situation was caused by "gaol or putrid fever."

NOTES

1. Hunter and George Fordyce wrote to Small as his "brethren in the medical society." George Fordyce and John Hunter to William Small, April 3, 1771, MS3783/13/199, Birmingham Central Library, Birmingham, England. Elected a physician at St. George's Hospital in 1768.

Dramatis Personae (1758–1764)

VIRGINIA

Williamsburg Friends and Associates (1758–1764)

Francis Fauquier (1703–1768)

The son of John Fauquier who was assistant to Sir Isaac Newton at the English Mint and Director of the Bank of England. Francis Fauquier was on the Board of the infamous South Sea Company and in 1753 he was elected to the Royal Society of London. In 1758, he was appointed lieutenant governor of the Colony of Virginia. Especially during his early years in Virginia, Fauquier elevated the scientific and cultural life of the colony by introducing institutions intended to cultivate a more sophisticated and enlightened approach to education and the sciences. He was a crucial factor in the success of the two societies associated with Small and Jefferson in Williamsburg; he hosted the intellectual soirées that Jefferson attended and sponsored the Virginia Society for the Encouragement of Arts and Manufacturing. Matthew Boulton would later reprise Fauquier's role in the founding of the Birmingham Lunar Society.

William Hunter (ca. 1720–1761)

The son of William Hunter of Yorktown, brother of Col. John Hunter. He apprenticed with the founder of the Williamsburg *Virginia Gazette*, William Parks, in the 1740s and succeeded him in 1751. Hunter became Benjamin Franklin's Co-Postmaster-General in 1753. Hunter recommended Franklin for an honorary degree at the College of William and Mary in 1755, which was the first degree that the college issued. In 1756, Hunter left to handle business in England and was ill when he returned in 1759. William Small attended to Hunter in his final sickness. He was an intimate friend of William Small, Francis Fauquier, and George Wythe.

Thomas Jefferson (1743–1826)

The most noted of Small's students from the College of William and Mary. Born at Shadwell, Virginia in 1743, In 1763, Jefferson went to Williamsburg to attend the College of William and Mary. His only professor was Small, who took Jefferson under his wing and included him in the exclusive intellectual society that he had formed with the governor, Francis Fauquier, and George Wythe. Jefferson was fascinated by Small's knowledge, instruction, and personality. Jefferson almost certainly studied with Small even after he had officially left the college and while he was reading law with George Wythe. Even by Jefferson's own account, Small had been the source of his philosophical viewpoints and love of science.

Peyton Randolph (1721–1775)

The son of Sir John Randolph of Tazewell Hall. He attended the College of William and Mary and studied law at Middle Temple at the Inns of Court in London. Randolph served several terms in the Virginia House of Burgesses, as attorney general, as a representative of the General Assembly to Parliament, as Rector of the College of William and Mary, and he was elected as President of both the First and Second Continental Congresses. He was a member of the Board of Visitors while Small was at the college and presided over the trial that dismissed Jacob Rowe, the only other collegiate professor at the institution when Jefferson arrived.

Selim the Algerine (ca. 1730–ca. 1780)

The most unusual and mysterious of Small's American friends. Selim was the son of wealthy Algerian parents; he was sent to Constantinople for a classical Muslim education. Returning to Algiers, his ship was captured by French privateers. He was taken to New Orleans and sold into slavery from which he escaped and made his way to the western part of Virginia. Selim was eventually sent to Williamsburg where he attracted the attention of Small because of his knowledge of ancient Greek and other Asian languages. Having been rejected by his parents because he had converted to Christianity, he lived in Virginia a guest of the Page and Randolph families for the rest of his life.

George Wythe (1726–1806)

George Wythe received his early and classical education from his mother at home; when he was of age he studied law with his uncle, Stephen Dewey, and was admitted to the bar in 1746. He was appointed as clerk to the House of Burgesses in 1748. He replaced Peyton Randolph, per interim, from 1753 to 1755. He was elected a Burgess for Williamsburg from 1755 to 1758; afterwards he became a Burgess for the College of William and Mary. Wythe joined Francis Fauquier and William Small in the establishment of the Virginia Society for the Encouragement of Arts and Manufacturing in 1759. He was a member of Fauquier's informal intellectual society the "partie quaree," along with Small, Fauquier and Jefferson. After 1762, he conducted informal legal instruction and mock trials at the college for present and former students. In 1779, Wythe became the first American professor of law at the College of William and Mary.

Dramatis Personae (1764–1775)

Friends and Associates in Birmingham and London (1764–1775)

John Ash (1723–1798)

Born in Coventry and was educated at Trinity College, Dublin: MA (1746), M.D. (1754). Ash became a member of the Royal College of Physicians in 1786. He established a flourishing medical practice in Birmingham and shared his house at 10 Temple Row with Small. Ash and Small were the leading players in establishing the Birmingham General Hospital.

John Baskerville (1706–1775)

Born in Wolverley, Worcestershire, he moved to Birmingham as a young man. There he was apprenticed as a maker of japanned trays and salvers, and perhaps worked for Boulton's father. Eventually, he moved into the printing business where he developed a new style of type set. He was an associate of Franklin and a friend of Boulton.

Nathaniel Jeffreys (1740?–1810)

The son of a London goldsmith, he was apprenticed to his uncle, Thomas Jeffreys, a prominent silversmith at Cockspur Street, Charing Cross, and upon his uncle's demise, he took over the business. He was a business acquaintance of Matthew Boulton, a friend of Benjamin Franklin and a member of his Honest Whigs Club at the

George and Vulture along with Joseph Priestley, John Whitehurst, Thomas Day, Dr. Daniel Solander, Rudolph Eric Raspe and Josiah Wedgwood. In 1765, Jeffreys sent a letter of recommendation to Boulton on Small's behalf.

William Legge, Earl of Dartmouth (1731–1801)
William Legge is the namesake of Dartmouth College and was the stepbrother of Lord North. He supported the Foundling Hospital in London, where Francis Fauquier had been Director, and was a central player in promoting and securing the passage of the Birmingham Canal Bill. He collaborated with Small, Boulton, and Samuel Garbett in establishing a canal system between Birmingham and other centers of trade in England.

John Roebuck (1718–1794)
Born in Sheffield, England. He attended University of Edinburgh, where he studied under William Cullen and Joseph Black; he continued his education in Holland and received an M.D. from the University of Leyden. In addition to his medical practice, he became involved in the production of iron and built a factory at Prestonpans, Scotland. Initially, he hired James Watt to help him develop a process to pump water out of his intermittently flooded mines. At an early stage of the steam engine's development, Roebuck lent Watt a substantial amount of money in return for a two-thirds share in his patent. Because of financial troubles Roebuck eventually sold his share in the patent to Matthew Boulton.

William Strahan (1715–1785)
Born in Edinburgh and early apprenticed at bookmaking. He next moved to London, where he became a freeman of the city. In the 1740s, he transitioned from printing to publishing; he became Samuel Johnson's chief publisher. At the same time, he was developing a thriving trade with the colonies and became acquainted with

Benjamin Franklin. During Small's busy season in London, he often went with Franklin to Strahan's home as a dinner guest.

BIRMINGHAM LUNAR SOCIETY

Matthew Boulton (1728–1809)

Born in Birmingham, he was the son of a manufacturer of toys, buttons, and buckles. He entered into his father's business in 1745, and by 1749, he was a partner. In 1760, he married the wealthy heiress, Anne Robinson of Lichfield; her fortune enabled him to expand his father's business, and when she suddenly died, he married her sister. Boulton opened his new factory, Soho Manufactures in 1760. With the illness of his daughter and the expansion of his factory, by 1765, Boulton was in the market for someone who could both attend to his family and advise him in technological and scientific matters. His friend Benjamin Franklin introduced him to William Small. Boulton's first priority for Small was the health of his daughter, but soon he enlisted Small as a scientific advisor and confidante. The two often dined together, discussing new and potentially useful technology and advancements—the immediate consequence of which was a model of a new type of steam engine that could facilitate the efficiency of Soho Factory. These "unconscious" dinners became the foundations of the celebrated Birmingham Lunar Society.

Erasmus Darwin (1731–1802)

The son of Robert Darwin, he was educated at St. John's College, Cambridge and the University of Edinburgh Medical School. He first practiced at Nottingham, but shortly thereafter moved to Lichfield, near Birmingham, where his reputation swiftly grew and he had a surplus of clients. In addition to medicine, Darwin was profoundly interested in science, mechanics, electricity, geology, botany, theories of evolution, and, above all, stream enginery. The conversations with Boulton and Small and later James Watt greatly excited Darwin's imagination. Erasmus Darwin was the grandfather of Charles Darwin and is considered by many as the true source of the theory of evolution.

Thomas Day (1748–1789)

He was born the only child of Thomas and Jane Day, a wealthy London couple. He attended Corpus Christi College at Oxford University. He returned to his home to Berkshire in 1767, where he met Richard Lovell Edgeworth, a talented scientist and inventor. Day was an ardent abolitionist and author. He wrote a sympathetic poem entitled "The Dying Negro," which described the trials of a runaway slave, and a moral tale "The History of Sandford and Merton," which told the story of how a poor but honorable boy changed the vicious character of his rich friend by his kind example. Day and Edgeworth became fast friends, and shared an eccentric sense of humor. Day also became a close and devoted friend of William Small.

Richard Lovell Edgeworth (1744–1817)

Born in Bath and educated at Trinity College, Dublin, he then attended Oxford. He was interested in technological improvements in agriculture and education and, along with Thomas Day, followed the progressive educational precepts of Jean-Jacques Rousseau.

James Keir (1735–1820)

Born in Scotland and studied medicine at the University of Edinburgh. He enlisted in the army in 1757, traveled abroad and spent time in the West Indies. In 1768, he resigned his commission and settled in West Bromwich, near Birmingham. He became involved with the scientific circle there and was active in experimentation and exploration. He was celebrated for his translation of *Macquer's Dictionary of Chemistry* from the French, he assisted Joseph Priestley in his experiments on the properties of gases, and was deeply involved in the development of the steam engine. He was a close friend of Small and handled most of the correspondence with William's brother Robert immediately following William's death.

James Watt (1736–1819)

Born in Greenock, Scotland, the son of a shipwright. As a youth, he was interested in the tools of the navigation trade and became proficient in making and repairing instruments. Through his mother's family, the Muirheads, he was introduced to several professors at the University of Glasgow and was hired by Robert Dick. Professor Dick encouraged Watt to go to London for further training and he apprenticed with John Morgan for a short period and then returned to Glasgow. He had a small shop in the commercial district of Glasgow, but continued to work for the scientific faculty at the university, particularly Professor John Anderson and Professor Black. In 1763, in the course of repairing an early prototype of a Newcomen steam engine, he realized that by employing a separate condenser he could greatly improve the efficiency and versatility of the apparatus. He shared his discovery with Professor Black, who, in turn, introduced him to Dr. John Roebuck. Roebuck quickly saw the potential of Watt's design and advanced him a substantial sum of money in return for a two-thirds partnership in his invention. In 1767, Watt made a journey to London, and on his return to Scotland stopped by Birmingham to visit Matthew Boulton's technologically advanced Soho Factory. Boulton was away on business, but his scientific adviser William Small escorted Watt around the complex. As they toured, the two men fell into a conversation about steam engines. Small became convinced that a partnership between his new friend and his employer would be a great advantage to both. Small urged and exhorted Boulton to hire Watt. In 1773, Boulton bought Roebuck's interest in the engine and Watt soon moved to Birmingham. The collaboration between Small and Watt resulted in a machine that turned Britain from an agrarian economy into an industrial society.

Josiah Wedgwood (1730–1795)

Born in Burslem, England, into a family of potters. He joined the family business at the age of nine and was especially interested in experimenting with chemicals and glazes. Like Boulton, his factory,

Etruria, was a model system utilizing a division of labor. With his organizational and artistic skills, Wedgwood's wares became universally sought out and endorsed by the royal family. Boulton, Wedgwood, and Small collaborated on several aspects of the technology, which he came to employ in a most utilitarian fashion. Both Wedgwood and Boulton were acoustical advocates of establishing a system of canals for transportation and industrial applications.

John Whitehurst (1718–1788)

Born in Cheshire, the son of a clockmaker. In 1736, he established a business in Derby making clocks and scientific apparatus. An ingenious innovator, he produced a number of devices that were connected both to the improvement of the steam engine and extracting ores. He was also involved with Small and Boulton in the Grand Trunk Canal, and with Darwin and Josiah Wedgwood in geological explorations. In 1763, he wrote to Franklin concerning his theory regarding the formation of the earth, which was gradually expanded and published in 1778.

Bibliography

PRIMARY SOURCES: ARCHIVES, MANUSCRIPTS, AND UNPUBLISHED PAPERS

Alderman Library, University of Virginia, Charlottesville, Virginia.

American Philosophical Society, Philadelphia, Pennsylvania.

Archives, University of St. Andrews, St. Andrews, Scotland.

Archives of Mt. Holyoke College, Mt. Holyoke College, Mt. Holyoke, Massachusetts.

Birmingham Central (Public) Library, Birmingham, England.

Boucher Papers, Swem Library, College of William and Mary, Williamsburg, Virginia.

Bursar Record Books, Special Collections, Swem Library, College of William and Mary, Williamsburg, Virginia.

Clemens Library, University of Michigan, Ann Arbor, Michigan.

Colonial Records Project, Fulham Palace Papers, Special Collections, Library of Virginia, Richmond.

Colonial Williamsburg Foundation, Rockefeller Library, Williamsburg, Virginia.

Dawson Papers, Library of Congress, Washington D.C.

Dundee Council Records, Archives, City of Dundee, Dundee, Scotland.

Edgehill-Randolph Papers, Special Collections, Alderman Library, University of Virginia, Charlottesville, Virginia.

Edrington Papers, Virginia Museum of History and Culture, Richmond, Virginia.

Erasmus Darwin Commonplace Book, Erasmus Darwin Centre, Lichfield, England.

Faculty-Alumni Files, Special Collections, Swem Library, College of William and Mary, Williamsburg, Virginia.

Franklin Papers, Archives, American Philosophical Society, Philadelphia, Pennsylvania.

Fulham Palace Papers, Virginia, Microfilm, Library of Congress, Washington D.C.

Ganter Collection, Archives, Swem Library, College of William and Mary, Williamsburg, Virginia.

Harrison Institute, University of Virginia, Charlottesville, Virginia.

Hughes, Robert M. "Norfolk Alumni of the College of William and Mary Prior to the Civil War," Archives, Swem Library, College of William and Mary, Williamsburg, Virginia.

Index of Matriculations and Graduations in the University of St. Andrews, Archives, St. Andrews University, St. Andrews, Scotland.

James Watt Papers, Archives, Birmingham Public Library, Birmingham, England.

John Page's Commonplace Book, Virginia Museum of History and Culture, Richmond, Virginia.

Jones Family Papers, Library of Congress, Washington, D.C.

Journal Book of the Royal Society, Archives, Royal Society of London, Royal Society, London, England.

Lee Collection, Virginia Museum of History and Culture, Richmond, Virginia.

Library of Congress, Washington, D.C.

Library of Virginia, Richmond.

Lord Lyons Office, New Register House, Edinburgh, Scotland.

Masters and Regents Records, Archives, University of Aberdeen, Aberdeen, Scotland.

Matthew Boulton Papers, Archives, Birmingham Public Library, Birmingham, England.

Meeting of the Visitors and Governors of the College of William and Mary, Virginia Colonial Records Project, Fulham Palace Papers, Library of Virginia, Richmond.

Meeting of the Principal and Masters of Marischal College, January 11, 1753, Archives, University of Aberdeen, Aberdeen, Scotland.

Meigle Kirk Session Records, National Archives of Scotland, New Register House, Edinburgh, Scotland.

Montagu Correspondence, Huntington Library, San Marino, California.

National Archives of Scotland, New Register House, Edinburgh, Scotland.

"Notes: A Compilation by Edwin Canaan Professor of Political Economy," University of London, Special Collections, Swem Library, College of William and Mary, Williamsburg, Virginia.

Old Parish Records, Archives, University of St. Andrews, St. Andrews, Scotland.

Papers of Sir John Pringle, Special Collections, Royal College of Physicians Edinburgh, Edinburgh, Scotland.

Records of the University of St. Andrews: Index of Matriculations and Graduations, 1579–1747, Compiled by Robert Smart, Archives, University of St. Andrews, St. Andrews, Scotland.

Rockefeller Library, Special Collections, Colonial Williamsburg Foundation, Williamsburg, Virginia.

St. Andrews Presbytery Minutes, Archives, University of St. Andrews, St. Andrews, Scotland.

St. Andrews Senatus Minutes, Archives, University of St. Andrews, St. Andrews, Scotland.

Stubbs, William Carter. Unpublished Notes, 1907, Students Attending the College of William and Mary before the Revolution, Archives, Swem Library, College of William and Mary, Williamsburg, Virginia.

Swem Library, Archives, College of William and Mary, Williamsburg, Virginia.

Taks and Teinds, Archives, University of St. Andrews, St. Andrews, Scotland.

Thomas Jefferson Papers, General Correspondence, Library of Congress, Washington, D.C.

Transcripts of the Forfar Town Council Minute Book, Angus Archives, Restenneth, Scotland.

Transcripts of the Meeting of the President and Board of Visitors, Colonial Williamsburg Foundation, Rockefeller Library, Williamsburg, Va.

University Library, Cambridge University, Cambridge, England.

University of Aberdeen Archives, Aberdeen, Scotland.

University of Edinburgh, Archives, Edinburgh, Scotland.

Virginia Colonial Records Project, Library of Virginia, Richmond.

Virginia Gazette Daybooks, Harrison Institute, University of Virginia, Charlottesville, Virginia.

Virginia Museum of History and Culture, Richmond.

William Yates, Personal Papers, Accession Number 26024, Archives, Library of Virginia, Richmond.

York County Records, Wills and Inventories, Book 21, Library of Virginia, Richmond.

PRIMARY SOURCES: PRINTED

Alumni Oxonienses, 1715–1886. Edited by Joseph Foster. Vol. 3. Oxford: Parker & Co., 1888.

The Annals of the Royal Society Club. London: Macmillan & Co, 1917.

Anonymous. *Letters from Virginia: By an Unknown Frenchman.* Translated by George Tucker. Baltimore: Fielding Lewis, 1816.

Bertie, David. *Scottish Episcopal Clergy, 1689–2000.* Edinburgh: T. & T. Clark, 2000.

Blomquist, Amy. *Vestry Book of Southam Parish, Cumberland County, Virginia, 1745–1792.* Westminster: Heritage Books, 2002.

Calendar of Virginia State Papers. Edited by E. H. Flournoy. Vol. 10. Richmond: James E. Goode, 1892.

Camm, John. *A Review of the Rector Detected: or, the Colonel Reconnoitred: Part the First.* Williamsburg: Joseph Royle, 1764.

A Catalogue of All Graduates in Divinity, Law, Medicine; and of Masters of Arts and Doctors of Music, Who Have Regularly Proceeded or Been Created in the University of Oxford, Between Oct. 10, 1659, and Oct. 10, 1800. Oxford: Clarendon Press, 1801.

Catalogue of Students at the College of William and Mary. Williamsburg: J. Hervey Ewing, 1855.

The Colonial Register. Edited by William and Mary Stanard. Albany: Joel Mussel's Sons, 1902.

Darwin, Erasmus. *The Letters of Erasmus Darwin.* Edited by Desmond King-Hele. New York: Cambridge University Press, 1981.

The Declaration of Independence, 1776, Literal Print. Washington: Department of State, 1911.

Dinwiddie, Robert. *The Official Records of Robert Dinwiddie.* Vol. I. Richmond: Virginia Historical Society, 1883.

Documents Relating to the Revolutionary History of the State of New Jersey, Vol. I: Extracts from American Newspapers, 1776–1777. Edited by William Stryker. Trenton: John Murphy Publishing, 1901.

Duncan, William. *The Elements of Logick.* Albany: E. F. Backus, 1814.

Evidence; Oral and Documentary. University of Aberdeen. Vol. 4. London: Clowes and Sons, 1837.

Extracts from the Carmylie Kirk Sessions, 1720–1771. Compiled by Muriel M. K. Thomson. Angus Archives, Hunter Library, Forfar, Scotland.

Extracts from the Itineraries and Other Miscellanies of Ezra Stiles. Edited by Franklin B. Dexter. New Haven: Yale University Press, 1916.

Fasti Academicae Mariscallanae Aberdonensis. Edited by P. J. Anderson. Vol. 2. Aberdeen: New Spalding Club, 1898.

Fasti Ecclesiae Scoticanae. Edited by Hew Scott. Vol. 5. Edinburgh: Oliver and Boyd, 1925.

Fauquier, Francis. *The Official Papers of Francis Fauquier.* Edited by George Reese. Vols. 1–2. Charlottesville: University Press of Virginia, 1981.

Fithian, Philip Vickers. *The Journal and Letters of Phillip Vickers Fithian.* Edited by Hunter Farish. Charlottesville: University Press of Virginia, 1968.

Franklin, Benjamin. *The Papers of Benjamin Franklin.* Edited by Leonard W. Labaree et al. New Haven: Yale University Press, 1965–1974.

Heberden, William, and Benjamin Franklin. *Some Account of the Success of Inoculation for the Small-Pox in England and America.* London: William Strahan, 1759.

Hertfordshire with a History and Description of the Various Towns and Villages. Hertford: Simson and Co., 1880.

Historical Collections Relating to the American Colonial Church. Edited by William Perry. Vol. 1. New York: AMS Press, 1969.

Historical Register of Officers of the Continental Army during the War of the Revolution. Edited by Francis Heitman. Washington: National Capitol Press, 1914.

The History of the College of William and Mary: From Its Foundation, 1660 to 1874. Richmond: Randolph & English, 1874.

Hume, David. *Essays: Moral, Political and Literary.* Indianapolis: Liberty Fund, 1985.

Jefferson, Thomas. *A Catalog with the Entries in His Own Order.* Edited by James Gilreath and Douglas Wilson. Washington, D.C.: Library of Congress, 2001.

———. *The Commonplace Book of Thomas Jefferson.* Edited by Gilbert Chinard. Baltimore: Johns Hopkins Press, 1926.

———. *Jefferson's Memorandum Books.* Edited by James Bear and Lucia Stanton. Vol. 1. Princeton: Princeton University Press, 1997.

———. *The Life and Selected Writings of Thomas Jefferson.* Edited by Adrienne Koch and William Peden. New York: Random House, 1944.

———. *Memoirs, Correspondence and Private Papers of Thomas Jefferson.* Edited by Thomas Jefferson Randolph. Vol. 2. London: Colburn and Bentley, 1829.

———. *Notes on the State of Virginia* Edited by William Peden. Chapel Hill: University of North Carolina Press, 1955.

———. *The Papers of Thomas Jefferson.* Edited by Julian P. Boyd et al. Princeton: Princeton University Press, 1950–2003.

———. *Thomas Jefferson's Garden Book, 1766–1824.* Edited by E. Morris Betts. Charlottesville: Thomas Jefferson Memorial Foundation, 1999.

————. *The Writings of Thomas Jefferson.* Edited by Albert Bergh. Washington: The Thomas Jefferson Memorial Association, 1903.

————. *The Writings of Thomas Jefferson.* Edited by H. A. Washington. Vol. 4. Washington D.C.: Taylor and Maury, 1854.

————. *The Writings of Thomas Jefferson: Autobiography.* Edited by Merrill Peterson. New York: Literary Classics of the United States, 1984.

————. *The Works of Thomas Jefferson.* Edited by Paul Leicester Ford. Vol. 11. New York: G. P. Putnam's Sons, 1905.

Journals of the House of Burgesses, 1752–1755, 1755–1758. Edited by H. R. McIlwaine. Richmond: Colonial Press, 1909.

Journals of the House of Burgesses of Virginia, 1761–1765. Edited by John P. Kennedy. Richmond: Virginia State Library, 1907.

Justices of the Peace of Colonial Virginia, 1757–1775, Bulletin of the Virginia State Library. Vol. 14, No. 2 (April 1921). Richmond: Public Printing, 1922.

Knox, John. *First Book of Discipline.* Edited by David Laing. Edinburgh: James Thin Co., 1895.

List of Members of the American Philosophical Society. Philadelphia: The Society, 1865.

List of the Revolutionary Soldiers of Virginia. Edited by H. J. Eckenrode. Richmond: Virginia State Library, 1912.

Miscellaneous Papers in the Collections of the Virginia Historical Society, 1762–1865. Edited by R. A. Brock. Vol. 4. Richmond: Virginia Historical Society, 1887.

The Minutes of the Aberdeen Philosophical Society, 1758–1773. Edited by H. Lewis Ulman. Aberdeen: Aberdeen University Press, 1990.

The Officers, Statutes and Charter of the College of William and Mary. Philadelphia: William Fry, 1817.

Owen, Goronwy. *The Letters of Goronwy Owen.* Edited by J. H. Davies. Cardiff: William Lewis Printers, 1924.

Reid, Thomas. *Inquiry into the Human Mind.* Edited by Timothy Duggan. Chicago: University of Chicago Press, 1970.

Rittenhouse, David. *The Scientific Writings of David Rittenhouse.* Edited by Brooke Hindle. New York: Arno Press, 1980.

The Statutes at Large, Being a Collection of All the Laws of Virginia. Edited by William Waller Hening. Richmond: Franklin Press, 1820–1823.

Stiles, Ezra. *Extracts from the Itineraries and Other Miscellanies of Ezra Stiles.* Edited by Franklin Bowditch Dexter. New Haven: Yale University Press, 1916.

Studies in the History and Development of the University of Aberdeen. Edited by P. J. Anderson. Aberdeen: Aberdeen University Press, 1906.

Transactions of the American Philosophical Society. Vol. 2. Philadelphia, Robert Aitken, 1786.

Wilson, James. *The Collected Works of James Wilson*. Edited by Kermit Hall and Mark David Hall. Vol. 2. Indianapolis: Liberty Fund, 2007.

Withering, William. *An Account of the Foxglove and Some of Its Medical Uses*. Birmingham: M. Sweeny, 1785.

SECONDARY SOURCES: BOOKS

The Aberdeen Enlightenment. Edited by Paul Wood. Aberdeen: Aberdeen University Press, 1993.

Adams, H. B. *The College of William and Mary: A Contribution to the History of Higher Education*. Whitefish: Kessinger Publishing Co, 2004.

Bailyn, Bernard. *Atlantic History: Concept and Contours*. Cambridge: Harvard University Press, 2005.

Baird, Ileana. *Social Networks in the Long Eighteenth Century*. Newcastle upon Tyne: Cambridge Scholars Publishing, 2014.

Ball, W. W. Rouse. *A History of the Study of Mathematics at Cambridge*. Cambridge: University Press, 1889.

Becker, Carl. *The Declaration of Independence*. New York: Harcourt, Brace and Co., 1922.

Bedini, Silvio. *Thomas Jefferson: Statesman of Science*. New York: Macmillan Publishing Company, 1990.

Brenaman, J. N. *A History of Virginia Conventions*. Richmond: J. L. Hill Printing Co, 1902.

Blair, Hugh. *History of the Virginia Federal Convention of 1788*. Richmond: Virginia Historical Society, 1891.

Blair, Robert, and William Row. *Life of ... Robert Blair ... Containing His Autobiography, From 1593 to 1636, With Supplement to His Life, and Continuation of the History of the Times to 1680*. Edited by Thomas McCrie. Publications 11. Edinburgh: Wodrow Society, 1848.

Boswell, James. *A Journey to the Western Islands of Scotland*. New York: Alfred Knopf Co., 2002.

Brock, R. A. *Virginia and Virginians*. Vol. I. Richmond: H. H. Hardesty Publishers, 1888.

Bryan, W. H. "Legal Education." In *Virginia Law Books: Essays and Bibliographies*. Edited by W. Hamilton Bryson. Philadelphia: American Philosophical Society, 2000.

Bulloch, J. M. *A History of the University of Aberdeen, 1495–1895*. London: Hodder and Stoughton, 1895.

Burk, John. *The History of Virginia from Its First Settlement to the Present Day*. Vol. 3. Petersburg: Dickson & Pescud, 1805.

Burn, Richard. *The Ecclesiastical Law*. London: Sweet, Stevens & Norton, 1842.

Burnaby, Andrew. *Travels through the Middle Settlements in North-America in the Years 1759–and 1760*. Dublin: R. Marchbank, 1775.

Campbell, Charles. *History of the Colony and Ancient Dominion of Virginia*. Philadelphia: Lippincott & Co., 1860.

Cant, Ronald G. *The University of St. Andrews: A Short History*. Edinburgh: Scottish Academic Press, 1970.

Carpenter, William. *Thomas Sherlock, 1678–1761*. London: The Society for the Promotion of Christian Knowledge, 1936.

Carter, Jennifer, and Colin McLaren. *Crown and Gown: An Illustrated History of the University of Aberdeen*. Aberdeen: Aberdeen University Press, 1995.

———, and Joan Pittock. *Aberdeen and the Enlightenment*. Aberdeen: Aberdeen University Press, 1987.

The Chesapeake in the Seventeenth Century. Edited by Thad Tate and David Ammerman. New York: W. W. Norton & Company, 1979.

Chitnis, Anand. *The Scottish Enlightenment*. London: Croom Helm Ltd., 1976.

Cicero, Marcus Tullius. *De Legibus*. London: W. Heinemann, 1928.

Clagett, Martin. *Scientific Jefferson: Revealed*. Charlottesville: University of Virginia Press, 2009.

———. *Portrait of William Small by Tilly Kettle*. Richmond: Earhart Foundation, 2006.

Cogliano, Francis. *Thomas Jefferson: Reputation and Legacy*. Charlottesville: University of Virginia Press, 2008.

Conant, James. *Thomas Jefferson and the Development of American Public Education*. Berkeley: University of California Press, 1963.

Cross, Arthur Lyon. *The Anglican Episcopate and the American Colonies*. New York: Longmans, Green and Co., 1902.

Defoe, Daniel. *A Tour Through the Whole Island of Great Britain*. Vol. 2. New York: Dutton, 1966.

Dent, Robert. *Old and New Birmingham*. Birmingham: Houghton and Hammond, 1880.

Dewey, Frank L. *Thomas Jefferson: Lawyer*. Charlottesville: University of Virginia Press, 1987.

Dickinson, H. W. *Matthew Boulton*. Cambridge: University Press, 1937.

Douglas, William. *Some Historical Remarks on the City of St. Andrews in North Briton*. London, 1728.

Duncan, William. *The Elements of Logick*. Albany: E. F. Backus, 1814.

Emerson, Roger. "Aberdeen Professors, 1690–1880: Two Structures, Two Professoriates, Two Careers." In Jennifer Carter and Colin McLaren. *Crown and Gown: An Illustrated History of the University of Aberdeen*, 62–78. Aberdeen: Aberdeen. University Press, 1995.

———. *Academic Patronage in the Scottish Enlightenment*. Edinburgh: Edinburgh University Press, 2008.

Emmerson, J. C. *The Emmersons and Portsmouth, 1785–1965*. Norfolk: Privately published, 1966.

Fischer, David Hackett. *Albion's Seed*. New York: Oxford University Press, 1989.

Flett, Iain. "Dundee Grammar School in the Eighteenth Century." In *Seven Hundred & Fifty Glorious Years: Some Facts and Facets of the High School of Dundee*. Dundee: Dundee City Council, 1994.

Flippen, Percy. *The Royal Government in Virginia, 1624–1775*. New York: Longmans, Green & Co., 1919.

Gill, Harold. The Apothecary in Colonial Virginia. Williamsburg: Colonial Williamsburg Foundation, 1972.

Girdwood, R. H. "The Influence of Scotland on North American Medicine." In *The Influence of Scottish Medicine*. Edited by Derek Dow. London: Butler & Tanner, 1988.

Godson, Susan, Ludwell Johnson, Richard Sherman, Thad Tate, and Helen Walker. *The College of William and Mary*. Williamsburg: King and Queen Press, 1985.

Goodwin, Mary R. M. *The College of William and Mary: A Brief History of the Main Building of the College, and the Rooms to be Restored to Their Eighteenth-Century Appearance*, 52–92. Williamsburg: Colonial Williamsburg Foundation, 1967.

The Green Bag. Edited by Horace Fuller. Vol. 5. Boston: Boston Book Co., 1893.

Greene, Jack. *Understanding the American Revolution: Issues and Actors*. Charlottesville: University Press of Virginia, 1995.

Grigsby, Hugh Blair. *The Virginia Convention of 1776*. Richmond: J. W. Randolph, 1855.

Harris, Malcolm. *Old New Kent County*. Baltimore: Genealogical Publishing Co., 2006.

The History of the College of William and Mary: From Its Foundation, 1660 to 1874. Richmond: J. W. Randolph & English, 1874.

Horner, Winifred H. *Nineteenth-Century Scottish Rhetoric: The American Connection*. Carbondale: Southern Illinois University Press, 1993.

Hume, David. *Essays: Moral, Political and Literary.* Indianapolis: Liberty Fund, 1985.

Jayne, Allen. *Jefferson's Declaration of Independence.* Lexington, University of Kentucky Press, 1998.

Jones, Dorothy. *Medical Surgical Nursing.* New York: McGraw-Hill, 1978.

Jones, John. "Goronwy Owen's Virginian Adventure." *Botetourt Bibliographical Society,* No.2. Williamsburg: College of William and Mary, 1969.

Jones, L. H. *Captain Roger Jones.* Albany: Joel Munsell's Sons, 1891.

Keir, James. *An Account of the Life and Writings of Thomas Day.* London: John Stockdale, 1791.

Kelly, Howard. *American Medical Biography.* Vol. 2. Philadelphia: W. B. Saunders Co., 1912.

Landsman, Ned. *From Colonials to Provincials: American Thought and Culture, 1680–1760.* New York: Twayne Publishers, 1997.

Lillywhite, Bryant. *London Coffee Houses.* London: Allen & Unwin, 1964.

Lyon, C. J. *The History of St. Andrews.* Edinburgh: William Tait, 1843.

Magnuson, Magnus. *Scotland: The Story of a Nation.* New York: Grove Press, 2000.

Maier, Pauline. *American Scripture.* New York: Alfred A. Knopf, 1997.

Malone, Dumas. *Jefferson the Virginian.* Boston: Little and Company, 1948.

Maxwell, Alexander. *The History of Old Dundee: Narrated Out of Town Council Records.* Dundee: William Kidd, 1884.

Maxwell, William. "Governor Page." *Virginia Historical Register.* Vol. 3. Richmond: MacFarlane & Ferguson, 1850.

Meade, William. *Old Churches, Ministers and Families of Virginia.* Vol. 2. Philadelphia: Lippincott & Co., 1878.

Meyer, Donald H. *The Democratic Enlightenment.* New York: G. P. Putnam's Sons, 1976.

Miller, E. I. *The Legislature of the Province of Virginia.* New York: Columbia University, 1907.

Morpurgo, J. E. *Their Majesties' Royall Colledge: William and Mary in the Seventeenth and Eighteenth Centuries.* Washington: Hennage Creative Printers, 1976.

Morton, Richard L. *Colonial Virginia.* Vol. 2. Chapel Hill: University of North Carolina Press, 1960.

Muirhead, James P. *The Origin and Progress of the Mechanical Inventions of James Watt.* Vols.1–2. London: John Murray, 1854–1856.

———. *The Life of James Watt: With Selections from His Correspondence.* London: John Murray, 1858.

Ossian. *The Works of Ossian.* Translated by James MacPherson. London: Becket and Dehondt, 1765.

Page, R. C. M. *Genealogy of the Page Family in Virginia.* New York: Press of the Publisher's Printing Co., 1893.

Philosophy and Science in the Scottish Enlightenment. Edited by Peter Jones. Edinburgh: John Donald Publishers, 1988.

Pocoke, Richard. *Tours in Scotland, 1747, 1750, 1760.* Edited by Daniel Kemp. Edinburgh: T. and A. Constable, 1887.

Porter, Albert. *County Government in Virginia: A Legislative History, 1607–1904.* New York: Columbia University Press, 1947.

Rait, Robert. "Buildings." In *Studies in the History and Development of the University of Aberdeen.* Edited by P. J. Anderson, 369–384. Aberdeen: Aberdeen University Press, 1906.

Rakove, Jack. *Original Meanings.* New York: Knopf, 1996.

Reid, Alan. *The Royal Burgh of Forfar.* Edinburgh: John Menzies & Co., 1902.

Reid, Thomas. *Inquiry into the Human Mind.* Edited by Timothy Duggan . Chicago, University of Chicago Press, 1970.

———. *An Inquiry into the Human Mind, on the Principles of Common Sense.* Edinburgh: Bell & Bradfute and Creech, 1801.

Report of the Virginia State Library, 1907–1908. Richmond: Davis Bottom, 1908.

Rittenhouse, David. *The Scientific Writings of David Rittenhouse.* Edited by Brooke Hindle. New York: Arno Press, 1980.

Rose, F. Clifford. *The Neurobiology of Painting: International Review of Neurobiology.* Vol. 74. Oxford: Elsevier Press, 2006.

Saunders, J. E. *Early Settlers of Alabama.* New Orleans: Graham & Sons, 1899.

Savage, Catherine. *The Wren Building, College of William and Mary: Preliminary Architectural Report,* 62–79. Williamsburg: Colonial Williamsburg Foundation, 1962.

Schofield, Robert. *The Lunar Society of Birmingham.* Oxford: Clarendon Press, 1963.

Schwarz, Philip. *Twice Condemned: Slaves and Criminal Laws of Virginia, 1705–1865.* Union, N.J.: The Lawbook Exchange, 1998.

Selby, John. *The Revolution in Virginia, 1775–1783.* Charlottesville: University Press of Virginia, 1988.

Shepard, Christine. "The Arts Curriculum at Aberdeen at the Beginning of the Eighteenth Century." In Jennifer Carter and Joan Pittock. *Aberdeen and the Enlightenment,* 146–154. Aberdeen: Aberdeen University Press, 1987.

Sher, Richard. "Professors of Virtue: the Edinburgh Chair." In M. A. Stewart. *Studies in the Philosophy of the Scottish Enlightenment,* 87–126. Oxford: Oxford University Press, 1991.

Singer, Michael. *Becoming Madison* (New York: Public Affairs, 2015).

Small, Robert. *History of Dundee from Its Origin Down to the Present Time with a Statistical Account of the Parish and Town in the Year 1792*. Dundee: J. Chalmers, 1842.

Smiles, Samuel. *Lives of the Engineers: Boulton and Watt*. London: John Murray, 1904.

Speed, John Gilmer. *The Gilmers in America*. New York: Private Distribution, 1897.

Stephenson, J. W. W. *Education in the Burgh of Dundee in the Eighteenth Century*, 2–48. Dundee: Dundee City Council, 1969.

Stith, William. *History of the Discovery and Settlement of Virginia*. Williamsburg: William Parks, 1747.

Studies in the History and Development of the University of Aberdeen. Edited by P. J. Anderson. Aberdeen: Aberdeen University Press, 1906.

Thomson, James. *The History of Dundee*. Dundee: John Durham & Son, 1874.

Thomson, Keith. *Before Darwin: Reconciling God and Nature*. New Haven: Yale University Press, 2005.

Torrence, William Clayton. *Virginia State Library: A Trial Biography of Colonial Virginia*. Richmond: Public Printing, 1908.

Tyler, Lyon Gardiner. *The Cradle of the Republic*. Richmond: The Hermitage Press, 1906.

_____. *The Making of the Union: Contributions of the College of William and Mary in Virginia*. Richmond: Whittet & Shepperson, 1888.

———. *Williamsburg: The Old Colonial Capital*. Richmond: Whittet & Shepperson, 1907.

Uglow, Jenny. *The Lunar Men*. New York: Farrar, Straus, and Giroux, 2002.

Wallis, P. J., and R. V. Wallis. *Eighteenth-Century Medics*. Newcastle upon Tyne: Project for Historic Bibliography, 1988.

Wills, Garry. *Inventing America: Jefferson's Declaration of Independence*. Garden City, N.Y.: Doubleday, 1978.

———. "Or Was Jefferson More Influenced by Scottish Thinkers?." In *What Did the Declaration Declare?*. Boston: Bedford/St. Martin's, 2000.

Wirt, William. *Sketches of the Life and Character of Patrick Henry*. New York: M'Elrath, Bangs, & Co., 1834.

Wolfe, John. *Brandy, Balloons, & Lamps*. Carbondale: Southern Illinois Press, 1999.

Woods, Paul. "Science and the Aberdeen Enlightenment." In *Philosophy and Science in the Scottish Enlightenment*. Edited by Peter Jones, 39–66. Edinburgh: John Donald Publishers, 1988.

SECONDARY SOURCES: ARTICLES

"Alexander Small." *European Magazine* (January 1799): 20–21.

"Alexander Small. Obituary of Remarkable Persons; with Biographical Anecdotes." *Gentleman's Magazine* 44 (September 6, 1794): 864–865.

Bell, Whitfield J., Jr. "Some American Students of That Shining Oracle of Physic, Dr. William Cullen of Edinburgh, 1755–1766." *Proceedings of the American Philosophical Society* 94, no. 3, Studies of Historical Documents in the Library of the American Philosophical Society (June 1950): 275–281.

Bowman, Larry. "The Virginia County Committees of Safety, 1774–1776." *Virginia Magazine of History and Biography* 79, no. 3 (July 1971): 322–337.

Brydon, G. MacLaren. "The Clergy of the Established Church in Virginia and the Revolution." *Virginia Magazine of History and Biography* 41, no. 2 (April 1933): 123–143.

———. "The Clergy of the Established Church in Virginia and the Revolution." *Virginia Magazine of History and Biography* 41, no. 3 (July 1933): 231–243.

Clagett, Martin. "James Wilson: His Scottish Background." *Pennsylvania History* 79, no. 2 (Spring 2012): 154–166.

Clive, John, and Bernard Bailyn. "England's Cultural Provinces: Scotland and America." *William and Mary Quarterly*, 3rd ser., vol. 11, no. 2 (April 1954): 200–213.

Coleman, Charles Washington. "The County Committees of 1774–'75 in Virginia." *William and Mary Quarterly*, 1st ser., vol. 5, no. 2 (October 1896): 94–106.

———. "The County Committees of 1774–1775 in Virginia." *William and Mary Quarterly*, 1st ser., vol. 5, no. 4 (April 1897): 245–255.

———. "Norborne, Baron de Botetourt, Governor-General of Virginia, 1768–1770." *William and Mary Quarterly*, 1st ser, vol. 5, no. 3 (January 1897): 165–171.

"Correspondence of Ezra Stiles, President of Yale College, and James Madison, President of William and Mary College, 1780." *William and Mary Quarterly*, 2nd ser., vol. 7, no. 4 (October 1927): 292–296.

Crane, Vernon. "The Honest Whig Society." *William and Mary Quarterly*, 3rd Ser., vol. 23, no. 2 (April 1966): 210–233.

Cutts, A. Bailey. "The Educational Influence of Aberdeen in Seventeenth Century Virginia." *William and Mary Quarterly*, 2nd ser., vol. 15, no. 3. (July 1935): 229–249.

Ewald, William. "James Wilson and the Drafting of the Constitution." *University of Pennsylvania. Journal of Constitutional Law* 10, no. 5 (June 2008): 901–1009.

Fauquier, Francis. "An Account of an Extraordinary Storm of Hail." *Gentleman's Monthly Intelligencer* 28 (November 1759).

"Francis Fauquier's Will." *William and Mary Quarterly*, 1st ser., vol. 8, no. 3 (January 1900): 171–177.

"Galt Family of Williamsburg." *William and Mary Quarterly*, 1st ser., vol. 8, no. 4 (April 1900): 259–262.

Garnett, James Mercer. "The Last Fifteen Years of the House of Burgesses of Virginia, 1761–1776." *Virginia Magazine of History and Biography* 18, no. 2 (April 1910): 213–223.

Greene, Jack. "Landon Carter and the Pistole Fee Dispute." *William and Mary Quarterly*, 3rd ser., vol. 14, no. 1 (January 1957): 66–69.

Hamowy, Ronald. "Jefferson and the Scottish Enlightenment: A Critique of Garry Wills's Inventing America." *William and Mary Quarterly*, 3rd ser., vol. 36, no. 4 (October 1979): 503–523.

"History of Dundee High School." *Dundee High School Magazine*, no. 60 (June 1934): 1–22.

Howell, Wilber S. "The Declaration of Independence and Eighteenth-Century Logic." *William and Mary Quarterly*, 3rd ser., vol. 18, no. 4 (October 1961): 463–484.

"Hubard Family." *William and Mary Quarterly*, 1st ser., vol. 5, no. 2 (October 1896): 106–109.

Hull, Gillian. "William Small, 1734–1775: No Publications, Much Influence." *Journal of the Royal Society of Medicine* 90 (February 1997): 102–105.

Isaac, Rhys. "Religion and Authority: Problems of the Anglican Establishment in Virginia in the Era of the Great Awakening and the Parsons' Cause." *William and Mary Quarterly*, 3rd ser., vol. 30, no. 1 (January 1973): 4–36.

"Journal of the Meetings of the President and Masters of William and Mary College." *William and Mary Quarterly*, 1st ser., vol. 2, no. 1 (July 1893): 50–57.

"Journal of the Meetings of the President and Masters of William and Mary College." *William and Mary Quarterly*, 1st ser., vol. 2, no. 4 (April 1894): 255–257.

"Journal of the Meetings of the President and Masters of William and Mary College." *William and Mary Quarterly*, 1st ser., vol. 4, no. 1 (July 1895): 43–46.

"Journals of the Meetings of the President and Masters of William and Mary College." *William and Mary Quarterly*, 1st ser., vol. 4, no. 2 (October 1895): 130–132.

"Justices of the Peace of Colonial Virginia, 1757–1775." *Bulletin of the Virginia State Library* 14, no. 2 (April 1921): 41–130.

Kingsland, Lawrence. "The United States Patent Office." *Law and Contemporary Problems* 13, no. 2 (Spring 1948): 354–367.

"Letters to Thomas Walker Gilmer." *William and Mary Quarterly*, 1st ser., vol. 15, no. 4 (April 1907): 225–234.

"List of the Inhabitants of Old Aberdeen, 1636." *Scottish Notes and Queries* 7, no. 1 (June 1893): 1–2.

"A List of Parishes, and the Ministers in Them." *William and Mary Quarterly*, 1st ser., vol. 5, no. 3 (January 1897): 200–203.

"The Ludwell Family." *William and Mary Quarterly*, 1st ser., vol. 19, no. 3 (January 1911): 199–214.

Lynn, Steven. "Johnson's Rambler and Eighteenth-Century Rhetoric." *Eighteenth Century Studies* 19, no. 4 (Summer 1986): 461–479.

Mason, George Carrington. "The Colonial Churches of King and Queen and King William Counties, Virginia," *William and Mary Quarterly*, 2nd ser., vol. 23, no. 4 (October 1943): 440–464.

———. "A Supplement to 'Colonial Churches of Tidewater Virginia.'" *Virginia Magazine of History and Biography* 66, no. 2 (April 1958): 167–177.

Masson, David. "Dead Men I Have Known." *Macmillan's Magazine* 9 (1863–1864): 352–374.

Miller, E. I. "The Virginia Committee of Correspondence, 1759–1770." *William and Mary Quarterly*, 1st ser., vol. 22, no. 1 (July 1913): 1–19.

———. "The Virginia Committee of Correspondence, 1773–1775." *William and Mary Quarterly*, 1st ser., vol. 22, no. 2 (October 1913): 99–113.

"Minutes of the Visitors and Governors of the College of William and Mary." *William and Mary Quarterly*, 2nd ser., vol. 1, no. 1 (January 1921): 24–26.

Mokyr, Joel. "The European Enlightenment, the Industrial Revolution, and Modern Economic Growth," 1–21. Max Weber Lecture, March 27, 2007. European University.

Neill, Edward. "Virginia Threads for the Future Historian." *William and Mary Quarterly*, 1st ser., vol. 1, no. 2 (October 1892): 79–80.

"Notes and Queries: Some Virginians Educated in Great Britain." *Virginia Magazine of History and Biography* 21, no. 2 (April 1913): 196–199.

"Notes Relating to Some of the Students Who Attended the College of William and Mary, 1753–1770." *William and Mary Quarterly*, 2nd ser., vol. 1, no. 1 (January 1921): 27–41.

"Obituary of Remarkable Persons; with Biographical Anecdotes." *Gentleman's Magazine* 64 (September 6, 1794): 864–865.

"The Old Capitol: Unveiling of a Tablet on the Site of the Capitol in Williamsburg." *William and Mary Quarterly*, 1st ser., vol. 13, no. 1 (July 1904): 64–66.

"Papers Relating to the College." *William and Mary Quarterly Magazine*, 1st ser., vol. 16, no. 3 (January 1908): 162–173.

Partington, J. R., and Douglas McKie. "Sir John Eliot and John Elliot." *Annals of Science* 6 (1948–1950): 262–267.

Pennypacker, Samuel W. "David Rittenhouse." *Harper's New Monthly Magazine* 44 (1882): 839–840.

Rankin, Hugh F. "The General Court of Colonial Virginia: Its Jurisdiction and Personnel." *Virginia Magazine of History and Biography* 70, no. 2 (April 1962): 142–153.

Reinhold, Meyer. "The Quest for Useful Knowledge in Eighteenth-Century America." *Proceedings of the American Philosophical Society* 119, no. 2 (April 16, 1975): 108–132.

Robinson, Eric. "The Lunar Society: Its Membership and Organization," 153–177. London: Newcomen Society Lecture, 1963.

Rude, G. T. "The Survey of the Continental Shelf." *Scientific Monthly* 34, no. 6 (June 1932): 547–550.

Schofield, Robert. "The Lunar Society of Birmingham: A Bicentenary Appraisal." *Notes and Records of the Royal Society of London* 21, no. 2 (December 1966): 144–161.

Smith, Daniel Blake. "Mortality and Family in the Colonial Chesapeake." *Journal of Interdisciplinary History* 8, no. 3 (Winter 1978): 403–427.

Smith, Glenn Curtis. "An Era of Non-Importation Associations, 1768–73." *William and Mary Quarterly*, 2nd ser., vol. 20, no. 1 (January 1940): 84–98.

"The Statutes of the College of William and Mary in Virginia." *William and Mary Quarterly*, 1st ser., vol. 16, no. 4 (April 1908): 239–256.

Stearns, Raymond Phineas. "Colonial Fellows of the Royal Society of London, 1661–1788." *William and Mary Quarterly*. 3rd ser., vol. 3, no. 2 (April 1946): 208–268.

"Students in 1754 at William and Mary College." *William and Mary Quarterly*, 1st ser., vol. 6, no. 3 (January 1898): 187–188.

Tate, Thad. "The Coming of the Revolution in Virginia: Britain's Challenge to Virginia's Ruling Class, 1763–1776." *William and Mary Quarterly*, 3rd ser., vol. 19, no. 3 (July 1962): 323–343.

Thomas, B. Bowen. "Goronwy Owen and the College of William and Mary." *Y Cymmrodor*, 43:19–44. London: Society of Cymmrodorion, 1932.

Thomson, Robert Polk. "The Reform of the College of William and Mary." *Proceedings of the American Philosophical Society* 115, no. 3 (June 17, 1971): 187–213.

"The Thruston Family of Virginia." *William and Mary Quarterly*, 1st ser., vol. 5, no. 2 (October 1896): 120–122.

"Trivia." *William and Mary Quarterly*, 3rd ser., vol. 12, no. 3 (July 1955): 55–57.

Tyler, Lyon G. "Early Courses and Professors at William and Mary College." *William and Mary Quarterly*, 1st ser., vol. 14, no. 2 (October 1905): 71–83.

———. "William and Mary College and Its Influence on the Founding of the Republic." *William and Mary Quarterly*, 2nd ser., vol. 15, no. 4 (October 1935): 324–333.

Wellford, Robert. "A Diary Kept by Dr. Robert Wellford, of Fredericksburg, Virginia, during the March of the Virginia Troops to Fort Pitt (Pittsburg) to Suppress the Whiskey Insurrection in 1794." *William and Mary Quarterly*, 1st ser., vol. 11, no. 1 (July 1902): 1–19.

Wells, R. V. "The Lunar Society." *School Science Magazine* 33, no. 119 (1951–1952): 13–14.

"William Lauder, The Literary Forger." *Blackwoods Edinburgh Magazine* 166 (July–December 1899): 381–396.

"William and Mary College in 1774: Letters in Rind's *Virginia Gazette.*" *William and Mary Quarterly*, 2nd ser., vol. 2, no. 2 (April 1922): 101–113.

"Williamsburg Lodge of Masons." *William and Mary Quarterly*, 1st ser., vol. 1, no. 1 (July 1892): 1–33.

REFERENCE—NEWSPAPERS, DISSERTATIONS, AND PAMPHLETS

American Biographical and Historical Dictionary. Edited by William Allen. Cambridge: Hilliard & Metcalf, 1809.

American Medical Biography. Edited by Howard Kelly. Vol. 2. Philadelphia: W. B. Saunders Co., 1912.

Aris's Birmingham Gazette.

Birmingham Evening Post.

Botetourt Bibliographical Society. No. 2. Williamsburg: College of William and Mary, 1969.

Clagett, Martin Richard. "William Small, 1734–1775: Teacher, Mentor, Scientist." Ph.D. diss., Virginia Commonwealth University, 2003.

Cule, J. E. "The Financial History of Matthew Boulton, 1759–1800." Master of Commerce thesis, University of Birmingham, 1935. C1. B35 C8.

Dictionary of National Biography. Edited by Leslie Stephen. Vol. 18. London: Smith, Elder & Co., 1889.

Dublin University Magazine.

Encyclopedia of Virginia Biography. Edited by Lyon Gardiner Tyler. New York: Lewis Historical Publishing Co., 1915.

Gentleman's Magazine.

Grafton Magazine of History and Genealogy. New York: Grafton Press, 1909.

London Magazine.

Supplement to Encyclopedia Britannica. Vol. 2. New York: Henry Allen Co., 1891.

Universal Magazine.

Virginia Gazette, 1 (1730–1765) Parks, Hunter, Royle.

Virginia Gazette, 1 (1766–1780) Purdie and Dixon.

Virginia Gazette, 2 (1766–1776) Rind, Pinkney.

Virginia Gazette, 3 (1775–1780) Purdie, Clarkson, and Davis.

Index

Illustration pages are given in italics.

Abercrombie, James, 60
Aberdeen, Scot., 26, 29. *See also* Marischal College (Aberdeen)
Aberdeen Philosophical Society (Wise Club), 34, 38, 39, 151, 155, 232, 311; members of, 312–314
Adams, John, 179, 180, 266
Adams, Samuel, 61
Anglican Church (Virginia), 54; clergy of, 54–57
Anson, Lord, 85
Arbroath, Scot., 19; Declaration of, 19
Argand, Ami, 140, 194
Ash, Dr. John, *223*, 285, 321; and William Small, 223, 257, 258, 259, 265, 266, 295, 296, 321
Afzelius, Adam, 233
Bacon, Francis, 35, 149, 166, 276
Baskerville, John, 224, 235, 295, 321
Berrington, Rev. Joseph, 235
Becker, Carl, 179
Birmingham General Hospital, 295, 296, 300, 321; Public Hospital, 254
Birmingham Lunar Society, 281–283, 284, 285, 286, 317, 323; accomplishments of, 235–237, 238–240, 282; characteristics of, 230–232; discussions and demonstrations of, 232, 237–238; dissolution of, 285–286; genesis of, 226–227, 281; and Industrial Revolution, 282; and Matthew Boulton, xxii, xxiii n1, 216, 227, 228, 231, 232, 234, 235, 236, 237–238, 239, 281, 282, 317, central role in, 241–242; members of, 227, 233–235, 236, 237, 238, 240, 241–242, 243, 262, 282, 286, 323–326; and William Small, xix, xx, xxii, xxiii n1, 1, 216, 221, 226, 227, 230, 231, 234, 236, 237, 241, 243, 253, 259, 279, 281, 283, 284, 285, 286, 287, 295, 298, 323, and founding of, 228, 279, 281, 283, 289
"Birmingham Philosophers," 228, 284
Bishop of London, 51, 56, 86, 100n13; and College of William and Mary, xxii, 42, 49, 54, 64, 65, 66, 68, 74, 75, 76, faculty chosen by, 87, 88, 89, 91, president of, 51, 118, and sacking of faculty of, 69, 70, 72; commissary for, 51, 88, 118; and William Small, 90, 94, 193, 201, 291

Blackwell, Thomas, 32, 33, 34, 148, 149, 151, 310

Blair, George, 22, 23, 309

Blair, Hugh, *Lectures on Rhetoric and Belles-Lettres*, 161, 233

Blair, James (president of College of William and Mary), 51, 52, 118

Blair, James (student of William Small), 163

Blair, John, 59, 60, 128, 136

Bland, Arthur Lee, 163

Bland, Richard, 55, 78n17, 114, 128

Bland, Theodorick, 131, 163

Boulton, Matthew, 233, 235, 236, 237–238, 241–242, 254, 295, 296, 280, 317, 321, 322, 323, 326; "Birmingham Philosopher," 226, 228; and Dr. John Roebuck, 250–252, 253, 261, 268, 325; and James Watt, 248, 249–253, 254, 255, 256, 265, 266, 276, 325, and steam-engine, 229, 284, firm, 255–257, 267–268, patent for, 256–257; portrait of, *241*; at Soho (Birmingham), 231, 264, 265, 231, 233, 242–243, 264, 265, 282, Soho Factory (Manufactory) of, 227, 228–229, 239, *239*, 242–243, *243*, 248, 249, 255, 259, 275, 281, 296, 297, 323, 325; and William Small, xx, xxi, xxii–xxiii, 19, 214, 224, 285, 287, 295, 296, 297, 326, and Argand Lamp, 140, 194, and canal scheme, 226, 254–255, and death of, 257–258, 260, 261, 262, 264, 265, 276, and estate of, 265–266, and memorial to, 266, personal physician to, 213, 221–222, 223, 292, 294, 323, and steam engine, 224–225, 226,

227, 228, 229, 249–253, 255–257, 281, firm, partner in, 267–268; and William Withering, 264, 284. *See also* Birmingham Lunar Society; Darwin, Erasmus; Franklin, Benjamin

Boulton, Mrs. Matthew, 225, 257, 258

Boulton, Watt, and Small (firm), 255, 267–268; patent for, 256–257

Brunskill, Rev. John, 64–67, 76

Burk, John, 85, 86

Burke, Edmund, 256

Burnaby, Rev. Andrew, 62, 63, 105–106, 107, 115, 191

Burwell, Lewis, 128, 129, 132

Burwell, Nathaniel, 131

Camm, John, 62, 66, 67, 97, 110, 116, 201; removed from faculty at College of William and Mary, 73, 74, 77, returned to faculty, 75, 76, 156, 191, 194–195

Carmylie, Scot.: parish of, 20, *20*

Carr, Dabney, 127, 131, 284; and Thomas Jefferson, 112, 161, 186

Carter, Charles, 78n17, 128, 130

Carter, Col. Landon, 58, 78n17, 129

Carter, Robert, 127, 129, 136

Carter family, 136, 137

Cary, Archibald, 129

Case of the Rev. Mr. Kay, 51, 57, 58, 63

Catesby, Mark, 111

Catherine the Great, 213, 224, 295

Clayton, John, 131

Cocke, Isabelle, 113, 114, 115

Cockler, Sir John, 197

Collard, John, *The Essentials of Logic*, 34, 150

College of William and Mary, 41, 42, 49; academic structure at, 152–154;

and Board of Visitors of, xxii, 42, 49, 51, 53, 54, 56, 57, 59, 66, 67, 68, 69, 70, 71, 72, 73, 74, 75, 84, 88, 89, 90, 91, 93, 94, 95, 96, 97, 114, 116, 118, 159, 192, 193, 194, 195, 200, 201, 202, 221, 291; and clergy, 54–57; conflicts at, 53–57, 84; courses taught at, 116–117, described, 110–115, apparel recommended at, 115–116, Wren Building at, 111, *111*; dual set of controlling boards, 53–54; established, 51, 52–53; and faculty (Society) of, xxii, 42, 49, 51, 53, 54, 55, 56, 57, 58, 64, 66–67, 68, 88, 89, 93, 94, 95, 113, 114, 118, 119, 126, 152, replacement of, 84–98, sacking of, 67–77, 91, salaries of, 118, 153; lower schools at, Grammar School at, 117, 118, 152, 153, 154, Indian School at, xxii, 72, 152, Master of, 98, 116–117, 153; scientific apparatus purchased for, 89, 157, 164–165, 192–193, 200, 291, 293; upper schools of (Moral and Natural Philosophy), 117, 152, 154, 155–162, and belle lettres, 160–161; Tilly Kettle portrait of William Small in president's office, 267. *See also* Bishop of London: and College of William and Mary; Blair, James (president of College of William and Mary); Camm, John; Dawson, Thomas; Digges, Cole; Dinwiddie, Lt. Gov. Robert; Franklin, Benjamin; Graham, Richard; Hawtrey, Edward; Hubard, Matthew; Jefferson, Thomas; Jones, Emmanuel; Lewis, Warner; Nichols, the Rt. Rev. Samuel; Owen, Goronwy; Preston, William, Robinson, Thomas; Robinson, William; Rowe, Jacob; Small, William: and College of William and Mary; Yates, William

Collins, John, 233

Common Sense Philosophy, 38, 49, 141n10, 161, 173, 175, 177, 277, 313. *See also* School of Common Sense Philosophy

Conrie, Walter, 5

Coutts, John, 23

Craig, Rev. John, 135, 136

Crawford, Henry, 9

Crie, John, 11

Crown (British), 55, 59

Cunn, Samuel, 157

Curthoys, Dr. Judith, 212

Cutts, Bailey, 53

Dalrymple, Hugh, 47n57, 211, 218

Dalrymple, Grace, 47n57, 211, *212*, 212, 218

Dalston, Catherine, 85

Dalston, Sir Charles, 85

Darwin, Charles, 324

Darwin, Erasmus, xx, 235, 236, 248, 254, 262, 285, 286, 323–324; and Matthew Boulton, 222, 225–226, 227, 228, 230, 231, 237, 238, 241; and steam engine, 281, efforts to get Parliamentary patent for, 256; and *Temple of Nature*, 238; and William Small, 254, 257, 258, 259, 264–265, 266, 284, 294, 295, 298, 299

Darwin, Robert, 323

Davidson, John, 23

Dawson, Thomas: president of College of William and Mary, 65, 74, 75, 88, 90, 91, 92, 93, 94, 97, 98

Dawson, William, 101n23

Day, Jane, 324

Day, Thomas, 322, 324; member of Birmingham Lunar Society, 227, 235, 237; and William Small, 260, 262, 290, and Small's estate, 266, 267

Declaration of Independence (American), 19. *See also* Jefferson, Thomas

Dickinson, Professor Harry, 7, 8

Dickinson, John (Pennsylvania), 61

Dickinson, Capt. John, 135

Digges, Coles, 51, 58, 67, 68, 71, 73

Digges, Dudley, 81n47, 90, 94, 193, 201, 279

Dinwiddie, Lt. Gov. Robert, 84, 86, 111, 125; and College of William and Mary, 84, 88, sacking faculty at, 69, and replacements thereof, 75, 76, 88, 90; and the Pistole Fee, 51, 57, 59, 60; and Rev. John Brunskill, 64, 65, 66

Doig, Andrew, 40

Dolland, Peter, 164

Drew, Joseph, 11

Duncan, William, 32, 33, 34, 38, 149–150, 151, 179, 181–185, 310; *Elements of Logick*, xxi, 32, 33–34, 150, 161, 181, 182, 186, 278

Dundee Grammar School (Aberdeen), xxi, 1, 20–25; instructors at, 20–22; William Small at, xxi, 1, 8, 20, 21, 22, 23, 25, 277, 309, family at, 8, 10, 20, 21, 22, Small's professors at, 309

Dunk, George Montagu, Earl of Halifax, 85, 86

Edgeworth, Marie, 266, 267

Edgeworth, Richard Lovell, 324; member of Birmingham Lunar Society, 227, 235, 236, 238, 262; and steam engine, 255; and William Small's estate, 266, 267

Edinburgh Society for the Encouragement of Arts, Sciences, Manufactures and Agriculture, 38, 150

Eliot, Sir John (Greenwich Hospital, London), 42, 212

Elliot, Sir John (king's physician), 212, 218; and William Small, 40, 210, 211, 292, 293, 314

Fauquier, Lt. Gov. Francis, 60, 62, 75, 107, 123, 124, 139, 193, 317, 318, 322; and the Partie Quarree, 125–128, 319; replaced Robert Dinwiddie, 84–86; and Rev. John Brunskill, 64; and Virginia Society for the Encouragement of Arts and Manufacturing, 128, 283; and William Small, 107, 124, 126, 192, 194, 279, 280; Williamsburg soirées of, 92, 107–108, 126, 232, 317

Fauquier, Dr. John Francis, 84–85, 125, 317

Fauquier, William, 125

Ferguson, James, 128, 157–158, 233, 280

Lindsay, Margaret, 7, 308

Fordyce, Dr. David, 34, 150, 310

Fordyce, George, 213, 220, 294, 295, 314–315

Fordyce, John, 315

Forbes, Elisabeth, 40, 311

Forbes, Lord, 40, 311

Forbes, Sir Samuel, 3

Fothergill, John, 248, 257, 267

Fothergill, Mrs., 257, 258

Foxcroft, John, 139, 193

Franklin, Benjamin, 86, 89, 128, 158, 162, 163, 164, 216, 217, 230, 233, 237, 248, 256, 275, 280, 291, 315, 316, 321, 323, 326; and honorary degree from College of William and Mary, 81n46, 138, 154, 318; and Matthew Boulton, 221, 222, 224, 225, 226, 229, 281, 292, 323; and Virginia Society for the Promotion of Useful Knowledge, 131; and William Small, xx, xxii, xxiii n1, 1, 19, 123, 138–140, 165, 193–194, 206, 208–209, 210, 213, 214, 221, 222, 224, 287, 292, 293, 294, 299, 323, lamp invented with, 194. *See also* Hunter, William

Froebel, Frederick, 235

Galt, John, 162, 163, 299

Galton, Francis, 286

Galton, Samuel, 235, 286

George III, 184

Gerard, Alexander, 31, 32, 34, 38, 150, 151, 161, 310–311, 312

Gilbert, Bishop of Brechin, 21

Gilmer, George, 162, 163, 299

Girardin, Louis Hue, 174

Givens, Samuel, 135

Gordon, Professor Thomas, 40

Graham, John, 135

Graham, Richard, 97, 201; removed from faculty of College of William and Mary, 73, 74, 75, 77; returned to faculty of College of William and Mary, 156, 159, 191–192, 194–195

Gray, Lord, 22

Gregorie, James (grandfather of John Gregory), 41

Gregory, David (cousin of John Gregory), 41

Gregory, James (brother of John Gregory), 40, 41, 212, 311; and William Small, 1, 41, 43, 290

Gregory, James (father of John Gregory), 41

Gregory, James (son of John Gregory), 41

Gregory, John (co-founder of Aberdeen Philosophical Society), 34, 151, 311

Gregory, John (physician), 41, 151; and William Small, xxii, 1, 34, 38, 39–41, 42, 43, 151, 162, 163, 210, 211, 212, 290, 292, 293, 299, 311

Gregory family, 41

Gronw, Owen, 86

Grymes, Philip, 78n17, 128

Gwatney, Thomas, 155

Hadow, James, 11

Haldane, Patrick, 11

Halyburton, Thomas, 11

Harrison, Benjamin, 112, 128

Hauksbee, Francis, the Younger, 164, 165

Hawtrey, Edward, 89, 90, 112, 115, 116, 210

Hawtrey, Stephen, 89, 112, 116, 118, 210, 292

Heberden, Dr. William, 125, 126, 213, 315; and William Small, 224, 257–258, 260, 294, 295

Helsham, Richard, *Lectures on Natural Philosophy*, 157

Henley, Professor Samuel, 131

Howell, Wilber, 161, 183

Hubard, James, 68

Hubard, Matthew, 51, 58, 67, 68, 71, 73

Hunter, John, 42, 213, 217, 290, 294, 295, 315–316

Hunter, William, 317–318; and Benjamin Franklin, 138, 139, 162, 193, 291, 318; proprietor of *Virginia Gazette*, 131, bookstore, 132, 162, 291; and William Small, 123, 124, 132, 138, 162, 193, 291, 318

Hunter, William (physician), 213, 294

Hutton, James, 233

Inglis, Mungo, 118

International Center of Jefferson Studies, xix

Jefferson, Thomas, 129, 130, 164, 282, 312, 317, 318, 319; biography of, 178, 179; and College of William and Mary, 76, 111, 132, 133, 159, roommates of, 112; and Common Sense Philosophy, 141n10, 161, 175, 177, 277; and Dabney Carr, 161, 186; and Declaration of Independence, 150, 178–186, 277, 278; description of Williamsburg Capitol, 109; and George Wythe, xxii, 98, 108, 123, 124, 132, 174, 178, 318; influences on, 34, 150, impact of Scottish Enlightenment on, 175–177, 179, 181, 183, 278; inventions by, 187; and John Page, 112, 127, 131, 132, 133, 134, 157, 178, 197, 198, 199, 200, 261, 284; letters of, 180, to grandson, Thomas Jefferson Randolph, 123–124, 174, 175–176; and library of, 133, 134, 160, 163; at Lt. Gov. Francis Fauquier's soirées, 107–108, 114, 317; and *Notes on the State of Virginia*, 176–177, *177*, 181, 186, 277, 278; and Partie Quarree, 127; and Peyton Randolph, 124, 174; and University of Virginia, 176, 178, 277; and William Duncan's

Elements of Logick, 179, 181–186; and William Small, xx, xxi, xxii, 1, 19, 38, 76, 98, 107–108, 123, 127, 131, 133, 134, 148, 150, 158, 160, 161, 162, 172–174, 178–179, 181, 186, 187, 274, 275, 276, 277, 278, 285, 287, 289, 318, "letter to unknown," 196–200, *197*, probably William Small, 198

Jeffreys, Nathaniel, 222, 258, 294, 321–322

Jeffreys, Thomas, 321

Johnson, Dr. Samuel, 23, 34, 150, 278, 322

Jones, Emmanuel, 67, 73, 74, 93, 117, 153

Jones, Thomas, 114, 156

Jones, Walter, 114, 119, 127, 156, 159–160, 162, 163, 299. *See also* Jones, Wat [Watt]

Jones, Wat [Watt], 132, 163

Kay, the Rev. Mr. William, 51, 57, 58, 63

Keir, James, 324; member of Birmingham Lunar Society, 235, 236, 239; and Tipton Works, 240; and William Small, 258, 262, 265, 266, 290, 324

Kettle, Tilly, xv, 267

King's College (Scotland), 26, 27, 39, 52

Kirkwood, James, *Grammatica Despauteriana*, 24

Knox, John, 23, 27; and *First Book of Discipline*, 37

Lauder, William, 22, 23–24, 309

Leclerc, George-Louis, Count of Buffon, 176, 181

Lee, Arthur, 283

Lee, Richard Henry, 61, 180–181

Legge, William, Earl of Dartmouth, 254, 322

Lewis, Warner: at College of William and Mary, 127, 132, 133, 156, 157, 160, 161, 163

Locke, John, 179, 180, 278

London, Eng., *207*; clubs, 208, 209; coffee houses, 208, *209*, 210

Lundie (Lundy), Gilbert, 22, 309

Lyons, Lord, office of, 7

MacPherson, James, 312

Madison, James, 167, 180

Marischal College (Aberdeen), xxi, 1, 25, 26, 27, *27*, 29, 39, 40; academics at, 29–34; Small's professors and colleagues at, 310–312

McClurg, James, 127, 131, 132, 162, 163, 284, 299

Mearns, John, 22, 23, 309

Melvil, Mr., 12

Miller, Perry, 38

Milton, John, 23

Moldrum, Robert, 12

Monboddo, Lord, 33

Montagu, Edward, 42, 43, 60, 61, 70

Montagu, Elizabeth, 40, 42, 43, 70, 311

Morgan, Dr. John, 131, 163

Morgan, John (London), 325

Morpurgo, J. E. "Jack," 70, 98, 110

Mortimer, John, 5

Muirhead, James Patrick, 1

Nairne, Edward, 164, 165, 187

Nelson, Thomas, 78n17, 129

Nelson, William, 78n17, 129

New Birmingham Lunar Society, xix. *See also* Birmingham Lunar Society

Newton, Sir Isaac, 37, 85, 134, 149, 155, 158, 165, 177, 274, 276, 317; *Philosophiae Naturalis Principia Mathematica*, 35

Nicholas, Robert Carter, 78n17, 101–102n26, 195, 291

Nichols (Nicholls), the Rt. Rev. Samuel: and faculty at College of William and Mary, xxii, 42, 43, 75, 76, 86, 88, 89, 90

Nicholson, Lt. Gov. Francis, 51

Ogilvie, Colonel, 309

Ogilvie, David, 6

Ogilvie, James, Earl of Airlie, 6, 25

Ogilvie, Susanna, 6, 7, 307

Ogilvie family, 12, 25

Owen, Goronwy: professor at College of William and Mary, xxii, 75, 76, 86–87, 91, 92, 93, 94, 95, 96, 97, 126

Owen, Mrs. Goronwy, 92, 93

Page, John, 131, 283–284; and Thomas Jefferson, 112, 127, 131, 132, 133, 134, 157, 178, 197, 198, 200, 261, 284; and Selim, 137; and William Small, 156, 157, 198

Page, Mann, 129, 284

Page, Margaret Lowther, 178, 200

Page family (Rosewell), 115, 124, 134, 136, 137, 197, 198, 319

Parliament (British), 4, 42, 59, 61, 64, 318; and James Watt's steam engine, 214, 249, 255, 256, 268

Partie Quarree (Williamsburg, Va.), 125–128, 166, 227, 286

Patton, Glenn, 106

Peale, Charles Willson, 137

Pestalozzi, Johann, 235

Pistole Fee (Virginia), 57–58, 58–60, 61, 62

Pitcairn, John, 23

Presbytery of St. Andrews (Scotland), 11, 12

Preston, William, 67, 71, 76

Priestley, Joseph, xx, 322, 324; member of Birmingham Lunar Society, 235, 236, 286

Prince of Wales, 212

Princess Dashkova of Russia, 233

Pringle, John, 42, 213, 216; and William Small, 257, 260, 290, 294, 298, 316

Privy Council (British), 4, 58, 60, 62, 63, 68, 194, 195

Randolph, Sir John, of Tazewell Hall, 318

Randolph, Peter, 78n17

Randolph, Peyton, 60, 78n17, 97, 115, 123, 124, 128, 279, 318, 319; and Francis Fauquier, 126, 127; and Partie Quarree, 166–167; and Thomas Jefferson, 124, 174

Randolph family, 319

Raspe, Rudolph Eric, 233, 322

Ravencroft, John, 163

Reid, Thomas, 151, 175, 181, 311, 312–313; *School of Common Sense Philosophy*, xxi, 38

Republic of Letters, xxiii, 1, 233, 274, 287, 289

Ricardo, David, 85

Rittenhouse, David, 131, 284

Robertson, Alexander, 4

Robertsone, John, 5

Robinson, Mr., 165

Robinson, Anne, of Lichfield, 323

Robinson, Eric, 227, 231, 233, 234, 235, 287

Robinson, John, 128

Robinson, Thomas, 71, 72, 74, 75, 97

Robinson, William, 66, 68, 72, 77, 88

Roebuck, Dr. John, 322, 325; and steam engine, 249–252, 253, 261, 268

Rousseau, Jean-Jacques, 235, 324

Rowe, Jacob: professor at College of William and Mary, xxii, 87, 91, 92, 93, 94, 95–97, 159, 160, 191, 195, 318

Ruddiman, Thomas, *Rudiments of Latin Grammar*, 24

Rush, Benjamin, 131

Russel, James, 8

Schofield, Robert, 227, 230, 231, 233, 234,

School of Common Sense Philosophy, 38

Scotland, 25–26

Scott, Anna, 13

Scott, Lillias (William Small's mother), 12–13, 260, 308

Scott, James, 13

Scottish Enlightenment, 27, 35–36, 149; and local ministers, 36–37; and Thomas Jefferson, 175–177, 179, 181, 183, 278; and William Small, 35, 77, 148, 161, 172, 175, 181, 274, 276, 278, 289

Scottish-naming tradition of children, 13

Scrymgeour, Alexander, 11

Selim the Algerine, 123, 134–138, 223, 319

Sherlock, Thomas (Bishop of London), 75, 100n13. *See also* Bishop of London

Simmonds, Joan, 98

Skene, David, 313

Skene, Francis, 32, 33, 34, 148, 149, 151, 211, 310

Small, Alexander, 139, 206, 207, 208, 213, 292, 294, 298, 316; and William Small's last illness, 257, 258, 260

Small, Anne (sister of William Small), 13

Small, David (brother of William Small), 13

Small, David (grandfather of William Small), 3, 6, 7–9, 10, 13, 20, 308. *See also* Lindsay, Margaret

Small, George (second great-grandfather of William Small), 2, 3, 307

Small, James (brother of William Small), 13, 268

Small, James (father of William Small), 1, 3, 7–8, 10–13, 41, 308. *See also* Scott, Lillias

Small, James (son of Thomas Small), 5, 7, 307

Small, John (brother of James Small), 7, 8

Small, Lillias Scott (mother of William Small), 12–13, 260, 308

Small, Robert (son of James Small and brother of William Small), 1, 8, 13, 260, 261, 265, 268, 285, 308–309; education of, 20, 21, 22, 41

Small, Susanna, 7. *See also* Ogilvie, Susanna

Small, Thomas (great-grandfather of William Small), 1, 2–7, 9, 41, 307; coat of arms of, 6–7, 7. *See also* Ogilvie, Susanna

Small, William
ancestors and family of, 1–13, 307–309
and Birmingham Lunar Society, xix, xx, xxii, xxiii n1, 1, 216, 221, 226, 227, 230, 231, 234, 236, 237, 241, 243, 253, 259, 279, 281, 283, 284, 285, 286, 287, 289, 295, 298, 323
and founding of, 228, 279, 281, 283, 289
"Birmingham Philosopher," 228
birth of, 13
books purchased by, 133–134
brother (Robert) of, 1, 8, 13, 20, 21, 22, 41, 260, 261, 265, 268, 285, 308–309
and canal project, 226, 255–257
and civil projects in Birmingham, 223–224
and College of William and Mary, xix, xx, xxi, 43, 49, 51, 77, 88, 94, 105, 110, 112, 113, 114, 118, 123, 153, 155–158, 277
and Bishop of London (Thomas Sherlock), 90, 94, 193, 201, 291
desire to return to England, 191, 192–193, 195
returning, 198, 200–202, 206
dinner companions of, 114–115
friendships of, 123–124
hiring of, 88–91, *91*, 152
professor at, xxii, 4
courses taught by, 150–151, 155–158
medicine, 157
"Professor of Mathematicks" at, 49–50, 51, 53, 57, 58, 90, 91
of Moral Philosophy, 160–162, 195
of Natural Philosophy, 156–158, 164–165, 195
quarters at, 112
salary of, 118, 119

scientific apparatus purchased by, 89, 157, 164–165, 192–193, 200, 291, 293

social circle of, 123–125

and students of, xix, xx, 49, 51, 88, 94, 108, 112, 118, 128, 130, 131, 153, 155–158, 159, 161, 163, 166–167, 172, 173, 192, 299

Thomas Jefferson, xx, xxi, xxii, 1, 19, 38, 76, 98, 107–108, 123, 127, 131, 133, 134, 148, 150, 158, 160, 161, 162, 172–174, 178–179, 181, 186, 187, 274, 275, 276, 277, 278, 285, 287, 318, "letter to unknown," 196–200, 197

taught all subjects at, 76, 98

teaching method of, 166–167

and Common Sense Philosophy, 35, 39, 49, 151, 161, 173, 175, 277

death of, 257–258, 264, 284

and burial of, 265

causes of, 258–261

desire for body after death, 125

irony of, 267–268

memorial to, 266

obituaries and tributes for, 261–263, 263, 290

early years of, xx, 1

education of

at Dundee Grammar School, xxi, 1, 8, 20, 21, 22, 23, 25, 277, 309

at Marischal College (Aberdeen), xxi, 1, 25, 27, 29, 33, 40, 159, 277

medical degree from, 210, 211, 216, 290, 292, 292, 293

professors for, 31–34, 38, 148, 149, 151, 310–311

and medical training, 39–42, 277, 290

study of scientific method, xxi

estate of, 265–266, 266–267

father of, 1, 3, 7–8, 10–13, 308

influence of, xix–xxi, 274–288

in London, Eng., 206–208, 209–210

at Lt. Gov. Francis Fauquier's soirées, 107–108, 126

and Partie Quarree, 125–128, 286

and medicine, xxii, 90, 157, 211, 276, 290–300

colleagues of, 293–294

opinion of, 295, 299

practiced in Birmingham, 213, 221–222, 223, 294–295, 300

and Birmingham General Hospital, 295, 296, 300, 321; Public, 254

and health insurance, 297–298

and hospital project, 223

practiced in Virginia, 162, 213, 259, 199, 211, 213, 222, 259, 300

medical students influenced by, 162, 163, 299

mother of, 12–13, 260, 308

portrait of, xv, 267

and Scottish Enlightenment, 35, 77, 148, 161, 172, 181, 274, 276, 278, 289

and Selim the Algerine, 134

and steam engine, 224–225, 226

and Virginia Society for the Encouragement of Arts and Manufacturing, 128, 130, 131, 283, 286

See also Ash, Dr. John; Boulton, Matthew; Darwin, Erasmus; Day,

Thomas; Franklin, Benjamin; Elliot, Sir John (king's physician); Gregory, James; Gregory, John; Heberden, Dr. William; Hunter, William; Jefferson, Thomas; Keir, James; Page, John; Pringle, John; Scottish Enlightenment; Watt, James; Wedgwood, Josiah; Withering, William; Wythe, George

Small coat of arms, 6–7, 7; family, 25, 41, tree, 2

Smeaton, John, 165, 233

Smiles, Samuel, 227, 228

Smith, Adam, 85, 312; *Wealth of Nations*, 242

Smith, William, 131

Society for the Encouragement of Arts, Manufactures and Commerce (Britain), 128, 129, 130

Solander, Daniel, 233, 322

Spotswood, Alexander, 111

Steptoe, George, 162

Steuart, Sir James, 85

Strahan, William, 139, 209, 217, 322–323

Syme, John, 11

Thomson, Robert P., 154, 155

Todd, Anthony, 138, 193

Trail, William, 313–314

Traill, James, 314

Traill, Robert, 313

Tucker, George, 178, 179

Tucker, St. George, 131, 163, 178

Tucker, Thomas Tudor, 163

Tucker family, 178

Two-Penny Act (Virginia), 51, 58, 62–64, 67, 92, 93

Tyler, Lyon G., 119, 160

Tyrie, James, 5

Uglow, Jenny, 228, 282

University of Cambridge, 27

University of Edinburgh, 26, 162–163, 211

University of Glasgow, 26

University of Oxford, 27

University of St. Andrews (Scotland), 3, 4, 5, 10–11, 25, 26; professors at, 11

University of Virginia, 176, 178, 277

Valentia, Lord, 211, 212

Virginia: Committee of Correspondence (1759), 61, 62; General Assembly, 59, 61, 130, 280, 318; Governor's Council, 59, 66, 67, 68, 70, 108, 128, 129, 136, 280; House of Burgesses, 51, 55, 56, 59–60, 62, 84, 92, 94, 95, 318, 319, and William Small, 192; power structure in, 54–57

Virginia Society for the Encouragement of Arts and Manufacturing, 128–131, 166, 283, 286, 317, 319

Virginia Society for the Promotion of Useful Knowledge, 131

Vilant, William, 11

Walker, John, 112, 127, 131, 132, 158, 284

Waller, Benjamin, 78n17

Ward, John, *The Young Mathematician's Guide*, 156–157

Washington, George, 129

Watt, Isaac, *Logick: or, the Right Use of Reason in the Enquiry After Truth*, 34, 150

Watt, James, xx, 233, 243, 282, 285, 322, 323, 325; and Birmingham Lunar Society, 227, 243, 255, 257; and canal schemes, 254; and Dr. John

Roebuck, 249–252; and Matthew Boulton, xxi, xxiii, 225, 227, 248, 249, 250, 251, 252, 253, 255, 256, 257, 258, 261, 262, 265, 266, 267–268, 276, 297; and steam engine, xxi, xxiii, 214, 225, 227, 249–253, 255, 260, and British Parliament patent for, 256–257, 259, 267, 268, and Newcomen, 248–249; and surveying canals, 253, 255; and William Small, xx, xxi, xxiii, 1, 19, 40, 151, 236, 237, 248, 249, 251, 252, 253, 254, 255, 256, 257, 258, 259–260, 261, 262, 266, 267, 268, 274, 275, 276, 287, 289, 295, 299

Watt, Peggy, 254, 260

Wedgwood, Josiah, 322, 325–326; and canal system, 254, 326; and Etruria Factory, 239, *239*; member of Birmingham Lunar Society, 227, 236, 241, 242, 253; and steam engine, 256; and William Small, 262, 326

Wells, R. V., 234

Whitehurst, John, 236, 322, 326

Wilson, James, 38

Williamsburg (Virginia): Capitol, 108–109, *108*; described, 105–107,
climate of, 115; Frenchman's Map of, *107*; Governor's Palace, 109, *110*

Wills, Garry, 181, 183; *Inventing America: Jefferson's Declaration of Independence*, 278

Wise Club of Aberdeen. *See* Aberdeen Philosophical Society

Withering, William: and Birmingham Lunar Society, 284, 285–286; took over William Small's medical practice in Birmingham, 264–265, 284, 285, 296, bought Small's portrait, 267, speculated on Small's patient numbers, 296, 298

Witherspoon, John, 38, 167

Wythe, George, 78n17, 128, 133, 275, 283, 318, 319; at Lt. Gov. Francis Fauquier's soirées, 107, 126, 127; and Thomas Jefferson, xxii, 98, 108, 123, 124, 132, 174, 178, 318; and students at College of William and Mary, 132, 166; and William Small, 98, 115, 123, 124, 195, 279, 280

Yates, William (president of College of William and Mary), 200, 201, 202

Old paint on canvas, as it ages, sometimes becomes transparent. When that happens it is possible, in some pictures, to see the original lines: a tree will show through a woman's dress, a child makes way for a dog, a large boat is no longer on an open sea. This is called pentimento because the painter "repented," changed his mind. Perhaps it would be as well to say that the old conception, replaced by a later choice, is a way of seeing and then seeing again.

Lillian Hellman: *Pentimento*